British Railways

LOCOMOTIVES &

COACHING STOCK

1999

The Complete Guide to all
Locomotives & Coaching Stock
Vehicles which run on
Britain's Mainline Railways

Neil Webster & Peter Fox

ISBN 1 902336 07 0

© 1999. Platform 5 Publishing Ltd., 3 Wyvern House, Sark Road, Sheffield,
S2 4HG, England.

CONTENTS

READERS' COMMENTS

With such a wealth of information as contained in this book, it is inevitable a few inaccuracies may be found. The authors will be pleased to receive notification from readers of any such inaccuracies, and also of any additional information to supplement our records and thus enhance future editions.

Please send comments to:

Peter Fox (Loco-Hauled Coaches) or Neil Webster (All other types),
Platform 5 Publishing Ltd.,
Wyvern House,
Sark Road,
Sheffield,
South Yorkshire,
S2 4HG
Tel: 0114 255 2625; Fax: 0114 255 2471
e-mail metent@globalnet.co.uk

Both the authors and staff of Platform 5 regret they are unable to answer specific queries regarding locomotives and rolling stock other than through the 'Q & A' section in the Platform 5 magazine *Today's Railways*.

UPDATES

A comprehensive update to *British Railways Locomotives & Coaching Stock* is published every month in the Platform 5 magazine, *Today's Railways*, which also contains news and rolling stock information on the railways of both Britain and Continental Europe. This is the ONLY commercial magazine to contain official Platform 5 rolling stock updates. For further details of *Today's Railways*, please see the advertisements inside the front and back covers of this book.

Information in this edition is intended to illustrate the actual situation on Britain's railways, rather than necessarily agree with TOPS, RSL and other computer records. Information is updated to 1st January 1999.

ORGANISATION & OPERATION OF BRITAIN'S RAILWAY SYSTEM

INFRASTRUCTURE & OPERATION

Britain's national railway infrastructure i.e. the track, signalling, stations and associated power supply equipment is owned by a public company – Railtrack PLC. Many stations and maintenance depots are leased to and operated by train operating companies (TOCs), but some larger stations remain under Railtrack control. The only exception is the infrastructure on the Isle of Wight, which is owned by the government and is leased to the Island Line franchisee.

Trains are operated by TOCs over the Railtrack network, regulated by access agreements between the parties involved. In general, TOCs are responsible for the provision and maintenance of the locomotives, rolling stock and staff necessary for the direct operation of services, whilst Railtrack is responsible for the provision and maintenance of the infrastructure and also for staff needed to regulate the operation of services.

DOMESTIC PASSENGER TRAIN OPERATORS

The large majority of passenger trains are operated by the TOCs on fixed term franchises. These are currently as follows:

Franchise	Owner	Trading Name
Anglia Railways	GB Railways	Anglia Railways
InterCity East Coast	Sea Containers	Great North Eastern Railway
InterCity West Coast	Virgin Rail	Virgin Train
Cross Country Trains	Virgin Rail	Virgin Trains
Great Eastern Railway	First Group	First Great Eastern
Great Western Trains	First Group	First Great Western
North West Regional Railways	First Group	First North Western
Midland Main Line	National Express	Midland Mainline
Gatwick Express	National Express	Gatwick Express

North London Railways	National Express	Silverlink Train Services
Central Trains	National Express	Central Trains
ScotRail	National Express	ScotRail
Merseyrail Electrics	MTL Rail	Merseyrail Electrics
Regional Railways North East	MTL Rail	Northern Spirit
LTS Rail	Prism Rail	LTS Rail
South Wales & West	Prism Rail	Wales & West Passenger Trains
Cardiff Railway	Prism Rail	Cardiff Railways
West Anglia Great Northern	Prism Rail	WAGN
South West Trains	Stagecoach	South West Trains
Island Line	Stagecoach	Island Line
Network South Central	Connex Rail	Connex South Central
South Eastern Trains	Connex Rail	Connex South Eastern
Thameslink Rail	GOVIA	Thameslink Rail
Chiltern Railways	M40 Trains	Chiltern Railways
Thames Trains	Victory Rail	Thames Trains

The above companies may also operate other services under 'Open Access' arrangements.

The following operators run non-franchised services only:

Operator	Trading Name	Route
British Airports Authority	Heathrow Express	London Paddington–Heathrow Airport
West Coast Railway	West Coast Railway	Fort William–Mallaig

INTERNATIONAL PASSENGER OPERATIONS

Eurostar (UK) operates international passenger services between the United Kingdom and continental Europe, jointly with French National Railways (SNCF) and Belgian National Railways (SNCB/NMBS). In addition, a service for the conveyance of accompanied road vehicles through the Channel Tunnel is provided by the tunnel operating company, Eurotunnel. Eurostar (UK) is a subsidiary of London & Continental Railways, which is now jointly owned by National Express Group and the British Airports Authority.

FREIGHT TRAIN OPERATIONS

TOCs currently engaged in freight train operation are:

English Welsh & Scottish Railway (EWS)
Freightliner
Direct Rail Services
Mendip Rail (comprises the rail interests of Foster Yeoman and Hanson Group).

Cover Photographs:
Front: Rail Express Systems liveried 47760 passes Otford Junction with a London Victoria–Folkestone Harbour VSOE Pullman service on 1st May 1997.
Rodney Lissenden

Back: North Western Trains liveried 158 757 & 158 758 arrive at Carlisle with a Sunday 'Dalesrail' working on 16th July 1998.
Kevin Conkey

1. LOCOMOTIVES

USING THIS SECTION – LAYOUT OF INFORMATION

Locomotives are listed in numerical order of class number, and then in numerical order of individual locomotives – using current numbers as allocated by the Rolling Stock Library. Where numbers carried are different to those officially allocated (e.g. former numbers); these are noted in class headings where appropriate.

Each locomotive entry is laid out as in one of the following examples:

Shunting Locomotives

RSL No.	Detail	Livery	Owner	Pool	Depot	Location
03179		**WA**	WA	HQXX	HE	*Hornsey EMUD*

Main Line Locomotives

RSL No.	Detail	Livery	Owner	Pool	Depot	Name
47777	x	**RX**	E	WHDP	CD	Restored

CLASS HEADINGS

Principal details and dimensions are quoted for each class in metric and/or imperial units as considered appropriate bearing in mind common usage in the UK. Abbreviations used are shown in Section 6.9.

All dimensions and weights are quoted for locomotives in an 'as new' condition with all necessary supplies (e.g. oil, water and sand) on board. Dimensions are quoted in the order Length – Width – Height. All lengths quoted are over buffers or couplings as appropriate. All width and height dimensions quoted are maxima.

DETAIL DIFFERENCES

Only detail differences which currently affect the areas and types of train which locomotives may work are shown. All other detail differences are specifically excluded – details of these may be found in more specialist publications. Where such differences occur within a class or part class, these are shown alongside the individual locomotive number. Standard abbreviations used are:

a	Train air brake equipment only
c	Scharfenberg couplers
j	RCH jumper cables for operating with Propelling Control Vehicles
m	Multiple working equipment
p	Train air, vacuum and electro-pneumatic brakes
r	Radio Electronic Token Block (RETB) equipment
s	Slow Speed Control equipment
v	Train vacuum brake only
x	Train air and vacuum brakes ('Dual brakes')
+	Additional fuel tank capacity
§	Sandite laying equipment.

In all cases use of the above abbreviations indicates the equipment indicated is normally operable. Meaning of non-standard abbreviations and symbols is detailed in individual class headings.

LIVERY CODES

Livery codes are used to denote the various liveries carried. Readers should note it is impossible in a publication of this size to list every livery variation which currently exists. In particular items ignored for the purposes of this book include:

* Minor colour variations;
* All numbering, lettering and branding;
* Omission of logos.

The descriptions quoted are thus a general guide only and may be subject to slight variation between individual locomotives. Logos as appropriate for each livery are normally deemed to be carried. A complete list of livery codes used appears in Section 6.1.

OWNER CODES

Owner codes are used to denote the owners of locomotives listed. Many locomotives are leased by the TOCs from specialist leasing companies. A complete list of owner codes used appears in Section 6.2.

POOL CODES

Locomotives are split into operational groups ('pools') for diagramming and maintenance purposes. The official codes used to denote these pools are shown in this publication.

A complete list of pool codes used appears in Section 6.3.

DEPOT & LOCATION CODES

Depot codes are used in this to denote the normal maintenance base of each operational locomotive. However, maintenance may be carried out at other locations and may also be carried out by mobile maintenance teams.

Location codes are used to denote the current actual location of stored vehicles. A location code will be followed by (S) to denote stored.

A complete list of depot and location codes used appears in Section 6.6.

A complete list of the abbreviations used to denote different types of depots appears in Section 6.7.

SHUNTING LOCOMOTIVE LOCATIONS

The actual location of operational shunting locomotives, updated to the date of going to press, is included as a guide to readers as to where these locomotives may be found. Whilst some locomotives remain at certain locations for some considerable length of time, others may move around far more frequently. Readers must appreciate the listing of a locomotive at a location is no absolute guarantee the locomotive concerned (or any other locomotive) will remain present on a subsequent date.

NAMES

Only names carried with official sanction are listed in this publication. As far as possible names are shown in UPPER/lower case characters as actually shown on the name carried on the locomotive. Names known to be carried on one side only are suffixed [1] (e.g. Back Tor[1]).

GENERAL INFORMATION

CLASSIFICATION AND NUMBERING

All locomotives are classified and allocated numbers under the TOPS numbering system, introduced in 1972. This comprises a two-digit class number followed by a three-digit serial number. Where the actual number carried by a locomotive differs from the allocated number, or where an additional number is carried to the allocated number, this is shown by a note in the class heading.

For diesel locomotives, class numbers offer an indication of engine horsepower as shown in the table below. However, it should be noted this system is no longer an infallible indicator of engine horsepower (e.g. Class 57).

Engine hp	Class No. Range
0–799	01–14
800–1000	15–20
1001–1499	21–31
1500–1999	32–39
2000–2999	40–54
3000+	55 onwards.

For electric locomotives class numbers are allocated in ascending numerical order under the following scheme:

Class 70–80	direct current and dc/diesel dual system locomotives.
Class 81 onwards	alternating current and ac/dc dual system locomotives.

Preserved diesel and electric locomotives authorised to run on the Railtrack system are either allocated their original TOPS numbers, or where a clash of numbers might occur, in the 89xxx series. 89xxx numbers are not actually carried externally on any preserved diesel or electric locos, but details of these numbers are quoted in class headings for reference purposes. Full details of all preserved locomotives can be found in the Platform 5 book *Preserved Locomotives of British Railways*.

WHEEL ARRANGEMENT

For main line diesel and electric locomotives the system whereby the number of driven axles on a bogie or frame is denoted by a letter (A = 1, B = 2, C = 3 etc.) and the number of undriven axles is denoted by a number is used. The use of a letter 'o' after a letter indicates each axle is individually powered, whilst the + symbol indicates bogies are intercoupled.

For shunting locomotives, the Whyte notation is used. In this notation, generally used in Britain for steam locomotives, the number of leading wheels are given, followed by the number of driving wheels and then the trailing wheels.

HAULAGE CAPABILITY OF DIESEL LOCOMOTIVES

The haulage capability of a diesel locomotive depends upon 3 basic factors:

1. Adhesive weight. The greater the weight on the driving wheels, the greater the adhesion and more tractive power can be applied before wheelslip occurs.

2. The characteristics of its transmission. To start a train the locomotive has to exert a pull at standstill. A direct drive diesel engine cannot do this, hence the need for transmission. This may be mechanical, hydraulic or electric. The current British Standard for locomotives is electric transmission. Here the diesel engine drives a generator or alternator and the current produced is fed to the traction motors. The force produced by each driven wheel depends on the current in its traction motor. In other words, the larger the current, the harder it pulls.

As the locomotive speed increases, the current in the traction motor falls, hence the *Maximum Tractive Effort* is the maximum force at its wheels the locomotive can exert at a standstill. The electrical equipment cannot take such high currents for long without overheating. Hence the *Continuous Tractive Effort* is quoted which represents the current which the equipment can take continuously.

3. The power of its engine. Not all power reaches the rail, as electrical machines are approximately 90% efficient. As the electrical energy passes through two such machines (the generator or alternator and the traction motors), the *Power at Rail* is approximately 81% (90% of 90%) of the engine power, less a further amount used for auxiliary equipment such as radiator fans, traction motor blowers, air compressors, battery charging, cab heating, Electric Train Supply (ETS) etc. The power of the locomotive is proportional to the tractive effort times the speed. Hence when on full power there is a speed corresponding to the continuous tractive effort.

HAULAGE CAPABILITY OF ELECTRIC LOCOMOTIVES

Unlike a diesel locomotive, an electric locomotive does not develop it power on board and its performance is determined only by two factors, namely its weight and the characteristics of its electrical equipment. Whereas a diesel locomotive tends to be a constant power machine, the power of an electric locomotive varies considerably. Up to a certain speed it can produce virtually a constant tractive effort. Hence power rises with speed according to the formula given in section three above, until a maximum speed is reached at which tractive effort falls, such that the power also falls. Hence the power at the speed corresponding to the maximum tractive effort is lower than the maximum speed.

BRAKE FORCE

The brake force is a measure of the braking power of a locomotive. This is shown on the locomotive data panels so operating staff can ensure sufficient brake power is available on freight trains.

ELECTRIC TRAIN SUPPLY (ETS)

A number of locomotives are equipped to provide a supply of electricity to the train being hauled to power auxiliaries such as heating, cooling fans, air conditioning and kitchen equipment. ETS is provided from the locomotive by means of a separate alternator, except in the case of Class 33 which have a dc generator. The ETS index of a locomotive is a measure of the electrical power available for train supply.

Similarly all loco hauled coaches also have an ETS index, which in this case is a measure of the power required to operate equipment mounted in the coach. The sum of the ETS indices of all the hauled vehicles in a train must not exceed the ETS index of the locomotive.

ETS is commonly known as ETH (Electric Train Heating), which is a throwback to the days before loco-hauled coaches were equipped with electrically powered auxiliary equipment.

ROUTE AVAILABILITY (RA)

This is a measure of a railway vehicle's axle load. The higher the axle load of a vehicle, the higher the RA number on a scale from 1 to 10. Each Railtrack route has a RA number and in general no vehicle with a higher RA number may travel on that route without special clearance.

MULTIPLE & PUSH-PULL WORKING

Multiple working between locomotives (i.e. between two and five locomotives being driven from one cab) is provided by jumper cables connecting the locomotives. However, not all types are compatible with each other, and a number of different systems are in use, each system being incompatible with any other.

Blue Star Coupling Code: Classes 20/0, 20/9, 31, 33, and 37. Locomotives 47971 and 47976.
DRS System: Classes 20/3 and 37/6.
GM System: Classes 59, 66, and 67.
Green Circle Coupling Code: Class 47 (not all equipped).
Orange Square Coupling Code: Class 50.
Red Diamond Coupling Code: Classes 56 and 58.
SR System: Classes 33/1, 73 and various 750 V d.c. EMUs.
Within Own Class only: Classes 43 and 60.

Class 47s nos. 47701–47717 use a time-division multiplex (TDM) system for push-pull working which utilises the existing Railway Clearing House (RCH) jumper cables between coaches. Previously these cables had only been used to control train lighting and public address systems.

A number of other locomotives are equipped with a more modern TDM system for push-pull working which also facilitates multiple working.

1.1 DIESEL LOCOMOTIVES

CLASS 03   BR/GARDNER   0–6–0

Built: 1962 by BR at Swindon Works.
Engine: Gardner 8L3 of 152 kW (204 hp) at 1200 rpm.
Transmission: Mechanical. Fluidrive type 23 hydraulic coupling to Wilson-Drewry CA5R7 gearbox with SCG type RF11 final drive.
Max. Tractive Effort: 68 kN (15300 lbf).
Cont. Tractive Effort: 68 kN (15300 lbf) at 3.75 mph.
Train Brakes: Air & vacuum.

Brake Force: 13 t.	**Dimensions:** 7.93 x 2.59 x 3.73 m.
Weight: 31.3 t.	**Wheel Diameter:** 1092 mm.
Design Speed: 28.5 mph.	**Max. Speed:** 28.5 mph.
Fuel Capacity: 1364 litres.	**RA:** 1.
Train Supply: Not equipped.	**Multiple Working:** Not equipped.

03179   **WN**   WN HQXX   HE   *Hornsey T&RSMD*

Name: 03179   CLIVE

CLASS 08   BR/ENGLISH ELECTRIC   0–6–0

Built: 1955–62 by BR at Crewe, Darlington, Derby, Doncaster or Horwich Works.
Engine: English Electric 6KT of 298 kW (400 hp) at 680 rpm.
Main Generator: English Electric 801.
Traction Motors: Two English Electric 506.
Max. Tractive Effort: 156 kN (35000 lbf).
Cont. Tractive Effort: 49 kN (11100 lbf) at 8.8 mph.
Power At Rail: 194 kW (260 hp).

	Train Brakes: Air & vacuum.
Brake Force: 19 t.	**Dimensions:** 8.92 x 2.59 x 3.89 m.
Weight: 49.6–50.4 t.	**Wheel Diameter:** 1372 mm.
Design Speed: 20 mph.	**Max. Speed:** 15 mph.
Fuel Capacity: 3037 litres.	**RA:** 5.
Train Supply: Not equipped.	**Multiple Working:** Not equipped.

Non-standard liveries/numbering:

- 08375/519/730/867 are BR style black.
- 08397 is as **F**, but with BR Railfreight General yellow & red logos.
- 08414 is as **DG**, but with BR & Railfreight Distribution logos and large bodyside numbers. Also carries number D3529.
- 08454/887/934 are in Virgin Trains 'Pitstop' livery of black with a large chequered flag on the bodyside.
- 08460 is light grey with black underframes, cab doors, window surrounds and roof. Also carries number D3575.
- 08500 is red, lined out in black and white. Also carries a large number '1' on the bodyside.
- 08527 is light grey with a black roof, blue bodyside stripe and 'Ilford Level 5' branding.
- 08593 is Great Eastern Railway style blue. Also carries number D3760.

- 08601 is London Midland & Scottish Railway style black.
- 08616 is Great Western Railway style green with cast numberplate 3783.
- 08617 is in Virgin Trains 'Pitstop' livery of black with a large red and white bodyside flag.
- 08642 is London & South Western Railway style black. Also carries number D3809.
- 08649 is grey with blue, white and red stripes and WTL logo. Also carries number D3816.
- 08682 is dark blue with a grey roof.
- 08689 is as **DG**, but with BR Railfreight General yellow & red logos and large bodyside numbers.
- 08715 is 'Dayglo' orange.
- 08721 is as **B**, but with a red and yellow stripe.
- 08724 is RFS style blue livery.
- 08743/903 are ICI Trafalgar blue.
- 08785 is silver grey.
- 08793 is LNER style apple green.
- 08805 is London Midland & Scottish Railway style maroon. Also carries number 3973.
- 08830 carries number D3998.
- 08870 is RMS Locotech blue and red. Also carries RMS number 024.
- 08879 is green and black with Railfreight Distribution logos.
- 08883 is Caledonian Railway style blue.
- 08907 is London & North Western Railway style black.
- 08928 is as **FR**, with large bodyside numbers and light blue solebar.
- 08938 is grey and red.

Notes: † – Equipped with remote control.

Class 08/0. Standard Design.

08077		**RF**	RF	DFLS	EH	*Southampton Maritime FLT*
08331		**GN**	RF	HBSH	EC	*Edinburgh Craigentinny T&RSMD*
08375		**0**	MO	MBDL	SD	*Sellafield T&RSMD*
08388	a	**FP**	E	WSXX	ZB(S)	
08389	a	**B**	E	EWOC	OC	*Wembley Yard*
08393	a	**FE**	E	EWOC	OC	*Temple Mills Yard*
08397	a	**0**	E	LWSP	CD	*Padeswood Hall Cement Works*
08401	a	**DG**	E	FDSI	IM	*Immingham TMD*
08402	a	**DG**	E	LWSP	CD	*Dee Marsh Sidings*
08405	a	**DG**	E	FDSI	IM	*Immingham TMD*
08410	a	**DG**	GW	HJXX	PM	*St. Philips Marsh T&RSMD*
08411	a	**B**	E	LGML	ML	*Motherwell TMD*
08413	a	**DG**	E	WSXX	ZB(S)	
08414	a	**0**	E	EWOC	OC	*Old Oak Common TMD*
08417	a	**B**	SO	CDJD	ZA(S)	
08418	a	**F**	E	FDSD	DR	*Doncaster TMD*
08419	a	**B**	E	WSYX	ZC(S)	
08428	a	**B**	E	WSXX	DR	*Doncaster TMD (in use)*
08441	a	**B**	E	WSXX	ZB(S)	
08442	a	**F**	E	FDSI	IM	*Immingham Yard*
08445	a	**B**	E	WSXX	ZB(S)	
08448	a	**B**	E	WSYX	BS(S)	

08449	a	**B**	E	WSYX	TT(S)	
08451		**B**	VW	HFSN	WN	Willesden TMD
08454		**O**	VW	HFSN	WN	Willesden TMD
08460	a	**O**	E	LWSP	CD	Warrington Arpley
08466	a	**FO**	E	WSXX	ZB(S)	
08472	a	**BR**	RF	HBSH	EC	Edinburgh Craigentinny T&RSMD
08473	v	**B**	E	WSYX	LR(S)	
08480	a	**G**	E	EWEH	EH	Eastleigh Yard
08481		**B**	E	LNCF	CF	Margam SD
08482	a	**DG**	E	EWOC	OC	Willesden Brent Sidings
08483	a	**DG**	GW	HJXX	PM	St. Philips Marsh T&RSMD
08484	a	**DG**	RC	KWSW	ZN	Railcare, Wolverton
08485	a	**B**	E	LWSP	CD	Warrington Arpley
08489	a	**F**	E	WSXX	WA(S)	
08492	a	**B**	E	WSXX	ZB(S)	
08493	a	**B**	E	LNCF	CF	Margam SD
08495		**B**	E	ENSN	TO	Worksop Yards
08499	a	**F**	E	FDSK	KY	Knottingley T&RSMD
08500		**O**	E	EWEH	EH	Stoke Gifford Yard
08506	a	**B**	E	LNWK	CF	Allied Steel & Wire, Cardiff
08509	a	**F**	E	FDSD	DR	Tinsley Yard
08510	a	**B**	E	FDSD	DR	Doncaster TMD
08511	a	**R**	E	ENSN	TO	Toton TMD
08512	a	**F**	E	FDSD	DR	Doncaster TMD
08514	a	**B**	E	FDSD	DR	Doncaster TMD
08515	a	**B**	E	WSYX	GD(S)	
08516	a	**DG**	E	ENSN	TO	Peterborough SD
08517	a	**B**	E	WSYX	SF(S)	
08519	a	**O**	E	WSXX	ZB(S)	
08523		**ML**	E	LBBS	BS	Bescot Yard
08525		**F**	MM	HISL	NL	Leeds Neville Hill (InterCity) T&RSMD
08526		**E**	E	EWOC	OC	Hither Green TMD
08527		**O**	AD	KCSI	ZI	Adtranz, Ilford
08528		**DG**	E	ENSN	TO	Toton TMD
08529		**B**	E	ENSN	TO	Worksop Yards
08530		**DG**	P	DFLS	OC	Tilbury FLT
08531	a	**DG**	P	DFLS	OC	Tilbury FLT
08534		**DG**	E	LGML	ML	Mossend Yard
08535		**DG**	E	LBBS	BS	Daventry International Railfreight Terminal
08536		**B**	MM	HISE	DY(S)	
08538		**DG**	E	ENSN	TO	Ketton
08540		**DG**	E	WSXX	ZB(S)	
08541		**DG**	E	EWOC	OC	Dagenham Dock Up Sidings
08542		**F**	E	LBBS	BS	Oxley T&RSMD
08543		**DG**	E	LBBS	BS	Bescot Yard
08561		**B**	E	WSXX	ZB(S)	
08567		**B**	E	LBBS	BS	Bescot TMD
08568	a	**B**	RC	KGSS	ZH	Railcare, Springburn
08569		**E**	E	ENSN	TO	Toton TMD
08571	a	**B**	RF	MBDL	ZB	RFS(E), Doncaster
08573		**B**	AD	KCSI	ZI	Adtranz, Ilford

08575		**BR**	P	DFLS	EH	*Southampton Maritime FLT*
08576		**B**	E	LNCF	CF	*Fowey Docks*
08577		**B**	E	FMSY	TE	*Tyne Yard*
08578		**RG**	E	LWSP	CD	*Blackburn Coal Concentration Depot*
08580		**B**	E	LBBS	BS	*Northampton*
08581		**BR**	E	WSYX	ZB(S)	
08582	a	**DG**	E	FMSY	TE	*Thornaby T&RSMD*
08585		**B**	P	DFLS	CD	*Crewe Basford Hall Yard*
08586	a	**F**	E	WSYX	AY(S)	
08587		**B**	E	FDSD	DR	*Doncaster Belmont Yard*
08588		**BR**	MM	HISL	NL	*Neville Hill (InterCity) T&RSMD*
08593		**0**	E	EWOC	OC	*Ipswich SD*
08594		**B**	E	WSYX	TT(S)	
08597		**B**	E	FDSK	KY	*Knottingley T&RSMD*
08599		**B**	E	WSXX	AN(S)	
08601		**0**	E	EWEH	EH	*Allerton T&RSMD*
08605		**B**	E	FDSK	KY	*Neville Hill (DMU/EMU) T&RSMD*
08607		**B**	E	WSYX	TT(S)	*Toton TMD*
08609		**B**	E	WSYX	ZB(S)	
08610		**B**	E	WSYX	ZB(S)	
08611		**V**	VW	HFSL	LO	*Edge Hill CSD*
08616		**0**	CT	HGSS	TS	*Tyseley T&RSMD*
08617		**0**	VW	HFSN	WN	*Willesden TMD*
08618		**B**	E	WSYX	GD(S)	
08619		**B**	E	WSYX	ZB(S)	
08622		**B**	E	WSYX	ML(S)	
08623		**B**	E	LBBS	BS	*Bescot TMD*
08624		**B**	P	DFLS	ML	*Coatbridge FLT*
08625		**B**	E	WSYX	CF(S)	
08628		**B**	E	LBBS	BS	*Bescot TMD*
08629		**RP**	RC	KWSW	ZN	*Railcare, Wolverton*
08630		**E**	E	LGML	ML	*Deanside Transit, Hillingdon*
08631		**FG**	FG	SDFR	TM	*Birmingham Railway Museum T&RSMD*
08632		**B**	E	FDSI	IM	*Immingham Yard*
08633		**RX**	E	FMSY	TE	*Heaton T&RSMD*
08634		**B**	E	WSYX	SF(S)	
08635		**B**	E	EWOC	OC	*Dagenham Dock Up Sidings*
08641		**DG**	GW	HJSL	LA	*Penzance*
08642		**0**	P	DFLS	CD	*Felixstowe North FLT*
08643		**DG**	GW	HJXX	PM	*St. Phillips Marsh T&RSMD*
08644		**IM**	GW	HJSL	LA	*Plymouth Laira T&RSMD*
08645		**DG**	GW	HJSL	LA	*Plymouth Laira T&RSMD*
08646		**F**	E	EWEH	EH	*Eastleigh Yard*
08648		**DG**	GW	HJSL	LA	*Plymouth Laira T&RSMD*
08649		**0**	AM	KESE	ZG	*Alstom, Eastleigh*
08651		**DG**	E	LNWK	CF	*Cardiff Canton (Loco) TMD*
08653		**FE**	E	LWSP	CD	*Allerton T&RSMD*
08655		**F**	E	FDSK	KY	*York WRD*
08661	a	**F**	E	WSYX	AN(S)	
08662		**B**	E	FDSK	KY	*Goole Docks*
08663	a	**DG**	GW	HJSL	LA	*Plymouth Station*

08664	B	E	EWEH	EH	Eastleigh Yard
08665	B	E	FDSI	IM	Immingham TMD
08666	B	E	WSYX	AN(S)	
08670 a	B	E	LGML	ML	Motherwell TMD
08673	IM	E	WSYX	AN(S)	
08675	F	E	LGML	ML	Millerhill SD
08676	B	E	FDSI	IM	Immingham TMD
08677	B	E	WSYX	ZB(S)	
08682	0	AD	KDSD	ZF	Adtranz, Doncaster
08683	B	E	LNWK	CF	Allied Steel & Wire, Cardiff
08685	B	E	LGML	ML	Polmadie T&RSMD
08689 a	0	E	FDSK	KY	Knottingley T&RSMD
08690	MM	MM	HISE	DY	Derby Etches Park T&RSMD
08691	G	FL	DFLS	CD	Trafford Park FLT
08693	B	E	WSYX	ML(S)	
08694 a	B	E	EWOC	OC	Euston Downside CARMD
08695 a	B	E	LWSP	CD	Crewe Gresty Lane
08696 a	V	VW	HFSL	LO	Longsight Diesel T&RSMD
08697	B	MM	HISE	DY	Derby Etches Park T&RSMD
08698 a	B	E	LBBS	BS	Bescot TMD
08700 a	B	E	WSYX	SF(S)	
08701 a	RX	E	LWSP	CD	Warrington Arpley
08702	B	E	WSXX	ZB(S)	
08703 a	B	E	LWSP	CD	Trafford Park EWS International Terminal
08706	B	E	ENSN	TO	Toton TMD
08709	B	E	LGML	ML	Carlisle Currock WRD
08711	RX	E	EWOC	OC	Wembley Yard
08713 a	B	E	WSYX	ZB(S)	
08714	RX	E	ENSN	TO	March Down Yard
08715 v	0	E	WSXX	SF(S)	
08718	B	E	WSYX	AY(S)	
08720 a	DG	E	LGML	ML	Motherwell TMD
08721	0	VW	HFSL	LO	Longsight International T&RSMD
08723	B	E	WSYX	TT(S)	
08724	0	RF	MBDL	ZB	ARC, Whatley
08730	0	RC	KGSS	ZH	Railcare, Springburn
08731	B	E	WSYX	ML(S)	
08733	B	E	WSYX	ML(S)	
08734	B	E	WSYX	CF(S)	
08735	DG	E	LGML	ML	Fort William SD
08737 a	FE	E	LWSP	CD	Warrington Arpley
08738	E	E	LWSP	CD	Crewe Diesel TMD
08739	B	E	WSXX	AN(S)	
08740	F	E	WSXX	SF(S)	
08742	RX	E	LWSP	AN(S)	
08743	0	IC	MBDL	BH	ICI, Billingham
08745	FE	P	DFLS	CD	Felixstowe North FLT
08746	DG	E	LGML	ML	Killoch Disposal Point
08750	B	E	WSXX	SF(S)	
08751	F	E	WSXX	ZB(S)	
08752	CE	E	ENSN	TO	Peterborough Crescent WRD

08754		B	SR	HASS	IS	Inverness
08755		B	E	WSYX	ZB(S)	
08756		DG	E	LNCF	CF	Cardiff Canton (Loco) TMD
08757		RX	E	WSXX	HT(S)	
08758		B	E	WSXX	SF(S)	
08762		B	SR	HASS	IS	Inverness Yard
08765		DG	E	LBBS	BS	Rugby
08768		B	E	LGML	ML	Motherwell TMD
08770	a	DG	E	LNCF	CF	Margam SD
08773		B	E	WSXX	TO(S)	
08775		E	E	EWOC	OC	Willesden Brent Yard
08776	a	DG	E	ENSN	TO	Toton TMD
08780		B	GW	HJSE	LE	Landore T&RSMD
08782	a	B	E	FDSK	KY	Knottingley T&RSMD
08783		B	E	FDSK	KY	Knottingley T&RSMD
08784		B	E	WSXX	AN(S)	
08785	a	O	FL	DFLS	CD	RFS(E) Doncaster
08786		DG	E	LNCF	CF	Plymouth Station
08790		B	VW	HFSL	LO	Longsight T&RSMD
08792		B	E	LNCF	CF	Exeter St. Davids
08793	a	O	E	WSYX	ZB(S)	
08795		IM	GW	HJSE	LE	Landore T&RSMD
08798		B	E	LNCF	CF	Tavistock Junction
08799		B	E	EWOC	OC	Stratford TMD
08801		B	E	LNCF	CF	Onllwyn
08802		RX	E	LWSP	CD	Dee Marsh Sidings
08804		B	E	EWEH	EH	Reading West Yard
08805		O	CT	HGSS	TS	Soho SD
08806	a	F	E	FMSY	TE	Tyne Yard
08807		BR	E	LBBS	BS	Bescot Yard
08810	a	B	AR	HSSN	NC	RMS Locotech, Dewsbury
08813	a	DG	E	FMSY	TE	Thornaby T&RSMD
08815		B	E	WSYX	AN(S)	
08817		BR	E	LWSP	CD	Allerton T&RSMD
08819		DG	E	LNWK	CF	Allied Steel & Wire, Cardiff
08822		IM	GW	HJSE	LE	Landore T&RSMD
08823	a	B	AD	KDSD	ZF	Adtranz, Doncaster
08824	a	F	E	FDSI	IM	Scunthorpe SD
08825	a	B	E	EWOC	OC	Euston Downside CARMD
08826	a	B	E	WSYX	ML(S)	
08827	a	B	E	LGML	ML	Motherwell TMD
08828	a	E	E	LNWK	CF	Cardiff Canton (Loco) TMD
08829	a	B	E	WSYX	TT(S)	
08830		G	CA	HLSV	CF	East Somerset Railway (on loan)
08834		FD	RF	HBSH	ZB(S)	
08836		I	GW	HJXX	OO	Old Oak Common TMD
08837		DG	E	LWSP	CD	Crewe International Electric Depot
08842		B	E	LWSP	CD	Allerton T&RSMD
08844		B	E	WSXX	ZB(S)	
08847		B	AM	KESE	ZG	Alstom, Eastleigh
08853	a	B	RF	HBSH	BN	Bounds Green T&RSMD

08854	E	E	LNWK	CF	Allied Steel & Wire, Cardiff
08855	B	E	WSZX	ZB(S)	
08856	B	E	EWEH	EH	Westbury Yard
08865	B	E	EWOC	OC	Parkeston Yard
08866	B	E	LWSP	CD	Trafford Park EWS International Terminal
08867	O	E	LWSP	CD	Brunner-Mond, Northwich
08868	B	HN	MBDL	CP	The Railway Age, Crewe
08869	G	AR	HSSN	NC(S)	
08870	O	HN	MBDL	NC	Norwich Crown Point T&RSMD
08872	DG	E	EWOC	OC	Three Bridges Yard
08873	RX	E	WSXX	ZB(S)	
08874	RF	MO	MBDL	ZB	Heys Chemicals, Sandbach
08877	DG	E	FDSD	DR	Rotherham Steel Terminal
08879	O	E	WSXX	ZB(S)	
08880	B	E	WSXX	AN(S)	
08881	DG	E	LGML	ML	Falkland Yard
08882	B	E	LGML	ML	Motherwell TMD
08883	O	E	LGML	ML	Perth New Yard
08884	B	E	LBBS	BS	Saltley SD
08886 †	E	E	WSTT	TO	Tyne Yard
08887 a	O	VW	HFSN	PC	Polmadie T&RSMD
08888	E	E	LBBS	BS	Bletchley T&RSMD
08890	DG	E	EWOC	OC	Stonebridge Park
08891	B	P	DFLS	CD	Garston FLT
08892	GN	RF	HBSH	BN	Bounds Green T&RSMD
08893	DG	E	WSYX	ZB(S)	
08894	B	E	WSXX	AN(S)	
08895	B	E	WSYX	MG(S)	
08896	E	E	EWEH	EH	Bristol Temple Meads
08897	DG	E	LWSP	CD	Crewe Diesel TMD
08899	MM	MM	HISE	DY	Derby Etches Park
08900	DG	E	LNWK	CF	Margam SD
08901	B	E	WSYX	ZB(S)	
08902	B	E	WSXX	AN(S)	
08903	O	IC	MBDL	BH	ICI, Billingham
08904	B	E	EWEH	EH	Didcot Yard
08905	B	E	LBBS	BS	Hams Hall
08906	B	E	LGML	ML(S)	
08907	O	E	LWSP	CD	Longport
08908	B	MM	HISL	NL	Neville Hill (InterCity) T&RSMD
08909	ML	E	LBBS	BS	Bescot TMD
08910	B	E	LGML	ML	Aberdeen Guild Street
08911	DG	E	LWSP	CD	Warrington Arpley
08912	B	E	LGML	ML	Carlisle
08913	DG	E	EWOC	OC	London International Freight Terminal
08914	B	E	WSXX	ZB(S)	
08915	F	E	LWSP	CD	Peak Forest
08918	DG	E	LWSP	CD	
08919	RX	E	EWOC	OC	Stratford TMD
08920	F	E	LBBS	BS	Wolverhampton Steel Terminal
08921 †	E	E	WSTT	TO	Wolverhampton Steel Terminal

08922		DG	E	LGML	ML	*Kingmoor Yard*
08924		DG	E	WSXX	ZB(S)	
08925		B	E	LWSP	CD	*Peak Forest*
08926		DG	E	WSXX	AN(S)	*Allerton T&RSMD*
08927		B	E	FDSI	IM	*Immingham TMD*
08928		0	AR	HSSN	NC(S)	
08931		B	E	WSYX	ZB(S)	
08932		B	E	LNWK	CF	*Allied Steel & Wire, Cardiff*
08933		E	E	WSXX	ZB(S)	
08934	a	0	VW	HFSN	WN	*Willesden TMD*
08938		0	E	WSYX	ML(S)	
08939		B	E	LWSP	CD	*Crewe International T&RSMD*
08940		B	E	WSYX	AN(S)	
08941		B	E	LNCF	CF	*Tavistock Junction*
08942		B	E	WSXX	ZB(S)	
08944		DG	E	WSXX	ZB(S)	
08946		FE	E	LBBS	BS	*Saltley SD*
08947		B	E	EWEH	EH	*Westbury Yard*
08948	c	EP	EU	GPSS	OC	*North Pole International T&RSMD*
08950		IM	MM	HISL	NL	*Neville Hill (InterCity) T&RSMD*
08951		DG	E	WSXX	ZB(S)	
08952		B	E	WSYX	ML(S)	
08953		DG	E	LNCF	CF	*St. Blazey T&RSMD*
08954		F	E	WSXX	ZB(S)	
08955		T	E	LNWK	CF	*Cardiff Canton (Loco) TMD*
08956		B	SO	CDJD	DY	*Railway Technical Centre, Derby)*
08957		E	E	LNWK	CF	*Newport Godfrey Road*
08958		B	E	WSXX	SF(S)	

Class 08/9. Reduced height cab. Details as Class 08/0 except:
Converted: 1985–87 by BR at Landore depot.
Dimensions: 8.92 x 2.59 x 3.60 m.

08993		T	E	LNCF	CF	*Cardiff Canton (Loco) TMD*
08994	a	FR	E	ENSN	TO	*Toton TMD*
08995	a	T	E	FMSY	TE	*Thornaby TMD*

Names:

08578	Lybert Dickinson	08869	The Canary
08629	BRML WOLVERTON LEVEL 5	08879	Sheffield Childrens Hospital
08649	G.H. Stratton	08888	Postman's Pride
08661	Europa	08896	STEPHEN DENT
08682	Lionheart	08919	Steep Holm
08701	The Sorter	08950	Neville Hill 1st
08714	Cambridge	08993	ASHBURNHAM
08743	ANGIE	08994	GWENDRAETH
08790	M.A. SMITH	08995	KIDWELLY

CLASS 09   BR/ENGLISH ELECTRIC   0–6–0

Built: 1959–62 by BR at Darlington or Horwich Works.
Engine: English Electric 6KT of 298 kW (400 hp) at 680 rpm.
Main Generator: English Electric 801.
Traction Motors: English Electric 506.
Max. Tractive Effort: 111 kN (25000 lbf).
Cont. Tractive Effort: 39 kN (8800 lbf) at 11.6 mph.

Power At Rail: 201 kW (269 hp).	**Train Brakes:** Air & vacuum.
Brake Force: 19 t.	**Dimensions:** 8.92 x 2.59 x 3.89 m.
Weight: 50 t.	**Wheel Diameter:** 1372 mm.
Design Speed: 27 mph.	**Max. Speed:** 27 mph.
Fuel Capacity: 3037 litres.	**RA:** 5.
Train Supply: Not equipped.	**Multiple Working:** Not equipped.

Note: 09017 was renumbered from 97806 during 1998.
Non-standard livery/numbering:
•   09017 is as **B**, but with a grey cab.

Class 09/0. Standard Design.

09001	**B**	E	LNCF	CF	*Margam SD*
09003	**B**	E	LNCF	CF	*Cardiff Canton (Loco) TMD*
09004	**B**	SC	HWSU	SU(S)	
09005	**DG**	E	FDSK	KY	*Healey Mills Yard*
09006	**ML**	E	EWOC	OC	*Hoo Junction*
09007	**ML**	E	FDSD	DR	*Tinsley Yard*
09008	**DG**	E	LNCF	CF	*Cardiff Canton (Loco) TMD*
09009	**E**	E	EWOC	OC	*Co-Steel, Sheerness*
09010	**DG**	E	EWOC	OC	*Parkeston Yard*
09011	**DG**	E	EWOC	OC	*Hither Green TMD*
09012	**DG**	E	EWOC	OC	*Wembley Yard*
09013	**DG**	E	LNCF	CF	*Tavistock Junction*
09014	**DG**	E	FDSD	DR	*Rotherham Steel Terminal*
09015	**DG**	E	LNCF	CF	*Barry WRD*
09016	**DG**	E	EWEH	EH	*Eastleigh Yard*
09017	**0**	E	LNCF	CF	*Sudbrook Pumping Station*
09018	**ML**	E	EWOC	OC	*Wembley Yard*
09019	**ML**	E	EWOC	OC	*Stewarts Lane T&RSMD*
09020	**B**	E	WSXX	ZB(S)	
09021	**FE**	E	LBBS	BS	*Saltley SD*
09022	**B**	E	WSXX	AN(S)	
09023	**ML**	E	LWSP	CD	*Allerton T&RSMD*
09024	**ML**	E	EWOC	OC	*Hoo Junction*
09025	**CX**	SC	HWSU	BI	*Brighton T&RSMD*
09026	**G**	SC	HWSU	BI	*Brighton T&RSMD*

Names:

09009	Three Bridges C.E.D.	09026	William Pearson
09012	Dick Hardy		

Class 09/1. Converted from Class 08/0. 110 V electrical equipment. Details as Class 09/0 except:
Built: 1960–61 by BR at Crewe, Derby or Horwich Works. Converted 1992–93 by RFS Industries, Kilnhurst.

09101	**DG**	E	EWEH	EH	*Swindon Cocklebury Yard*
09102	**DG**	E	EWEH	EH	*Wembley Yard*
09103	**DG**	E	LGML	ML	*Motherwell TMD*
09104	**DG**	E	LGML	ML	*Motherwell TMD*
09105	**DG**	E	LNCF	CF	*Newport ADJ*
09106	**DG**	E	FMSY	TE	*Thornaby TMD*
09107	**DG**	E	LNCF	CF	*Cardiff Canton (Loco) TMD*

Class 09/2. Converted from Class 08/0. 90 V electrical equipment. Details as Class 09/0 except:
Built: 1958–60 by BR at Crewe or Derby Works. Converted 1992 by RFS Industries, Kilnhurst.

09201	a	**DG**	E	FDSK	KY	*Knottingley T&RSMD*
09202		**DG**	E	LGML	ML	*Aberdeen Guild Street*
09203		**DG**	E	LNCF	CF	*Newport ADJ*
09204		**DG**	E	FMSY	TE	*Thornaby TMD*
09205		**DG**	E	LGML	ML	*Millerhill Yard*

CLASS 20   ENGLISH ELECTRIC   Bo–Bo

Built: 1957–68 by English Electric Company at Vulcan Foundry, Newton le Willows or by Robert Stephenson & Hawthorn at Darlington.
Engine: English Electric 8SVT Mk. II of 746 kW (1000 hp) at 850 rpm.
Main Generator: English Electric 819/3C.
Traction Motors: English Electric 526/5D or 526/8D.
Max. Tractive Effort: 187 kN (42000 lbf).
Cont. Tractive Effort: 111 kN (25000 lbf) at 11 mph.
Power At Rail: 574 kW (770 hp).   **Train Brakes:** Air & vacuum.
Brake Force: 35 t.   **Dimensions:** 14.25 x 2.67 x 3.86 m.
Weight: 73.4–73.5 t.   **Wheel Diameter:** 1092 mm.
Design Speed: 75mph.   **Max. Speed:** 60 mph.
Fuel Capacity: 1727 litres.   **RA:** 5.
Train Supply: Not equipped.   **Multiple Working:** Blue Star.
Non-standard livery/numbering:
• 20092/169 are in British Railways Board Central Services livery of red and grey.

Class 20/0. Standard Design.

20007	s	**B**	DR	XHSS	ZB(S)
20016	s	**B**	E	WNZX	BS(S)
20032	s	**B**	DR	XHSS	ZB(S)
20057	s	**B**	E	WNZX	BS(S)
20059	s	**FR**	E	WNXX	MG(S)
20066		**B**	E	WNZX	BS(S)
20072	s	**B**	DR	XHSS	ZB(S)
20073	s	**B**	E	WHZX	BS(S)
20081	s	**B**	E	WNZX	BS(S)

20087	s	**BR**	E	WNZX	BS(S)	
20088	s	**RF**	DR	XHSS	SD(S)	
20092		**0**	E	WNZX	BS(S)	
20105	s	**RF**	DR	XHSS	ZB(S)	
20118		**FR**	E	WNZX	BS(S)	
20119		**B**	E	WNZX	TT(S)	
20121	s	**B**	DR	XHSS	ZB(S)	
20132	s	**FR**	E	WNZX	BS(S)	
20138		**FR**	E	WNZX	BS(S)	
20145		**RF**	DR	XHSS	BS(S)	
20154	s	**B**	E	WNZX	TT(S)	
20159	s	**RF**	DR	XHSS	ZB(S)	
20165		**FR**	E	WNZX	BS(S)	
20168	s	**B**	E	WNZX	MG(S)	
20169	s	**0**	E	WNZX	BS(S)	
20177	s	**B**	E	WNZX	TT(S)	
20209	s	**B**	DR	XHSS	ZK(S)	
20215	s	**FR**	DR	XHSS	ZB(S)	

Class 20/3. Direct Rail Services refurbished locos. Details as Class 20/0 except:
Refurbished: 1995–96 by Brush Traction at Loughborough (20301–305) or 1997–98 by RFS(E) at Doncaster (20306–315).
Train Brakes: Air.   **Max. Speed:** 75 mph.
Brake Force: 31 t.   **Fuel Capacity:** 4727 litres.
Multiple Working: DRS System (20301–305 at nose end only).

20301			**DR**	DR	XHSD	SD	FURNESS RAILWAY 150
20302			**DR**	DR	XHSD	SD	
20303			**DR**	DR	XHSD	SD	
20304			**DR**	DR	XHSD	SD	
20305			**DR**	DR	XHSD	SD	
20306	(20131)		**DR**	DR	XHSD	SD	
20307	(20128)		**DR**	DR	XHSD	SD	
20308	(20187)		**DR**	DR	XHSD	SD	
20309	(20075)		**DR**	DR	XHSD	SD	
20310	(20190)		**DR**	DR	XHSD	SD	
20311	(20102)		**DR**	DR	XHSD	SD	
20312	(20042)		**DR**	DR	XHSD	SD	
20313	(20194)		**DR**	DR	XHSD	SD	
20314	(20117)		**DR**	DR	XHSD	SD	
20315	(20104)		**DR**	DR	XHSD	SD	

Class 20/9. Direct Rail Services (former Hunslet-Barclay) refurbished locos. Details as Class 20/0 except:

Refurbished: 1989 by Hunslet-Barclay at Kilmarnock.
Train Brakes: Air.   **Fuel Capacity:** 1727 (+ 4727) litres.

20901		**HB**	DR	XHSS	SD(S)
20902	+	**HB**	DR	XHSS	SD(S)
20903	+	**HB**	DR	XHSS	KD(S)
20904		**HB**	DR	XHSS	KD(S)
20905	+	**HB**	DR	XHSS	KD(S)
20906		**HB**	DR	XHSS	KD(S)

CLASS 25   BR/BEYER PEACOCK/SULZER   Bo–Bo

Built: 1963–65 by BR at Derby Locomotive Works (25083) or Beyer Peacock at Gorton (25278).
Engine: Sulzer 6LDA28-B of 930 kW (1250 hp) at 750 rpm.
Main Generator: AEI RTB15656.   **Traction Motors:** AEI 253AY.
Max. Tractive Effort: 200 kN (45000 lbf).
Cont. TE: 93 kN (20800 lbf) at 17.1 mph.
Power At Rail: 708 kW (949 hp).   **Train Brakes:** See below.
Brake Force: 38 t.   **Dimensions:** 15.39 x 2.73 x 3.86 m.
Weight: 73.75 t. (25083); 71.45 t. (25278).
Design Speed: 90 mph.   **Wheel Diameter:** 1143 mm.
Maximum Speed: 90 mph (25083); 60 mph (25278).
Fuel Capacity: 2270 litres.   **RA:** 5.
Train Supply: Steam (25083); Not equipped (25278).
Multiple Working: Blue Star.

Class 25/2. GEC Series 2 Control Equipment.

25083   v   **B**   E   WNZX   CP(S)

Class 25/3. GEC Series 3 Control Equipment.

25278   x   **G**   NY   MBDL   NY   SYBILIA

CLASS 31   BRUSH/ENGLISH ELECTRIC   A1A–A1A

Built: 1958–62 by Brush Traction at Loughborough.
Engine: English Electric 12SVT of 1100 kW (1470 hp) at 850 rpm.
Main Generator: Brush TG160-48.
Traction Motors: Brush TM73-68.
Max. Tractive Effort: 160 or * 190 kN (35900 or * 42800 lbf).
Cont. TE: 83 kN (18700 lbf) at 23.5 mph. (* 99 kN (22250 lbf) at 19.7 mph.).
Power At Rail: 872 kW (1170 hp).   **Train Brakes:** Air & vacuum.
Brake Force: 49 t.   **Dimensions:** 17.30 x 2.67 x 3.87 m.
Weight: 106.7–111 t.   **Wheel Diameter:** 1092/1003 mm.
Design Speed: 90 (* 80) mph.   **Max. Speed:** 60 mph.
Fuel Capacity: 2409 litres.   **RA:** 5 or 6.
Train Supply: Not equipped.   **Multiple Working:** Blue Star.
Note: 31452 was renumbered from 31552 during 1998.
Non-standard livery/numbering:
•   31116 is grey and yellow with red stripes.

Class 31/1. Standard Design. RA: 5.

31102		**CE**	E	WNYX	CD(S)
31105	*	**T**	E	WNZX	BS(S)
31106	*	**CE**	E	WNZX	BS(S)
31107		**CE**	E	WNZX	BS(S)
31110		**CE**	E	WMAN	BS
31112	*	**TC**	E	WNXX	BS(S)
31113		**CE**	E	WMAN	BS
31116		**0**	E	WNZX	TU(S)

31119	CE	E	WNXX	CL(S)	
31125	CE	E	WNZX	BS(S)	
31126	CE	E	WNYX	SP(S)	
31128	FO	E	WNZX	BS(S)	
31130	FC	E	WNZX	BS(S)	
31132	FO	E	WNXX	BS(S)	
31134	CE	E	WNYX	SP(S)	
31135	CE	E	WNZX	TU(S)	
31142	CE	E	WMAN	BS	
31144	CE	E	WNXX	CL(S)	
31145 r	CE	E	WNYX	SP(S)	
31146 r	CE	E	WNYX	WA(S)	Brush Veteran
31147	CE	E	WNZX	BS(S)	
31149	FR	E	WNYX	TT(S)	
31154	CE	E	WMAN	BS	
31155	FA	E	WNZX	BS(S)	
31158	CE	E	WNZX	BS(S)	
31160	F	E	WNYX	SP(S)	
31163	CE	E	WMAN	BS	
31164	FO	E	WNZX	BS(S)	
31166 r	CE	E	WMAN	BS	
31168	B	E	WNZX	BS(S)	
31171	FO	E	WNZX	BS(S)	
31174	CE	E	WNZX	BS(S)	
31178	CE	E	WNZX	BS(S)	
31180	FR	E	WNZX	TU(S)	
31181	CE	E	WNZX	TU(S)	
31184	FO	E	WNZX	TU(S)	
31185	CE	E	WNZX	BS(S)	
31186	CE	FG	SDXL	TM(S)	
31187	CE	E	WNZX	TU(S)	
31188	CE	E	WMAN	BS	
31190	CE	E	WMAN	BS	
31191	CE	FG	SDXL	TM(S)	
31196	CE	E	WNZX	SF(S)	
31199	FC	E	WNYX	TT(S)	
31200	FC	E	WNYX	BA(S)	
31201	FC	E	WMAN	BS	
31203	CE	E	WMAN	BS	
31205	FR	E	WNZX	TU(S)	
31206	CE	E	WNXX	BS(S)	
31207	CE	E	WMAN	BS	
31209	FA	E	WNZX	TU(S)	
31219	CE	E	WNZX	TU(S)	
31224	CE	E	WNXX	CL(S)	
31229	CE	E	WNZX	BS(S)	
31230 *	FO	E	WNZX	TU(S)	
31232	CE	E	WNZX	BS(S)	
31233	CE	E	WMAN	BS	Severn Valley Railway
31235	CE	E	WNXX	CL(S)	
31237	CE	E	WNZX	BS(S)	

31238	CE	E	WNYX	SP(S)
31242	CE	E	WNXX	SP(S)
31247	FR	E	WNZX	TU(S)
31248	FO	E	WNZX	BS(S)
31250	CE	E	WNZX	TU(S)
31252	FO	E	WNYX	PB(S)
31255	CE	E	WMAN	BS
31263	CE	E	WNZX	BS(S)
31268	CE	E	WNZX	TU(S)
31270	F	E	WNXX	CL(S)
31273	CE	E	WNYX	BS(S)
31276	FC	E	WNZX	TU(S)
31282	FR	E	WNZX	BS(S)
31283	B	E	WNZX	SF(S)
31285	CE	E	WNXX	CL(S)
31286	B	E	WNZX	BS(S)
31289	B	E	WNZX	BS(S)
31290	CE	E	WNZX	TU(S)
31294	FA	E	WNZX	TU(S)
31296	FA	E	WHZX	CP(S)
31299	FO	E	WNZX	SF(S)
31301	FR	E	WNZX	BS(S)
31302	FP	E	WNYX	SP(S)
31304	FC	E	WNYX	SP(S)
31306	CE	E	WMAN	BS
31308	CE	E	WMAN	BS
31312	FC	E	WNYX	SP(S)
31317	FO	E	WNZX	BS(S)
31319	FC	E	WNYX	BS(S)
31320	B	E	WNZX	SF(S)
31327	FR	E	WNXX	CL(S)

Class 31/4. Electric Train Supply equipment. Details as Class 31/1 except:
Max. Speed: 90 mph.   **RA:** 6.
Train Supply: Electric, but not operational (e – Electric, index 66).

31402		B	E	WNZX	BS(S)
31403		B	E	WNZX	TU(S)
31405		IM	E	WNXX	ZF(S)
31407		ML	E	WNZX	BS(S)
31408		B	E	WNYX	SP(S)
31411		DG	E	WNZX	BS(S)
31415		B	E	WNZX	BS(S)
31417		DG	E	WNZX	BS(S)
31420	e	IM	E	WMAN	BS
31421		RR	E	WNYX	BA(S)
31422		IM	E	WNXX	BS(S)
31423		IM	E	WNZX	BS(S)
31427		B	E	WNXX	BS(S)
31428		B	E	WNZX	BS(S)
31432		B	E	WNYX	SP(S)
31434		B	E	WNYX	BS(S)

31435		CE	E	WNZX	BS(S)	North Yorkshire Moors Railway
31439		RR	E	WNXX	BS(S)	
31442		B	E	WNYX	BA(S)	
31444		CE	E	WNYX	SP(S)	
31450		B	E	WNXX	SP(S)	
31452	e	FG	FG	SDFR	TM	
31455		RR	E	WNYX	SP(S)	
31459		B	FG	SDXL	TM(S)	
31460		B	E	WNZX	BS(S)	
31461		DG	FG	SDXL	TM(S)	
31462		DG	E	WNZX	BS(S)	
31465	e	RR	E	WMAN	BS	
31466	e	E	E	WMAN	BS	
31467		B	E	WNZX	BS(S)	
31468	e	FG	FG	SDFR	TM	

Class 31/1 ("31/5"). Electric Train Supply equipment fitted, but isolated.
Details as Class 31/1 except: **RA:** 6.
Max. Speed: 60 mph.   **Train Supply:** Electric, isolated.

31512	CE	E	WNZX	BS(S)
31514	CE	E	WMAN	BS
31516	CE	E	WNZX	BS(S)
31519	CE	E	WNYX	SP(S)
31524	CE	E	WNZX	BS(S)
31526	CE	E	WNZX	BS(S)
31530	CE	E	WMAN	BS
31531	CE	E	WNZX	TU(S)
31533	CE	E	WNZX	BS(S)
31537	CE	E	WNXX	BS(S)
31538	B	E	WNXX	CL(S)
31541	CE	E	WNYX	OC(S)
31545	B	E	WNZX	BS(S)
31546	CE	E	WNZX	BS(S)
31547	CE	E	WNZX	TU(S)
31548	CE	E	WNZX	BS(S)
31549	CE	FG	SDXL	TM(S)
31553	CE	E	WNZX	TU(S)
31554	CE	E	WMAN	BS
31556	CE	E	WNXX	CL(S)
31558	CE	FG	SDXL	TM(S)
31569	CE	E	WNZX	TU(S)

CLASS 33   BRCW/SULZER   Bo–Bo

Built: 1960–62 by the Birmingham Railway Carriage & Wagon Company at Smethwick.
Engine: Sulzer 8LDA28 of 1160 kW (1550 hp) at 750 rpm.
Main Generator: Crompton Parkinson CG391B1.
Traction Motors: Crompton Parkinson C171C2.
Max. Tractive Effort: 200 kN (45000 lbf).
Cont. Tractive Effort: 116 kN (26000 lbf) at 17.5 mph.

Power At Rail: 906 kW (1215 hp).
Brake Force: 35 t.
Weight: 77.7 t.
Design Speed: 85 mph.
Fuel Capacity: 3410 litres.
Train Supply: Electric, not operational (e – index 48 (750 V dc only).
Multiple Working: Blue Star.

Train Brakes: Air & vacuum.
Dimensions: 15.47 x 2.82 x 3.86 m.
Wheel Diameter: 1092 mm.
Max. Speed: 60 (* 75, † 85) mph.
RA: 6.

Non-standard livery/numbering:
* 33012 carries number 6515.
* 33051 also carries number 6569.
* 33116 also carries number D6535.
* 33208 carries number D6593.

Class 33/0. Standard Design.

33012	e†	**B**	71	MBDL	RL	
33019		**CE**	E	WNWX	IM(S)	
33021	e†	**R**	FG	SDFR	TM	Eastleigh
33025		**CE**	E	WNXX	IM(S)	
33026		**CE**	E	WNXX	EH(S)	
33030		**E**	E	WNWX	IM(S)	
33038		**B**	E	WNZX	SF(S)	
33046		**CE**	E	WNZX	EH(S)	
33051		**B**	E	WNXX	EH(S)	Shakespeare Cliff

Class 33/1. Buckeye Couplings and SR Multiple Working Equipment. Details as Class 33/0 except:
Train Brakes: Air, vacuum & electro-pneumatic.
Weight: 78.5 t.   **Multiple Working:** Blue Star & SR System.

33103	e†	**G**	CM	CTLO	TM
33109	e	**B**	71	MBDL	RL
33116		**B**	E	WNXX	OC(S)

Class 33/2. Narrow body profile. Details as Class 33/0 except:
Weight: 77.5 t.   **Dimensions:** 15.47 x 2.64 x 3.86 m.

33202		**CE**	E	WNWX	IM(S)
33205		**FD**	E	WNZX	OC(S)
33208	e*	**G**	71	MBDL	RL

CLASS 37   ENGLISH ELECTRIC TYPE 3   Co-Co

Built: 1960–65 by English Electric Company at Vulcan Foundry, Newton le Willows or by Robert Stephenson & Hawthorn at Darlington.
Engine: English Electric 12CSVT of 1300 kW (1750 hp) at 850 rpm.
Main Generator: English Electric 822/10G.
Traction Motors: English Electric 538/A.
Max. Tractive Effort: 245 kN (55500 lbf).
Cont. Tractive Effort: 156 kN (35000 lbf) at 13.6 mph.
Power At Rail: 932 kW (1250 hp).
Brake Force: 50 t.
Weight: 102.8–108.4 t.
Design Speed: 90 mph.

Train Brakes: Air & vacuum.
Dimensions: 18.75 x 2.74 x 3.94 or 3.99 m.
Wheel Diameter: 1092 mm.
Max. Speed: 80 mph.

Fuel Capacity: 4046 (+ 7678) litres.   **RA:** 5.
Train Supply: Not equipped.   **Multiple Working:** Blue Star.
Notes: 37072–074/131–298/358/370–384 have roof mounted horns and are
3.99 m. high. Others have nose mounted horns and are 3.94 m. high.

Non-standard liveries/numbering:
• 37101 is officially numbered 37345, but it is doubtful it has ever carried
  this number.
• 37116 is as **B**, but with Transrail markings.
• 37330 is blue with yellow cabs and black window surrounds.
• 37350 also carries number D6700.
• 37403 carries number D6607.

Class 37/0. Standard Design. Details as above.

37010		**CE**	E	WKBN	TO
37012	§	**CE**	E	WKBN	TO
37013	+	**ML**	E	WKBN	TO
37019	+	**FD**	E	WNYX	HM(S)
37023	r	**ML**	E	WKMB	ML	Stratford TMD Quality Approved
37025		**BL**	E	WKBN	TO	Inverness TMD
37026	+	**FD**	E	WNYX	SP(S)
37037		**F**	E	WKBN	TO
37038		**CE**	E	WKBN	TO
37040		**E**	E	WKBN	TO
37042	+	**E**	E	WKBN	TO
37043	r§	**TC**	E	WKMB	ML
37045	+	**F**	E	WNYX	TT(S)
37046		**CE**	E	WKBN	TO
37047	+	**ML**	E	WKBN	TO
37048		**MG**	E	WNYX	TT(S)
37051		**E**	E	WKBN	TO	Merehead
37054		**CE**	E	WKBN	TO
37055	+	**ML**	E	WKBN	TO
37057	+	**E**	E	WKBN	TO	Viking
37058	+	**CE**	E	WKBN	TO
37059	+	**FD**	E	WKBN	TO
37063	a+	**FD**	E	WNYX	ZB(S)
37065	+	**ML**	E	WKBN	TO
37068	+	**FD**	E	WNYX	IM(S)
37069	+	**CE**	E	WKBN	TO
37071	+	**CE**	E	WKBN	TO
37072	+	**DG**	E	WNYX	ZB(S)
37073	+	**T**	E	WKBN	TO	Fort William/An Gearasdan
37074	+	**ML**	E	WKBN	TO
37075	+	**F**	E	WNXX	IM(S)
37077		**ML**	E	WKBN	TO
37078	+	**FM**	E	WNYX	ML(S)
37079	+	**FD**	E	WNYX	ZH(S)	Medite
37083	+	**CE**	E	WNYX	DR(S)
37087		**CE**	E	WNXX	BA(S)
37088		**TC**	E	WNYX	ML(S)	Clydesdale
37092		**CE**	E	WNYX	TT(S)

37095	+	CE	E	WNYX	ZB(S)	
37097		CE	E	WNYX	MH(S)	
37098	+	CE	E	WNYX	OC(S)	
37100	+	T	E	WKBN	TO	
37101	+	FD	E	WNZX	IM(S)	
37104		CE	E	WNYX	IM(S)	
37106	+	CE	E	WKBN	TO	
37107	+	FD	E	WNYX	SP(S)	
37108	+	F	E	WNYX	BS(S)	
37109	a	E	E	WKBN	TO	
37110	+	F	E	WNYX	IM(S)	
37114	r+	E	E	WKMB	ML	City of Worcester
37116	r+	O	E	WKMB	ML	Sister Dora
37131	+§	F	E	WKBN	TO	
37133	a§	CE	E	WKBN	TO	
37137		MG	E	WNYX	TT(S)	
37139	+	FC	E	WNYX	TE(S)	
37140		CE	E	WKBN	TO	
37141		CE	E	WNYX	ZC(S)	
37142		CE	E	WNYX	BA(S)	
37144	r	FA	E	WNYX	IM(S)	
37146		CE	E	WKBN	TO	
37152	r§	IS	E	WKMB	ML	
37153	r§	TC	E	WKMB	ML	
37154	+§	T	E	WKBN	TO	
37156		T	E	WKBN	TO	
37158		CE	E	WKBN	TO	
37162	+	DG	E	WKBN	TO	
37165	r+	TC	E	WKMB	ML	
37170	r	TC	E	WKMB	ML	
37174	a	E	E	WKBN	TO	
37175	a	CE	E	WKBN	TO	
37178	+§	F	E	WKBN	TO	
37184	§	CE	E	WNYX	BS(S)	
37185	+	CE	E	WKBN	TO	Lea & Perrins
37188		TC	E	WNYX	TT(S)	
37191	a§	CE	E	WKBN	TO	
37194	+	MG	E	WKBN	TO	British International Freight Association
37196	§	CE	E	WKBN	TO	
37197	+§	TC	E	WKBN	TO	
37198	+	ML	E	WKBN	TO	
37201		TC	E	WNXX	BS(S)	
37203		ML	E	WKBN	TO	
37207		CE	E	WNXX	BS(S)	
37209		BL	E	WNYX	DR(S)	
37211		CE	E	WKBN	TO	
37212	+	T	E	WKBN	TO	
37213	+	FC	E	WNYX	TT(S)	
37214	+	T	E	WNXX	BS(S)	
37216	r+	ML	E	WKBN	TO	
37217	+	B	E	WNXX	AY(S)	

▲ Increasing numbers of Class 08 are being repainted into EWS corporate red and gold livery. 08828 is seen here at Margam Yard on 28th January 1998.

Rodney Lissenden

▼ BR 'general grey' liveried 09014 shunts type HAA coal hopper wagons at Milford West Sidings on 2nd October 1997.

John G. Teasdale

British Nuclear Fuels subsidiary Direct Rail Services is progressively taking over the haulage of nuclear flask trains from EWS. Here 20301 and 20302 wait at Lydd Town level crossing on the branch to Dungeness Power Station whilst on a crew training trip on 21st April 1997.

Rodney Lissenden

BR blue liveried 31434 pulls away from a signal check at Warrington Arpley with five salt hoppers forming a Runcorn–Arpley 'Enterprise' trip. The wagons are eventually destined for Dalry, in South West Scotland. **Nic Joynson**

▲ D6593 (33208) arrives at Ystrad Mynach with the 17.38 Rhymney–Cardiff Central service whilst on hire to Cardiff Railways on 30th April 1998.

Hugh Ballantyne

▼ 37153 (nearest camera) and 37154 carry the two different varieties of Transrail livery. They are seen here stabled at the erstwhile Stratford TMD on 30th May 1998.

Kevin Conkey

▲ Regional Railways liveried 37420 'The Scottish Hosteller' arrives at Holyhead with the 14.23 service from Birmingham New Street on 15th August 1998.
Nic Joynson

▼ 43101, complete with new style Virgin name 'The Irish Mail Trên Post Gwyddelig' leads on the 09.10 Aberdeen–Plymouth on 23rd September 1998. **Dave McAlone**

▲ Fragonset Railways' 47703 departs from Crewe with the 06.42 Poole–Liverpool Lime Street on 31st March 1998. **Bob Sweet**

▼ 47750 'Royal Mail Cheltenham' passes Barry Town with the all Rail Express Systems liveried 10.25 Bristol Temple Meads–Swansea empty van train on 2nd April 1998. **Rodney Lissenden**

Privately owned 50050 'Fearless' made its first outing on the main line journeying to Bournemouth TMD Open Day on 16th May 1998. It is one of only two preserved locos authorised for main line use at 90 mph.

Nic Joynson

56047 passes Hasland with the 08.37 Tees Yard–Erruria empty bogie bolster train on 28th April 1998. **Rodney Lissenden**

▲ Freightliner's 57001 takes on fuel at the company's recently opened fuelling point at Crewe Basford Hall Yard on 17th August 1998. **Neil Webster**

▼ Mainline blue liveried 58021 'Hither Green Depot' stands, appropriately, at Hither Green depot on 14th May 1998. **Rodney Lissenden**

▲ All the Class 59/2 locomotives acquired by EWS from National Power have now been repainted in EWS corporate livery. 59203 'Vale of Pickering', is seen here at Knottingley at the head of a Drax–Milford empty wagon train on 4th September 1998. **Michael J. Collins**

▼ Transrail liveried 60061 'Alexander Graham Bell' passes through the industrial landscape of Widnes with a train of empty 'merry-go-round' hoppers en route to Gladstone Dock on 24th September 1997. **Nic Joynson**

English Welsh & Scottish Railway is receiving deliveries of its order for 250 Class 66 locomotives from General Motors in Canada at quite a fast pace. 66001 was exhibited at Foster Yeoman's 75th anniversary event at Merehead on 27th June 1998.

Hugh Ballantyne

▲ With both loco and coaches looking in smart in Gatwick Express corporate livery, 73205 passes Horley with the 16.30 London Victoria–Gatwick Airport on 9th May 1998. **Nic Joynson**

▼ In its 'home' county, 87025 'County of Cheshire' passes Red Bank, near Winwick Junction with the 11.20 Preston–London Euston on 15th May 1997. **Nic Joynson**

Anglia Railways 86215, then un-named but now named 'Norfolk & Norwich Festival' passes Stratford with the 10.05 Norwich–London Liverpool Street on 17th September 1998.
Brian Denton

▲ Unique 89001 operates on a self-contained diagram between London King's Cross and Leeds. It is seen here awaiting departure time at King's Cross at the head of the 07.50 'Yorkshire Pullman' on 8th May 1998. **Hugh Ballantyne**

▼ Railfreight Distribution liveried 90134 departs from Wembley Yard with the 13.08 Dagenham Dock–Mossend Yard on 21st May 1998. **Brian Denton**

▲ 91014 approaches Doncaster with the 10.00 London King's Cross–Glasgow Central on 19th August 1998. **Les Nixon**

▼ Eurotunnel 'Shuttle' loco 9024 arrives at the UK terminal at Cheriton with a car shuttle on 17th May 1997. **Hugh Ballantyne**

92023 'Ravel' passes Kemsing with the 09.33 Wembley–Dollands Moor freight on 24th March 1998.   Rodney Lissenden

37218	+	F	E	WNXX	IM(S)	
37219		ML	E	WKBN	TO	
37220	r+	E	E	WKMB	ML	
37221	r	T	E	WKMB	ML	
37222	+	MG	E	WNYX	CF(S)	
37223	+	FC	E	WNXX	IM(S)	
37225	+	F	E	WKBN	TO	
37227	+	MG	E	WNYX	SL(S)	
37229	+§	FC	E	WKBN	TO	
37230	+§	TC	E	WKBN	TO	
37232	r§	TC	E	WNXX	ML(S)	The Institution of Railway Signal Engineers
37235	+	F	E	WNYX	DR(S)	
37238	+	F	E	WKBN	TO	
37240	+	CE	E	WNXX	BS(S)	
37241		MG	E	WNYX	TT(S)	
37242	+	ML	E	WKBN	TO	
37244	+	F	E	WKBN	TO	
37245		CE	E	WNWX	TO(S)	
37248	+	ML	E	WKBN	TO	Midland Railway Centre
37250	+	T	E	WKBN	TO	
37251	a+	IS	E	WNYX	ML(S)	The Northern Lights[1]
37252		FD	E	WNYX	DR(S)	
37254	+	CE	E	WNYX	ZH(S)	
37255	+§	CE	E	WKBN	TO	
37261	a+	FD	E	WKBN	TO	Caithness
37262	+§	DG	E	WKBN	TO	Dounreay[1]
37263	§	CE	E	WKBN	TO	
37264		CE	E	WKBN	TO	
37274	+	ML	E	WKBN	TO	
37275	+§	B	E	WKBN	TO	Oor Wullie
37278	+	FC	E	WNYX	TT(S)	
37293	+	ML	E	WKBN	TO	
37294	r+	CE	E	WKMB	ML	
37298	+	E	E	WKBN	TO	

Class 37/3. Re-geared (CP7) bogies. Details as Class 37/0 except:
Max. Tractive Effort: 250 kN (56180 lbf).
Cont. Tractive Effort: 184 kN (41250 lbf) at 11.4 mph.
Design Speed: 80 mph.　　　　　**Max. Speed:** 80 mph.
Notes: 37334 is mounted on standard bogies, but has not been renumbered back to Class 37/0. 37384 was renumbered from 37258 during 1998.

37330	+§	O	E	WNYX	TT(S)	
37331		FM	E	WNYX	DR(S)	
37332	+§	FC	E	WNXX	TO(S)	The Coal Merchants' Association of Scotland
37334	a+§	F	E	WNXX	IM(S)	
37335	+	F	E	WNYX	IM(S)	
37340	+	FD	E	WNYX	IM(S)	
37341	+	F	E	WNYX	TE(S)	
37343		CE	E	WNYX	TT(S)	

37344	+	**FD**	E	WNYX	IM(S)	
37350	+	**G**	E	WKBN	TO	NATIONAL RAILWAY MUSEUM
37351	+	**TC**	E	WKBN	TO	
37358	+	**F**	E	WNXX	IM(S)	
37359		**FP**	E	WNYX	TE(S)	
37370		**E**	E	WKBN	TO	
37371	+	**ML**	E	WKBN	TO	
37372		**ML**	E	WKBN	TO	
37375	+	**ML**	E	WKBN	TO	
37376	+	**F**	E	WKBN	TO	
37377	+	**CE**	E	WKBN	TO	
37379	r	**ML**	E	WKBN	TO	Ipswich WRD Quality Approved
37380		**MG**	E	WKBN	TO	
37381	+	**FD**	E	WNYX	FH(S)	
37382		**FP**	E	WNYX	IM(S)	
37383	+	**ML**	E	WKBN	TO	
37384	+§	**CE**	E	WKBN	TO	

Class 37/4. Refurbished locos with train supply equipment. Main generator replaced by alternator. Re-geared (CP7) bogies. Details as class 37/0 except:
Main Alternator: Brush BA1005A.   **Power At Rail:** 935 kW (1254 hp).
Max. Tractive Effort: 256 kN (57440 lbf).
Cont. Tractive Effort: 184 kN (41250 lbf) at 11.4 mph.
Dimensions: 18.75 x 2.74 x 3.99 m.   **Weight:** 107 t.
Design Speed: 80 mph.   **Max. Speed:** 80 mph.
Fuel Capacity: 7678 litres.   **Train Supply:** Electric, index 38.

37401	r	**E**	E	WKCD	CD	Mary Queen of Scots
37402		**F**	E	WKCN	TO	Bont Y Bermo
37403	r	**G**	E	WKMB	ML	Ben Cruachan
37404	r	**T**	E	WKMB	ML	Loch Long
37405	r	**E**	E	WKMB	ML	
37406	r	**T**	E	WKMB	ML	The Saltire Society
37407		**T**	E	WKCN	TO	Blackpool Tower
37408		**E**	E	WKCD	CD	
37409	r	**T**	E	WKMB	ML	Loch Awe
37410	r	**T**	E	WKMB	ML	Aluminium 100
37411		**E**	E	WKCN	TO	Ty Hafan
37412		**T**	E	WKCN	TO	Driver John Elliott
37413	r	**E**	E	WKMB	ML	The Scottish Railway Preservation Society
37414		**RR**	E	WKCN	TO	Cathays C & W Works 1846-1993
37415		**E**	E	WKCD	CD	
37416		**E**	E	WKCN	TO	
37417		**E**	E	WKCN	TO	RAIL MAGAZINE
37418		**E**	E	WKCD	CD	East Lancashire Railway
37419	r	**E**	E	WKMB	ML	
37420		**RR**	E	WKCD	CD	The Scottish Hosteller
37421		**E**	E	WKCD	CD	
37422		**RR**	E	WKCD	CD	Robert F. Fairlie Locomotive Engineer 1831–1885

37423	r	**T**	E	WKMB	ML	Sir Murray Morrison 1873-1948 Pioneer of the British Aluminium Industry
37424	r	**T**	E	WKMB	ML	
37425	r	**RR**	E	WKMB	ML	Sir Robert McAlpine/Concrete Bob
37426		**E**	E	WKCD	CD	
37427	r	**E**	E	WKMB	ML	
37428	r	**GS**	E	WKMB	ML	
37429		**RR**	E	WKCN	TO	Eisteddfod Genedlaethol
37430	r	**T**	E	WKMB	ML	Cwmbrân
37431	r	**IM**	E	WKMB	ML	

Class 37/5. Refurbished locos without train supply equipment. Main generator replaced by alternator. Re-geared (CP7) bogies. Details as class 37/4 except:
Max. Tractive Effort: 248 kN (55590 lbf).
Dimensions: 18.75 x 2.74 x 3.94 or 3.99 m.
Weight: 106.1–107.3 t.   **Train Supply:** Not equipped.
Notes: 37610–679/682–698/800–899 have roof mounted horns and are 3.99 m. high. Others have nose mounted horns and are 3.94 m. high.

37503	§	**E**	E	WKFN	TO	
37505		**T**	E	WKFN	TO	British Steel Workington
37509		**F**	E	WKFN	TO	
37510		**IS**	E	WKFN	TO	
37513	s	**LH**	E	WKFN	TO	
37515	s	**FM**	E	WKFN	TO	
37516	s	**LH**	E	WKFN	TO	
37517	rs	**LH**	E	WKMB	ML	
37518		**FM**	E	WKFN	TO	
37519	§	**FM**	E	WKFN	TO	
37520	r	**E**	E	WKMB	ML	
37521		**E**	E	WKFN	TO	English China Clays

Class 37/6. Refurbished locos for the aborted Nightstar services. Main generator replaced by alternator, re-geared bogies and UIC jumpers. Details as class 37/5 except:
Max. Speed: 80 († 75) mph.   **Train Brake:** Air.
Train Supply: Not equipped, but electric through wired.
Multiple Working: TDM († plus DRS System).

37601		**EP**	EU	GPSV	OC	
37602		**EP**	EU	GPSV	OC	
37603		**EP**	EU	GPSV	OC	
37604		**EP**	EU	DFLT	ML	
37605		**EP**	EU	GPSV	OC	
37606		**EP**	EU	GPSV	OC	
37607	†	**DR**	DR	XHSD	SD	
37608	†	**DR**	DR	XHSD	SD	
37609	†	**DR**	DR	XHSD	SD	
37610	†	**DR**	DR	XHSD	SD	
37611	†	**DR**	DR	XHSD	SD	
37612	†	**DR**	DR	XHSD	SD	

Class 37/5 (Continued).

37667	rs	E	E	WKMB	ML	Meldon Quarry Centenary
37668	s	E	E	WKFN	TO	
37669		E	E	WKFN	TO	
37670		E	E	WKFN	TO	St.Blazey T&RS Depot
37671		T	E	WKFN	TO	Tre Pol and Pen
37672	s	T	E	WKFN	TO	
37673		T	E	WKFN	TO	
37674		T	E	WKFN	TO	St. Blaise Church 1445-1995
37675	s	T	E	WKFN	TO	
37676		F	E	WKFN	TO	
37677	§	F	E	WKFN	TO	
37678		F	E	WKFN	TO	
37679		F	E	WKFN	TO	
37680	§	FA	E	WKFN	TO	
37682	r	E	E	WKMB	ML	Hartlepool Pipe Mill
37683		T	E	WKFN	TO	
37684	r	E	E	WKMB	ML	Peak National Park
37685		IS	E	WKFN	TO	
37686		FA	E	WKFN	TO	
37688	§	E	E	WKFN	TO	
37689		F	E	WKFN	TO	
37692	s	FC	E	WKFN	TO	The Lass O' Ballochmyle
37693	s	T	E	WKFN	TO	
37694		E	E	WKFN	TO	
37695	s	E	E	WKFN	TO	
37696	s	T	E	WKFN	TO	
37697	s§	E	E	WKFN	TO	
37698	s	LH	E	WKFN	TO	

Class 37/7. Refurbished locos. Main generator replaced by alternator. Re-geared (CP7) bogies. Ballast weights added. Details as class 37/5 except: Main Alternator: GEC G564AZ (37796–803) Brush BA1005A (others). **Max. Tractive Effort:** 276 kN (62000 lbf).
Weight: 120 t.   **RA:** 7.

37701	as	T	E	WKGN	TO	
37702	s	T	E	WKGN	TO	Taff Merthyr
37703		E	E	WKGN	TO	
37704	s	E	E	WKGN	TO	
37705		MG	E	WKGN	TO	
37706		E	E	WKGN	TO	
37707		E	E	WKGN	TO	
37708		FP	E	WKGN	TO	
37709		MG	E	WKGN	TO	
37710		LH	E	WKGN	TO	
37711		FM	E	WKGN	TO	
37712	a	E	E	WKGN	TO	
37713		LH	E	WKGN	TO	
37714	a	E	E	WKGN	TO	
37715		MG	E	WKGN	TO	British Petroleum
37716		E	E	WKGN	TO	

37717		E	E	WKGN	TO	Berwick Middle School, Railsafe Trophy Winners 1998
37718		E	E	WKGN	TO	
37719	a	FP	E	WKGN	TO	
37796	s	FC	E	WKGN	TO	
37797	as	E	E	WKGN	TO	
37798		ML	E	WKGN	TO	
37799	s	T	E	WKGN	TO	Sir Dyfed/County of Dyfed
37800		MG	E	WKGN	TO	
37801	s	E	E	WKGN	TO	
37802	s	T	E	WKGN	TO	
37803		ML	E	WKGN	TO	
37883		E	E	WKGN	TO	
37884		LH	E	WKGN	TO	Gartcosh
37885		E	E	WKGN	TO	
37886		E	E	WKGN	TO	
37887	s	T	E	WKGN	TO	
37888		F	E	WKGN	TO	
37889		T	E	WKGN	TO	
37890	a	MG	E	WKGN	TO	The Railway Observer
37891		MG	E	WKGN	TO	
37892		MG	E	WKGN	TO	Ripple Lane[1]
37893		E	E	WKGN	TO	
37894	s	FC	E	WKGN	TO	
37895	as	E	E	WKGN	TO	
37896	s	T	E	WKGN	TO	
37897	s	T	E	WKGN	TO	
37898	s	T	E	WKGN	TO	Cwmbargoed DP
37899	s	E	E	WKGN	TO	

Class 37/9. Refurbished locos. New power unit. Main generator replaced by alternator. Ballast weights added. Details as Class 37/4 except:
Engine: Mirrlees MB275T of 1340 kW (1800 hp) at 1000 rpm (‡ Ruston RK270T of 1340 kW (1800 hp) at 900 rpm).
Main Alternator: Brush BA1005A (‡ GEC G564AZ).
Max. Tractive Effort: 279 kN (62680 lbf).
Cont. Tractive Effort: 184 kN (41250 lbf) at 11.4 mph.
Weight: 120 t.   **RA:** 7.
Train supply: Not equipped.

37901		T	E	WNXX	CF(S)	Mirrlees Pioneer
37902		FM	E	WNYX	MG(S)	
37903		FM	E	WNXX	IM(S)	
37904		FM	E	WNYX	CF(S)	
37905	‡s	FM	E	WNXX	IM(S)	
37906	‡s	T	E	WKHN	CF	

CLASS 43   BREL/PAXMAN   Bo–Bo

Built: 1976–82 by BREL at Crewe Works.
Engine: Paxman Valenta 12RP200L of 1680 kW (2250 hp) at 1500 rpm († Paxman 12VP185 of 2010 kW (2700 hp) at ?? rpm).
Main Alternator: Brush BA1001B.
Traction Motors: Brush TMH68–46 or GEC G417AZ, frame mounted.
Max. Tractive Effort: 80 kN (17980 lbf).
Cont. Tractive Effort: 46 kN (10340 lbf) at 64.5 mph.
Power At Rail: 1320 kW (1770 hp).   **Train Brakes:** Air.
Brake Force: 35 t.   **Dimensions:** 17.79 x 2.71 x 3.88 m.
Weight: 70 t.   **Wheel Diameter:** 1020 mm.
Design Speed: 125 mph.   **Max. Speed:** 125 mph.
Fuel Capacity: 4500 litres.   **RA:** 5.
Train Supply: Three-phase electric.
Multiple Working: Within Class, jumpers at non-driving end only.

43002	GW	A	IWRP	PM	Techni?uest
43003	GW	A	IWRP	PM	
43004	GW	A	IWRP	PM	Borough of Swindon
43005	GW	A	IWRP	PM	
43006	IS	A	IWCP	LA	
43007	IS	A	IWCP	LA	
43008	V	A	IWCP	LA	
43009	GW	A	IWRP	PM	
43010	GW	A	IWRP	PM	
43011	GW	A	IWRP	PM	Reader 125
43012	GW	A	IWRP	PM	
43013	V	P	ICCP	LA	
43014	IS	P	ICCP	LA	
43015	GW	A	IWRP	PM	
43016	GW	A	IWRP	PM	
43017	GW	A	IWRP	LA	
43018	GW	A	IWRP	LA	The Red Cross
43019	GW	A	IWRP	LA	Dinas Abertawe/City of Swansea
43020	GW	A	IWRP	LA	John Grooms
43021	GW	A	IWRP	LA	
43022	GW	A	IWRP	LA	
43023	GW	A	IWRP	LA	County of Cornwall
43024	GW	A	IWRP	LA	
43025	GW	A	IWRP	LA	Exeter
43026	GW	A	IWRP	LA	City of Westminster
43027	GW	A	IWRP	LA	Glorious Devon
43028	GW	A	IWRP	LA	
43029	IS	A	IWRP	LA	
43030	GW	A	IWRP	PM	
43031	GW	A	IWRP	PM	
43032	GW	A	IWRP	PM	The Royal Regiment of Wales
43033	GW	A	IWRP	PM	
43034	GW	A	IWRP	PM	The Black Horse
43035	IS	A	IWRP	PM	

43036	IS	A	IWRP	PM	
43037	IS	A	IWRP	PM	
43038	GN	A	IECP	EC	
43039	GN	A	IECP	EC	
43040	GW	A	IWRP	PM	
43041	IS	A	IWRP	LA	City of Discovery
43042	GW	A	IWRP	LA	
43043	MM	P	IMLP	NL	LEICESTERSHIRE COUNTY CRICKET CLUB
43044	MM	P	IMLP	NL	Borough of Kettering
43045	MM	P	IMLP	NL	
43046	MM	P	IMLP	NL	Royal Philharmonic
43047 †	MM	P	IMLP	NL	
43048	MM	P	IMLP	NL	
43049	MM	P	IMLP	NL	Neville Hill
43050	MM	P	IMLP	NL	
43051	MM	P	IMLP	NL	
43052	MM	P	IMLP	NL	
43053	MM	P	IMLP	NL	Leeds United
43054	MM	P	IMLP	NL	
43055	MM	P	IMLP	NL	Sheffield Star
43056	MM	P	IMLP	NL	
43057	MM	P	IMLP	NL	
43058	MM	P	IMLP	NL	MIDLAND PRIDE
43059 †	MM	P	IMLP	NL	
43060	MM	P	IMLP	NL	County of Leicestershire
43061	MM	P	IMLP	NL	
43062	V	P	ICCP	LA	
43063	V	P	ICCP	LA	Maiden Voyager
43064	MM	P	IMLP	NL	
43065	V	P	ICCP	LA	
43066	MM	P	IMLP	NL	Nottingham Playhouse
43067	IS	P	ICCP	LA	
43068	V	P	ICCP	LA	The Red Nose
43069	V	P	ICCP	LA	
43070	IS	P	ICCP	LA	
43071	IS	P	ICCP	LA	Forward Birmingham
43072	MM	P	IMLP	NL	Derby Etches Park
43073	MM	P	IMLP	NL	
43074 †	MM	P	IMLP	NL	BBC EAST MIDLANDS TODAY
43075 †	MM	P	IMLP	NL	
43076	MM	P	IMLP	NL	THE MASTER CUTLER 1947-1997
43077	MM	P	IMLP	NL	
43078	IS	P	ICCP	LA	Golowan Festival Penzance
43079	IS	P	ICCP	LA	
43080	IS	P	ICCP	LA	
43081	MM	P	IMLP	NL	
43082	MM	P	IMLP	NL	DERBYSHIRE FIRST
43083	MM	P	IMLP	NL	
43084	V	P	ICCP	LA	County of Derbyshire
43085	MM	P	IMLP	NL	

43086	IS	P	ICCP	LA	
43087	IS	P	ICCP	LA	
43088	IS	P	ICCP	LA	XIII Commonwealth Games Scotland 1986
43089	IS	P	ICCP	LA	
43090	V	P	ICCP	LA	
43091	IS	P	ICCP	LA	Edinburgh Military Tattoo
43092	V	P	ICCP	LA	Institution of Mechanical
					Engineers 150th Anniversary
43093	V	P	ICCP	LA	Lady in Red
43094	IS	P	ICCP	LA	
43095	GN	A	IECP	EC	
43096	GN	A	IECP	EC	The Great Racer
43097	IS	P	ICCP	LA	
43098	V	P	ICCP	LA	railway children
43099	IS	P	ICCP	LA	
43100	V	P	ICCP	LA	Blackpool Rock
43101	V	P	ICCP	LA	The Irish Mail Trên Post Gwyddelig
43102	V	P	ICCP	LA	
43103	V	P	ICCP	LA	
43104	IS	A	SCXL	LA(S)	County of Cleveland
43105	GN	A	IECP	EC	
43106	GN	A	IECP	EC	
43107	GN	A	IECP	EC	
43108	GN	A	IECP	EC	
43109	GN	A	IECP	EC	
43110	GN	A	IECP	EC	
43111	GN	A	IECP	EC	
43112	GN	A	IECP	EC	
43113	GN	A	IECP	EC	
43114	GN	A	IECP	EC	
43115	GN	A	IECP	EC	
43116	GN	A	IECP	EC	
43117	GN	A	IECP	EC	
43118	GN	A	IECP	EC	
43119	GN	A	IECP	EC	
43120	GN	A	IECP	EC	
43121	V	P	ICCP	LA	
43122	IS	P	ICCP	LA	South Yorkshire Metropolitan County
43123	IS	P	ICCP	LA	
43124	GW	A	IWRP	PM	
43125	IS	A	IWRP	PM	Merchant Venturer
43126	GW	A	IWRP	PM	City of Bristol
43127	IS	A	IWRP	PM	
43128	GW	A	IWRP	PM	
43129	GW	A	IWRP	PM	
43130	IS	A	IWRP	PM	Sulis Minerva
43131	GW	A	IWRP	PM	Sir Felix Pole
43132	GW	A	IWRP	PM	
43133	GW	A	IWRP	PM	
43134	GW	A	IWRP	PM	County of Somerset
43135	GW	A	IWRP	PM	

43136	GW	A	IWRP	PM	
43137	GW	A	IWRP	PM	Newton Abbot 150
43138	GW	A	IWRP	PM	
43139	GW	A	IWRP	PM	
43140	GW	A	IWRP	PM	
43141	GW	A	IWRP	PM	
43142	GW	A	IWRP	PM	
43143	IS	A	IWRP	PM	
43144	IS	A	IWRP	PM	
43145	GW	A	IWRP	PM	
43146	IS	A	IWRP	PM	
43147	IS	A	IWRP	PM	
43148	GW	A	IWRP	PM	
43149	GW	A	IWRP	PM	B.B.C. Wales Today
43150	GW	A	IWRP	PM	Bristol Evening Post
43151	GW	A	IWRP	PM	
43152	GW	A	IWRP	PM	
43153	V	P	ICCP	LA	THE ENGLISH RIVIERA TORQUAY
43154	V	P	ICCP	LA	INTERCITY
43155	V	P	ICCP	LA	City of Aberdeen
43156	IS	P	ICCP	LA	
43157	V	P	ICCP	LA	HMS Penzance
43158	V	P	ICCP	LA	
43159	IS	P	ICCP	LA	
43160	V	P	ICCP	LA	
43161	IS	P	ICCP	LA	Reading Evening Post
43162	IS	P	ICCP	LA	Borough of Stevenage
43163	IS	A	IWRP	LA	
43164	IS	A	IWRP	LA	
43165	IS	A	IWRP	LA	
43166	IS	A	IWRP	LA	
43167 †	GN	A	IECP	EC	
43168 †	GW	A	IWRP	LA	
43169 †	GW	A	IWRP	LA	The National Trust
43170 †	GW	A	IWRP	LA	Edward Paxman
43171	GW	A	IWRP	LA	
43172	IS	A	IWRP	LA	
43173 †	GW	A	SCXL	ZC(S)	
43174	GW	A	IWRP	LA	Bristol-Bordeaux
43175 †	IS	A	IWRP	LA	
43176	IS	A	IWRP	LA	
43177 †	GW	A	IWRP	LA	University of Exeter
43178	V	A	IWCP	LA	
43179 †	GW	A	IWRP	LA	Pride of Laira
43180	V	P	ICCP	LA	City of Newcastle upon Tyne
43181	GW	A	IWRP	LA	Devonport Royal Dockyard 1693-1993
43182	IS	A	IWRP	LA	
43183	GW	A	IWRP	LA	
43184	V	A	IWCP	LA	
43185	GW	A	IWRP	LA	Great Western
43186	GW	A	IWRP	LA	Sir Francis Drake

43187	**GW**	A	IWRP	LA	
43188	**GW**	A	IWRP	LA	City of Plymouth
43189	**GW**	A	IWRP	LA	RAILWAY HERITAGE TRUST
43190	**GW**	A	IWRP	LA	
43191	† **GW**	A	IWRP	LA	Seahawk
43192	**GW**	A	IWRP	LA	City of Truro
43193	**IS**	P	ICCP	LA	Plymouth SPIRIT OF DISCOVERY
43194	**IS**	P	ICCP	LA	
43195	**IS**	P	ICCP	LA	British Red Cross 125th Birthday 1995
43196	**IS**	P	ICCP	LA	The Newspaper Society Founded 1836
43197	**IS**	P	ICCP	LA	Railway Magazine Centenary 1897-1997
43198	**IS**	P	ICCP	LA	

CLASS 46   BR/SULZER   1Co–Co1

Built: 1963 by BR at Derby Locomotive Works.
Engine: Sulzer 12LDA28B of 1860 kW (2500 hp) at 750 rpm.
Main Generator: Brush TG160-60.
Traction Motors: Brush TM73-68 Mk3 (axle hung).
Max. Tractive Effort: 245 kN (55000 lbf).
Cont. Tractive Effort: 141 kN (31600 lbf) at 22.3 mph.
Power At Rail: 1460 kW (1960 hp).   **Train Brakes:** Air & vacuum.
Brake Force: 63 t.   **Dimensions:** 20.70 x 2.78 x 3.92 m.
Weight: 140 t.   **Wheel Diameter:** 914/1143 mm.
Design Speed: 90 mph.   **Max. Speed:** 75 mph.
Fuel Capacity: 3591 litres.   **RA:** 7.
Train Supply: Not equipped.   **Multiple Working:** Not equipped.
Non-standard livery/numbering:
•   46035 carries number D172. Official RSL number is 89472.

46035	**G**	CN	MBDL	CQ	Ixion

CLASS 47   BR/BRUSH/SULZER   Co–Co

Built: 1963–67 by Brush Traction, at Loughborough or by BR at Crewe Works.
Engine: Sulzer 12LDA28C of 1920 kW (2580 hp) at 750 rpm.
Main Generator: Brush TG160-60 Mk4 or TM172-50 Mk1.
Traction Motors: Brush TM64-68 Mk1 or Mk1A.
Max. Tractive Effort: 267 kN (60000 lbf).
Cont. Tractive Effort: 133 kN (30000 lbf) at 26 mph.
Power At Rail: 1550 kW (2080 hp).   **Train Brakes:** Air.
Brake Force: 61 t.   **Dimensions:** 19.38 x 2.79 x 3.9 m.
Weight: 111.5–120.6 t.   **Wheel Diameter:** 1143 mm.
Design Speed: 95 mph.   **Max. Speed:** 75 mph.
Fuel Capacity: 3273 (+ 5550; † 4410 litres).
Train Supply: Not equipped.
Multiple Working: Not equipped (m – Green Circle).
Non-standard liveries/numbering:
•   47016 also carries number 1546.
•   47114 is two-tone green with Freightliner logos.
•   47145 is dark blue with Railfreight Distribution logos.

- 47484 is Great Western Railway style green, with cast numberplates.
- 47515 is livery **IM** on one side and all-over white on the other side).
- 47519 also carries number D1102.
- 47803 is yellow and white with a red stripe.
- 47972 is in British Railways Board Central Services livery of red and grey.

Class 47/0 (Dual braked locos) or Class 47/2 (Air braked locos). Standard Design. Details as above.

47004	x	**G**	E	WNZX	SP(S)	Old Oak Common Traction & Rolling Stock Depot
47016	x	**F0**	E	WNZX	SP(S)	ATLAS[1]
47033	m+	**FE**	E	WHBF	BS	The Royal Logistic Corps
47049	m+	**FE**	E	WNXX	BA(S)	GEFCO
47051	m+	**FE**	E	WNZX	SP(S)	
47052		**FF**	P	DFLT	CD	
47053	m+	**FE**	E	WNYX	BS(S)	Dollands Moor International
47060		**FF**	P	DHLT	LB(S)	
47079		**FF**	FL	DFFT	CD	
47085	m+	**FE**	E	WNXX	BA(S)	REPTA 1893-1993
47095	m+	**FE**	E	WNYX	CD(S)	
47114	m+	**0**	FL	DFLM	CD	Freightlinerbulk
47125	m+	**FE**	E	WNXX	BA(S)	
47145	m+	**0**	E	WHBF	BS	Merddin Emrys
47146	m+	**FE**	E	WNYX	CD(S)	Loughborough Grammar School
47150	m+	**FF**	FL	DFLM	CD	
47152	m+	**FF**	FL	DFLM	CD	
47156	m+	**FD**	FL	DFYX	BA(S)	
47157	m+	**FF**	FL	DFLM	CD	Johnson Stevens Agencies
47186	m+	**FE**	E	WNYX	BS(S)	Catcliffe Demon
47188	m+	**FE**	E	WNYX	CD(S)	
47193	x	**F**	P	DFLT	CD	
47194	m+	**FD**	E	WHBF	BS	
47197		**FF**	P	DFFT	CD	
47200	m+	**FE**	E	WHBF	BS	Herbert Austin
47201	m+	**FE**	E	WNYX	BS(S)	
47204	m+	**FF**	FL	DFLM	CD	
47205	m+	**FF**	FL	DFLM	CD	
47206		**FF**	P	DFLT	CD	The Morris Dancer
47207	m+	**FF**	P	DFLM	CD	The Felixstowe Partnership
47209	m+	**FF**	P	DFLM	CD	
47210	m+	**FD**	E	WNZX	SP(S)	
47211	m+	**FD**	E	WNYX	EH(S)	
47212	x†	**FF**	P	DFLT	CD	
47213	m+	**FD**	E	WHBF	BS	Marchwood Military Port
47217	m+	**FE**	E	WHBF	BS	
47218	m+	**FE**	E	WHBF	BS	United Transport Europe
47219	m+	**FE**	E	WHBF	BS	Arnold Kunzler
47221	x†	**FP**	FL	DHLT	TO(S)	
47223	x†	**F**	E	WNYX	BA(S)	
47224	x†	**FP**	FL	DFLT	EH(S)	
47225		**FF**	P	DFLT	CD	

47226	m+**FD**	E	WHBF	BS	
47228	m+**FE**	E	WHBF	BS	axial
47229	m+**FD**	E	WNYX	??(S)	
47231	**FF**	P	DFLT	CD	
47234	m+**FF**	FL	DFLM	CD	
47236	m+**FE**	E	WHBF	BS	ROVER GROUP QUALITY ASSURED
47237	m+**FE**	E	WHBF	BS	
47238	x **FD**	E	WNYX	BS(S)	
47241	m+**FE**	E	WNYX	AN(S)	Halewood Silver Jubilee 1988
47245	m+**FE**	E	WHBF	BS	The Institute of Export
47256	x **FD**	E	WNZX	DR(S)	
47258	m+**FE**	FL	DFLM	CD	
47270	**FF**	P	DFFT	CD	Cory Brothers 1842-1992
47276	m†**F**	E	WHBF	BS	
47277	x†**FD**	E	WNYX	IM(S)	
47278	x **FP**	E	WNYX	SP(S)	
47279	m+**FF**	FL	DFLM	CD	
47280	m+**FD**	E	WHBF	BS	Pedigree
47281	m+**FD**	E	WNZX	SP(S)	
47283	**FF**	FL	DFLT	CD	
47284	m+**FD**	E	WHBF	BS	
47285	m+**FE**	E	WHBF	BS	
47286	m+**FE**	E	WHBF	BS	Port of Liverpool
47287	m+**FE**	FL	DFLM	CD	
47289	m+**FF**	P	DFLM	CD	
47290	m+**FF**	FL	DFLM	CD	
47292	m+**F**	P	DFLM	CD	
47293	m+**FE**	E	WHBF	BS	TRANSFESA
47294	s†**FD**	E	WNYX	TT(S)	
47295	† **F**	FL	DFFT	CD	
47296	x **FF**	P	DFLT	CD	
47297	m+**FE**	E	WHBF	BS	Cobra RAILFREIGHT
47298	m+**FD**	E	WHBF	BS	Pegasus
47299	m†**FE**	E	WNXX	LB(S)	

Class 47/3 (Dual braked locos) or Class 47/2 (Air braked locos). Details as Class 47/0 except: Weight: 113.7 t.

47300	x **CE**	E	WNYX	BS(S)	
47301	m+**FF**	P	DFLM	CD	Freightliner Birmingham
47302	m+**FF**	FL	DFLM	CD	
47303	m+**FF**	P	DFLM	CD	Freightliner Cleveland
47304	m+**FD**	E	WHBF	BS	
47305	**FF**	P	DFLT	CD	
47306	m+**FE**	E	WHBF	BS	The Sapper
47307	m+**FE**	E	WHBF	BS	
47308	m **FF**	FL	DFLT	CD	
47309	m+**FF**	FL	DHLT	CD	European Freight Operator of the Year - IFW Freighting Industry Awards 1998
47310	m+**FE**	E	WHBF	BS	Henry Ford
47312	m+**FE**	E	WHBF	BS	Parsec of Europe

47313	m+**FD**	E	WHBF	BS	
47314	m+**FD**	E	WHBF	BS	Transmark
47315	xs **CE**	E	WHBF	BS	
47316	m+**FE**	E	WHBF	BS	
47318	x **F0**	E	WNZX	BS(S)	
47319	x† **FP**	E	WNZX	IM(S)	
47323	m+**FF**	P	DFFT	CD	
47326	m+**FE**	E	WHBF	BS	Saltley Depot Quality Approved
47328	m+**FD**	E	WNXX	CD(S)	
47329	x **CE**	FL	DFLT	CD	
47330	m+**FF**	FL	DFLM	CD	
47331	xs **CE**	E	WHBF	BS	
47332	x **CE**	FL	DHLT	LB(S)	
47334	**FF**	P	DFLT	CD	P & O Nedlloyd
47335	m+**FD**	E	WHBF	BS	
47337	m+**FF**	FL	DFLM	CD	
47338	m+**FE**	E	WHBF	BS	
47339	**FF**	P	DFLT	CD	
47341	x **CE**	E	WNYX	TT(S)	
47344	m+**FE**	E	WHBF	BS	
47345	x **FF**	P	DFLT	CD	
47348	m+**FE**	E	WHBF	BS	St. Christopher's Railway Home
47349	x **FF**	P	DFLT	CD	
47351	m+**FE**	E	WNYX	LB(S)	
47352	x **CE**	E	WNZX	FH(S)	
47353	x **FF**	FL	DFLT	CD	
47354	**FF**	FL	DFLT	CD	
47355	m+**FD**	E	WHBF	BS	
47357	x **CE**	E	WNYX	BS(S)	
47358	m+**FF**	P	DFLM	CD	
47360	m+**FE**	E	WHBF	BS	
47361	m+**FF**	FL	DFLM	CD	Wilton Endeavour
47362	m+**FD**	E	WHBF	BS	
47363	m+**F**	E	WHBF	BS	
47365	m+**FE**	E	WNYX	CF(S)	Diamond Jubilee
47366	x **CE**	E	WNYX	SP(S)	
47367	m+**FF**	P	DFLM	CD	
47368	x **F**	E	WNYX	SF(S)	
47370	m+**FF**	P	DFLM	CD	Andrew A Hodgkinson
47371	x **FF**	P	DHLT	TO(S)	
47372	x **FF**	FL	DFLT	CD	
47375	m+**FE**	E	WHBF	BS	Tinsley Traction Depot (Quality Approved)
47376	x **FF**	P	DFLT	CD	Freightliner 1995
47377	**FF**	P	DFLT	CD	
47379	m† **F**	E	WHBF	BS	

Class 47/4. Electric Train Supply equipment. Details as Class 47/0 except:
Weight: 120.4–125.1 t.   **Max. Speed:** 95 (* 75, † 100) mph.
Fuel Capacity: 3273 (+ 5887) litres.   **RA:** 7.
Train Supply: Electric, index 66.
Multiple Working: Not equipped († Blue Star).

47462	x*	RG	E	WNYX	TT(S)	
47467	x*	BL	E	WNZX	SP(S)	
47471	x	I	E	WNYX	BA(S)	
47474	x*	RG	E	WHBF	BS	Sir Rowland Hill
47475	x*	RX	E	WHBF	BS	Restive
47476	x*	RG	E	WHBF	BS	Night Mail
47478	x*	B	E	WNYX	BS(S)	
47481	x	BL	E	WNYX	BA(S)	
47484	x*	0	E	WNXX	CD(S)	
47488	x	G	FG	SDFR	TM	
47489		RG	E	WNYX	BS(S)	
47492	x*	RX	E	WHBF	BS	
47501	x	RG	E	WHCN	CD	Craftsman
47513	x*	BL	E	WNYX	CD(S)	
47515	x	0	E	WNYX	BA(S)	
47519	x+*		G	E	WHBF	BS
47522	x*	RG	E	WNZX	SP(S)	Doncaster Enterprise
47523	*	IM	E	WNZX	SP(S)	
47524	x*	RX	E	WNYX	BA(S)	
47525	x*	FE	E	WNYX	CD(S)	
47526	x*	BL	E	WNYX	BA(S)	
47528	x*	IM	E	WNYX	DR(S)	The Queen's Own Mercian Yeomanry
47530	x*	RX	E	WNYX	BA(S)	
47532	x*	RX	E	WNYX	CD(S)	
47535	x*	RX	E	WHBF	BS	
47536	x*	RX	E	WNYX	CD(S)	
47539		RX	E	WNYX	BA(S)	
47540	xm*	CE	E	WNYX	BA(S)	The Institution of Civil Engineers
47547		N	E	WNZX	CD(S)	
47550	x*	IM	E	WNYX	IM(S)	
47555	x*	FE	E	WNZX	TO(S)	The Commonwealth Spirit
47565	x	RX	E	WHDT	CD	Responsive
47566	x*	RX	E	WNYX	CD(S)	
47572	x	RG	E	WHCN	CD	Ely Cathedral
47574	x*	RG	E	WNXX	CD(S)	
47575	x	RG	E	WHCN	CD	City of Hereford
47576	x*	RX	E	WNYX	CD(S)	
47584	x	RX	E	WHCN	CD	THE LOCOMOTIVE & CARRIAGE INSTITUTION 1911
47596	x	RX	E	WHCN	CD	
47624	xj*	RX	E	WNYX	AN(S)	Saint Andrew
47627	x	R	E	WHCN	CD	
47628	j*	RX	E	WNYX	BA(S)	
47634	x	RG	E	WHCN	CD	Holbeck
47635	xj	RG	E	WHCN	CD	
47640	j*	RG	E	WHBF	BS	University of Strathclyde

**Class 47/7. Electric Train Supply and Push & Pull equipment (RCH System).
Details as Class 47/4 except:**

Weight: 118.7 t.   **Fuel Capacity:** 5887 litres.

| 47701 | x | FG | FG | SDFR | TM | Waverley |

47702	x	**V**	E	ILRA	TO	County of Suffolk
47703	x	**FG**	FG	SDFR	TM	
47704	*	**RX**	E	WNZX	CD(S)	
47707	x	**RX**	E	WNYX	BA(S)	Holyrood
47709	x	**FG**	FG	SDFR	TM	
47710	x	**FG**	FG	SDFR	TM(S)	
47711	x	**V**	E	ILRA	TO	County of Hertfordshire
47712	x	**N**	FG	SDFR	TM	
47714	x	**RX**	E	WNYX	BA(S)	
47715	*	**N**	E	WNYX	BA(S)	
47716	x*	**RX**	E	WNYX	BA(S)	
47717	x	**RG**	E	WNYX	BA(S)	

Class 47/7. Electric Train Supply equipment and RCH Jumper Cables for use on Railnet services. Details as Class 47/4 except:
Weight: 118.7 t.   **Fuel Capacity:** 5887 litres.

47721		**RX**	E	WHDP	CD	Saint Bede
47722		**RX**	E	WHDP	CD	The Queen Mother
47725		**RX**	E	WHDP	CD	The Railway Mission
47726		**RX**	E	WHDP	CD	Manchester Airport Progress
47727		**RX**	E	WHDP	CD	Duke of Edinburgh's Award
47732	x	**RX**	E	WHDP	CD	Restormel
47733		**RX**	E	WHDP	CD	Eastern Star
47734		**RX**	E	WHDP	CD	Crewe Diesel Depot Quality Approved
47736		**RX**	E	WHDP	CD	Cambridge Traction & Rolling Stock Depot
47737		**RX**	E	WHDP	CD	Resurgent
47738		**RX**	E	WHDP	CD	Bristol Barton Hill
47739		**RX**	E	WHDP	CD	Resourceful
47741		**RX**	E	WHDP	CD	Resilient
47742		**RX**	E	WHDP	CD	The Enterprising Scot
47744		**E**	E	WHDP	CD	
47745	x	**RX**	E	WHDP	CD	Royal London Society for the Blind
47746		**RX**	E	WHDP	CD	The Bobby
47747		**RX**	E	WHDP	CD	Res Publica
47749		**RX**	E	WHDP	CD	Atlantic College
47750		**RX**	E	WHDP	CD	Royal Mail Cheltenham
47756		**RX**	E	WHDC	ML	Royal Mail Tyneside
47757		**RX**	E	WHDP	CD	Restitution
47758		**E**	E	WHDP	CD	Regency Rail Cruises
47759		**RX**	E	WHDP	CD	
47760		**RX**	E	WHDP	CD	Restless
47761		**RX**	E	WHDP	CD	
47762	x	**RX**	E	WHDP	CD	
47763		**RX**	E	WHDP	CD	
47764		**RX**	E	WHDP	CD	Resounding
47765	x	**RX**	E	WHDP	CD	Ressaldar
47766	x	**RX**	E	WHDP	CD	Resolute
47767		**RX**	E	WHDC	ML	Saint Columba
47768	x	**E**	E	WHDP	CD	Resonant
47769		**RX**	E	WHDP	CD	Resolve
47770		**RX**	E	WHDP	CD	Reserved

47771		**RX**	E	WHDP	CD	Heaton Traincare Depot
47772	x	**RX**	E	WHDP	CD	
47773		**RX**	E	WHDP	CD	Reservist
47774	x	**RX**	E	WHDP	CD	Poste Restante
47775		**RX**	E	WHDP	CD	Respite
47776	x	**RX**	E	WHDP	CD	Respected
47777	x	**RX**	E	WHDP	CD	Restored
47778		**RX**	E	WHDP	CD	Irresistible
47779		**RX**	E	WHDP	CD	
47780		**RX**	E	WHDP	CD	
47781		**RX**	E	WHDP	CD	Isle of Iona
47782		**RX**	E	WHDP	CD	
47783		**RX**	E	WHDP	CD	Saint Peter
47784		**RX**	E	WHDP	CD	Condover Hall
47785		**E**	E	WHDP	CD	Fiona Castle
47786		**E**	E	WHDP	CD	Roy Castle OBE
47787		**RX**	E	WHDP	CD	Victim Support
47788		**RX**	E	WHDP	CD	Captain Peter Manisty RN
47789		**RX**	E	WHDP	CD	Lindisfarne
47790		**RX**	E	WHDC	ML	Dewi Sant/Saint David
47791		**RX**	E	WHDC	ML	
47792		**RX**	E	WHDP	CD	Saint Cuthbert
47793		**RX**	E	WHDP	CD	Saint Augustine

Class 47/7. Electric Train Supply equipment. Locos dedicated for Royal Trai & (occasional) Charter Train use. Details as Class 47/4 except:
Weight: 118.7 t.   **Fuel Capacity**: 5887 litres.

47798		**RP**	E	WHDA	CD	Prince William
47799		**RP**	E	WHDA	CD	Prince Henry

Class 47/4 ("47/8" & "47/9") Continued.
Note: 47977 is expected to be renumbered from 47565 during 1999.

47802	*	**IS**	E	WNZX	ZC(S)	
47803	*	**O**	E	WNYX	SF(S)	
47805		**IS**	P	ILRA	TO	
47806		**V**	P	ILRA	TO	
47807		**V**	P	ILRA	TO	The Lion of Vienna
47810		**IS**	P	ILRA	TO	PORTERBROOK
47811		**GW**	P	IWLA	LE	
47812		**IS**	P	ILRA	TO	
47813		**GW**	P	IWLA	LE	S.S. Great Britain
47814		**V**	P	ILRA	TO	Totnes Castle
47815		**GW**	P	IWLA	LE	
47816		**IS**	P	IWLA	LE	Bristol Bath Road Quality Approved
47817		**V**	P	ILRA	TO	
47818		**V**	P	ILRA	TO	
47822		**V**	P	ILRA	TO	Pride of Shrewsbury
47825		**IS**	P	ILRB	TO	Thomas Telford
47826		**IS**	P	ILRA	TO	
47827		**V**	P	ILRA	TO	
47828		**IS**	P	ILRA	TO	

47829		IS	P	ILRA	TO	
47830		GW	P	IWLA	LE	
47831		IS	P	ILRA	TO	Bolton Wanderer
47832		IS	P	IWLX	LE	Tamar
47839		IS	P	ILRA	TO	
47840		IS	P	ILRA	TO	NORTH STAR
47841		IS	P	ILRA	TO	The Institution of Mechanical Engineers
47843		IS	P	ILRA	TO	
47844		V	P	ILRA	TO	
47845		V	P	ILRA	TO	County of Kent
47846		GW	P	IWLA	LE	THOR
47847		IS	P	ILRA	TO	
47848		IS	P	ILRA	TO	
47849		IS	P	ILRA	TO	
47851		IS	P	ILRA	TO	
47853		IS	P	ILRA	TO	
47854		IS	P	ILRA	TO	Women's Royal Voluntary Service
47971	x†	BL	E	WNYX	CD(S)	Robin Hood
47972	†	O	E	WNYX	CD(S)	The Royal Army Ordnance Corps
47976	x†	CE	E	WHDT	CD	Aviemore Centre
47977						

Class 47/3 ("47/9") Continued.

| 47981 | xs* | CE | E | WNYX | LB(S) | |

CLASS 50   ENGLISH ELECTRIC   Co–Co

Built: 1967–68 by English Electric at Vulcan Foundry, Newton-le-Willows.
Engine: English Electric 16CVST of 2010 kW (2700 hp) at 850 rpm.
Main Generator: English Electric 840/4B.
Traction Motors: English Electric 538/5A.
Max. Tractive Effort: 216 kN (48500 lbf).
Cont. Tractive Effort: 147 kN (33000 lbf) at 23.5 mph.
Power At Rail: 1540 kW (2070 hp).   **Train Brakes:** Air & vacuum.
Brake Force: 59 t.   **Dimensions:** 20.88 x 2.78 x 3.96 m.
Weight: 116.9 t.   **Wheel Diameter:** 1092 mm.
Design Speed: 105 mph.   **Max. Speed:** 90 (* 75) mph.
Fuel Capacity: 4796 litres.   **RA:** 6.
Train Supply: Electric, index 66.   **Multiple Working:** Orange Square.

| 50031 | * | BL | 50 | MBDL | KR | Hood |
| 50050 | † | BL | HS | MBDL | NC | Fearless |

CLASS 55   ENGLISH ELECTRIC   Co–Co

Built: 1961 by English Electric at Vulcan Foundry, Newton-le-Willows.
Engine: Two Napier-Deltic D18-25 of 1230 kW (1650 hp) at 1500 rpm.
Main Generators: Two English Electric EE829.
Traction Motors: English Electric E538/A.
Max. Tractive Effort: 222 kN (50000 lbf).
Cont. Tractive Effort: 136 kN (30500 lbf) at 32.5 mph.

Power At Rail: 1969 kW (2640 hp)			**Train Brakes:** Air & vacuum.	
Brake Force: 51 t.			**Dimensions:** 21.18 x 2.68 x 3.94 m.	
Weight: 104.7 t.			**Wheel Diameter:** 1092 mm.	
Design Speed: 100 mph.			**Max. Speed:** 100 mph.	
Fuel Capacity: 3755 litres.			**RA:** 5.	
Train Supply: Electric, index 66.			**Multiple Working:** Not equipped.	

Non-standard livery/numbering:
• 55022 carries number D9000. Official RSL number is 89500.

55022	**G**	90	MBDL	NC	ROYAL SCOTS GREY

CLASS 56   BRUSH/BR/PAXMAN   Co–Co

Built: 1976–84 by Electroputere at Craiova, Romania (as sub contractors for Brush) or BREL at Doncaster or Crewe Works.
Engine: Ruston Paxman 16RK3CT of 2460 kW (3250 hp) at 900 rpm.
Main Alternator: Brush BA1101A.
Traction Motors: Brush TM73-62.
Max. Tractive Effort: 275 kN (61800 lbf).
Cont. Tractive Effort: 240 kN (53950 lbf) at 16.8 mph.
Power At Rail: 1790 kW (2400 hp).   **Train Brakes:** Air.
Brake Force: 60 t.   **Dimensions:** 19.36 x 2.79 x 3.9 m.
Weight: 125.2 t.   **Wheel Diameter:** 1143 mm.
Design Speed: 80 mph.   **Max. Speed:** 80 mph.
Fuel Capacity: 5228 litres.   **RA:** 7.
Train Supply: Not equipped.   **Multiple Working:** Red Diamond.
Note: All equipped with Slow Speed Control.

56003	**LH**	E	WGAN	IM	
56004	**B**	E	WGAN	IM	
56006	**LH**	E	WGAN	IM	Ferrybridge 'C' Power Station
56007	**T**	E	WGAN	IM	
56008	**B**	E	WNYX	IM(S)	
56010	**T**	E	WGAN	IM	
56011	**E**	E	WGAN	IM	
56012	**FC**	E	WNYX	IM(S)	
56013	**FC**	E	WNYX	TT(S)	
56014	**FC**	E	WNYX	IM(S)	
56018	**E**	E	WGAN	IM	
56019	**FR**	E	WGAN	IM	
56021	**LH**	E	WGAN	IM	
56022	**T**	E	WGAN	IM	
56023	**FC**	E	WNYX	TT(S)	
56025	**T**	E	WGAN	IM	
56027	**LH**	E	WGAN	IM	
56029	**T**	E	WGAN	IM	
56031	**CE**	E	WGAN	IM	
56032	**E**	E	WGAN	IM	
56033	**T**	E	WGAN	IM	Shotton Paper Mill
56034	**LH**	E	WGAN	IM	Castell Ogwr/Ogmore Castle
56035	**LH**	E	WGAN	IM	
56036	**TC**	E	WGAN	IM	

56037	E	E	WGAN	IM	
56038	E	E	WNXX	LB(S)	Western Mail
56039	LH	E	WGAN	IM	
56040	T	E	WGAN	IM	Oystermouth
56041	E	E	WGAN	IM	
56043	FM	E	WGAN	IM	
56044	T	E	WGAN	IM	Cardiff Canton Quality Approved
56045	LH	E	WGAN	IM	British Steel Shelton
56046	CE	E	WGAN	IM	
56047	TC	E	WGAN	IM	
56048	E	E	WGAN	IM	
56049	TC	E	WGAN	IM	
56050	LH	E	WGAN	IM	British Steel Teesside
56051	E	E	WGAN	IM	
56052	T	E	WGAN	IM	The Cardiff Rod Mill
56053	T	E	WGAN	IM	Sir Morgannwg Ganol/County of Mid Glamorgan
56054	T	E	WGAN	IM	British Steel Llanwern
56055	LH	E	WGAN	IM	
56056	T	E	WGAN	IM	
56057	E	E	WGAN	IM	British Fuels
56058	E	E	WGAN	IM	
56059	E	E	WGAN	IM	
56060	E	E	WGAN	IM	
56061	FM	E	WGAN	IM	
56062	E	E	WGAN	IM	
56063	F	E	WGAN	IM	Bardon Hill
56064	T	E	WGAN	IM	
56065	E	E	WGAN	IM	
56066	T	E	WGAN	IM	
56067	E	E	WGAN	IM	
56068	E	E	WGAN	IM	
56069	E	E	WGAN	IM	Wolverhampton Steel Terminal
56070	T	E	WGAN	IM	
56071	E	E	WGAN	IM	
56072	T	E	WGAN	IM	
56073	T	E	WGAN	IM	Tremorfa Steelworks
56074	LH	E	WGAN	IM	Kellingley Colliery
56075	F	E	WGAN	IM	West Yorkshire Enterprise
56076	T	E	WGAN	IM	
56077	LH	E	WGAN	IM	Thorpe Marsh Power Station
56078	E	E	WGAN	IM	
56079	T	E	WGAN	IM	
56080	F	E	WGAN	IM	Selby Coalfield
56081	E	E	WGAN	IM	
56082	F	E	WGAN	IM	
56083	LH	E	WGAN	IM	
56084	LH	E	WGAN	IM	
56085	LH	E	WGAN	IM	
56086	T	E	WGAN	IM	The Magistrates' Association
56087	E	E	WGAN	IM	ABP Port of Hull

56088	E	E	WGAN	IM	
56089	E	E	WGAN	IM	
56090	LH	E	WGAN	IM	
56091	E	E	WGAN	IM	Stanton
56092	T	E	WGAN	IM	
56093	T	E	WGAN	IM	
56094	E	E	WGAN	IM	Eggborough Power Station
56095	E	E	WGAN	IM	
56096	E	E	WGAN	IM	
56097	FM	E	WGAN	IM	
56098	F	E	WGAN	IM	
56099	T	E	WGAN	IM	Fiddlers Ferry Power Station
56100	LH	E	WGAN	IM	
56101	T	E	WGAN	IM	Mutual Improvement
56102	LH	E	WGAN	IM	
56103	E	E	WGAN	IM	STORA
56104	FC	E	WGAN	IM	
56105	E	E	WGAN	IM	
56106	LH	E	WGAN	IM	
56107	LH	E	WGAN	IM	
56108	F	E	WGAN	IM	
56109	LH	E	WGAN	IM	
56110	LH	E	WNXX	ZC(S)	Croft
56111	LH	E	WGAN	IM	
56112	LH	E	WGAN	IM	Stainless Pioneer
56113	E	E	WGAN	IM	
56114	E	E	WGAN	IM	
56115	E	E	WGAN	IM	
56116	LH	E	WGAN	IM	
56117	E	E	WGAN	IM	
56118	LH	E	WGAN	IM	
56119	E	E	WGAN	IM	
56120	E	E	WGAN	IM	
56121	E	E	WGAN	IM	
56123	T	E	WGAN	IM	Drax Power Station
56124	T	E	WGAN	IM	
56125	T	E	WGAN	IM	
56126	FC	E	WGAN	IM	
56127	T	E	WGAN	IM	
56128	T	E	WGAN	IM	
56129	T	E	WGAN	IM	
56130	LH	E	WGAN	IM	Wardley Opencast
56131	F	E	WGAN	IM	Ellington Colliery
56132	T	E	WGAN	IM	
56133	T	E	WGAN	IM	Crewe Locomotive Works
56134	FC	E	WGAN	IM	Blyth Power
56135	F	E	WGAN	IM	Port of Tyne Authority

CLASS 57 BRUSH/GM Co–Co

Built: 1965 by Brush Traction at Loughborough as Class 47. Rebuilt 1997–99 by Brush Traction at Loughborough.
Engine: General Motors 645-12E3 of 1860 kW (2500 hp) at 900 rpm.
Main Alternator: Brush BA1101A.
Traction Motors: Brush TM68-46.
Maximum Tractive Effort: 244.5 kN (55000 lbf).
Continuous Tractive Effort: 140 kN (31500 lbf) at ?? mph.
Power at Rail: 1507 kW (2025 hp). | **Train Brakes:** Air.
Brake Force: 80 t. | **Dimensions:** 19.38 x 2.79 x 3.9 m.
Weight: 120.6 t. | **Wheel Diameter:** 1143 mm.
Design Speed: 75 mph. | **Max. Speed:** 75 mph.
Fuel Capacity: | **RA:** 6
Train Supply: Not equipped. | **Multiple Working:** Not equipped.

57001	(47356)	**FL**	FL	DFHZ	CD	Freightliner Pioneer
57002	(47322)	**FL**	FL	DFHZ	CD	Freightliner Phoenix
57003	(47317)	**FL**	FL	DFHZ	LB(S)	Freightliner Evolution
57004	(47347)	**FL**	FL	DFHZ	LB(S)	
57005	(47350)	**FL**	FL	DFHZ	LB(S)	
57006	(47187)	**FL**	FL	DFHZ	LB(S)	
57007						
57008						

CLASS 58 BREL/PAXMAN Co–Co

Built: 1983–87 by BREL at Doncaster Works.
Engine: Ruston Paxman RK3ACT of 2460 kW (3300 hp) at 1000 rpm.
Main Alternator: Brush BA1101B.
Traction Motors: Brush TM73-62.
Max. Tractive Effort: 275 kN (61800 lbf).
Cont. Tractive Effort: 240 kN (53950 lbf) at 17.4 mph.
Power At Rail: 1780 kW (2387 hp). | **Train Brakes:** Air.
Brake Force: 62 t. | **Dimensions:** 19.13 x 2.72 x 3.93 m.
Weight: 130 t. | **Wheel Diameter:** 1120 mm.
Design Speed: 80 mph. | **Max. Speed:** 80 mph.
Fuel Capacity: 4214 litres. | **RA:** 7.
Train Supply: Not equipped. | **Multiple Working:** Red Diamond.
Note: All equipped with Slow Speed Control.

58001	**MG**	E	WFAN	TO	
58002	**ML**	E	WFAN	TO	Daw Mill Colliery
58003	**MG**	E	WFAN	TO	Markham Colliery
58004	**MG**	E	WFAN	TO	
58005	**ML**	E	WFAN	TO	Ironbridge Power Station
58006	**MG**	E	WFAN	TO	
58007	**MG**	E	WFAN	TO	Drakelow Power Station
58008	**ML**	E	WFAN	TO	
58009	**MG**	E	WFAN	TO	
58010	**MG**	E	WFAN	TO	

58011	**MG**	E	WFAN	TO	Worksop Depot
58012	**MG**	E	WFAN	TO	
58013	**ML**	E	WFAN	TO	
58014	**ML**	E	WFAN	TO	Didcot Power Station
58015	**MG**	E	WFAN	TO	
58016	**E**	E	WFAN	TO	
58017	**MG**	E	WFAN	TO	Eastleigh Depot
58018	**MG**	E	WFAN	TO	High Marnham Power Station
58019	**MG**	E	WFAN	TO	Shirebrook Colliery
58020	**MG**	E	WFAN	TO	Doncaster Works
58021	**ML**	E	WFAN	TO	Hither Green Depot
58022	**MG**	E	WFAN	TO	
58023	**ML**	E	WFAN	TO	Peterborough Depot
58024	**E**	E	WFAN	TO	
58025	**MG**	E	WFAN	TO	
58026	**MG**	E	WFAN	TO	
58027	**MG**	E	WFAN	TO	
58028	**MG**	E	WFAN	TO	
58029	**MG**	E	WFAN	TO	
58030	**E**	E	WFAN	TO	
58031	**MG**	E	WFAN	TO	
58032	**ML**	E	WFAN	TO	Thoresby Colliery
58033	**E**	E	WFAN	TO	
58034	**MG**	E	WFAN	TO	Bassetlaw
58035	**MG**	E	WFAN	TO	
58036	**ML**	E	WFAN	TO	
58037	**E**	E	WFAN	TO	
58038	**ML**	E	WFAN	TO	
58039	**E**	E	WFAN	TO	
58040	**MG**	E	WFAN	TO	Cottam Power Station
58041	**MG**	E	WFAN	TO	Ratcliffe Power Station
58042	**ML**	E	WFAN	TO	Petrolea
58043	**MG**	E	WFAN	TO	
58044	**MG**	E	WFAN	TO	Oxcroft Opencast
58045	**E**	E	WFAN	TO	
58046	**ML**	E	WFAN	TO	Asfordby Mine
58047	**E**	E	WFAN	TO	
58048	**E**	E	WFAN	TO	
58049	**E**	E	WFAN	TO	Littleton Colliery
58050	**E**	E	WFAN	TO	Toton Traction Depot

CLASS 59   GENERAL MOTORS   Co–Co

Built: 1985 (59001/002/004) or 1989 (59005) by General Motors, La Grange, Illinois, USA or 1990 (59101–4), 1994 (59201) and 1995 (59202–6) by General Motors, London, Ontario, Canada.
Engine: General Motors 645E3C two stroke of 2460 kW (3300 hp) at 900 rpm.
Main Alternator: General Motors AR11 MLD-D14A.
Traction Motors: General Motors D77B.
Max. Tractive Effort: 506 kN (113 550 lbf).
Cont. Tractive Effort: 291 kN (65 300 lbf) at 14.3 mph.

Power At Rail: 1889 kW (2533 hp).
Brake Force: 69 t.
Weight: 121 t.
Design Speed: 60 (* 75) mph.
Fuel Capacity: 4546 litres.
Train Supply: Not equipped.

Train Brakes: Air.
Dimensions: 21.35 x 2.65 x 3.9 m.
Wheel Diameter: 1067 mm.
Max. Speed: 60 (* 75) mph.
RA: 7.
Multiple Working: GM System.

Class 59/0. Owned by Foster-Yeoman Ltd.

59001	**FY**	FY	XYPO	MD	YEOMAN ENDEAVOUR
59002	**FN**	FY	XYPO	MD	ALAN J DAY
59004	**FN**	FY	XYPO	MD	PAUL A HAMMOND
59005	**FY**	FY	XYPO	MD	

Class 59/1. Owned by Hanson Quarry Products.

59101	**AC**	HA	XYPA	MD	Village of Whatley
59102	**AO**	HA	XYPA	MD	Village of Chantry
59103	**AO**	HA	XYPA	MD	Village of Mells
59104	**AO**	HA	XYPA	MD	Village of Great Elm

Class 59/2. Owned by English Welsh & Scottish Railway.

59201	*	E	E	WDAN	FB	Vale of York
59202	*	E	E	WDAN	FB	Vale of White Horse
59203	*	E	E	WDAN	FB	Vale of Pickering
59204	*	E	E	WDAN	FB	Vale of Glamorgan
59205	*	E	E	WDAN	FB	L. Keith McNair
59206	*	E	E	WDAN	FB	Pride of Ferrybridge

CLASS 60   BRUSH/MIRRLEES   Co–Co

Built: 1989–1993 by Brush Traction at Loughborough.
Engine: Mirrlees 8MB275T of 2310 kW (3100 hp) at 1000 rpm.
Main Alternator: Brush BA1000.   **Traction Motors:** Brush TM216.
Max. Tractive Effort: 500 kN (106500 lbf).
Cont. Tractive Effort: 336 kN (71570 lbf) at 17.4 mph.
Power At Rail: 1800 kW (2415 hp).   **Train Brakes:** Air.
Brake Force: 74 (+ 62) t.   **Dimensions:** 21.34 x 2.64 x 3.95 m.
Weight: 129 (+ 131) t.   **Wheel Diameter:** 1118 mm.
Design Speed: 62 mph.   **Max. Speed:** 60 mph.
Fuel Capacity: 4546 (+ 5225) litres.   **RA:** 7.
Train Supply: Not equipped.   **Multiple Working:** Within class.
Note: All equipped with Slow Speed Control.
Non-standard livery/numbering:
• 60006/033 are in British Steel livery of blue with white logos.
• 60064/070 are as **F**, with Loadhaul logos.

60001		E	E	WCAN	TO	
60002	+	E	E	WCAN	TO	High Peak
60003	+	E	E	WCAN	TO	FREIGHT TRANSPORT ASSOCIATION
60004	+	E	E	WCAN	TO	
60005	+	E	E	WCAN	TO	
60006		0	E	WCAN	TO	Scunthorpe Ironmaster
60007	+	LH	E	WCAN	TO	
60008		LH	E	WCAN	TO	GYPSUM QUEEN II
60009	+	MG	E	WCAN	TO	Carnedd Dafydd
60010	+	E	E	WCAN	TO	
60011		ML	E	WCAN	TO	
60012	+	E	E	WCAN	TO	
60013		F	E	WCAN	TO	Robert Boyle
60014		FP	E	WCAN	TO	Alexander Fleming
60015	+	T	E	WCAN	TO	Bow Fell
60016		E	E	WCAN	TO	
60017	+	E	E	WCAN	TO	Shotton Works Centenary Year 1996
60018		E	E	WCAN	TO	
60019		E	E	WCAN	TO	
60020	+	E	E	WCAN	TO	
60021	+	F	E	WCAN	TO	Pen-y-Ghent
60022	+	E	E	WCAN	TO	
60023	+	E	E	WCAN	TO	
60024	+	E	E	WCAN	TO	
60025	+	LH	E	WCAN	TO	
60026	+	E	E	WCAN	TO	
60027	+	E	E	WCAN	TO	
60028	+	E	E	WCAN	TO	John Flamsteed
60029		E	E	WCAN	TO	Clitheroe Castle
60030		E	E	WCAN	TO	
60031		FM	E	WCAN	TO	Ben Lui[1]
60032		T	E	WCAN	TO	William Booth
60033		0	E	WCAN	TO	Tees Steel Express

60034		T	E	WCAN	TO	Carnedd Llewelyn
60035		T	E	WCAN	TO	Florence Nightingale
60036		E	E	WCAN	TO	
60037	+	E	E	WCAN	TO	Aberthaw/Aberddawan
60038	+	LH	E	WCAN	TO	
60039		E	E	WCAN	TO	
60040		E	E	WCAN	TO	
60041	+	E	E	WCAN	TO	
60042	+	E	E	WCAN	TO	
60043		E	E	WCAN	TO	
60044		ML	E	WCAN	TO	Ailsa Craig
60045		E	E	WCAN	TO	The Permanent Way Institution
60046	+	T	E	WCAN	TO	William Wilberforce[1]
60047	+	E	E	WCAN	TO	
60048		E	E	WCAN	TO	Eastern
60049	+	E	E	WCAN	TO	
60050	+	E	E	WCAN	TO	
60051	+	E	E	WCAN	TO	
60052	+	E	E	WCAN	TO	Glofa Twr The last deep mine in Wales Tower Colliery
60053	+	E	E	WCAN	TO	Nordic Terminal
60054	+	FP	E	WCAN	TO	Charles Babbage
60055	+	T	E	WCAN	TO	Thomas Barnardo
60056	+	T	E	WCAN	TO	William Beveridge
60057		FC	E	WCAN	TO	Adam Smith
60058		T	E	WCAN	TO	John Howard
60059	+	LH	E	WCAN	TO	Swinden Dalesman
60060		FC	E	WCAN	TO	James Watt
60061		T	E	WCAN	TO	Alexander Graham Bell
60062		T	E	WCAN	TO	Samuel Johnson
60063		T	E	WCAN	TO	James Murray
60064	+	O	E	WCAN	TO	Back Tor[1]
60065		T	E	WCAN	TO	Kinder Low
60066		FC	E	WCAN	TO	John Logie Baird
60067	+	F	E	WCAN	TO	James Clerk-Maxwell
60068		F	E	WCAN	TO	Charles Darwin
60069		F	E	WCAN	TO	Humphry Davy
60070	+	O	E	WCAN	TO	John Loudon McAdam
60071	+	MG	E	WCAN	TO	Dorothy Garrod
60072		MG	E	WCAN	TO	Cairn Toul
60073		MG	E	WCAN	TO	Cairn Gorm[1]
60074		MG	E	WCAN	TO	Braeriach
60075		MG	E	WCAN	TO	Liathachl
60076		MG	E	WCAN	TO	
60077	+	MG	E	WCAN	TO	Canisp[1]
60078		ML	E	WCAN	TO	
60079		MG	E	WCAN	TO	Foinaven
60080	+	T	E	WCAN	TO	Kinder Scout
60081	+	T	E	WCAN	TO	Bleaklow Hill[1]
60082		T	E	WCAN	TO	Mam Tor
60083		E	E	WCAN	TO	Mountsorrel

60084	T	E	WCAN	TO	Cross Fell
60085	T	E	WCAN	TO	
60086	MG	E	WCAN	TO	Schiehallion
60087	MG	E	WCAN	TO	Slioch
60088	MG	E	WCAN	TO	Buachaille Etive Mor
60089	T	E	WCAN	TO	Arcuil
60090	+ FC	E	WCAN	TO	Quinag
60091	+ FC	E	WCAN	TO	An Teallach
60092	FT	E	WCAN	TO	Reginald Munns
60093	T	E	WCAN	TO	Jack Stirk
60094	MG	E	WCAN	TO	Tryfan
60095	F	E	WCAN	TO	
60096	+ T	E	WCAN	TO	Ben Macdui
60097	T	E	WCAN	TO	
60098	+ E	E	WCAN	TO	Charles Francis Brush
60099	MG	E	WCAN	TO	Ben More Assynt
60100	MG	E	WCAN	TO	Boar of Badenoch

CLASS 66   GENERAL MOTORS   Co–Co

Built: 1998–2000 by General Motors, London, Ontario, Canada (Model JT42CWR).
Engine: General Motors 12N-7103GB-EC two stroke of 2385 kW (3200 hp) at 900 rpm.
Main Alternator: General Motors AR8/C86.

Traction Motors: General Motors D43TR.	**Max. Tractive Effort:** 409 kN (92000 lbf).
Cont. Tractive Effort: 260 kN (58390 lbf) at 15.9 mph.	
Power At Rail: 1850 Kw (2480 hp).	**Train Brakes:** Air.
Brake Force: 68 t.	**Dimensions:** 21.35 x 2.64 x 3.90 m.
Weight: 126 t.	**Wheel Diameter:** 1120 mm.
Design Speed: 75 mph.	**Max. Speed:** 75 mph.
Fuel Capacity: 6550 litres.	**RA:** 7.
Train Supply: Not equipped.	**Multiple Working:** GM System.

66001	E	A	WBAN	TO
66002	E	A	WBAN	
66003	E	A	WBAN	TO
66004	E	A	WBAN	TO
66005	E	A	WBAN	TO
66006	E	A	WBAN	TO
66007	E	A	WBAN	TO
66008	E	A	WBAN	TO
66009	E	A	WBAN	TO
66010	E	A	WBAN	TO
66011	E	A	WBAN	TO
66012	E	A	WBAN	TO
66013	E	A	WBAN	TO
66014	E	A	WBAN	TO
66015	E	A	WBAN	TO
66016	E	A	WBAN	TO
66017	E	A	WBAN	TO
66018	E	A	WBAN	TO
66019	E	A	WBAN	TO

66020	E	A	WBAN	TO
66021	E	A	WBAN	TO
66022	E	A	WBAN	TO
66023	E	A	WBAN	TO
66024	E	A	WBAN	TO
66025	E	A	WBAN	TO
66026	E	A	WBAN	TO
66027	E	A	WBAN	TO
66028	E	A	WBAN	TO
66029	E	A	WBAN	TO
66030	E	A	WBAN	TO
66031	E	A	WBAN	TO
66032	E	A	WBAN	TO
66033	E	A	WBAN	TO
66034	E	A	WBAN	TO
66035	E	A	WBAN	TO
66036	E	A	WBAN	TO
66037	E	A	WBAN	TO
66038	E	A	WBAN	TO
66039	E	A	WBAN	TO
66040	E	A	WBAN	TO
66041	E	A	WBAN	TO
66042	E	A	WBAN	TO
66043	E	A	WBAN	TO
66044	E	A	WBAN	TO
66045	E	A	WBAN	
66046	E	A	WBAN	
66047	E	A	WBAN	
66048	E	A	WBAN	
66049	E	A	WBAN	
66050	E	A	WBAN	
66051	E	A	WBAN	
66052	E	A	WBAN	
66053	E	A	WBAN	
66054	E	A	WBAN	
66055	E	A	WBAN	
66056	E	A	WBAN	
66057	E	A	WBAN	
66058	E	A	WBAN	
66059	E	A	WBAN	
66060	E	A	WBAN	
66061	E	A	WBAN	
66062	E	A	WBAN	
66063	E	A	WBAN	
66064	E	A	WBAN	
66065	E	A	WBAN	
66066	E	A	WBAN	
66067	E	A	WBAN	
66068	E	A	WBAN	
66069	E	A	WBAN	
66070	E	A	WBAN	

66071	E	A	WBAN
66072	E	A	WBAN
66073		A	WBAN
66074		A	WBAN
66075		A	WBAN
66076		A	WBAN
66077		A	WBAN
66078		A	WBAN
66079		A	WBAN
66080		A	WBAN
66081		A	WBAN
66082		A	WBAN
66083		A	WBAN
66084		A	WBAN
66085		A	WBAN
66086		A	WBAN
66087		A	WBAN
66088		A	WBAN
66089		A	WBAN
66090		A	WBAN
66091		A	WBAN
66092		A	WBAN
66093		A	WBAN
66094		A	WBAN
66095		A	WBAN
66096		A	WBAN
66097		A	WBAN
66098		A	WBAN
66099		A	WBAN
66100		A	WBAN
66101		A	WBAN
66102		A	WBAN
66103		A	WBAN
66104		A	WBAN
66105		A	WBAN
66106		A	WBAN
66107		A	WBAN
66108		A	WBAN
66109		A	WBAN
66110		A	WBAN
66111		A	WBAN
66112		A	WBAN
66113		A	WBAN
66114		A	WBAN
66115		A	WBAN
66116		A	WBAN
66117		A	WBAN
66118		A	WBAN
66119		A	WBAN
66120		A	WBAN
66121		A	WBAN

66122	A	WBAN
66123	A	WBAN
66124	A	WBAN
66125	A	WBAN
66126	A	WBAN
66127	A	WBAN
66128	A	WBAN
66129	A	WBAN
66130	A	WBAN
66131	A	WBAN
66132	A	WBAN
66133	A	WBAN
66134	A	WBAN
66135	A	WBAN
66136	A	WBAN
66137	A	WBAN
66138	A	WBAN
66139	A	WBAN
66140	A	WBAN
66141	A	WBAN
66142	A	WBAN
66143	A	WBAN
66144	A	WBAN
66145	A	WBAN
66146	A	WBAN
66147	A	WBAN
66148	A	WBAN
66149	A	WBAN
66150	A	WBAN
66151	A	WBAN
66152	A	WBAN
66153	A	WBAN
66154	A	WBAN
66155	A	WBAN
66156	A	WBAN
66157	A	WBAN
66158	A	WBAN
66159	A	WBAN
66160	A	WBAN
66161	A	WBAN
66162	A	WBAN
66163	A	WBAN
66164	A	WBAN
66165	A	WBAN
66166	A	WBAN
66167	A	WBAN
66168	A	WBAN
66169	A	WBAN
66170	A	WBAN
66171	A	WBAN
66172	A	WBAN

66173	A	WBAN
66174	A	WBAN
66175	A	WBAN
66176	A	WBAN
66177	A	WBAN
66178	A	WBAN
66179	A	WBAN
66180	A	WBAN
66181	A	WBAN
66182	A	WBAN
66183	A	WBAN
66184	A	WBAN
66185	A	WBAN
66186	A	WBAN
66187	A	WBAN
66188	A	WBAN
66189	A	WBAN
66190	A	WBAN
66191	A	WBAN
66192	A	WBAN
66193	A	WBAN
66194	A	WBAN
66195	A	WBAN
66196	A	WBAN
66197	A	WBAN
66198	A	WBAN
66199	A	WBAN
66200	A	WBAN
66201	A	WBAN
66202	A	WBAN
66203	A	WBAN
66204	A	WBAN
66205	A	WBAN
66206	A	WBAN
66207	A	WBAN
66208	A	WBAN
66209	A	WBAN
66210	A	WBAN
66211	A	WBAN
66212	A	WBAN
66213	A	WBAN
66214	A	WBAN
66215	A	WBAN
66216	A	WBAN
66217	A	WBAN
66218	A	WBAN
66219	A	WBAN
66220	A	WBAN
66221	A	WBAN
66222	A	WBAN
66223	A	WBAN
66224	A	WBAN

66225	A	WBAN
66226	A	WBAN
66227	A	WBAN
66228	A	WBAN
66229	A	WBAN
66230	A	WBAN
66231	A	WBAN
66232	A	WBAN
66233	A	WBAN
66234	A	WBAN
66235	A	WBAN
66236	A	WBAN
66237	A	WBAN
66238	A	WBAN
66239	A	WBAN
66240	A	WBAN
66241	A	WBAN
66242	A	WBAN
66243	A	WBAN
66244	A	WBAN
66245	A	WBAN
66246	A	WBAN
66247	A	WBAN
66248	A	WBAN
66249	A	WBAN
66250	A	WBAN

CLASS 67   GENERAL MOTORS   Bo–Bo

Built: 1998–99 by Alstom at Valencia, Spain, as sub-contractors for General Motors.
Engine: General Motors 12N-7103GB-EC two stroke of 2385 kW (3200 hp) at 900 rpm.
Main Alternator: General Motors AR8/C86.
Traction Motors: General Motors D43TR.

Max. Tractive Effort:	**Cont. Tractive Effort:**
Power At Rail:	**Train Brakes:** Air.
Brake Force:	**Dimensions:** 21.02 x 2.72 x 3.95 m.
Weight: 88 t.	**Wheel Diameter:** 1120 mm.
Design Speed: 125 mph.	**Max. Speed:** 125 mph.
Fuel Capacity:	**RA:**
Train Supply: Electric.	**Multiple Working:** GM System.

67001	A	WAAN
67002	A	WAAN
67003	A	WAAN
67004	A	WAAN
67005	A	WAAN
67006	A	WAAN
67007	A	WAAN
67008	A	WAAN
67009	A	WAAN
67010	A	WAAN
67011	A	WAAN
67012	A	WAAN
67013	A	WAAN
67014	A	WAAN
67015	A	WAAN
67016	A	WAAN
67017	A	WAAN
67018	A	WAAN
67019	A	WAAN
67020	A	WAAN
67021	A	WAAN
67022	A	WAAN
67023	A	WAAN
67024	A	WAAN
67025	A	WAAN
67026	A	WAAN
67027	A	WAAN
67028	A	WAAN
67029	A	WAAN
67030	A	WAAN

1.2. ELECTRIC & ELECTRO-DIESEL LOCOMOTIVES

CLASS 71   BR/ENGLISH ELECTRIC   Bo–Bo

Built: 1959 by BR at Doncaster Works.
Electric Supply System: 750 V dc from third rail.
Traction Motors: English Electric 532.
Max. Tractive Effort: 195 kN (43800 lbf).
Continuous Rating: 1716 kW (2300 hp) giving a tractive effort of 55 kN (12400 lbf) at 69.6 mph.   **RA:** 6.
Maximum Rail Power: 2239 kW (3000 hp).
Train Brakes: Air, vacuum & electro-pneumatic.
Brake Force: 41 t.   **Dimensions:** 15.42 x 2.82 x 3.99 m.
Weight: 76.2 t.   **Wheel Diameter:** 1219 mm.
Design Speed: 90 mph   **Max. Speed:** 90 mph.
Train Supply: Electric (300 kW maximum).
Multiple Working: SR System.
Non-standard livery/numbering:
• 71001 carries number E5001.

71001   **G**   NR   MBEL   SE

UNCLASSIFIED   METROPOLITAN VICKERS   Bo–Bo

Built: 1922 by Metropolitan Vickers at Gorton.
Electric Supply System: 750 V dc from third rail or four rail system.
Traction Motors:
Max. Tractive Effort: 100 kN (22600 lbf).
Continuous Rating: 895 kW (1200 hp) giving a tractive effort of 65 kN (14700 lbf) at   mph.   **RA:**
Maximum Rail Power: **Train Brakes:** Air.
Brake Force: **Dimensions:**
Weight: 76.2 t.   **Wheel Diameter:** 1105 mm.
Design Speed: 65 mph   **Max. Speed:** 65 mph.
Train Supply: Not equipped.   **Multiple Working:** Not equipped.
Non-standard livery/numbering:
• L12 is London Transport red. Official RSL number is 89212.

L12   **0**   LU   MBEL   SARAH SIDDONS

CLASS 73   BR/ENGLISH ELECTRIC   Bo–Bo

Built: 1962 by BR at Eastleigh Works.
Engine: English Electric 4SRKT of 447 kW (600 hp) at 850 rpm.
Main Generator: English Electric 824/3D.
Electric Supply System: 750 V dc from third rail.

Traction Motors: English Electric 542A.
Max. Tractive Effort: Electric 187 kN (42000 lbf). Diesel 152 kN (34100 lbf).
Continuous Rating: Electric 1060 kW (1420 hp) giving a tractive effort of 43 kN (9600 lbf) at 55.5 mph.
Cont. Tractive Effort: Diesel 72 kN (16100 lbf) at 10 mph.
Maximum Rail Power: Electric 1830 kW (2450 hp) at 37 mph.
Train Brakes: Air, vacuum & electro-pneumatic († Air & electro-pneumatic).
Brake Force: 31 t.   **Dimensions:** 16.36 x 2.64 x 3.8 m.
Weight: 76.3 t.   **Wheel Diameter:** 1016 mm.
Design Speed: 80 mph   **Max. Speed:** 60 mph.
Fuel Capacity: 1545 litres.   **RA:** 6.
Train Supply: Electric, index 66 (on electric power only). May also deliver a reduced electric train supply when on diesel power whilst stationary.
Multiple Working: SR System.

Non-standard livery/numbering:
- 73005 is in non-standard blue livery with white roof.

Class 73/0. First build. Details as above.

73002	**BL**	ME	HEBD	KK(S)
73005	**0**	ME	HEBD	BD

Class 73/1. Later build. Revised details.
Built: 1965–67 by English Electric Co. at Vulcan Foundry, Newton le Willows.
Main Generator: English Electric 824/5D.
Traction Motors: English Electric 546/1B.
Max. Tractive Effort: Electric 179 kN (40000 lbf). Diesel 160 kN (36000 lbf).
Continuous Rating: Electric 1060 kW (1420 hp) giving a tractive effort of 35 kN (7800 lbf) at 68 mph.
Cont. Tractive Effort: Diesel 60 kN (13600 lbf) at 11.5 mph.
Maximum Rail Power: Electric 2350 kW (3150 hp) at 42 mph.
Weight: 77 t.   **Dimensions:** 16.36 x 2.64 x 3.81m.
Design Speed: 90 mph   **Max. Speed:** 60 (90*) mph.
Fuel Capacity: 1409 litres.
Note: ‡ Modified cabs for use on route learning duties.

73101	*	**PC**	E	WPAN	EH	The Royal Alex'
73103		**I**	E	WPAN	EH	
73104	*	**I**	E	WPAN	EH	
73105	*	**CE**	E	WPAN	EH	
73106		**DG**	E	WPAN	EH	
73107	*	**CE**	E	WPAN	EH	Redhill 1844-1994
73108		**CE**	E	WPAN	EH	
73109	*	**ST**	SW	HYSB	BM	Battle of Britain 50th Anniversary
73110		**CE**	E	WPAN	EH	
73114	*	**ML**	E	WPAN	EH	Stewarts Lane Traction Maintenance Depot
73117		**I**	E	WPAN	EH	University of Surrey
73118	†c	**EP**	EU	GPSN	OC	
73119	*	**CE**	E	WPAN	OC(S)	Kentish Mercury
73126		**N**	E	WNYX	OC(S)	
73128	*	**E**	E	WPAN	EH	
73129	*	**N**	E	WPAN	EH	City of Winchester

73130	†c	EP	EU	GPSN	OC	
73131	*	E	E	WPAN	EH	
73132		I	E	WNXX	OC(S)	
73133	‡	ML	E	WPAN	EH	The Bluebell Railway
73134		I	E	WPAN	EH	Woking Homes 1885-1985
73136		ML	E	WPAN	EH	Kent Youth Music
73138		CE	E	WPAN	EH	
73139		I	E	WPAN	EH	
73140		I	E	WNXX	OC(S)	
73141		I	E	WPAN	EH	

Class 73/2. Gatwick Express locomotives. Details as Class 73/1 except:
Max. Speed: 90 mph.   **Train Brakes:** Air & electro-pneumatic.

73201	GX	GX	IVGA	SL	Broadlands
73202	GX	GX	IVGA	SL	Royal Observer Corps
73203	GX	GX	IVGA	SL	
73204	GX	GX	IVGA	SL	Stewarts Lane 1860-1985
73205	GX	GX	IVGA	SL	
73206	GX	GX	IVGA	SL	Gatwick Express
73207	GX	GX	IVGA	SL	County of East Sussex
73208	GX	GX	IVGA	SL	Croydon 1883-1983
73209	GX	GX	IVGA	SL	
73210	GX	GX	IVGA	SL	Selhurst
73211	GX	GX	IVGA	SL	
73212	GX	GX	IVGA	SL	Airtour Suisse
73213	GX	GX	IVGA	SL	University of Kent at Canterbury
73235	GX	GX	IVGA	SL	

Class 73/9. Merseyrail Electrics engineering and sandite train locomotives.
Details as Class 73/0.

73901	MD	ME	HEBD	BD	
73906	MD	ME	HEBD	BD	

NOTES FOR CLASSES 86–91

The following common features apply to all locos of Classes 86–91.

Supply System: 25 kV a.c. 50 Hz overhead.
Multiple Working: Time division multiplex system.

CLASS 86   BR/ENGLISH ELECTRIC   Bo–Bo

Built: 1965–66 by English Electric Co. at Vulcan Foundry, Newton le Willows or by BR at Doncaster Works.
Traction Motors: AEI 282BZ frame mounted.
Max. Tractive Effort: 207 kN (46500 lbf).
Continuous Rating: 3010 kW (4040 hp) giving a tractive effort of 85 kN (19200 lbf) at 77.5 mph.
Maximum Rail Power: 4550 kW (6100 hp) at 49.5 mph.
Train Brakes: Air.

Brake Force: 40 t.
Weight: 83–86.8 t.
Design Speed: 100 mph
Train Supply: Electric, index 74.

Dimensions: 17.83 x 2.65 x 3.98 m.
Wheel Diameter: 1156 mm.
Max. Speed: 100 mph
RA: 6.

Class 86/1. Class 87 type bogies and motors. Details as above except:
Max. Tractive Effort: 258 kN (58000 lbf).
Traction Motors: GEC 412AZ.
Continuous Rating: 3730 kW (5000 hp) giving a TE of 95 kN (21300 lbf) at 87 mph.
Maximum Rail Power: 5860 kW (7860 hp) at 50.8 mph.
Weight: 86.8 t.
Design Speed: 110 mph

Wheel Diameter: 1150 mm.
Max. Speed: 110 mph.

86101	**IS**	F	WEMF	CE	Sir William A Stanier FRS
86102	**IS**	F	WEMF	CE .	Robert A Riddles
86103	x	**IS**	F	SAXL	CE(S)	André Chapelon

Class 86/2. Standard Design. Details as in main class heading except:
Weight: 85–86.2 t.
Non-standard livery/numbering:
*   86245 is as **V**, but with blue replacing red as the main colour and red rather than white stripes.

86204	**IS**	F	SAXL	ZH(S)	City of Carlisle
86205	**IS**	F	ICCA	LG	City of Lancaster
86206	**IS**	F	SAXL	ZH(S)	City of Stoke on Trent
86207	**IS**	F	SAXL	ZH(S)	City of Lichfield
86208	**IS**	E	WEMP	CE	City of Chester
86209	**IS**	F	IANA	NC	City of Coventry
86210	x	**RX**	E	WEMP	CE	C.I.T. 75th Anniversary
86212	**IS**	F	ICCA	LG	Preston Guild 1328-1992
86213	**IS**	F	SAXL	ZH(S)	Lancashire Witch
86214	**IS**	F	ICCA	LG	Sans Pareil
86215	**AR**	F	IANA	NC	Norwich and Norfolk Festival
86216	**IS**	F	SAXL	ZH(S)	Meteor
86217	**IS**	F	IANA	NC	City University
86218	**AR**	F	IANA	NC	NHS 50
86219	**IS**	F	SAXL	ZH(S)	Phoenix
86220	**IS**	F	IANA	NC	The Round Tabler
86221	**IS**	F	IANA	NC	B.B.C. Look East
86222	**IS**	F	ICCA	LG	Clothes Show Live
86223	**IS**	F	IANA	NC	Norwich Union
86224	**IS**	F	ICCA	LG	
86225	**IS**	F	ICCA	LG	Hardwicke
86226	**IS**	F	ICCA	LG	CHARLES RENNIE MACKINTOSH
86227	**IS**	F	SAXL	PC(S)	Sir Henry Johnson
86228	**IS**	F	SAXL	ZH(S)	Vulcan Heritage
86229	**V**	F	IWPA	WN	Lions Clubs International
86230	**IS**	F	IANA	NC	
86231	**IS**	F	ICCA	LG	Starlight Express
86232	**IS**	F	IANA	NC	
86233	**IS**	F	IWPA	WN	Laurence Olivier
86234	**IS**	F	ICCA	LG	J B Priestley OM

86235	**AR**	F	IANA	NC	Crown Point
86236	**IS**	F	ICCA	LG	Josiah Wedgwood MASTER POTTER 1736-1795
86237	**AR**	F	IANA	NC	University of East Anglia
86238	**IS**	F	IANA	NC	European Community
86240	**IS**	F	ICCA	LG	Bishop Eric Treacy
86241	**RX**	E	WEMP	CE	Glenfiddich
86242	**V**	F	ICCA	LG	James Kennedy GC
86243 x	**RX**	E	WEMP	CE	
86244	**IS**	F	ICCA	LG	The Royal British Legion
86245	**O**	F	IWPA	WN	Caledonian
86246	**AR**	F	IANA	NC	Royal Anglian Regiment
86247	**IS**	F	IWPA	WN	Abraham Darby
86248	**IS**	F	ICCA	LG	Sir Clwyd/County of Clwyd
86249	**IS**	F	SAXL	ZH(S)	County of Merseyside
86250	**AR**	F	IANA	NC	
86251	**IS**	F	ICCA	LG	The Birmingham Post
86252	**IS**	F	IANA	NC	The Liverpool Daily Post
86253	**IS**	F	ICCA	LG	The Manchester Guardian
86254 x	**RX**	E	WEMP	CE	
86255	**IS**	F	SAXL	LG(S)	Penrith Beacon
86256	**IS**	F	ICCA	LG	Pebble Mill
86257	**AR**	F	IANA	NC	
86258	**IS**	F	ICCA	LG	Talyllyn-The First Preserved Railway
86259	**IS**	F	IWPA	WN	Greater MANCHESTER THE LIFE & SOUL OF BRITAIN
86260	**IS**	F	IWPA	WN	Driver Wallace Oakes G.C.
86261 x	**E**	E	WEMP	CE	THE RAIL CHARTER PARTNERSHIP

Class 86/4. EWS (Rail Express Services) locomotives. Details as Class 86/2 except:
Max. Tractive Effort: 258 kN (58000 lbf).
Traction Motors: AEI 412AZ. **Weight:** 83–83.9 t.
Continuous Rating: 2680 kW (3600 hp) giving a tractive effort of 89 kN (20000 lbf) at 67 mph.
Maximum Rail Power: 4400 kW (5900 hp) at 38 mph.

86401		**E**	E	WEMP	CE	Hertfordshire Rail Tours
86416	x	**RX**	E	WEMP	CE	
86417	x	**RX**	E	WEMP	CE	
86419	x	**RX**	E	WEMP	CE	
86424	x	**RX**	E	WEMP	CE	
86425	x	**RX**	E	WEMF	CE	Saint Mungo
86426	x	**E**	E	WEMP	CE	Pride of the Nation
86430	x	**RX**	E	WEMP	CE	Saint Edmund

Class 86/6. Freightliner locomotives. Details as Class 86/4 except:
Max. Speed: 75 mph. **Train Supply:** Electric, isolated.

86602	**F**	FL	DFNC	CE
86603	**FE**	FL	DFNC	CE
86604	**FF**	FL	DFNC	CE
86605	**FF**	FL	DFNC	CE
86606	**FF**	FL	DFNC	CE

86607	F	FL	DFNC	CE	The Institution of Electrical Engineers
86608	FE	FL	DFNC	CE	St John Ambulance
86609	F	FL	DFNC	CE	
86610	F	FL	DFNC	CE	
86611	FF	FL	DFNC	CE	Airey Neave
86612	FF	P	DFNC	CE	Elizabeth Garrett Anderson
86613	FF	P	DFNC	CE	County of Lancashire
86614	FF	P	DFNC	CE	Frank Hornby
86615	F	P	DFNC	CE	Rotary International
86618	FF	P	DFNC	CE	
86620	FL	P	DFNC	CE	Philip G Walton
86621	FF	P	DFNC	CE	London School of Economics
86622	FF	P	DFNC	CE	
86623	FF	P	DFNC	CE	
86627	F	P	DFNC	CE	The Industrial Society
86628	FF	P	DFNC	CE	Aldaniti
86631	FL	P	DFNC	CE	
86632	F	P	DFNC	CE	Brookside
86633	FF	P	DFNC	CE	Wulfruna
86634	FL	P	DFNC	CE	University of London
86635	F	P	DFNC	CE	
86636	F	P	DFNC	CE	
86637	FF	P	DFNC	CE	
86638	FF	P	DFNC	CE	
86639	FF	P	DFNC	CE	

CLASS 87   BREL/GEC   Bo–Bo

Built: 1973–75 by BREL at Crewe Works.
Traction Motors: GEC G412AZ frame mounted.
Max. Tractive Effort: 258 kN (58000 lbf).
Continuous Rating: 3730 kW (5000 hp) giving a TE of 95 kN (21300 lbf) at 87 mph.
Maximum Rail Power: 5860 kW (7860 hp) at 50.8 mph.
Train Brakes: Air.
Brake Force: 40 t.
Weight: 83.3 t.
Design Speed: 110 mph
Train Supply: Electric, index 95 (* 66).

Dimensions: 17.83 x 2.65 x 3.96 m.
Wheel Diameter: 1150 mm.
Max. Speed: 110 mph
RA: 6.

Class 87/0. Standard Design.

87001		IS	P	IWCA	WN	
87002		IS	P	IWCA	WN	Royal Sovereign
87003		V	P	IWCA	WN	Patriot
87004		V	P	IWCA	WN	Britannia
87005		IS	P	IWCA	WN	City of London
87006		V	P	IWCA	WN	George Reynolds
87007		IS	P	IWCA	WN	City of Manchester
87008		V	P	IWCA	WN	Royal Scot
87009	*	V	P	IWCA	WN	
87010		IS	P	IWCA	WN	King Arthur

87011	IS		P	IWCA	WN	
87012	V		P	IWCA	WN	
87013	V		P	IWCA	WN	
87014	IS		P	IWCA	WN	Knight of the Thistle
87015	IS		P	IWCA	WN	Howard of Effingham
87016	V		P	IWCA	WN	Willesden Intercity Depot
87017	IS		P	IWCA	WN	Iron Duke
87018	IS		P	IWCA	WN	Lord Nelson
87019	IS		P	IWCA	WN	Sir Winston Churchill
87020	IS		P	IWCA	WN	North Briton
87021	IS		P	IWCA	WN	Robert The Bruce
87022	V		P	IWCA	WN	Lew Adams The Black Prince
87023	IS		P	IWCA	WN	Velocity
87024	IS		P	IWCA	WN	Lord of the Isles
87025	V		P	IWCA	WN	County of Cheshire
87026	IS		P	IWCA	WN	Sir Richard Arkwright
87027	IS		P	IWCA	WN	Wolf of Badenoch
87028	IS		P	IWCA	WN	Lord President
87029	IS	*	P	IWCA	WN	Earl Marischal
87030	IS		P	IWCA	WN	Black Douglas
87031	V		P	IWCA	WN	Hal o' the Wynd
87032	V		P	IWCA	WN	Kenilworth
87033	IS		P	IWCA	WN	Thane of Fife
87034	IS		P	IWCA	WN	William Shakespeare
87035	IS		P	IWCA	WN	Robert Burns

Class 87/1. Thyristor Control. Details as Class 87/0 except:
Traction Motors: GEC G412BZ frame mounted.
Continuous Rating: 3620 kW (4850 hp) giving a TE of 96 kN (21600 lbf) at 84 mph.
Max. Speed: 75 mph.

87101	B	E	WEMF	CE	STEPHENSON

CLASS 89   BRUSH   Co–Co

Built: 1986 by BREL at Crewe Works (as sub-contractors for Brush).
Traction Motors: Brush. Frame mounted.
Max. Tractive Effort: 205 kN (46000 lbf).
Continuous Rating: 4350 kW (5850 hp) giving a TE of 105 kN (23600 lbf) at 92 mph.

Maximum Rail Power:	**Train Brakes:** Air.
Brake Force: 50 t.	**Dimensions:** 19.80 x 2.74 x 3.98 m.
Weight: 104 t.	**Wheel Diameter:** 1150 mm.
Design Speed: 125 mph	**Max. Speed:** 125 mph.
Train Supply: Electric, index 95.	**RA:** 6.

89001	GN	SS	IECB	BN

CLASS 90   GEC   Bo–Bo

Built: 1987–90 by BREL at Crewe Works (as sub contractors for GEC).
Traction Motors: GEC G412CY frame mounted.
Max. Tractive Effort: 258 kN (58000 lbf).
Continuous Rating: 3730 kW (5000 hp) giving a TE of 95 kN (21300 lbf) at 87 mph.
Max. Rail Power: 5860 kW (7860 hp) at 68.3 mph.
Train Brakes: Air.
Brake Force: 40 t.   **Dimensions:** 18.80 x 2.74 x 3.97 m.
Weight: 84.5 t.   **Wheel Diameter:** 1156 mm.
Design Speed: 110 mph   **Max. Speed:** 110 mph.
Train Supply: Electric, index 95.   **RA:** 7.
Note: 90025–90029 were renumbered from 90125–129 respectively in 1998.
Non-standard liveries/numbering:
* 90028 is in Belgian National Railways style blue and yellow.
* 90029 is in German Federal Railways style red and white.
* 90130 is in French National Railways style two-tone grey.
* 90136 is as **FE**, but has a yellow roof.

Class 90/0. Standard Design. Details as above.

90001	**IS**	P	IWCA	WN	BBC Midlands Today
90002	**V**	P	IWCA	WN	Mission: Impossible
90003	**IS**	P	IWCA	WN	THE HERALD
90004	**V**	P	IWCA	WN	
90005	**IS**	P	IWCA	WN	Financial Times
90006	**IS**	P	IWCA	WN	High Sheriff
90007	**IS**	P	IWCA	WN	Lord Stamp
90008	**IS**	P	IWCA	WN	The Birmingham Royal Ballet
90009	**IS**	P	IWCA	WN	
90010	**IS**	P	IWCA	WN	275 Railway Squadron (Volunteers)
90011	**IS**	P	IWCA	WN	The Chartered Institute of
90012	**V**	P	IWCA	WN	British Transport Police
90013	**IS**	P	IWCA	WN	The Law Society
90014	**V**	P	IWCA	WN	The Big Dish
90015	**V**	P	IWCA	WN	The International Brigades SPAIN 1936-1939
90016	**RX**	E	WEMP	CE	
90017	**RX**	E	WEMP	CE	Rail Express Systems Quality Assured
90018	**RX**	E	WEMP	CE	
90019	**RX**	E	WEMP	CE	
90020	**E**	E	WEMP	CE	Sir Michael Heron
90021	**FE**	E	WEMP	CE	
90022	**FE**	E	WEMP	CE	Freightconnection
90023	**FE**	E	WEMP	CE	
90024	**FE**	E	WEMP	CE	
90025	**FD**	E	WEMF	CE	
90026	**FE**	E	WEMP	CE	Crewe International Electric Maintenance Depot
90027	**FD**	E	WEMF	CE	Allerton T & RS Depot Quality Approved
90028	**0**	E	WEMP	CE	Vrachtverbinding
90029	**0**	E	WEMF	CE	Frachtverbindungen

Class 90/1. EWS & Freightliner locomotives. Details as Class 90/0 except:
Max. Speed: 75 mph.   **Train Supply**: Electric, isolated.

90130	0	E	WEMF	CE	Fretconnection
90131	FE	E	WEMF	CE	Intercontainer
90132	FE	E	WEMF	CE	Cerestar
90133	FE	E	WEMF	CE	
90134	FE	E	WEMF	CE	
90135	FE	E	WEMF	CE	Crewe Basford Hall
90136	0	E	WEMF	CE	
90137	FD	E	WEMF	CE	
90138	FE	E	WEMF	CE	
90139	FD	E	WEMF	CE	
90140	FD	E	WEMF	CE	
90141	FF	P	DFLC	CE	
90142	FF	P	DFLC	CE	
90143	FF	P	DFLC	CE	Freightliner Coatbridge
90144	FF	P	DFLC	CE	
90145	FF	P	DFLC	CE	
90146	FF	P	DFLC	CE	
90147	FF	P	DFLC	CE	
90148	FF	P	DFLC	CE	
90149	FF	P	DFLC	CE	
90150	FF	P	DFLC	CE	

CLASS 91   GEC   Bo–Bo

Built: 1988–91 by BREL at Crewe Works (as sub contractors for GEC).
Traction Motors: GEC G426AZ.
Continuous Rating: 4540 kW (6090 hp).
Maximum Rail Power: 4700 kW (6300 hp).
Train Brakes: Air.
Brake Force: 45 t.   **Dimensions**: 19.41 x 2.74 x 3.76 m.
Weight: 84 t.   **Wheel Diameter**: 1000 mm.
Design Speed: 140 mph   **Max. Speed**: 125 mph.
Train Supply: Electric, index 95.   **RA**: 7.

91001	GN	F	IECA	BN	
91002	GN	F	IECA	BN	
91003	GN	F	IECA	BN	
91004	GN	F	IECA	BN	
91005	GN	F	IECA	BN	
91006	GN	F	IECA	BN	
91007	GN	F	IECA	BN	
91008	GN	F	IECA	BN	
91009	GN	F	IECA	BN	The Samaritans
91010	GN	F	IECA	BN	
91011	GN	F	IECA	BN	
91012	GN	F	IECA	BN	
91013	GN	F	IECA	BN	
91014	GN	F	IECA	BN	
91015	GN	F	IECA	BN	

91016	**GN**	F	IECA	BN
91017	**GN**	F	IECA	BN
91018	**GN**	F	IECA	BN
91019	**GN**	F	IECA	BN
91020	**GN**	F	IECA	BN
91021	**GN**	F	IECA	BN
91022	**GN**	F	IECA	BN
91023	**GN**	F	IECA	BN
91024	**GN**	F	IECA	BN
91025	**GN**	F	IECA	BN
91026	**GN**	F	IECA	BN
91027	**GN**	F	IECA	BN
91028	**GN**	F	IECA	BN
91029	**GN**	F	IECA	BN
91030	**GN**	F	IECA	BN
91031	**GN**	F	IECA	BN

CLASS 92 BRUSH Co–Co

Built: 1993–96 by Brush Traction at Loughborough.
Supply System: 25 kV a.c. 50 HZ overhead and 750 V d.c. third rail.
Traction Motors: Brush. **Max. Tractive Effort:** 400 kN (90 000 lbf).
Continuous Rating: 5040 kW (6760 hp) on a.c, 4000 kW (5360 hp) on d.c.
Maximum Rail Power: **Train Brakes:** Air.
Brake Force: 63 t. **Dimensions:** 21.34 x ?? x ?? m.
Weight: 126 t. **Wheel Diameter:** 1160 mm.
Design Speed: 140 km/h (87½ mph). **Max. Speed:** 140 km/h (87½ mph).
Train Supply: Electric, index 108 (ac), 70 (dc). **RA:** 8..
Multiple Working: Time division multiplex system.

92001	**E**	E	WTWN	CE	Victor Hugo
92002	**EP**	E	WTAN	CE	H.G. Wells
92003	**EP**	E	WTWN	CE	Beethoven
92004	**EP**	E	WTAN	CE	Jane Austen
92005	**EP**	E	WTAN	CE	Mozart
92006	**EP**	SF	WTAN	CE	Louis Armand
92007	**EP**	E	WTAN	CE	Schubert
92008	**EP**	E	WTWN	CE	Jules Verne
92009	**EP**	E	WTAN	CE	Elgar
92010	**EP**	SF	WTAN	CE	Molière
92011	**EP**	E	WTAN	CE	Handel
92012	**EP**	E	WTWN	CE	Thomas Hardy
92013	**EP**	E	WTWN	CE	Puccini
92014	**EP**	SF	WTAN	CE	Emile Zola
92015	**EP**	E	WTAN	CE	D.H. Lawrence
92016	**EP**	E	WTAN	CE	Brahms
92017	**EP**	E	WTAN	CE	Shakespeare
92018	**EP**	SF	WTAN	CE	Stendhal
92019	**EP**	E	WTWN	CE	Wagner
92020	**EP**	EU	WTAN	CE	Milton
92021	**EP**	EU	WTAN	CE	Purcell

92022	**EP**	E	WTAN	CE	Charles Dickens
92023	**EP**	SF	WTAN	CE	Ravel
92024	**EP**	E	WTWN	CE	J.S. Bach
92025	**EP**	E	WTAN	CE	Oscar Wilde
92026	**EP**	E	WTWN	CE	Britten
92027	**EP**	E	WTAN	CE	George Eliot
92028	**EP**	SF	WTAN	CE	Saint Saëns
92029	**EP**	E	WTAN	CE	Dante
92030	**EP**	E	WTAN	CE	Ashford
92031	**EP**	E	WTAN	CE	
92032	**EP**	EU	WTAN	CE	César Franck
92033	**EP**	SF	WTAN	CE	Berlioz
92034	**EP**	E	WTWN	CE	Kipling
92035	**EP**	E	WTAN	CE	Mendelssohn
92036	**EP**	E	WTAN	CE	Bertolt Brecht
92037	**EP**	E	WTWN	CE	Sullivan
92038	**EP**	SF	WTAN	CE	Voltaire
92039	**EP**	E	WTAN	CE	Johann Strauss
92040	**EP**	EU	WTEN	CE	Goethe
92041	**EP**	E	WTAN	CE	Vaughan Williams
92042	**EP**	E	WTAN	CE	Honegger
92043	**EP**	SF	WTAN	CE	Debussy
92044	**EP**	EU	WTAN	CE	Couperin
92045	**EP**	EU	WTAN	CE	Chaucer
92046	**EP**	EU	WTAN	CE	Sweelinck

1.3. MISCELLANEOUS VEHICLES

POWER UNIT TRANSPORTER/MAINTENANCE VEHICLE

Built: 1962-63 by English Electric Company at Vulcan Foundry, Newton le Willows (025031) or by Robert Stephenson & Hawthorn at Darlington (025032) as Class 37 locomotives. Converted to present use 1996 at Toton depot. Also carry local numbers 1 & 2 respectively.

| 025031 (37070) | **DG** | E | | TO |
| 025032 (37138) | **DG** | E | | TO |

1.4. LOCOMOTIVES AWAITING DISPOSAL

Included in this section are locomotives awaiting disposal of classes which do not otherwise feature in this publication.

Class 45

| 45015 | **B** | E | WNZX | TT(S) |

1.5 EUROTUNNEL LOCOMOTIVES

Depot: Coquelles (France).

0001–0005   MAK   Bo-Bo

Built: 1992–93 by MaK at Kiel, Germany (Model DE1004).
Engine: MTU 12V 396 Tc of 1180 kW (1580 hp) at 1800 rpm.
Main Alternator: BBC.   **Traction Motors:** BBC.
Max. Tractive Effort: 305 kN (68600 lbf).
Cont. Tractive Effort: 140 kN (31500 lbf) at 20 mph.
Power At Rail: 750 kW (1012 hp).
Brake Force: 120 kN.   **Dimensions:** 16.50 x ?? x ?? m.
Weight: 84 t.   **Wheel Diameter:** 1000 mm.
Design Speed: 120 km/h.   **Max. Speed:** 120 km/h.
Fuel Capacity: **Train Brakes:** Air.
Train Supply: Not equipped.   **Multiple Working:** Within class.
Livery: Grey and yellow.

0001	0002	0003	0004	0005

0032–0042   HUNSLET/SCHÖMA   0-4-0

Built: 1989–90 by Hunslet Engine Company at Leeds as 900 mm. gauge.
Rebuilt: 1993-94 by Schöma in Germany as 1435 mm. gauge.
Engine: Deutz of 270 kW (200 hp) at ???? rpm.
Transmission: Mechanical.   **Max. Tractive Effort:**
Cont. Tractive Effort: **Power At Rail:**
Brake Force: **Dimensions:**
Weight: **Wheel Diameter:**
Design Speed: 50 km/h.   **Max. Speed:** 50 km/h.
Fuel Capacity: **Train Brakes:** Air.
Train Supply: Not equipped.   **Multiple Working:** Not equipped.
Livery: Plain yellow.

0031	FRANCES	0037	LYDIE
0032	ELISABETH	0038	JENNY
0033	SILKE	0039	PACITA
0034	AMANDA	0040	JILL
0035	MARY	0041	KIM
0036	LAWRENCE	0042	NICOLE

9001–9105   BRUSH/ABB   Bo-Bo-Bo

Built: 1993–99 by Brush Traction at Loughborough. 9105 remained to be delivered at the time of going to press.
Supply System: 25 kV a.c. 50 Hz overhead.
Traction Motors: ABB 6PH.   **Max. Tractive Effort:** 400 kN (90 000 lbf).
Continuous Rating: 5760 kW (7725 hp) giving a TE of 310 kN at 65 km/h.

Maximum Rail Power:
Brake Force: 50 t.   **Dimensions:** 22.00 x ?? x ?? m.
Weight: 132 t.   **Wheel Diameter:** 1090 mm.
Design Speed: 175 km/h.   **Max. Speed:** 160 km/h.
Train Supply: Electric.   **Train Brakes:** Air.
Multiple Working: Time division multiplex system.

9001	LESLEY GARRETT
9002	STUART BURROWS
9003	BENJAMIN LUXON
9004	VICTORIA DE LOS ANGELES
9005	JESSYE NORMAN
9006	REGINE CRISPIN
9007	DAME JOAN SUTHERLAND
9008	ELISABETH SODERSTROM
9009	FRANÇOISE POLLET
9010	JEAN-PHILLIPE COURTIS
9011	JOSÉ VAN DAM
9012	LUCIANO PAVAROTTI
9013	MARIA CALLAS
9014	LUCIA POPP
9015	LÖTSCHBERG
9016	WILLARD WHITE
9017	JOSÉ CARRERAS
9018	WILHELMENA FERNANDEZ
9019	EMARIA EWING
9020	NICOLAI GHIAROV
9021	THERESA BERGANZA
9022	DAME JANET BAKER
9023	DAME ELIZABETH LEGGE-SCHWARZKOPF
9024	GOTTHARD 1882
9025	JUNGFRAUJOCH
9026	FURKATUNNEL
9027	BARBARA HENDRICKS
9028	DAME KIRI TE KANAWA
9029	THOMAS ALLEN
9031	PLACIDO DOMINGO
9032	RENATA TEBALDI
9033	MONTSERRAT CABALLE
9034	MIRELLA FRENI
9035	NICOLAI GEDDA
9036	ALAIN FONDARY
9037	GABRIEL BACQUIER
9038	HILDEGARD BEHRENS
9040	
9101	
9102	
9103	
9104	
9105	

2. COACHING STOCK

USING THIS SECTION – LAYOUT OF INFORMATION

Coaches are listed in numerical order of painted number in batches according to type.

Each coach entry is laid out as in the following example (former number column may be omitted where not applicable):

No.	Prev. No.	Notes	Livery	Owner	Operation	Depot/Location
2918	(40518)	*	**RP**	RT	*OR*	ZN

DETAILED INFORMATION & CODES

Under each type heading, the following details are shown:

- Diagram Code. This consists of the first three characters of the TOPS type code followed by two numbers which relate to the particular design of vehicle.
- 'Mark' of coach (see below).
- Number of first class seats , standard class seats, lavatory compartments and wheelchair spaces shown as F/S nT nW respectively.
- Bogie type (see below).
- Additional features.
- ETH Index.

TOPS TYPE CODES

TOPS type codes are allocated to all coaching stock. For vehicles numbered in the passenger stock number series the code consists of:

(1) Two letters denoting the layout of the vehicle as follows:

AA	Gangwayed Corridor
AB	Gangwayed Corridor Brake
AC	Gangwayed Open (2+2 seating)
AD	Gangwayed Open (2+1 seating)
AE	Gangwayed Open Brake
AF	Gangwayed Driving Open Brake
AG	Micro-Buffet
AH	Brake Micro-Buffet
AI	As 'AC' but with drop-head buckeye and gangway at one end only
AJ	Restaurant Buffet with Kitchen
AK	Kitchen Car
AL	As 'AC' but with disabled person's toilet (Mark 4 only)
AN	Miniature Buffet
AP	Pullman First with Kitchen
AQ	Pullman Parlour First
AR	Pullman Brake First

AS	Sleeping Car	
AT	Royal Train Coach	
AU	Sleeping Car with Pantry	
AX	Generator Van	
AZ	Special Saloon	
GF	DMU/EMU/Mark 4 Barrier Vehicle	
NM	Sandite Coach	

(2) A digit denoting the class of passenger accommodation:

1	First	4	Unclassified
2	Standard (formerly second)	5	None
3	Composite (first & standard)		

(3) A suffix relating to the build of coach.

1	Mark 1	C	Mark 2C	G	Mark 3 or 3A
Z	Mark 2	D	Mark 2D	H	Mark 3B
A	Mark 2A	E	Mark 2E	J	Mark 4
B	Mark 2B	F	Mark 2F		

OPERATING CODES

Operating codes used by train company operating staff (and others) to denote vehicle types in general. These are shown in parentheses adjacent to TOPS type codes. Letters use are:

B	Brake	K	Side corridor with lavatory
C	Composite	O	Open
F	First Class	S	Standard Class (formerly second)

Various other letters are in use and the meaning of these can be ascertained by referring to the titles at the head of each type.

Readers should note the distinction between an SO (Open Standard) and a TSO (Tourist Open Standard) The former has 2 + 1 seating layout, whilst the latter has 2 + 2.

BOGIE TYPES

BR Mark 1 (BR1)
Double bolster leaf spring bogie. Generally 90 m.p.h., but BR1 bogies may be permitted to run at 100 m.p.h. with special maintenance. Weight: 6.1 t.

BR Mark 2 (BR2)
Single bolster leaf-spring bogie used on certain types of non-passenger stock and suburban stock (all now withdrawn). Weight: 5.3 t.

COMMONWEALTH (C)
Heavy, cast steel coil spring bogie. 100 m.p.h. Weight: 6.75 t.

B4
Coil spring fabricated bogie. Generally 100 m.p.h., but B4 bogies may be permitted to run at 110 m.p.h. with special maintenance. Weight: 5.2 t.

B5.
Heavy duty version of B4. 100 m.p.h. Weight: 5.3 t.

B5 (SR)
A bogie originally used on Southern Region EMUs, similar in design to B5. Now also used on locomotive hauled coaches. 100 m.p.h.

BT10
A fabricated bogie designed for 125 m.p.h. Air suspension.

T4
A 125 m.p.h. bogie designed by BREL (now Adtranz).

BT41
Fitted to Mark 4 vehicles, designed by SIG in Switzerland. At present limited to 125 m.p.h., but designed for 140 m.p.h.

BRAKES

Air braking is now standard on British main line trains. Vehicles with other equipment are denoted:

v   Vacuum braked.
x   Dual braked (air and vacuum).

HEATING

Electric heating is now standard on British main-line trains. Certain coaches for use on charter services may in addition also have steam heating facilities, or be steam heated only.

PUBLIC ADDRESS

It is assumed all coaches are now fitted with public address equipment, although certain stored vehicles may not have this feature. In addition, it is assumed all vehicles with a conductor's compartment have public address transmission facilities, as have catering vehicles. Mark 1 catering vehicles have gas powered cooking equipment, whilst Mark 2, 3 and 4 catering vehicles all have electric powered cooking equipment.

ADDITIONAL FEATURE CODES

d   Secondary door locking.
dg   Driver–Guard communication equipment.
f   Facelifted or fluorescent lighting.
k   Composition brake blocks (instead of cast iron).
n   Day/night lighting.
p   Public telephone.
pg   Public address transmission and driver-guard communication.
pt   Public address transmission facility.
q   Catering staff to shore telephone.
w   Wheelchair space.
z   Disabled persons' toilet.

Standard class coaches with wheelchair space also have one tip-up seat per space.

NOTES ON ETH INDICES

The sum of ETH indices in a train must not be more than the ETS index of the locomotive. The normal voltage on British trains is 1000 V. Suffix 'X' denotes 600 amp wiring instead of 400 amp. Trains whose ETH index is higher than 66 must be formed completely of 600 amp wired stock. Class 55 locomotives cannot provide a consistent electric train supply for Mark 2E or 2D FO 3192/ 3202, FK 13585–13607 & BFK 17163–17172. Class 33 locomotives cannot provide a suitable electric train supply for Mark 2D, Mark 2E, Mark 2F, Mark 3, Mark 3A, Mark 3B or Mark 4 coaches.

BUILD DETAILS

Lot Numbers
Vehicles ordered under the auspices of BR were allocated a lot (batch) number when ordered and these are quoted in class headings and sub-headings.

Vehicle Numbers
Where a coach has been renumbered, the former number is shown in parentheses. If a coach has been renumbered more than once, the original number is shown first in parentheses, followed by the most recent previous number. Where the former number of a coach due to be converted or renumbered is known and the conversion and/or renumbering has not yet taken place, the coach is listed under both current number (with depot allocation) and under new number (without allocation).

Numbering Systems
Seven different numbering systems were in use on BR. These were the BR series, the four pre-nationalisation companies' series', the Pullman Car Company's series and the UIC (International Union of Railways) series. BR number series coaches, former Pullman Car Company series and UIC series coaches are listed separately. There is also a separate listing of 'Saloon' type vehicles which are registered to run on the Railtrack network. Please note the Mark 2 Pullman vehicles were ordered after the Pullman Car Company had been nationalised and are therefore numbered in the BR series.

THE DEVELOPMENT OF BR STANDARD COACHES

The standard BR coach built from 1951 to 1963 was the Mark 1. This type features a separate underframe and body. The underframe is normally 64 ft. 6 in. long, but certain vehicles were built on shorter (57 ft.) frames. Tungsten lighting was standard and until 1961, BR Mark 1 bogies were generally provided. In 1959 Lot No. 30525 (TSO) appeared with fluorescent lighting and melamine interior panels, and from 1961 onwards Commonwealth bogies were fitted in an attempt to improve the quality of ride which became very poor when the tyre profiles on the wheels of the BR1 bogies became worn. Later batches of TSO and BSO retained the features of Lot No. 30525, but compartment vehicles – whilst utilising melamine panelling in standard class – still retained tungsten lighting. Wooden interior finish was retained in first class vehicles where the only change was to fluorescent lighting in open vehicles (except Lot No. 30648, which had tungsten lighting). In later years many Mark 1 coaches had BR 1 bogies replaced by B4.

In 1964, a new prototype train was introduced. Known as 'XP64', it featured new seat designs, pressure heating & ventilation, aluminium compartment doors and corridor partitions, foot pedal operated toilets and B4 bogies. The vehicles were built on standard Mark 1 underframes. Folding exterior doors were fitted, but these proved troublesome and were later replaced with hinged doors. All XP64 coaches have been withdrawn, but some have been preserved.

The prototype Mark 2 vehicle (W 13252) was produced in 1963. This was an FK of semi-integral construction and had pressure heating & ventilation, tungsten lighting, and was mounted on B4 bogies. This vehicle has been preserved by the National Railway Museum. The production build was similar, but wider windows were used. The TSO and SO vehicles used a new seat design similar to that in the XP64 and fluorescent lighting was provided. Interior finish reverted to wood. Mark 2 vehicles were built from 1964–66.

The Mark 2A design, built 1967–68, incorporated the remainder of the features first used in the XP64 coaches, i.e. foot pedal operated toilets (except BSO), new first class seat design, aluminium compartment doors and partitions together with fluorescent lighting in first class compartments. Folding gangway doors (lime green coloured) were used instead of the traditional one-piece variety.

The following list summarises the changes made in the later Mark 2 variants:

Mark 2B: Wide wrap around doors at vehicle ends, no centre doors, slightly longer body. In standard class, one toilet at each end instead of two at one end as previously. Red folding gangway doors.

Mark 2C: Lowered ceiling with twin strips of fluorescent lighting and ducting for air conditioning, but air conditioning not fitted.

Mark 2D: Air conditioning. No opening top-lights in windows.

Mark 2E: Smaller toilets with luggage racks opposite. Fawn folding gangway doors.

Mark 2F: Plastic interior panels. Inter-City 70 type seats. Modified air conditioning system.

The Mark 3 design has BT10 bogies, is 75 ft. (23 m.) long and is of fully integral construction with Inter-City 70 type seats. Gangway doors were yellow (red in RFB) when new, although these are being changed on refurbishment. Loco-hauled coaches are classified Mark 3A, Mark 3 being reserved for HST trailers. A new batch of FO and BFO, classified Mark 3B, was built in 1985 with Advanced Passenger Train-style seating and revised lighting. The last vehicles in the Mark 3 series were the driving brake vans built for West Coast Main Line services.

The Mark 4 design was built by Metro-Cammell for use on the East Coast Main Line after electrification and features a body profile suitable for tilting trains, although tilt is not fitted, and is not intended to be. This design is suitable for 140 m.p.h. running, although is restricted to 125 m.p.h. pending installation of a more advanced signalling system on the route. The bogies for these coaches were built by SIG in Switzerland and are designated BT41. Power operated sliding plug exterior doors are standard.

2.1. BR NUMBER SERIES STOCK

AJ11 (RF)   RESTAURANT FIRST

Dia. AJ106. Mark 1. 24/–. 325 spent most of its life as a Royal Train vehicle and was numbered 2907 for a time. Built with Commonwealth bogies, but B5 bogies substituted on 325. ETH 2.

Lot No. 30633 Swindon 1961. 42.5 t C, 41 t B5.

324	x **CH**	NY	*ON*	NY	
325	**WV**	VS		SL	

AP1Z (PK)   PULLMAN FIRST WITH KITCHEN

Dia. AP101. Mark 2. Pressure ventilated. 18/– 2T. B5 bogies. ETH 6.

Lot No. 30755 Derby 1966. 40 t.

Non-Standard Livery: Maroon & beige.

504	**0**	WC	*ON*	CS	THE WHITE ROSE
506	**0**	WC	*ON*	CS	THE RED ROSE

AQ1Z (PC)   PULLMAN PARLOUR FIRST

Dia. AQ101. Mark 2. Pressure ventilated. 36/– 2T. B4 bogies. ETH 5.

Lot No. 30754 Derby 1966. 35 t.

Non-Standard Livery: Maroon & beige.

546	**0**	WC	*ON*	CS	CITY OF MANCHESTER
548	**0**	WC	*ON*	CS	ELIZABETHAN
549	**0**	WC	*ON*	CS	PRINCE RUPERT
550	**0**	WC	*ON*	CS	GOLDEN ARROW
551	**0**	WC	*ON*	CS	CALEDONIAN
552	**0**	WC	*ON*	CS	SOUTHERN BELLE
553	**0**	WC	*ON*	CS	KNNG ARTHUR

AR1Z (PB)   PULLMAN BRAKE FIRST

Dia. AR101. Mark 2. Pressure ventilated. 30/– 2T. B4 bogies. ETH 4.

Lot No. 30753 Derby 1966. 35 t.

Non-Standard Livery: Maroon & beige.

586	**0**	WC	*ON*	CS	TALISMAN

AJ1F (RFB)   BUFFET OPEN FIRST

Dia. AJ104. Mark 2F. Air conditioned. Converted 1988–9/91 at BREL, Derby from Mark 2F FOs. 1200/1/3/6/11/14–17/20/21/50/2/5/6/9 have Stones equipment, others have Temperature Ltd. 25/– 1T plus wheelchair space (except 1217 and 1253 which are 26/– 1T). B4 bogies. p. q. d. ETH 6X.

1200/3/6/11/14/16/20/52/5/6. Lot No. 30845 Derby 1973. 33 t.
1201/4/5/7/8/10/12/13/15/17–9/21/50/1/4/7/9. Lot No. 30859 Derby 1973–4. 33 t.
1202/9/53/8. Lot No. 30873 Derby 1974–5. 33 t.

* Refurbished with new seat trim.
r Refurbished with new seat trim and new m.a. sets.

1200	(3287, 6459)	r	V	F	VX	MA
1201	(3361, 6445)	r	V	F	VX	MA
1202	(3436, 6456)	r	V	F	VX	MA
1203	(3291)	*		F	VX	MA
1204	(3401)	r	V	F	VX	MA
1205	(3329, 6438)	r	V	F	VX	MA
1206	(3319)	r	V	F	VX	MA
1207	(3328, 6422)	r	V	F	VX	MA
1208	(3393)			F	VX	MA
1209	(3437, 6457)	r	V	F	VX	MA
1210	(3405, 6462)	r	V	F	VX	MA
1211	(3305)	*		F	VX	MA
1212	(3427, 6453)	r	V	F	VX	MA
1213	(3419)	r	V	F	VX	MA
1214	(3317, 6433)	*		F	VX	MA
1215	(3377)	*		F	VX	MA
1216	(3302)	r	V	F	VX	MA
1217	(3357, 6444)			F	SR	IS
1218	(3332)			F	VX	MA
1219	(3418)			F	VX	MA
1220	(3315, 6432)			F	VX	MA
1221	(3371)	*		F	VX	MA
1250	(3372)	r	V	F	VX	MA
1251	(3383)	r	V	F	VX	MA
1252	(3280)	r	V	F	VX	MA
1253	(3432)	r	V	F	VX	MA
1254	(3391)	r	V	F	VX	MA
1255	(3284)			F	VX	MA
1256	(3296)	*		F	VX	MA
1258	(3322)	r	V	F	VX	MA
1259	(3439)	r	V	F	VX	MA
1260	(3378)	r	V	F	VX	MA

AK51 (RKB)   KNTCHEN BUFFET

Dia. AK502. Mark 1. No seats. B5 bogies. ETH 1.

Lot No. 30624 Cravens 1960–1. 41 t.

1566	**G**	VS	ON	CP	

AJ41 (RBR)   RESTAURANT BUFFET

Dia. AJ403. Mark 1. Built with 23 loose chairs (Dia. AJ402). All remaining vehicles refurbished with 23 (21 w) fixed polypropylene chairs and fluorescent lighting. ETH 2 (2X*).

r Further refurbished with 21 chairs, payphone, wheelchair space and carpets (Dia. AJ417).

1644–1699. Lot No. 30628 Pressed Steel 1960–61. Commonwealth bogies. 39 t.
1730. Lot No. 30512 BRCW 1960–61. B5 bogies. 37 t.

1691 is leased to the Venice Simplon Orient Express.

1644			WC		CS	1679		**G**	RS	*ON*	BN
1649	w		F		KN	1680	*w	**WV**	RS	*ON*	BN
1650	w		WC		CS	1683	r	**FT**	F	*ON*	CP
1652	w		WC		CS	1684	x*	**BG**	WC		KM
1653	w		CN		FK	1686	r		F		LM
1655			WC		KM	1688	w	**BG**	WC		CS
1658		**BG**	RS	*ON*	BN	1689	r		F		LM
1659	x	**PC**	WT	*ON*	CS	1691	r	**G**	F	*ON*	SL
1663	x*		WC		CS	1692	xr	**CH**	RV	*ON*	CP
1666	x*		WC		CS	1696		**G**	RS	*ON*	BN
1667	x		RS	*ON*	BN	1697	r		F		CP
1670	x*w	**BG**	WC		CS	1698		**WV**	RS	*ON*	BN
1671	x*	**CC**	RS	*ON*	BN	1699	r		F		CP
1673	w		F		KN	1730	x	**M**	SP	*ON*	BT
1674			RS	*ON*	BN						

AN21 (RMB)   MINIATURE BUFFET CAR

Dia. AN203. Mark 1. –/44 2T. These vehicles are basically an open standard with two full window spaces removed to accommodate a buffet counter, and four seats removed to allow for a stock cupboard. All remaining vehicles have fluorescent lighting. All vehicles have Commonwealth bogies except 1850 (B5). ETH 3.

1813–1832. Lot No. 30520 Wolverton 1960. 38 t.
1840–1850. Lot No. 30507 Wolverton 1960. 37 t (1850 is 36 t).
1853–1863. Lot No. 30670 Wolverton 1961–2. 38 t.
1871–1882. Lot No. 30702 Wolverton 1962. 38 t.

1842/50/71 have been been refurbished and are fitted with a microwave oven and payphone. Dia. AN208.

1813	x	**CC**	RS	*ON*	BN	1859	x	**M**	SP	*ON*	BT
1832	x		RS	*ON*	BN	1860	x	**M**	WC	*ON*	CS
1840	v	**G**	MH	*ON*	RL	1861	x	**M**	WT	*ON*	CS
1842	x		F	*AR*	NC	1863	x	**CH**	RV	*ON*	CP
1850			F	*AR*	NC	1871	x		F	*AR*	NC
1853	x		RS	*ON*	BN	1882	x		**M**	WC	*ON*	CS

AJ41 (RBR)   RESTAURANT BUFFET

Dia. AJ414. Mark 1. This vehicle was built as an unclassified restaurant (RU). It was rebuilt with buffet counter and 23 fixed polypropylene chairs (RBS), then further refurbished by fitting fluorescent lighting and reclassified RBR. B4/B5 bogies. ETH 2X.

Lot No. 30575 Swindon 1960. 36.5 t.

| 1953 | **RB** VS | *ON* | CP |

AS41   FIRST CLASS SLEEPING CAR

Dia. AS101. Mark 1. Pressure ventilated. 11 single-berth compartments plus an attendant's compartment with gas cooking. ETH 3 (3X*).

2013. Lot No. 30159 Wolverton 1958. B5 bogies. 39 t.
2127. Lot No. 30687 Wolverton 1961. Commonwealth bogies. 41 t.

2013 was numbered 2908 for a time when in use with the Royal Train.

| 2013 | **M** FS | SZ | | 2127 * | **M** GS | CS |

AU51   CHARTER TRAIN STAFF COACHES

Dia. AU501. Mark 1. Converted from BCK in 1988. Commonwealth bogies. ETH 2.

Lot No. 30732 Derby 1964. 37 t.

| 2833 (21270) | RS *ON* | BN | | 2834 (21267) | **WV** RS *ON* | BN |

AT5G   HM THE QUEEN'S SALOON

Dia. AT525. Mark 3. Converted from FO built 1972. Consists of a lounge, bedroom and bathroom for HM The Queen, and a combined bedroom and bathroom for the Queen's dresser. One entrance vestibule has double doors. Air conditioned. BT10 bogies. ETH 9X.

Lot No. 30886 Wolverton 1977. 36 t.

| 2903 | (11001) | **RP** RT *OR* | ZN |

AT5G   HRH THE DUKE OF EDINBURGH'S SALOON

Dia. AT526. Mark 3. Converted from TSO built 1972. Consists of a combined lounge/dining room, a bedroom and a shower room for the Duke, a kitchen and a valet's bedroom and bathroom. Air conditioned. BT10 bogies. ETH 15X.

Lot No. 30887 Wolverton 1977. 36 t.

| 2904 | (12001) | **RP** RT *OR* | ZN |

AT5B   ROYAL HOUSEHOLD COUCHETTES

Dia. AT527. Mark 2B. Converted from BFK built 1969. Consists of luggage accommodation, guard's compartment, 350 kW diesel generator and staff sleeping accommodation. Pressure ventilated. B5 bogies. ETH 5X.

Lot No. 30888 Wolverton 1977. 46 t.

2905 (14105)   **RP** RT *OR*   ZN

.Dia. AT528. Mark 2B. Converted from BFK built 1969. Consists of luggage accommodation, guards compartment and staff accommodation. Pressure ventilated. B5 bogies. ETH 4X.

Lot No. 30889 Wolverton 1977. 35.5 t.

2906 (14112)   **RP** RT *OR*   ZN

AT5G   ROYAL HOUSEHOLD SLEEPING CARS

Dia. AT531. Mark 3A. Built to similar specification to SLE 10646–732 .12 sleeping compartments for use of Royal Household with a fixed lower berth and a hinged upper berth. 2T. Shower room. Air conditioned. BT10 bogies. ETH 11X.

Lot No. 31002 Derby/Wolverton 1985. 42.5 t (44 t*).

2914   **RP** RT *OR*   ZN
2915 *   **RP** RT *OR*   ZN

AT5G   ROYAL KNTCHEN/DINING CAR

Dia AT537. Mark 3. Converted from HST TRUK built 1976. Large kitchen retained, but dining area modified for Royal use seating up to 14 at central table(s). Air conditioned. BT10 bogies. ETH 13X.

Lot No. 31059 Wolverton 1988. 43 t.

2916 (40512)   **RP** RT *OR*   ZN

AT5G   ROYAL HOUSEHOLD KNTCHEN/DINING CAR

Dia. AT539. Mark 3. Converted from HST TRUK built 1977. Large kitchen retained and dining area slightly modified with seating for 22 Royal Household members. Air conditioned. BT10 bogies. ETH 13X.

Lot No. 31084 Wolverton 1990. 43 t.

2917 (40514)   **RP** RT *OR*   ZN

AT5G   ROYAL HOUSEHOLD CARS

Dia. AT538 (AT540*). Mark 3. Converted from HST TRUK built 1976/7. Air conditioned. BT10 bogies. ETH 10X.

Lot Nos. 31083 (31085*) Wolverton 1989. 41.05 t.

2918 (40515)   **RP** RT *OR*   ZN
2919 (40518) *   **RP** RT *OR*   ZN

AT5B   ROYAL HOUSEHOLD COUCHETTES

Dia. AT536. Mark 2B. Converted from BFK built 1969. Consists of luggage accommodation, guard's compartment, workshop area, 350 kW diesel generator and staff sleeping accommodation. B5 bogies. ETH2X.

Lot No. 31044 Wolverton 1986. 48 t.

| 2920 | (14109, 17109) | **RP** RT | *OR* | ZN |

Dia. AT541. Mark 2B. Converted from BFK built 1969. Consists of luggage accommodation, kitchen, brake control equipment and staff accommodation. B5 bogies. ETH7X.

Lot No. 31086 Wolverton 1990. 41.5 t.

| 2921 | (14107, 17107) | **RP** RT | *OR* | ZN |

AT5G HRH THE PRINCE OF WALES'S SLEEPING CAR

Dia. AT534. Mark 3B. BT10 bogies. Air conditioned. ETH 7X.

Lot No. 31035 Derby/Wolverton 1987.

| 2922 | **RP** RT | *OR* | ZN |

AT5G   HRH THE PRINCE OF WALES'S SALOON

Dia. AT535. Mark 3B. BT10 bogies. Air conditioned. ETH 6X.

Lot No. 31036 Derby/Wolverton 1987.

| 2923 | **RP** RT | *OR* | ZN |

AD11 (FO)   OPEN FIRST

Dia. AD103. Mark 1. 42/– 2T. ETH 3. Many now fitted with table lamps.

3063–3069. Lot No. 30169 Doncaster 1955. B4 bogies. 33 t.
3085. Lot No. 30472 BRCW 1957. B4 bogies. 33 t.
3096–3100. Lot No. 30576 BRCW 1959. B4 bogies. 33 t.

3064, 3068 and 3085 were numbered DB 975607, DB 975606 and DB 977492 for a time when in departmental service for British Rail. 3065 has BR Mark 1 bogies and weighs 34 t.

3063	**BG**	VS		SL		3085	**BG**	VS		SL
3064	**BG**	VS		SL		3096	x **M**	SP	*ON*	BT
3065	v **PC**	WT		CS		3097	**WV**	RS	*ON*	BN
3066	**G**	VS	*ON*	CP		3098	x **CH**	RV	*ON*	CP
3068	**G**	VS	*ON*	CP		3100	x **CC**	RS	*ON*	BN
3069	**G**	VS	*ON*	CP						

Later design with fluorescent lighting, aluminium window frames and Commonwealth bogies.

3105–3128. Lot No. 30697 Swindon 1962–3. 36 t.
3130–3150. Lot No. 30717 Swindon 1963. 36 t.

3128/36/41/3/4/6/7/8 were renumbered 1058/60/3/5/6/8/9/70 when reclassified RUO, then 3600/5/8/9/2/6/4/10 when declassified, but have now regained their original numbers.

3105	× **M**	WC	*ON*	CS	3128	× **M**	WC	*ON*	CS
3107	× **BG**	RS	*ON*	BN	3130	v **M**	WC		CS
3110	× **CC**	RS	*ON*	BN	3131	× **CC**	RS	*ON*	BN
3112	× **CH**	RV	*ON*	CP	3132	× **CC**	RS	*ON*	BN
3113	× **M**	WC	*ON*	CS	3133	× **CC**	RS	*ON*	BN
3114	**G**	RS	*ON*	BN	3136		RS	*ON*	BN
3115	× **BG**	RS	*ON*	BN	3140	×	CN		CP
3117	× **M**	WC	*ON*	CS	3141	**WV**	RS	*ON*	BN
3119	× **CC**	RS	*ON*	BN	3143		FS		SZ
3120	**WV**	RS	*ON*	BN	3144	× **CC**	RS	*ON*	BN
3121	**WV**	RS	*ON*	BN	3146	**WV**	RS	*ON*	BN
3122	× **CH**	RV	*ON*	CP	3147	**WV**	RS	*ON*	BN
3123	**G**	RS	*ON*	BN	3148		RS	*ON*	BN
3124		CN		BN	3149		RS	*ON*	BN
3125	**RB**	VS	*ON*	CP	3150	**G**	RS	*ON*	BN
3127	**G**	RS	*ON*	BN					

AD1D (FO)   OPEN FIRST

Dia. AD105. Mark 2D. Air conditioned. 3172–88 have Stones equipment. 3192/ 3202 have Temperature Ltd and require at least 800 V train heating supply. 42/ – 2T. B4 bogies. ETH 5.

Lot No. 30821 Derby 1971–2. 32.5 t.

3172		CN		DY	3186		CN		DY
3174		VS		CP	3187		E		KM
3178		VS		DY	3188	**RB**	VS	*ON*	CP
3181	**RB**	VS	*ON*	CP	3192		E		DY
3182		VS		DY	3202		E		KM

AD1E (FO)   OPEN FIRST

Dia. AD106. Mark 2E. Air conditioned. Stones equipment. Require at least 800 V train heating supply. 42/– 2T (w 41/– 2T 1W). B4 bogies. ETH 5.

* Seats removed to accommodate catering module. 40F 1T.
§ Fitted with power supply for adjacent Mk. 1 RBR.

Lot No. 30843 Derby 1972–3. 32.5 t.

3221	w	F		ZC	3239		VS		CP
3223		CN		OM	3240	**CH**	RV	*ON*	CP
3225		E		KN	3241	d	F		LM
3226		E		KN	3242	w§	F		LM
3228	d§	F	*VW*	OY	3244	dw	F	*VW*	OY
3229	d	F	*VW*	OY	3246	w	RA		CP
3230		CN		DY	3247		VS		CP
3231		RA		CP	3248		CN		DY
3232	dw	F		LM	3251	*	CN		FK
3234	w	VS		CP	3252		F		LM
3235	§	F		LM	3256	w	F		LM
3237		CN		FK	3257	w	VS		CP

3258	n		E		KN	3270	VS	CP
3261	dw		F		CP	3272	VS	CP
3267		**CH** RV *ON*			CP	3273	**CH** RV *ON*	CP
3268			CN		KN	3275	VS	CP
3269	d		F		CP			

AD1F (FO)   OPEN FIRST

Dia. AD107. Mark 2F. Air conditioned. 3277–3318/58–81 have Stones equipment, others have Temperature Ltd. 42/– 2T. All refurbished with power-operated vestibule doors, new panels and new seat trim. B4 bogies. d. ETH 5X.

3277–3318. Lot No. 30845 Derby 1973. 33 t.
3325–3428. Lot No. 30859 Derby 1973–4. 33 t.
3429–3438. Lot No. 30873 Derby 1974–5. 33 t.

§ Fitted with power supply for adjacent Mk. 1 RBR.
r Further refurbished with table lamps and new burgundy seat trim.

3403 was numbered 6450 for a time when declassified.

3277			F	*AR*	NC		3351			F	*AR*	NC
3278	r	**V**	F	*VW*	OY		3352	r	**V**	F	*VW*	OY
3279	§	**AR**	F	*AR*	NC		3353			F	*VW*	OY
3285	r		F	*VW*	OY		3354			F	*VW*	OY
3290			F	*AR*	NC		3356	r		F	*VW*	OY
3292			F	*AR*	NC		3358		**AR**	F	*AR*	NC
3293			F	*VW*	OY		3359			F	*VW*	OY
3295			F	*AR*	NC		3360			F	*VW*	OY
3299	r	**V**	F	*VW*	OY		3362			F	*VW*	OY
3300	r		F	*VW*	OY		3363			F	*VW*	OY
3303			F	*AR*	NC		3364	r		F	*VW*	OY
3304	r	**V**	F	*VW*	OY		3366			F	*VW*	OY
3309			F	*AR*	NC		3368		**AR**	F	*AR*	NC
3312			F	*VW*	OY		3369			F	*VW*	OY
3313	r	**V**	F	*VW*	OY		3373			F	*AR*	NC
3314	r	**V**	F	*VW*	OY		3374			F	*AR*	NC
3318			F	*AR*	NC		3375			F	*AR*	NC
3325	r	**V**	F	*VW*	OY		3379	§		F	*AR*	NC
3326	r	**V**	F	*VW*	OY		3381			F	*AR*	NC
3330	r	**V**	F	*VW*	OY		3384	r	**V**	F	*VW*	OY
3331			F	*AR*	NC		3385	r	**V**	F	*VW*	OY
3333	r	**V**	F	*VW*	OY		3386	r	**V**	F	*VW*	OY
3334			F	*AR*	NC		3387			F	*VW*	OY
3336	§		F	*AR*	NC		3388			F	*AR*	NC
3337	r	**V**	F	*VW*	OY		3389			F	*VW*	OY
3338	§	**AR**	F	*AR*	NC		3390	r	**V**	F	*VW*	OY
3340	r	**V**	F	*VW*	OY		3392	r	**V**	F	*VW*	OY
3344	r	**V**	F	*VW*	OY		3395	r	**V**	F	*VW*	OY
3345	r	**V**	F	*VW*	OY		3397	r	**V**	F	*VW*	OY
3348	r	**V**	F	*VW*	OY		3399	§	**AR**	F	*AR*	NC
3350	r	**V**	F	*VW*	OY		3400		**AR**	F	*AR*	NC

▲ **Pullman Stock.** Umber and cream liveried Pullman Kitchen First No. 284 'VERA' at London Victoria on 8th May 1998. B5(SR) bogies are fitted. **Hugh Ballantyne**

▼ **Mark 1 Stock.** Converted for use on Anglo-Scottish sleeper services but now used on charter services, Generator Van No. 6311 is pictured on one such working at London Victoria on 13th December 1997. This vehicle carries a non-standard purple livery. **Stephen Widdowson**

Mark 1 Stock. Intercity liveried Open First No. 3107 on the rear of a charter train at Worcester Shrub Hill on 6th December 1997. **Stephen Widdowson**

▲ **Mark 2A Stock.** Open Standard No. 5364 'Andrea' at Carlisle on 28th August 1998. It carries a blue and white livery which Forward Trust Rail has applied to some of its Mark 2A vehicles which are available for short term hire. **Dave McAlone**

▼ **Mark 2B Stock.** South Wales & West blue liveried Open Standard No. 5478 at Weymouth on 18th January 1997. **Denise Johnson**

Mark 2D Stock. Open Standard No. 5647 at Weymouth on 18th January 1997. This vehicle is in a non-standard Waterman Railways purple & cream livery.
Denise Johnson

▲ **Mark 2E Stock.** Open Brake Standard No. 9502 is seen passing Hay Fell on the rear of a down Virgin Cross Country service on 10th April 1997.

Dave McAlone

▼ **Mark 2F Stock.** Virgin Trains liveried Buffet Open First No. 1252 in the formation of the 12.40 Glasgow Central–Brighton at Wigan North Western on 21st June 1998. **Martyn Hilbert**

Open Standard No. 6064 in the formation of the 14.20 Brighton–Manchester Piccadilly on 29th October 1997.

Chris Wilson

▲ **Mark 3 Stock.** Great Western Trains liveried Trailer First No. 41021 at Plymouth on 19th August 1998. The company has recently dropped the Intercity branding from its stock and now applies the Great Western branding at both ends of its coaches as can be seen here. **Stephen Widdowson**

▼ Midland Mainline liveried Trailer Guard's Standard No. 44044 at London St Pancras on 1st December 1997. **Stephen Widdowson**

Mark 3A Stock. Restaurant Buffet First No. 10246 is pictured leaving Carlisle in the formation of the 16.15 Glasgow Central–London Euston on 24th May 1998.

Kevin Conkey

Mark 3 B Stock. One of only three coaches built to this design, Brake Open First No. 17174 leaves Carlisle on 24th May 1998 in the formation of the 16.15 Glasgow Central–London Euston.

Kevin Conkey

Mark 4 Stock. Great North Eastern Railway liveried Restaurant Buffet First No. 10318 leaves London King's Cross on 12th May 1998 as part of the 15.40 to Bradford Foster Square.

Kevin Conkey

Non-Passenger Carrying Coaching Stock. Post Office Sorting Van No. 80353 in the formation of a travelling post office (TPO) train stabled at Carlisle station on 3rd May 1998. The vehicle carries Royal Mail livery.

Kevin Conkey

Virgin Trains liveried Mark 3B Driving Van Trailer No. 82119 at Carlisle on 24th May 1998.

Kevin Conkey

Great North Eastern Railway liveried Mark 4 Driving Van Trailer No. 82226 leaves London King's Cross on the rear of the 15.40 to Bradford Foster Square on 12th May 1998.

Kevin Conkey

▲ Rail Express Systems liveried High Security General Utility Van No. 94166 at Plymouth on 19th August 1998. **Stephen Widdowson**

▼ Propelling Control Vehicle No. 94307, operating in control mode, leads a mail train into the sidings at Carlisle station on 10th April 1998. **Dave McAlone**

▲ High Security Brake Van No. 94403 at Carlisle on 3rd May 1998. **Kevin Conkey**

▼ Super General Utility Van No. 95759 at Carlisle on 16th June 1998. The vehicle has Rail Express Systems branding but carries plain red livery. **Kevin Conkey**

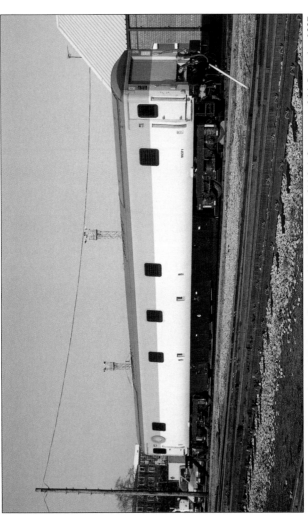

European Passenger Services liveried Nightstar Generator Van No. 96371 at Old Oak Common on 14th December 1997. These vehicles are now without work following the decision not to operate Nightstar services. **Kevin Conkey**

3402	F	VW	OY		3425		F	VW	OY
3403	F	VW	OY		3426	r	F	VW	OY
3408	F	VW	OY		3428		F	VW	OY
3411	F	VW	OY		3429	r V	F	VW	OY
3414	F	AR	NC		3431	r V	F	VW	OY
3416	F	AR	NC		3433	r V	F	VW	OY
3417	F	AR	NC		3434		F	VW	OY
3424	F	AR	NC		3438		F	VW	OY

AG1E (FOT)   OPEN FIRST (PANTRY)

Dia. AG101. Mark 2E. Air conditioned. Converted from FO. Fitted with pantry, microwave oven and payphone for use on sleeping car services. 36/– 1T. B4 bogies. d. ETH 5X.

Lot No. 30843 Derby 1972–3. 32.5 t.

3520 (3253)	F	GW	LA		3523 (3238)	F	SR	IS
3521 (3271)	F	GW	LA		3524 (3254)	F	SR	IS
3522 (3236)	F	GW	LA		3525 (3255)	F		ZC

AC21 (TSO)   OPEN STANDARD

Dia. AC204. Mark 1. These vehicles have 2+2 seating and are classified TSO ('Tourist second open'–a former LNER designation). –/64 2T. ETH 4.

3766. Lot No. 30079 York 1953. Commonwealth bogies (originally built with BR Mark 1 bogies). This coach has narrower seats than later vehicles. 36 t.
4198. Lot No. 30172 York 1956. BR Mark 1 bogies. 33 t.

| 3766 | x | M | WC ON | CS | | 4198 | v | CH | NY ON | NY |

AD21 (SO)   OPEN STANDARD

Dia. AD201. Mark 1. These vehicles have 2+1 seating and were often used as second class dining cars when new. –/48 2T. BR Mark 1 bogies. ETH 4.

4786. Lot No. 30376 York 1957. 33 t.
4817–4828. Lot No. 30473 BRCW 1957–59. 33 t (4828 has B4 bogies 32 t).

| 4786 | v | CH | NY ON | NY | | 4828 | v | M | VS | SL |
| 4817 | v | CH | NY ON | NY | | | | | |

AC21 (TSO)   OPEN STANDARD

Dia. AC201. Mark 1. These vehicles are a development of Dia. AC204 with fluorescent lighting and modified design of seat headrest. Built with BR Mark 1 bogies. –/64 2T. ETH 4.

4831–4836. Lot No. 30506 Wolverton 1959. Commonwealth bogies. 33 t.
4842–4880. Lot No. 30525 Wolverton 1959–60. B4 bogies. 33 t.

4831	x	M	SP ON	BT		4842	x		RV	FK
4832	x	M	SP ON	BT		4849	x	RR F	NW	OY
4836	x	M	SP ON	BT		4854	x	RR F	NW	OY

4856	x	**M**	SP	*ON*	BT
4858	x		WC		KM
4860	x	**M**	WC		CS
4866	x	**RR**	F	*NW*	OY
4869	x		CN		FK

4873	x	**RR**	F	*NW*	OY
4875	x	**RR**	F	*NW*	OY
4876	x	**RR**	F	*NW*	OY
4880	x	**RR**	F	*NW*	OY

Lot No. 30646 Wolverton 1961. Built with Commonwealth bogies, but BR Mark 1 bogies substituted by the SR on 4902/5/9/10/12/15/16. All now re-rebogied. 34 t B4, 36 t C.

4902	x B4	**CH**	RV	*ON*	CP
4905	v C	**M**	WT	*ON*	CS
4909	x B4		CN		FK
4910	v C	**M**	WT	*ON*	CS

4912	x C	**M**	WC	*ON*	CS
4915	x B4	**CC**	RS	*ON*	BN
4916	x B4		CN		BN
4917	x C	**RR**	F	*NW*	OY

Lot No. 30690 Wolverton 1961–2. 37 t. Commonwealth bogies and aluminium window frames.

4925		**G**	RS	*ON*	BN
4927	f	**CH**	RV	*ON*	CP
4931	v	**M**	WC	*ON*	CS
4932	v	**N**	WC		CS
4936	v	**M**	WC		CS
4938		**W**	RS	*ON*	BN
4939			RS	*ON*	BN
4940	v	**M**	WT	*ON*	CS
4946	x	**CC**	RS	*ON*	BN
4949			RS	*ON*	BN
4951	v	**M**	WT	*ON*	CS
4954	v	**M**	WC	*ON*	CS
4956			RS	*ON*	BN
4958	v	**M**	WC	*ON*	CS
4959			RS	*ON*	BN
4960	v	**M**	WT	*ON*	CS
4963	x	**CH**	RV	*ON*	CP
4973	v	**M**	WT	*ON*	CS
4977			RS	*ON*	BN
4984	v	**M**	WT	*ON*	CS
4986		**G**	RS	*ON*	BN
4991		**W**	RS	*ON*	BN
4993			RS	*ON*	BN
4994	v	**M**	WT	*ON*	CS

4996	xf	**CC**	RS	*ON*	BN
4997	v	**BG**	WC		CS
4998			RS	*ON*	BN
4999		**BG**	RS	*ON*	BN
5002		**W**	RS	*ON*	BN
5005		**W**	RS	*ON*	BN
5007	f	**G**	RS	*ON*	BN
5008	x	**CC**	RS	*ON*	BN
5009	x	**CH**	RV	*ON*	CP
5010			RV		CP
5023		**G**	RS	*ON*	BN
5025	x	**CH**	RV	*ON*	CP
5027		**G**	RS	*ON*	BN
5028	x	**M**	SP	*ON*	BT
5029	x	**CH**	RV	*ON*	CP
5030	x	**CH**	RV	*ON*	CP
5032	x	**M**	WC	*ON*	CS
5033	x	**M**	WC	*ON*	CS
5035	x	**M**	WC	*ON*	CS
5037		**G**	RS	*ON*	BN
5038	x		E		OM
5040		**CH**	RV	*ON*	CP
5042	x		CN		FK
5044	x	**M**	WC	*ON*	CS

AC2Z (TSO)   OPEN STANDARD

Dia. AC205. Mark 2. Pressure ventilated. –/64 2T. B4 bogies. ETH 4.

Lot No. 30751 Derby 1965–7. 32 t.

5125	v	**G**	MH	*ON*	RL
5132	v	**LN**	F		LT
5135	v	**RR**	F		LT

5148	v	**RR**	F	LT
5154	v	**LN**	F	LT
5156	v	**RR**	F	LT

5157	v	RR	F		LT		
5158	v	RR	F		LT		
5161	v	RR	F		LT		
5163	v	RR	F		LT		
5166	v	LN	F		LT		
5167	v	RR	F		LT		
5174	v	RR	F		LT		
5177	v	RR	F		LT		
5179	v	RR	F		LT		
5180	v	RR	F		LT		
5183	v	RR	F		LT		
5186	v	RR	F		LT		
5191	v	LN	F		TM		
5193	v	LN	F		LT		
5194	v	RR	F		LT		
5198	v	RR	F		TM		
5200	v	G	MH ON		RL		
5207	v	RR	F		LT		
5209	v	RR	F		LT		
5212	v	LN	F		LT		
5213	v	RR	F		LT		
5216	v	G	MH ON		RL		
5221	v	RR	F		LT		
5222	v	G	MH ON		RL		
5225	v	RR	F		LT		
5226	v	RR	F		LT		

AD2Z (SO)   OPEN STANDARD

Dia. AD203. Mark 2. Pressure ventilated. –/48 2T. B4 bogies. ETH 4.

Lot No. 30752 Derby 1966. 32 t.

5237	v	G	MH ON	RL	
5249	v	G	MH ON	RL	
5254		BG	F		DY

AC2A (TSO)   OPEN STANDARD

Dia. AC206. Mark 2A. Pressure ventilated. –/64 2T (–/62 2T w). B4 bogies. ETH 4.

5265–5345. Lot No. 30776 Derby 1967–8. 32 t.
5350–5433. Lot No. 30787 Derby 1968. 32 t.

5265		RR	F		LM
5266		RR	F		Cw
5267		RR	F		LM
5271		RR	F		LM
5272		RR	F		CP
5275		FT	F	CA	CF
5276		RR	F	NW	OY
5277		BG	F		LM
5278		RR	F	NW	OY
5279		BG	F		LM
5282		RR	F		LM
5290		NB	F		LM
5291		RR	F		ZB
5292		RR	F		CP
5293		NB	F		LM
5299		M	WC ON		CS
5300		BG	F		LM
5304		RR	F		Cw
5307		RR	F	ON	CP
5309		RR	F	NW	OY
5314		BG	F		LM
5316		RR	F		LM
5322		RR	F	NW	OY
5323		RR	F		LM
5331		RR	F	NW	OY
5335		RR	F	NW	OY
5337		BG	F		LM
5341		RR	F		CP
5345		RR	F	NW	OY
5350		FT	F	CA	CF
5353		RR	F		LM
5354		RR	F		LM
5364		FT	F	CA	CF
5365		FT	F	CA	CF
5366		RR	F		LM
5373		FT	F	CA	CF
5376		FT	F	CA	CF
5378		FT	F	CA	CF
5379		RR	F		LM
5381 w		RR	F	NW	OY
5384		N	F		Cw
5386 w		RR	F	NW	OY
5389 w		RR	F	NW	OY
5392		BG	F		LM
5393		RR	F		LM
5396		RR	F		LM

5401	**RR**	F		LM		5419	w	**RR**	F	*NW*	OY
5410	**N**	F		LM		5420	w	**RR**	F	*NW*	OY
5412	w **RR**	F	*NW*	OY		5433	w	**RR**	F	*NW*	OY

AC2B (TSO)   OPEN STANDARD

Dia. AC207. Mark 2B. Pressure ventilated. –/62 2T. B4 bogies. ETH 4.

Lot No. 30791 Derby 1969. 32 t.

Non-Standard Livery: 5453, 5478 and 5491 are royal blue with white lining.

5439	**N**	F		LM		5464	**N**	RV		CP
5443	**N**	F		LM		5471	**N**	F		LM
5446	**N**	F		LM		5472	**N**	F		LM
5447	**N**	F		LM		5475	**N**	F		LM
5449	**N**	RV		CP		5478	d **0**	WC	*WW*	CF
5450	**N**	F		LM		5480	**N**	F		LM
5453	d **0**	WC	*WW*	CF		5487	d **M**	WC	*WW*	CF
5454	**N**	F		LM		5491	d **0**	WC	*WW*	CF
5462	**N**	RV		CP		5494	**N**	RV		CP
5463	d **M**	WC	*WW*	CF						

AC2C (TSO)   OPEN STANDARD

Dia. AC208. Mark 2C. Pressure ventilated. –/62 2T. B4 bogies. ETH 4.

Lot No. 30795 Derby 1969–70. 32 t.

5505	**RR**	WC		CS		5600	**M**	WC	*ON*	CS
5554	**RR**	F		CW		5614	**RR**	F		CW
5569	d **M**	WC	*WW*	CF						

AC2D (TSO)   OPEN STANDARD

Dia. AC209. Mark 2D. Air conditioned. Stones equipment. –/62 2T. B4 bogies. ETH 5.

Non-Standard Livery: 5630, 5647, 5732 & 5739 are **WV** without lining.

Lot No. 30822 Derby 1971. 33 t.

5616		CN		FK		5645		WC	CS
5618		F		LM		5647	**0**	RV	CP
5620		F		LT		5650		F	LT
5623		F		LT		5657	d	F	ZC
5628		F		LM		5661		F	KN
5629		F		LT		5662		F	LM
5630	**0**	RV		CP		5663		F	KN
5631	d	F		LM		5665		F	LM
5632	d	F		LM		5669	d	F	LT
5634		F		LM		5674		F	KN
5636	d	F		ZC		5676		F	LM
5640		F		LT		5679	d	F	ZC
5642		WC		CS		5686		F	LM

5687	F		KN
5690	F		LT
5692	F		LM
5694	F		KN
5699	F		LM
5700 d	F		LM
5701	F		KN
5704	**M**	WC *ON*	CS
5709	**BG**	WC	CS
5710 d	F		LM
5711	F		LT
5712		WC	CS
5714	**M**	WC *ON*	CS
5715	F		LT

5716	F		KN
5718	F		KN
5722	E		KM
5724	F		LT
5726	F		LM
5727	**M**	WC *ON*	CS
5728	F		LM
5731	F		KN
5732	**0**	RV	CP
5735	F		LM
5737 d	F		ZC
5738	F		KN
5739	**0**	RV	CP
5740 d	F		LM

AC2E (TSO)   OPEN STANDARD

Dia. AC210. Mark 2E. Air conditioned. Stones equipment. –/64 2T (w –/62 2T 1W). B4 bogies. Require at least 800 V train heat supply. d (except 5756, 5803 and 5879). ETH 5.

5744–5803. Lot No. 30837 Derby 1972. 33.5 t.
5810–5906. Lot No. 30844 Derby 1972–3. 33.5 t.

* Refurbished with green seat trim.
† Refurbished with green seat trim, modified design of seat headrest and centre luggage stack. –/60 2T (w –/58 2T 1W).
§ Facelifted with modified design of seat headrest and new red seat trim.
• Facelifted with new-style individual seats.

5744		F	*VX*	MA
5745 †	**V**	F	*VX*	MA
5746		F	*VX*	MA
5748 * pt		F	*VX*	MA
5750 †	**V**	F	*VX*	MA
5751 w§		F	*VW*	OY
5752 *		F	*VX*	MA
5754 w†	**V**	F	*VX*	MA
5756		**M** WC *ON*		CS
5760 §		F	*VX*	MA
5769 *		F	*VX*	MA
5772 w§		F	*VX*	MA
5773 † pt	**V**	F	*VX*	MA
5775 †	**V**	F	*VX*	MA
5776 *		F	*VX*	MA
5778 w		F	*VX*	MA
5779 *		F	*VX*	MA
5780 w		F	*VX*	MA
5781 w		F	*VX*	MA
5784		F	*VX*	MA
5787 †	**V**	F	*VX*	MA

5788 *		F	*VX*	MA
5789 * pt		F	*VX*	MA
5791 w*		F	*VX*	MA
5792 *		F	*VX*	MA
5793 w†pt	**V**	F	*VX*	MA
5794 w*		F	*VX*	MA
5796 w*		F	*VX*	MA
5797 *		F	*VX*	MA
5799 w•		F	*VW*	OY
5800		F	*VW*	OY
5801		F	*VX*	MA
5803		F		PC
5810 †	**V**	F	*VX*	MA
5812 w*		F	*VX*	MA
5814 *		F	*VX*	MA
5815 w†	**V**	F	*VX*	MA
5816 * pt		F	*VX*	MA
5821		F	*VX*	MA
5822 w†pt	**V**	F	*VX*	MA
5824 *w		F	*VX*	MA
5826 §		F	*VX*	MA

5827	*		F	VX	MA
5828	w†	V	F	VX	MA
5831			F	VW	OY
5833			F	VX	MA
5836			F	VW	OY
5840	§		F	VW	OY
5843	w*		F	VX	MA
5845	†	V	F	VX	MA
5847	w		F	VX	MA
5851	§		F	VW	OY
5852			F	VW	OY
5853			F	AR	NC
5854	*		F	VX	MA
5859	†	V	F	VX	MA
5863			F	VW	OY
5866	* pt		F	VX	MA
5868	† pt	V	F	VX	MA
5869			F	AR	NC
5871	§		F	VX	MA

5874	w		F	AR	NC
5876	† pt	V	F	VX	MA
5879			E		OM
5881	w†	V	F	VX	MA
5886	†	V	F	VX	MA
5887	w*		F	VX	MA
5888	w*		F	VX	MA
5889	†	V	F	VX	MA
5890	§		F	VW	OY
5892			F	VX	MA
5893	†	V	F	VX	MA
5897	*		F	VX	MA
5899	†	V	F	VX	MA
5900	w†	V	F	VX	MA
5901	†	V	F	VX	MA
5902	†	V	F	VX	MA
5903	†	V	F	VX	MA
5905	†	V	F	VX	MA
5906	*		F	VX	MA

AC2F (TSO)   OPEN STANDARD

Dia. AC211. Mark 2F. Air conditioned. Temperature Ltd. equipment. –/64 2T. (w –/62 2T 1W) Inter-City 70 seats. All were refurbished in the 1980s with power-operated vestibule doors and new panels and new seat trim. B4 bogies. d. ETH 5X.

5908–5958. Lot No. 30846 Derby 1973. 33 t.
5959–6170. Lot No. 30860 Derby 1973–4. 33 t.
6171–6184. Lot No. 30874 Derby 1974–5. 33 t.

* Early Mark 2 style seats.

These vehicles are now undergoing a second refurbishment with new carpets, new motor-alternator sets and new seat trim as follows:

r Standard refurbished vehicles.

Cross-Country vehicles:

§ Centre luggage stack. –/60 2T.
• Centre luggage stack. –/60 2T plus pt.
† Centre luggage stack. –/58 2T 1W.

West Coast vehicles:

‡ Refurbished. –/60 2T 2W.

5908	r	V	F	VW	OY
5910	‡	V	F	VW	OY
5911	§	V	F	VX	MA
5912	§	V	F	VX	MA
5913	r		F	VX	MA
5914	‡	V	F	VW	OY
5915	r	V	F	VW	OY
5916	rw		F	VX	MA

5917	§	V	F	VX	MA
5918	†	V	F	VX	MA
5919	•	V	F	VX	MA
5920			F	VW	OY
5921			F	AR	NC
5922		AR	F	AR	NC
5924		AR	F	AR	NC
5925	r		F	VX	MA

5926		F	AR	NC		5984	r	V	F	VW	OY
5927	AR	F	AR	NC		5985		F	AR	NC
5928		F	AR	NC		5986	r	V	F	VW	OY
5929		F	AR	NC		5987	r	V	F	VW	OY
5930	† V	F	VX	MA		5988	r	V	F	VW	OY
5931	w	F	VW	OY		5989	† V	F	VX	MA
5932	r	V F	VW	OY		5991	§	F	VX	MA
5933	r	V F	VW	OY		5993	w*	F	AR	NC
5934		F	VW	OY		5994	*	F	VX	MA
5935		F	AR	NC		5995	§	F	VX	MA
5936	AR	F	AR	NC		5996	• V	F	VX	MA
5937	r	V F	VW	OY		5997	r	V	F	VW	OY
5939	r	V F	VW	OY		5998		F	AR	NC
5940	w	F	VW	OY		5999	§ V	F	VX	MA
5941	r	V	F	VW	OY		6000	† V	F	VX	MA
5943	rw	V F	VW	OY		6001	‡ V	F	VW	OY
5944	w	F	AR	NC		6002		F	VW	OY
5945	r	V	F	VW	OY		6005	*	F	VX	MA
5946	r	V	F	VW	OY		6006		F	AR	NC
5947		F	VX	MA		6008	§ V	F	VX	MA
5948	‡ V	F	VW	OY		6009	r	V	F	VW	OY
5949	‡ V	F	VW	OY		6010	§ V	F	VX	MA
5950		F	AR	NC		6011	§ V	F	VX	MA
5951		F	VX	MA		6012	r	V	F	VW	OY
5952	r	V	F	VW	OY		6013	r		F	VX	MA
5953	r		F	VW	OY		6014	r		F	VX	MA
5954	AR	F	AR	NC		6015	† V	F	VX	MA
5955	r	V	F	VW	OY		6016	r	V	F	VW	OY
5956		F	AR	NC		6018	† V	F	VX	MA
5957	r	V	F	VW	OY		6021		F	VW	OY
5958	§	F	VX	MA		6022	§ V	F	VX	MA
5959	n	AR	F	AR	NC		6024	§ V	F	VX	MA
5960	§ V	F	VX	MA		6025	w*	F	VX	MA
5961	• V	F	VX	MA		6026	§	F	VX	MA
5962	• V	F	VX	MA		6027	‡ V	F	VW	OY
5963	*	F	VW	OY		6028		F	AR	NC
5964		F	AR	NC		6029	r	V	F	VW	OY
5965	rw	F	VX	MA		6030	† V	F	VX	MA
5966		F	AR	NC		6031	r	V	F	VW	OY
5967	† V	F	VX	MA		6034		F	AR	NC
5968		F	AR	NC		6035	rw	F	VX	MA
5969	‡ V	F	VW	OY		6036	*	AR	F	AR	NC
5971	§	F	VX	MA		6037		F	AR	NC
5973	AR	F	AR	NC		6038	§ V	F	VX	MA
5975	§ V	F	VX	MA		6041	§ V	F	VX	MA
5976	† V	F	VX	MA		6042		F	AR	NC
5977	r	V	F	VW	OY		6043		F	VW	OY
5978	r	V	F	VW	OY		6045	w	F	VW	OY
5980	r	V	F	VW	OY		6046	§ V	F	VX	MA
5981	§	F	VX	MA		6047	n*	F	VW	OY
5983	§ V	F	VX	MA		6049	r	V	F	VW	OY

6050	r		F	VX	MA
6051	r	V	F	VW	OY
6052	†w		F	VX	MA
6053	*		F	AR	NC
6054	r	V	F	VW	OY
6055			F	VW	OY
6056			F	VW	OY
6057	r		F	VW	OY
6059	§	V	F	VX	MA
6060	rw		F	VW	OY
6061	•	V	F	VX	MA
6062			F	VW	OY
6063	w		F	VW	OY
6064	§	V	F	VX	MA
6065	r	V	F	VW	OY
6066	r		F	VX	MA
6067	•	V	F	VX	MA
6073	§	V	F	VX	MA
6100	*		F	VW	OY
6101	r	V	F	VW	OY
6102	r		F	VW	OY
6103			F	AR	NC
6104	r	V	F	VW	OY
6105	†pt	V	F	VX	MA
6106	r		F	VW	OY
6107	r	V	F	VW	OY
6110	w		F	AR	NC
6111			F	VW	OY
6112	•	V	F	VX	MA
6113			F	VW	OY
6115	r		F	VX	MA
6116			F	VW	OY
6117	†	V	F	VX	MA
6119	§	V	F	VX	MA
6120	§	V	F	VX	MA
6121			F	VW	OY
6122	§	V	F	VX	MA
6123			F	AR	NC
6124	r		F	VX	MA
6134			F	VW	OY
6135	r		F	VX	MA
6136	r	V	F	VW	OY
6137	•	V	F	VX	MA
6138			F	VW	OY
6139	n*		F	AR	NC
6141	w		F	VW	OY
6142	*		F	VW	OY
6144	*		F	VW	OY
6145	•	V	F	VX	MA
6146	*		F	AR	NC
6147	r		F	VW	OY
6148	r		F	VX	MA
6149	‡	V	F	VW	OY
6150	r*		F	VX	MA
6151	*		F	VW	OY
6152	*	AR	F	AR	NC
6153	r		F	VW	OY
6154	r*		F	VX	MA
6155	`*	AR	F	AR	NC
6157	§	V	F	VX	MA
6158	r	V	F	VW	OY
6159	•	V	F	VX	MA
6160	*		F	AR	NC
6161	*		F	VW	OY
6162	•	V	F	VX	MA
6163	r	V	F	VW	OY
6164			F	VW	OY
6165	r	V	F	VW	OY
6166			F	AR	NC
6167			F	AR	NC
6168	r		F	VX	MA
6170	§	V	F	VX	MA
6171			F	VW	OY
6172	§	V	F	VX	MA
6173	§	V	F	VX	MA
6174			F	AR	NC
6175	r	V	F	VW	OY
6176	†	V	F	VX	MA
6177	§	V	F	VX	MA
6178	§		F	VX	MA
6179	r	V	F	VW	OY
6180	w		F	VW	OY
6181	wn		F	VW	OY
6182	§	V	F	VX	MA
6183	§	V	F	VX	MA
6184	§	V	F	VX	MA

AC2D (TSO)   OPEN STANDARD

Dia. AC217. Mark 2D. Air conditioned. Stones equipment.. –/58 2T. (–/58 1T*).
B4 bogies. ETH 5X. Rebuilt from FO with new style 2+2 seats.

Lot No. 30821 Derby 1971–2. 33.5 t.

* One toilet converted to store room for use of sleeping car attendant.

6200	(3198)	d	F	GW	LA		6213	(3208)	d	F		CP
6202	(3191)	d*	F		CP		6216	(3179)		F		LM
6203	(3180)	d	F		CP		6219	(3213)	d	F		CP
6206	(3183)	d	F	GW	LA		6221	(3173)	d	F		CP
6207	(3204)	d	F		CP		6226	(3203)	d	F	GW	LA
6212	(3176)	d	F		CP							

GX51   GENERATOR VAN

Dia. GX501. Mark 1. Renumbered 1989 from BR departmental series. Converted from NDA in 1973 to three-phase supply generator van for use with HST trailers. Currently used to test overhauled HST trailers. B4 bogies.

Lot No. 30400 Pressed Steel 1958.

6310	(81448, 975325)	**P**	P	P	ZG

AX51   GENERATOR VAN

Dia. AX501. Mark 1. Converted from NDA in 1992 to generator vans for use on Anglo-Scottish sleeping car services. Now normally used on trains hauled by steam locomotives. B4 bogies. ETH75.

6311. Lot No. 30162 Pressed Steel 1958. 37.25 t.
6312. Lot No. 30224 Cravens 1956. 37.25 t.
6313. Lot No. 30484 Pressed Steel 1958. 37.25 t.

Non-Standard Livery: 6311 is purple.

6313 is leased to the Venice Simplon Orient Express.

6311	(80903, 92911)	**B**	RS	ON	BN
6312	(81023, 92925)		FS		SZ
6313	(81553, 92167)	**PC**	P	ON	SL

GS5 (HSBV)   HST BARRIER VEHICLE

Various diagrams. Renumbered from departmental stock or converted from various types. B4 bogies (Commonwealth bogies *).

6330. Mark 2A. Lot No. 30786 Derby 1968. 32 t.
6334. Mark 1. Lot No. 30400 Pressed Steel 1957–8. 31.5 t.
6336/8/44. Mark 1. Lot No. 30715 Gloucester 1962. 31 t.
6340. Mark 1. Lot No. 30669 Swindon 1962. 36 t.
6346. Mark 2A. Lot No. 30777 Derby 1967. 31.5 t.
6347. Mark 2A. Lot No. 30787 Derby 1968. 31.5 t.
6348. Mark 1. Lot No. 30163 Pressed Steel 1957. 31.5 t.

6330	(14084, 975629)			A	A	LA
6334	(81478, 92128)	**P**	P	P	A	LA
6336	(81591, 92185)			A	A	LA
6338	(81581, 92180)			A	A	LA
6340	(21251, 975678)	*		A	A	LA
6344	(81263, 92080)			A	A	EC

6346	(9422)		A	*A*	EC
6347	(5395)		A	*A*	LA
6348	(81233, 92963)		A	*A*	LA

GF5 (MFBV)   MARK 4 BARRIER VEHICLE

Various diagrams. Renumbered from departmental stock, or converted from FK, BSO or BG. B4 bogies.

6351. Mark 1. Lot No. 30091 Doncaster 1954. 33 t.
6352/3. Mark 2A. Lot No. 30774 Derby 1968. 33 t.
6354–6. Mark 2C. Lot No. 30820 Derby 1970. 32 t.
6357. Mak 2C. Lot No. 30798 Derby 1970. 32 t.
6358–9. Mark 2A. Lot No. 30788 Derby 1968. 31.5 t.
6390. Mark 1. Lot No. 30136 Metro-Cammell 1955. 31.5 t.

6351	(3050, 975435)			F	*GN*	EC
6352	(13465, 19465)	BG	F	*GN*	BN
6353	(13478, 19478)	BG	F	*GN*	EC
6354	(9459)			F	*GN*	BN
6355	(9477)	BG	F	*GN*	BN
6356	(9455)	BG	F	*GN*	BN
6357	(9443)	BG	F	*GN*	BN
6358	(9432)	BG	F	*GN*	BN
6359	(9429)	BG	F	*GN*	BN
6390	(80723, 92900)			F	*GN*	BN

GF5 (BV)   DMU/EMU* BARRIER VEHICLE

Various diagrams. Converted 1992 from BSO or BG*.

6360. Mark 2A. Lot No. 30777 Derby 1967. B4 bogies. 31.5 t.
6361. Mark 2C. Lot No. 30820 Derby 1970. B4 bogies. 32 t.
6364. Mark 1. Lot No. 30039 Derby 1954. BR Mark 1 bogies. 32 t.
6365. Mark 1. Lot No. 30323 Pressed Steel 1957. BR Mark 1 bogies. 32 t.

6360	(9420)		RR	P	*P*	NL
6361	(9460)		RR	P	*P*	NL
6364	(80565)	*	RR	P	*P*	TS
6365	(81296, 84296)	*	RR	P	*P*	TS

GS5 (HSBV)   HST BARRIER VEHICLE

Dia. GS507. Mark 1. Converted from BG in 1994–5. B4 bogies.

6392. Lot No. 30715 Gloucester 1962. 29.5 t.
6393/6/7. Lot No. 30716 Gloucester 1962. 29.5 t.
6394. Lot No. 30162 Pressed Steel 1956–7. 30.5 t.
6395. Lot No. 30484 Pressed Steel 1958. 30.5 t.
6398/9. Lot No. 30400 Pressed Steel 1957–8. 30.5 t.

6392	(81588, 92183)	P	P	*P*	NL
6393	(81609, 92196)	P	P	*P*	NL
6394	(80878, 92906)	P	P	*P*	NL

6395	(81506, 92148)	**P**	P	*P*	NL
6396	(81606, 92195)	**P**	P	*P*	LA
6397	(81600, 92190)	**P**	P	*P*	LA
6398	(81471, 92126)	**P**	P	*P*	NL
6399	(81367, 92994)	**P**	P	*P*	NL

AG2C (TSOT)   OPEN STANDARD (TROLLEY)

Dia. AG201. Mark 2C. Converted from TSO by removal of one seating bay and replacing this by a counter with a space for a trolley. Adjacent toilet removed and converted to steward's washing area/store. Pressure ventilated. –/54 1T. B4 bogies. ETH 4.

Lot No. 30795 Derby 1969–70. 32.5 t.

| 6513 | (5538) | **N** | F | | OM | | 6523 | (5569) | **BG** | WC | | CS |
| 6517 | (5499) | **N** | F | | OM | | 6528 | (5592) | **M** | WC | *ON* | CS |

AG2D (TSOT)   OPEN STANDARD (TROLLEY)

Dia. AG202. Mark 2D. Converted from TSO by removal of one seating bay and replacing this by a counter with a space for a trolley. Adjacent toilet removed and converted to steward's washing area/store. Air conditioned. Stones equipment. –/54 1T. B4 bogies. ETH 5.

Lot No. 30822 Derby 1971. 33 t.

| 6609 | (5698) | | F | | KN | | 6619 | (5655) | | F | | KN |

AN2D (RMBT)   MINIATURE BUFFET CAR

Dia. AN207. Mark 2D. Converted from TSOT by the removal of another seating bay and fitting a proper buffet counter with boiler and microwave oven. Air conditioned. Stones equipment. –/46 1T. B4 bogies. p. q. d. ETH 5.

Lot No. 30822 Derby 1971. 33 t.

6652	(5622, 6602)	F	ZC		6662	(5641, 6612)	F	LM
6660	(5627, 6610)	F	ZC		6665	(5721, 6615)	F	ZC
6661	(5736, 6611)	F	ZC					

AN1F (RLO)   SLEEPER RECEPTION CAR

Dia. AN101 (AN102*). Mark 2F. Converted from FO, these vehicles consist of pantry, microwave cooking facilities, seating area for passengers, telephone booth and staff toilet. 6703–8 also have a bar. Converted at RTC, Derby (6700), Ilford (6701–5) and Derby (6706–8). Air conditioned. 6700/1/3/5/6–8 have Stones equipment, 6702/4 Temperature Ltd. 26/– 1T. B4 bogies. p. q. d. ETH 5X.

6700–2/4/8. Lot No. 30859 Derby 1973–4. 33.5 t.
6703/5–7. Lot No. 30845 Derby 1973. 33.5 t.

| 6700 | (3347) | | | F | *SR* | IS |
| 6701 | (3346) | | * | F | *SR* | IS |

6702	(3421)	*	F	*SR*	IS
6703	(3308)		F	*SR*	IS
6704	(3341)		F	*SR*	IS
6705	(3310, 6430)		F	*SR*	IS
6706	(3283, 6421)		F	*SR*	IS
6707	(3276, 6418)		F	*SR*	IS
6708	(3370)		F	*SR*	IS

AC2F (TSO)   OPEN STANDARD

Dia. AC224. Mark 2F. Renumbered from FO and declassified in 1985–6. Converted 1990 to TSO with mainly unidirectional seating and power-operated vestibule doors. Air conditioned. B4 bogies. –/74 2T. 6800–14 were converted by BREL Derby and have Temperature Ltd. air conditioning. 6815–29 were converted by RFS Industries Doncaster and have Stones air conditioning. d. ETH 5X.

6800–07. 6810–12. 6813–14. 6819/22/28. Lot No. 30859 Derby 1973–4. 33 t.
6808–6809. Lot No. 30873 Derby 1974–5. 33.5 t.
6815–18. 6820–21. 6823–27. 6829. Lot No. 30845 Derby 1973. 33 t.

6800	(3323, 6435)	**AR**	F	*AR*	NC
6801	(3349, 6442)		F	*AR*	NC
6802	(3339, 6439)		F	*AR*	NC
6803	(3355, 6443)		F	*AR*	NC
6804	(3396, 6449)		F	*AR*	NC
6805	(3324, 6436)		F	*AR*	NC
6806	(3342, 6440)		F	*AR*	NC
6807	(3423, 6452)		F	*AR*	NC
6808	(3430, 6454)		F	*AR*	NC
6809	(3435, 6455)	**AR**	F	*AR*	NC
6810	(3404, 6451)		F	*AR*	NC
6811	(3327, 6437)		F	*AR*	NC
6812	(3394, 6448)		F	*AR*	NC
6813	(3410, 6463)		F	*AR*	NC
6814	(3422, 6465)		F	*AR*	NC
6815	(3282, 6420)	**AR**	F	*AR*	NC
6816	(3316, 6461)	**AR**	F	*AR*	NC
6817	(3311, 6431)		F	*AR*	NC
6818	(3298, 6427)		F	*AR*	NC
6819	(3365, 6446)		F	*AR*	NC
6820	(3320, 6434)		F	*AR*	NC
6821	(3281, 6458)	**AR**	F	*AR*	NC
6822	(3376, 6447)		F	*AR*	NC
6823	(3289, 6424)		F	*AR*	NC
6824	(3307, 6429)	**AR**	F	*AR*	NC
6825	(3301, 6460)	**AR**	F	*AR*	NC
6826	(3294, 6425)		F	*AR*	NC
6827	(3306, 6428)	**AR**	F	*AR*	NC
6828	(3380, 6464)		F	*AR*	NC
6829	(3288, 6423)		F	*AR*	NC

NM51   MERSEYRAIL SANDITE COACH

Dia. NM504. Mark 1. Former Class 501 750 V d.c. third rail EMU driving trailers converted for use as Sandite/de-icing coaches. BR Mark 1 Bogies.

Lot No. 30328 Ashford/Eastleigh 1958.   . t.

6910	(75178, 977346)	**MD** RT	*OD*	BD	
6911	(75180, 977348)	**MD** RT	*OD*	BD	

AH2Z (BSOT)   OPEN BRAKE STANDARD (MICRO-BUFFET)

Dia. AH203. Mark 2. Converted from BSO by removal of one seating bay and replacing this by a counter with a space for a trolley. Adjacent toilet removed and converted to a steward's washing area/store. –/23 0T. ETH 4.

Lot No. 30757 Derby 1966. 31 t.

9100	(9405)	v	**RR** F			LT
9101	(9398)	v	**RR** F			LT
9104	(9401)	v	**G** MH	*ON*		RL
9105	(9404)	v	**RR** F			LT

AE21 (BSO)   OPEN BRAKE STANDARD

Dia. AE201. Mark 1. –/39 1T. BR Mark 1 bogies. ETH 3.

Lot No. 30170 Doncaster 1955–6. 34 t.

9227	xk	**M** SP	*ON*	BT	9274	v	**CH** NY	*ON*	NY

AE2Z (BSO)   OPEN BRAKE STANDARD

Dia. AE203. Mark 2. These vehicles use the same body shell as the Mark 2 BFK and have first class seat spacing and wider tables. Pressure ventilated. –/31 1T. B4 bogies. ETH 4.

Lot No. 30757 Derby 1966. 31.5 t.

9385	v	**LN** F		LT	9388	v	**LN** F	LT

AE2A (BSO)   OPEN BRAKE STANDARD

Dia. AE204. Mark 2A. These vehicles use the same body shell as the mark 2A BFK and have first class seat spacing and wider tables. Pressure ventilated. –/31 1T. B4 bogies. ETH 4.

9417–9424. Lot No. 30777 Derby 1967. 31.5 t.
9428–9438. Lot No. 30788 Derby 1968. 31.5 t.

9417	**FT** F	*CA*	CF	9428	**RR** F		CP
9418	**RR** F		LM	9431	**RR** F		LM
9419	**RR** F		LM	9434	**RR** F		ZB
9421	**RR** F		CP	9435	**RR** F		LM
9424	**RR** F		CP	9438	**RR** F		CP

AE2C (BSO)   OPEN BRAKE STANDARD

Dia. AE205. Mark 2C. Pressure ventilated. –/31 1T. B4 bogies. ETH 4.

9440–48. Lot No. 30798 Derby 1970. 32 t.
9458–70. Lot No. 30820 Derby 1970. 32 t.

Non-Standard Livery: 9440 is in Royal blue with white lining.

9440	d	**0**	WC	WW	CF	9458	**RR** F	ZB
9448	d	**M**	WC	WW	CF			

AE2D (BSO)   OPEN BRAKE STANDARD

Dia. AE206. Mark 2D. Air conditioned. Stones equipment. –/31 1T. B4 bogies. pg. ETH 5.

* Refurbished with green seat trim.

Lot No. 30824 Derby 1971. 33 t.

9479	d*	F	VX	MA	9486		F	LM
9480	d	F	VX	MA	9488	d	F	ZC
9481	d	F	GW	LA	9489	d	F	VX	MA
9482		F		NL	9490	d	F		LT
9483		F		LM	9492	d	F	GW	LA
9484	d	F		LT	9493	d	F	VX	MA
9485		F		LT	9494	d	F		ZC

AE2E (BSO)   OPEN BRAKE STANDARD

Dia. AE207. Mark 2E. Air conditioned. Stones equipment. –/32 1T. B4 bogies. d. pg. ETH 5.

Lot No. 30838 Derby 1972. 33 t.

r Refurbished with green seat trim.
† Refurbished with modified design of seat headrest and green seat trim.

9496	r		F	VX	MA	9504		F	VX	MA
9497	r		F	VX	MA	9505	r	F	VX	MA
9498			F	VX	MA	9506	†	**V** F	VX	MA
9500	r		F	VX	MA	9507	†	**V** F	VX	MA
9501			F	GW	LA	9508	†	**V** F	VX	MA
9502	†	**V** F	VX	MA	9509	†	**V** F	VX	MA
9503	†	**V** F	VX	MA					

AE2F (BSO)   OPEN BRAKE STANDARD

Dia. AE208. Mark 2F. Air conditioned. Temperature Ltd. equipment. All now refurbished with power-operated vestibule doors, new panels and seat trim. –/32 1T. B4 bogies. d. pg. ETH 5X.

Lot No. 30861 Derby 1974. 34 t.

r Further refurbished with green seat trim.

9513	r	**V**	F	*VX*	MA		9526	r		F	*VX*	MA

9513 r **V** F *VX* MA | 9526 r   F *VX* MA
9516 r **V** F *VX* MA | 9527 r **V** F *VX* MA
9520 r **V** F *VX* MA | 9529   F *VX* MA
9521 r **V** F *VX* MA | 9531 r **V** F *VX* MA
9522 r **V** F *VX* MA | 9537 r **V** F *VX* MA
9523   F *VX* MA | 9538 r **V** F *VX* MA
9524 r **V** F *VX* MA | 9539 r **V** F *VX* MA
9525 r **V** F *VX* MA

AF2F (DBSO)   DRIVING OPEN BRAKE STANDARD

Dia. AF201. Mark 2F. Air conditioned. Temperature Ltd. equipment. Push &
pull (t.d.m. system). Converted from BSO, these vehicles originally had half
cabs at the brake end. They have since been refurbished and have had their
cabs widened and the outer gangways removed. Fitted with cowcatchers.
Cab to shore communication. BR Cellnet phone and data transmitter. d. –/32
1T. B4 bogies. pg. ETH 5X.

9701–9710. Lot No. 30861 Derby 1974. Converted Glasgow 1979. Disc brakes. 34 t.
9711–9713. Lot No. 30861 Derby 1974. Converted Glasgow 1985. 34 t.
9714. Lot No. 30861 Derby 1974. Converted Glasgow 1986. Disc brakes. 34 t.

9701 (9528)   F *AR* NC | 9709 (9515) **AR** F *AR* NC
9702 (9510)   F *AR* NC | 9710 (9518) **AR** F *AR* NC
9703 (9517)   F *AR* NC | 9711 (9532)   F *AR* NC
9704 (9512)   F *AR* NC | 9712 (9534)   F *AR* NC
9705 (9519)   F *AR* NC | 9713 (9535) **AR** F *AR* NC
9707 (9511) **AR** F *AR* NC | 9714 (9536)   F *AR* NC
9708 (9530) **AR** F *AR* NC

AJ1G (RFM)   RESTAURANT BUFFET FIRST (MODULAR)

Dia. AJ103 (10200/1 are Dia. AJ101). Mark 3A. Air conditioned. Converted
from HST TRFK, RFB and FO. 22/– (*24/–, §18/_). BT10 bogies. p. q. d. ETH
14X.

10200–10211. Lot No. 30884 Derby 1977.
10212–10229. Lot No. 30878 Derby 1975–6. 39.8 t.
10230–10260. Lot No. 30890 Derby 1979. 39.8 t.

r Refurbished with table lamps and burgundy set trim.

10200 (40519) *   P *AR* NC | 10210 (40509)   P *VW* PC
10201 (40520) r **V**   P *VW* OY | 10211 (40510) r **V**   P *VW* PC
10202 (40504) r **V**   P *VW* MA | 10212 (11049) r§ **V** P *VW* MA
10203 (40506) *   P *AR* NC | 10213 (11050) r§ **V** P *VW* MA
10204 (40502) r **V**   P *VW* MA | 10214 (11034) * **AR** P *AR* NC
10205 (40503) r **V**   P *VW* OY | 10215 (11032) r§ **V** P *VW* PC
10206 (40507) r **V**   P *VW* MA | 10216 (11041) * **AR** P *AR* NC
10207 (40516) §   P *VW* PC | 10217 (11051) r **V**   P *VW* MA
10208 (40517) r **V**   P *VW* MA | 10218 (11053)   P *VW* PC
10209 (40508)   P *VW* PC | 10219 (11047) r§ **V** P *VW* PC

10220 (11056) r§ **V**	P	*VW*	OY		10240 (10003) r§ **V**	P	*VW*	OY
10221 (11012) r§ **V**	P	*VW*	PC		10241 (10009) *	P	*AR*	NC
10222 (11063) r **V**	P	*VW*	MA		10242 (10002) r§	P	*VW*	OY
10223 (11043) *	P	*AR*	NC		10245 (10019) r **V**	P	*VW*	PC
10224 (11062) §	P	*VW*	MA		10246 (10014) r **V**	P	*VW*	PC
10225 (11014) r§	P	*VW*	OY		10247 (10011) * **AR** P	*AR*	NC
10226 (11015) r **V**	P	*VW*	MA		10248 (10005) r **V**	P	*VW*	OY
10227 (11057) §	P	*VW*	PC		10249 (10012) r§ **V**	P	*VW*	PC
10228 (11035) * **AR** P	*AR*	NC		10250 (10020) r **V**	P	*VW*	OY
10229 (11059) r§ **V**	P	*VW*	MA		10251 (10024) r **V**	P	*VW*	OY
10230 (10021) r **V**	P	*VW*	PC		10252 (10008) r§ **V**	P	*VW*	OY
10231 (10016) r§ **V**	P	*VW*	OY		10253 (10026)	P	*VW*	PC
10232 (10027) r	P	*VW*	OY		10254 (10006)	P	*VW*	PC
10233 (10013) §	P	*VW*	PC		10255 (10010) r§ **V**	P	*VW*	PC
10234 (10004)	P	*VW*	PC		10256 (10028) r§ **V**	P	*VW*	PC
10235 (10015) r	P	*VW*	OY		10257 (10007) r§ **V**	P	*VW*	PC
10236 (10018) §	P	*VW*	PC		10258 (10023)	P	*VW*	OY
10237 (10022) r **V**	P	*VW*	MA		10259 (10025) §	P	*VW*	OY
10238 (10017) r **V**	P	*VW*	OY		10260 (10001) r **V**	P	*VW*	MA

AJ1J (RFM) RESTAURANT BUFFET FIRST (MODULAR)

Dia. AJ105. Mark 4. Air conditioned. 20/– 1T. BT41 bogies. ETH 6X.

Lot No. 31045 Metro-Cammell 1989 onwards. 45.5 t.

10300	**GN**	F	*GN*	BN		10317	**GN**	F	*GN*	BN
10301	**GN**	F	*GN*	BN		10318	**GN**	F	*GN*	BN
10302	**GN**	F	*GN*	BN		10319	**GN**	F	*GN*	BN
10303	**GN**	F	*GN*	BN		10320	**GN**	F	*GN*	BN
10304	**GN**	F	*GN*	BN		10321	**GN**	F	*GN*	BN
10305	**GN**	F	*GN*	BN		10322	**GN**	F	*GN*	BN
10306	**GN**	F	*GN*	BN		10323	**GN**	F	*GN*	BN
10307	**GN**	F	*GN*	BN		10324	**GN**	F	*GN*	BN
10308	**GN**	F	*GN*	BN		10325	**GN**	F	*GN*	BN
10309	**GN**	F	*GN*	BN		10326	**GN**	F	*GN*	BN
10310	**GN**	F	*GN*	BN		10327	**GN**	F	*GN*	BN
10311	**GN**	F	*GN*	BN		10328	**GN**	F	*GN*	BN
10312	**GN**	F	*GN*	BN		10329	**GN**	F	*GN*	BN
10313	**GN**	F	*GN*	BN		10330	**GN**	F	*GN*	BN
10314	**GN**	F	*GN*	BN		10331	**GN**	F	*GN*	BN
10315	**GN**	F	*GN*	BN		10332	**GN**	F	*GN*	BN
10316	**GN**	F	*GN*	BN		10333	**GN**	F	*GN*	BN

AU4G (SLEP)   SLEEPING CAR WITH PANTRY

Dia. AU401. Mark 3A. Air conditioned. 12 compartments with a fixed lower berth and a hinged upper berth, plus an attendants compartment with 2T (controlled emission). BT10 bogies. ETH 7X.

Lot No. 30960 Derby 1981–3. 41 t.

Note: 10569 is leased to Venice Simplon Orient Express.

10500		SS		YS		10562	d	P	*SR*	IS
10501	d	P	*SR*	IS		10563	d	P	*GW*	LA
10502	d	P	*SR*	IS		10565	d	P	*SR*	IS
10503		SS		YS.		10566	d	P		ZD
10504	d	P	*SR*	IS		10567		P		ZG
10506	d	P	*SR*	IS		10569	d **PC**	P	*ON*	SL
10507	d	P	*SR*	IS		10570		P		KN
10508	d	P	*SR*	IS		10571		SS		BN
10510	d	P	*SR*	IS		10572	d	P		ZD
10512	d	P		ZG		10573	d	P		DY
10513	d	P	*SR*	IS		10574		CN		FK
10514		SS		YS		10575		SS		YS
10515	d	P	*SR*	IS		10577	**BG**	P		ZD
10516	d	P	*SR*	IS		10578		P		KN
10519	d	P	*SR*	IS		10579	**BG**	P		KN
10520	d	P	*SR*	IS		10580	d	P	*SR*	IS
10522	d	P	*SR*	IS		10582	d	P		ZD
10523	d	P	*SR*	IS		10583	d **GW**	P	*GW*	LA
10526	d	P	*SR*	IS		10584	d	P	*GW*	LA
10527	d	P	*SR*	IS		10586	d	P		KN
10529	d	P	*SR*	IS		10588	d	P	*GW*	LA
10530	d	P		ZD		10589	d	P	*GW*	LA
10531	d	P	*SR*	IS		10590	d **GW**	P	*GW*	LA
10532	d **GW**	P	*GW*	LA		10591		P		KN
10533		P		ZD		10592		P		KN
10534	d **GW**	P	*GW*	LA		10593	d	P		KN
10535	d	P		ZD		10594	d	P	*GW*	LA
10536	d	P		KN		10595	**BG**	P		KN
10537	d	P		ZD		10596	d	P		KN
10538	d	P		KN		10597	d	P	*SR*	IS
10539	d	P		KN		10598	d	P	*SR*	IS
10540	d	P		ZD		10599		P		KN
10542	d	P	*SR*	IS		10600	d	P	*SR*	IS
10543	d	P	*SR*	IS		10601		P		ZD
10544	d	P	*SR*	IS		10602		P		ZD
10546		P		ZD		10603		P		KN
10547	d	P	*SR*	IS		10604		P		ZD
10548	d	P	*SR*	IS		10605	d	P	*SR*	IS
10549	d	P		ZD		10606		P		KN
10550	d	P		ZD		10607	d	P	*SR*	IS
10551	d	P	*SR*	IS		10608	**BG**	P		ZN
10553	d	P	*SR*	IS		10609	**BG**	P		ZG
10554	d	P		ZD		10610	d	P	*SR*	IS
10555	d	P		KN		10612	d	P	*GW*	LA
10557	d	P		ZD		10613	d	P	*SR*	IS
10558	d	P		ZH		10614	d	P	*SR*	IS
10559	d	P		KN		10616	d	P	*GW*	LA
10560	d	P		ZD		10617	d	P	*SR*	IS
10561	d	P	*SR*	IS						

AS4G (SLE)   SLEEPING CAR

Dia. AS403. Mark 3A. Air conditioned. 13 compartments with a fixed lower berth and a hinged upper berth. 2T (controlled emission). BT10 bogies. ETH 6X.

Note: 10664/7/9/76/7/81/94/5/8/721 were sold to the Danish State Railways (DSB) and numbered in the UIC system. They have since been purchased by Angel Train Contracts and returned to Britain.

Lot No. 30961 Derby 1980–4. 43.5 t.

10646	d		CN	FK	10690	d		P	SR	IS
10647	d		P	KN	10691	d		P	ZD
10648	d		P	SR	IS	10692	d		P	ZD
10649	d		P	KN	10693	d		P	SR	IS
10650	d		P	SR	IS	10694		DS	A	KN
10651	d		P	ZD	10695		DS	A	KN
10653	d		P	ZD	10696			P	KN
10654	d		P	ZD	10697			P	KN
10655			SS	YS	10698		DS	A	KN
10656			P	KN	10699	d		P	SR	IS
10657			SS	YS	10700		BG	P	KN
10658	d		P	KN	10701	d		P	KN
10660	d		P	ZD	10702			SS	YS.
10662			P	ZD	10703	d		P	SR	IS
10663	d		P	SR	IS	10704	d		P	ZD
10664		DS	A	KN	10706	d		P	SR	IS
10665		BG	P	ZG	10707			P	ZG
10666			P	SR	IS	10708	d		P	ZD
10667		DS	A	KN	10709	d		P	ZD
10668	d		P	ZD	10710	d		P	KN
10669		DS	A	KN	10711	d		P	ZD
10670			P	KN	10712	d		P	ZD
10672	d		P	ZG	10713	d		P	ZD
10674	d		P	ZG	10714	d		P	SR	IS
10675	d		P	SR	IS	10715	d		P	ZD
10676		DS	A	KN	10716	d		P	ZD
10677		DS	A	KN	10717	d		P	ZD
10678		BG	P	KN	10718	d		P	SR	IS
10679		BG	P	KN	10719	d		P	SR	IS
10680	d		P	SR	IS	10720			P	KN
10681		DS	A	KN	10721		DS	A	KN
10682	d		P	ZD	10722	d		P	SR	IS
10683	d		P	SR	IS	10723	d		P	SR	IS
10684		BG	P	KN	10724			SS	FK
10685	d		P	ZH	10725			SS	YS
10686	d		P	ZD	10726			SS	YS
10687	d		P	ZD	10727			SS	YS
10688	d		P	ZD	10728			P	ZN
10689	d		P	SR	IS	10729			SS	FK

| 10730 d | P | ZD | | 10732 d | P | KN |
| 10731 d | P | KN | | | | |

AD1G (FO)   OPEN FIRST

Dia. AD108. Mark 3A. Air conditioned. 11905–7. 48/– 2T (w 47/– 2T 1W). BT10 bogies. d. ETH 6X.

11005–7 were open composites 11905–7 for a time.

Lot No. 30878 Derby 1975–6. 34.3 t.

r Further refurbished with table lamps and burgundy seat trim.
* Disabled toilet, but no wheelchair space (48/_ 1T 1TD).
† Cellnet mobile phones display area. 44/– 2T.

Non-standard Livery: 0 As **V** but blue instead of red and Cellnet logos.

11005		P	VW	PC		11031 r	V	P	VW	MA
11006		P	VW	PC		11033		P	VW	PC
11007 w		P	VW	PC		11036 r	V	P	VW	MA
11011 r*	V	P	VW	MA		11037 r	V	P	VW	PC
11013		P	VW	PC		11038 r	V	P	VW	PC
11016 r	V	P	VW	PC		11039 w		P	VW	PC
11017		P	VW	PC		11040 r	V	P	VW	MA
11018 r	V	P	VW	MA		11042 r	V	P	VW	MA
11019 r	V	P	VW	PC		11044 r	V	P	VW	MA
11020 r	V	P	VW	MA		11045 r	V	P	VW	PC
11021 w		P	VW	PC		11046 r	V	P	VW	PC
11023 r	V	P	VW	PC		11048 r	V	P	VW	MA
11024 r	V	P	VW	MA		11052 r	V	P	VW	MA
11026 r†	0	P	VW	MA		11054 r	V	P	VW	PC
11027 r	V	P	VW	MA		11055		P	VW	PC
11028 r	V	P	VW	MA		11058 r	V	P	VW	MA
11029 r	V	P	VW	MA		11060 r	V	P	VW	PC
11030 r	V	P	VW	MA						

AD1H (FO)   OPEN FIRST

Dia. AD109. Mark 3B. Air conditioned. Inter-City 80 seats. 48/– 2T (w 47/– 2T 1W). BT10 bogies. d. ETH 6X.

Lot No. 30982 Derby 1985. 36.5 t.

r Further refurbished with table lamps and new burgundy seat trim.

11064 r	V	P	VW	MA		11072 r	V	P	VW	PC
11065		P	VW	MA		11073 r	V	P	VW	MA
11066		P	VW	PC		11074 r	V	P	VW	MA
11067 r	V	P	VW	PC		11075 w		P	VW	MA
11068		P	VW	MA		11076 r	V	P	VW	PC
11069		P	VW	PC		11077 w		P	VW	MA
11070 w		P	VW	MA		11078 w		P	VW	PC
11071 r	V	P	VW	PC		11079 r	V	P	VW	MA

11080	r	**V**	P	*VW*	MA	11091	pw		P	*VW*	MA
11081	r	**V**	P	*VW*	PC	11092	p		P	*VW*	PC
11082	w		P	*VW*	PC	11093	pw		P	*VW*	PC
11083	pr	**V**	P	*VW*	MA	11094	pr	**V**	P	*VW*	MA
11084	pr	**V**	P	*VW*	MA	11095	p		P	*VW*	PC
11085	pr	**V**	P	*VW*	MA	11096	p		P	*VW*	PC
11086	pr	**V**	P	*VW*	PC	11097	pr	**V**	P	*VW*	MA
11087	p		P	*VW*	PC	11098	p		P	*VW*	PC
11088	p		P	*VW*	PC	11099	pr	**V**	P	*VW*	PC
11089	pr	**V**	P	*VW*	PC	11100	p		P	*VW*	PC
11090	p		P	*VW*	PC	11101	pw		P	*VW*	MA

AD1J (FO)   OPEN FIRST

Dia. AD111. Mark 4. Air conditioned. Known as 'Pullman Open' by GNER.
46/– 1T. BT41 bogies. ETH 6.

11264–71 were cancelled.

Lot No. 31046 Metro-Cammell 1989–92. 39.7 t.

11200		**GN**	F	*GN*	BN	11231	p	**GN**	F	*GN*	BN
11201	p	**GN**	F	*GN*	BN	11232		**GN**	F	*GN*	BN
11202		**GN**	F	*GN*	BN	11233	p	**GN**	F	*GN*	BN
11203	p	**GN**	F	*GN*	BN	11234		**GN**	F	*GN*	BN
11204	p	**GN**	F	*GN*	BN	11235	p	**GN**	F	*GN*	BN
11205		**GN**	F	*GN*	BN	11236		**GN**	F	*GN*	BN
11206		**GN**	F	*GN*	BN	11237	p	**GN**	F	*GN*	BN
11207	p	**GN**	F	*GN*	BN	11238		**GN**	F	*GN*	BN
11208		**GN**	F	*GN*	BN	11239	p	**GN**	F	*GN*	BN
11209		**GN**	F	*GN*	BN	11240		**GN**	F	*GN*	BN
11210		**GN**	F	*GN*	BN	11241		**GN**	F	*GN*	BN
11211	p	**GN**	F	*GN*	BN	11242	p	**GN**	F	*GN*	BN
11212		**GN**	F	*GN*	BN	11243	p	**GN**	F	*GN*	BN
11213	p	**GN**	F	*GN*	BN	11244		**GN**	F	*GN*	BN
11214	p	**GN**	F	*GN*	BN	11245	p	**GN**	F	*GN*	BN
11215		**GN**	F	*GN*	BN	11246	p	**GN**	F	*GN*	BN
11216		**GN**	F	*GN*	BN	11247	p	**GN**	F	*GN*	BN
11217	p	**GN**	F	*GN*	BN	11248		**GN**	F	*GN*	BN
11218		**GN**	F	*GN*	BN	11249	p	**GN**	F	*GN*	BN
11219	p	**GN**	F	*GN*	BN	11250		**GN**	F	*GN*	BN
11220		**GN**	F	*GN*	BN	11251	p	**GN**	F	*GN*	BN
11221	p	**GN**	F	*GN*	BN	11252		**GN**	F	*GN*	BN
11222	p	**GN**	F	*GN*	BN	11253	p	**GN**	F	*GN*	BN
11223		**GN**	F	*GN*	BN	11254		**GN**	F	*GN*	BN
11224		**GN**	F	*GN*	BN	11255	p	**GN**	F	*GN*	BN
11225	p	**GN**	F	*GN*	BN	11256		**GN**	F	*GN*	BN
11226		**GN**	F	*GN*	BN	11257	p	**GN**	F	*GN*	BN
11227	p	**GN**	F	*GN*	BN	11258		**GN**	F	*GN*	BN
11228	p	**GN**	F	*GN*	BN	11259	p	**GN**	F	*GN*	BN
11229	p	**GN**	F	*GN*	BN	11260		**GN**	F	*GN*	BN
11230		**GN**	F	*GN*	BN	11261	p	**GN**	F	*GN*	BN

11262		**GN**	F	*GN*	BN
11263 p		**GN**	F	*GN*	BN
11272		**GN**	F	*GN*	BN
11273		**GN**	F	*GN*	BN

11274		**GN**	F	*GN*	BN
11275		**GN**	F	*GN*	BN
11276		**GN**	F	*GN*	BN

AC2G (TSO)   OPEN STANDARD

Dia. AC213 (AC220 z). Mark 3A. Air conditioned. All now refurbished with modified seat backs and new layout. 12169–72 have been converted from open composites 11908–10/22, formerly FOs 11008–10/22. –/76 2T (w –/74 2T 1W, z _/74 1TD 1T 1W) BT10 (BREL T4 §) bogies. d. ETH 6X.

Lot No. 30877 Derby 1975–7. 34.3 t.

r Further refurbished with new light blue seat trim.
* Further refurbished with new light blue seat trim. –/70 1TD 1T 2W.

12004			P	*VW*	PC
12005			P	*VW*	PC
12007	r	**V**	P	*VW*	MA
12008	r	**V**	P	*VW*	MA
12009			P	*VW*	PC
12010	r	**V**	P	*VW*	MA
12011	r	**V**	P	*VW*	PC
12012			P	*VW*	PC
12013	r	**V**	P	*VW*	MA
12014			P	*VW*	PC
12015			P	*VW*	PC
12016			P	*VW*	PC
12017	r	**V**	P	*VW*	MA
12019			P	*VW*	PC
12020	r	**V**	P	*VW*	MA
12021			P	*VW*	PC
12022	r	**V**	P	*VW*	MA
12023			P	*VW*	PC
12024	w		P	*VW*	PC
12025	r	**V**	P	*VW*	MA
12026			P	*VW*	PC
12027	r	**V**	P	*VW*	MA
12028	r	**V**	P	*VW*	MA
12029			P	*VW*	PC
12030			P	*VW*	PC
12031			P	*VW*	PC
12032	r	**V**	P	*VW*	PC
12033	z*	**V**	P	*VW*	MA
12034	r	**V**	P	*VW*	MA
12035	r	**V**	P	*VW*	PC
12036	w		P	*VW*	PC
12037	r	**V**	P	*VW*	PC
12038			P	*VW*	PC
12040	r	**V**	P	*VW*	PC
12041	r	**V**	P	*VW*	PC
12042	*	**V**	P	*VW*	PC
12043	r	**V**	P	*VW*	MA
12044	r	**V**	P	*VW*	MA
12045	r	**V**	P	*VW*	MA
12046	r	**V**	P	*VW*	PC
12047	z		P	*VW*	PC
12048	r	**V**	P	*VW*	PC
12049			P	*VW*	PC
12050	*	**V**	P	*VW*	PC
12051			P	*VW*	PC
12052			P	*VW*	PC
12053	r	**V**	P	*VW*	MA
12054	*	**V**	P	*VW*	MA
12055			P	*VW*	PC
12056			P	*VW*	PC
12057	r	**V**	P	*VW*	MA
12058	r	**V**	P	*VW*	PC
12059	w		P	*VW*	PC
12060			P	*VW*	PC
12061	w		P	*VW*	PC
12062			P	*VW*	PC
12063	r	**V**	P	*VW*	MA
12064			P	*VW*	MA
12065	r	**V**	P	*VW*	MA
12066	r	**V**	P	*VW*	MA
12067	r	**V**	P	*VW*	MA
12068			P	*VW*	PC
12069	r	**V**	P	*VW*	MA
12070	w		P	*VW*	PC
12071			P	*VW*	PC
12072	r	**V**	P	*VW*	MA
12073	r	**V**	P	*VW*	MA
12075	r	**V**	P	*VW*	PC

12076		P	VW	PC	12124		P	VW	PC
12077 r	V	P	VW	PC	12125		P	VW	MA
12078 r	V	P	VW	MA	12126 r	V	P	VW	MA
12079		P	VW	PC	12127 r	V	P	VW	PC
12080 r	V	P	VW	PC	12128 *	V	P	VW	MA
12081 r	V	P	VW	PC	12129		P	VW	PC
12082 r	V	P	VW	PC	12130 r	V	P	VW	MA
12083 r	V	P	VW	MA	12131 r	V	P	VW	PC
12084		P	VW	PC	12132		P	VW	PC
12085 *	V	P	VW	MA	12133 r	V	P	VW	MA
12086 *	V	P	VW	MA	12134 r	V	P	VW	PC
12087 *	V	P	VW	PC	12135		P	VW	PC
12088 r	V	P	VW	PC	12136 r	V	P	VW	PC
12089		P	VW	PC	12137 r	V	P	VW	PC
12090		P	VW	PC	12138 r	V	P	VW	PC
12091		P	VW	PC	12139 r	V	P	VW	MA
12092 r	V	P	VW	MA	12140 *§	V	P	VW	PC
12093 r	V	P	VW	PC	12141		P	VW	PC
12094 r	V	P	VW	PC	12142 *	V	P	VW	PC
12095 r	V	P	VW	MA	12143 r	V	P	VW	PC
12096 r	V	P	VW	PC	12144 w		P	VW	PC
12097		P	VW	PC	12145 r	V	P	VW	MA
12098 r	V	P	VW	PC	12146		P	VW	PC
12099 r	V	P	VW	PC	12147 r	V	P	VW	PC
12100 *z	V	P	VW	PC	12148 r	V	P	VW	PC
12101 *	V	P	VW	PC	12149 r	V	P	VW	PC
12102 r	V	P	VW	PC	12150 r	V	P	VW	PC
12103 w		P	VW	PC	12151 r	V	P	VW	PC
12104 r	V	P	VW	MA	12152 r	V	P	VW	PC
12105		P	VW	PC	12153 r	V	P	VW	PC
12106 r	V	P	VW	MA	12154 r	V	P	VW	MA
12107		P	VW	PC	12155 *	V	P	VW	PC
12108 w		P	VW	PC	12156 r	V	P	VW	MA
12109 w		P	VW	MA	12157		P	VW	MA
12110		P	VW	MA	12158 r	V	P	VW	PC
12111 r	V	P	VW	MA	12159		P	VW	PC
12112 z*	V	P	VW	MA	12160 w		P	VW	PC
12113 r	V	P	VW	MA	12161 *z	V	P	VW	MA
12114 r	V	P	VW	PC	12163 r	V	P	VW	MA
12115 w		P	VW	PC	12164 r	V	P	VW	PC
12116 r	V	P	VW	PC	12165 r	V	P	VW	MA
12117 r	V	P	VW	MA	12166 r	V	P	VW	PC
12118 r	V	P	VW	MA	12167		P	VW	PC
12119 r	V	P	VW	MA	12168 *	V	P	VW	PC
12120		P	VW	MA	12169 *	V	P	VW	MA
12121 r	V	P	VW	PC	12170 *	V	P	VW	MA
12122 z*	V	P	VW	MA	12171 w		P	VW	PC
12123 r	V	P	VW	PC	12172 z		P	VW	PC

AI2J (TSOE)   OPEN STANDARD (END)

Dia. AI201. Mark 4. Air conditioned. –/74 2T. BT41 bogies. ETH 6.

Lot No. 31047 Metro-Cammell 1989–91. 39.5 t.

12232 was converted from the original 12405.

12200	**GN**	F	*GN*	BN		12216	**GN**	F	*GN*	BN
12201	**GN**	F	*GN*	BN		12217	**GN**	F	*GN*	BN
12202	**GN**	F	*GN*	BN		12218	**GN**	F	*GN*	BN
12203	**GN**	F	*GN*	BN		12219	**GN**	F	*GN*	BN
12204	**GN**	F	*GN*	BN		12220	**GN**	F	*GN*	BN
12205	**GN**	F	*GN*	BN		12222	**GN**	F	*GN*	BN
12206	**GN**	F	*GN*	BN		12223	**GN**	F	*GN*	BN
12207	**GN**	F	*GN*	BN		12224	**GN**	F	*GN*	BN
12208	**GN**	F	*GN*	BN		12225	**GN**	F	*GN*	BN
12209	**GN**	F	*GN*	BN		12226	**GN**	F	*GN*	BN
12210	**GN**	F	*GN*	BN		12227	**GN**	F	*GN*	BN
12211	**GN**	F	*GN*	BN		12228	**GN**	F	*GN*	BN
12212	**GN**	F	*GN*	BN		12229	**GN**	F	*GN*	BN
12213	**GN**	F	*GN*	BN		12230	**GN**	F	*GN*	BN
12214	**GN**	F	*GN*	BN		12231	**GN**	F	*GN*	BN
12215	**GN**	F	*GN*	BN		12232	**GN**	F	*GN*	BN

AL2J (TSOD) OPEN STANDARD (DISABLED ACCESS)

Dia. AL201. Mark 4. Air conditioned. –/72 1TD 1W. BT41 bogies. p. ETH 6.

Lot No. 31048 Metro-Cammell 1989–91. 39.4 t.

12300	**GN**	F	*GN*	BN		12316	**GN**	F	*GN*	BN
12301	**GN**	F	*GN*	BN		12317	**GN**	F	*GN*	BN
12302	**GN**	F	*GN*	BN		12318	**GN**	F	*GN*	BN
12303	**GN**	F	*GN*	BN		12319	**GN**	F	*GN*	BN
12304	**GN**	F	*GN*	BN		12320	**GN**	F	*GN*	BN
12305	**GN**	F	*GN*	BN		12321	**GN**	F	*GN*	BN
12306	**GN**	F	*GN*	BN		12322	**GN**	F	*GN*	BN
12307	**GN**	F	*GN*	BN		12323	**GN**	F	*GN*	BN
12308	**GN**	F	*GN*	BN		12324	**GN**	F	*GN*	BN
12309	**GN**	F	*GN*	BN		12325	**GN**	F	*GN*	BN
12310	**GN**	F	*GN*	BN		12326	**GN**	F	*GN*	BN
12311	**GN**	F	*GN*	BN		12327	**GN**	F	*GN*	BN
12312	**GN**	F	*GN*	BN		12328	**GN**	F	*GN*	BN
12313	**GN**	F	*GN*	BN		12329	**GN**	F	*GN*	BN
12314	**GN**	F	*GN*	BN		12330	**GN**	F	*GN*	BN
12315	**GN**	F	*GN*	BN						

AC2J (TSO)   OPEN STANDARD

Dia. AC214. Mark 4. Air conditioned. –/74 2T. BT41 bogies. ETH 6X.

Lot No. 31049 Metro-Cammell 1989 onwards. 39.9 t.

12405 is the second coach to carry that number. It was built from the bodyshell originally intended for 12221. The original 12405 is now 12232. 12490–12512 were cancelled.

12400	GN	F	GN	BN	12441	GN	F	GN	BN
12401	GN	F	GN	BN	12442	GN	F	GN	BN
12402	GN	F	GN	BN	12443	GN	F	GN	BN
12403	GN	F	GN	BN	12444	GN	F	GN	BN
12404	GN	F	GN	BN	12445	GN	F	GN	BN
12405	GN	F	GN	BN	12446	GN	F	GN	BN
12406	GN	F	GN	BN	12447	GN	F	GN	BN
12407	GN	F	GN	BN	12448	GN	F	GN	BN
12408	GN	F	GN	BN	12449	GN	F	GN	BN
12409	GN	F	GN	BN	12450	GN	F	GN	BN
12410	GN	F	GN	BN	12451	GN	F	GN	BN
12411	GN	F	GN	BN	12452	GN	F	GN	BN
12412	GN	F	GN	BN	12453	GN	F	GN	BN
12413	GN	F	GN	BN	12454	GN	F	GN	BN
12414	GN	F	GN	BN	12455	GN	F	GN	BN
12415	GN	F	GN	BN	12456	GN	F	GN	BN
12416	GN	F	GN	BN	12457	GN	F	GN	BN
12417	GN	F	GN	BN	12458	GN	F	GN	BN
12418	GN	F	GN	BN	12459	GN	F	GN	BN
12419	GN	F	GN	BN	12460	GN	F	GN	BN
12420	GN	F	GN	BN	12461	GN	F	GN	BN
12421	GN	F	GN	BN	12462	GN	F	GN	BN
12422	GN	F	GN	BN	12463	GN	F	GN	BN
12423	GN	F	GN	BN	12464	GN	F	GN	BN
12424	GN	F	GN	BN	12465	GN	F	GN	BN
12425	GN	F	GN	BN	12466	GN	F	GN	BN
12426	GN	F	GN	BN	12467	GN	F	GN	BN
12427	GN	F	GN	BN	12468	GN	F	GN	BN
12428	GN	F	GN	BN	12469	GN	F	GN	BN
12429	GN	F	GN	BN	12470	GN	F	GN	BN
12430	GN	F	GN	BN	12471	GN	F	GN	BN
12431	GN	F	GN	BN	12472	GN	F	GN	BN
12432	GN	F	GN	BN	12473	GN	F	GN	BN
12433	GN	F	GN	BN	12474	GN	F	GN	BN
12434	GN	F	GN	BN	12475	GN	F	GN	BN
12435	GN	F	GN	BN	12476	GN	F	GN	BN
12436	GN	F	GN	BN	12477	GN	F	GN	BN
12437	GN	F	GN	BN	12478	GN	F	GN	BN
12438	GN	F	GN	BN	12479	GN	F	GN	BN
12439	GN	F	GN	BN	12480	GN	F	GN	BN
12440	GN	F	GN	BN	12481	GN	F	GN	BN

12482	**GN**	F	*GN*	BN	12522	**GN**	F	*GN*	BN
12483	**GN**	F	*GN*	BN	12523	**GN**	F	*GN*	BN
12484	**GN**	F	*GN*	BN	12524	**GN**	F	*GN*	BN
12485	**GN**	F	*GN*	BN	12525	**GN**	F	*GN*	BN
12486	**GN**	F	*GN*	BN	12526	**GN**	F	*GN*	BN
12487	**GN**	F	*GN*	BN	12527	**GN**	F	*GN*	BN
12488	**GN**	F	*GN*	BN	12528	**GN**	F	*GN*	BN
12489	**GN**	F	*GN*	BN	12529	**GN**	F	*GN*	BN
12513	**GN**	F	*GN*	BN	12530	**GN**	F	*GN*	BN
12514	**GN**	F	*GN*	BN	12531	**GN**	F	*GN*	BN
12515	**GN**	F	*GN*	BN	12532	**GN**	F	*GN*	BN
12516	**GN**	F	*GN*	BN	12533	**GN**	F	*GN*	BN
12517	**GN**	F	*GN*	BN	12534	**GN**	F	*GN*	BN
12518	**GN**	F	*GN*	BN	12535	**GN**	F	*GN*	BN
12519	**GN**	F	*GN*	BN	12536	**GN**	F	*GN*	BN
12520	**GN**	F	*GN*	BN	12537	**GN**	F	*GN*	BN
12521	**GN**	F	*GN*	BN	12538	**GN**	F	*GN*	BN

AA11 (FK)   CORRIDOR FIRST

Dia. AA101. Mark 1. 42/– 2T. ETH 3.

13225–13230. Lot No. 30381 Swindon 1959. B4 bogies. 33 t.
13306–13341. Lot No. 30667 Swindon 1962. Commonwealth bogies. 36 t.

f Fluorescent lighting.

13225	k	**RR**	F		CP			
13227	xk	**CH**	RV	*ON*	CP			
13228	xk	**M**	SP		BT			
13229	xk	**M**	SP	*ON*	BT			
13230	xk	**M**	SP	*ON*	BT			
13306	v	**BG**	WC		KM			
13318			CN		FK			
13320	v	**BG**	WC		CS			
13321	x	**M**	WC	*ON*	CS			
13323	xf	**M**	WC		CS			
13331	vf	**N**	LW		CP			
13341	f	**W**	CN		FK			

AA1D (FK)   CORRIDOR FIRST

Dia. AA109. Mark 2D. Air conditioned. Stones equipment. 42/– 2T. B4 bogies.
13585–13607 require at least 800 V train supply. ETH 5.

Lot No. 30825 Derby 1971–2. 34.5 t.

13575	**N**	F		OM	13604	CN	BN
13582		E		KN	13607	CN	FK
13585		CN		KN			

AA31 (CK)   CORRIDOR COMPOSITE

Dia. AA301. Mark 1. 24/18 1T. ETH 2.

Lot No. 30665 Derby 1961. Commonwealth bogies and metal window frames.
37 t. Numbered 7167 for a time.

16167 v   **N**   VS   SL

AB11 (BFK)   CORRIDOR BRAKE FIRST

Dia. AB101. Mark 1. 24/– 1T. Commonwealth bogies. ETH 2.

17007. Lot No. 30382 Swindon 1959. 35 t.
17013–17019. Lot No. 30668 Swindon 1961. 36 t.
17023. Lot No. 30718 Swindon 1963. Metal window frames. 36 t.

Originally numbered 14007/13/15/19/23.

17007 x	**PC**	O	*OS*	SZ		17019 v	**M**	O	*OS*	BQ
17013 v	**M**	FS		SZ		17023 x	**G**	RS	*ON*	BN
17015 x	**BG**	RS	*ON*	BN						

AB1Z (BFK)   CORRIDOR BRAKE FIRST

Dia. AB102. Mark 2. Pressure ventilated. 24/– 1T. B4 bogies. ETH 4.

Lot No. 30756 Derby 1966. 31.5 t.

Originally numbered 14039.

17039 v	**RX**	F	*E*	CD

AB1A (BFK)   CORRIDOR BRAKE FIRST

Dia. AB103. Mark 2A. Pressure ventilated. 24/– 1T. B4 bogies. ETH 4.

17056–17077. Lot No. 30775 Derby 1967–8. 32 t.
17086–17102. Lot No. 30786 Derby 1968. 32 t.

Originally numbered 14056–102. 17090 was numbered 35503 for a time when declassified.

17096 is leased to the Venice Simplon Orient Express.

17056	**N**	RV		CP		17090 v	**RR**	F		LT
17058	**N**	F		LM		17091 v	**RR**	F		LT
17064 v	**RR**	F		LT		17096	**G**	F	*ON*	SL
17073	**N**	F		LM		17099 v	**RR**	F		LT
17077	**FT**	F	*CA*	CF		17102	**M**	WC	*ON*	CS
17086	**FT**	F	*CA*	CF						

AB1D (BFK)   CORRIDOR BRAKE FIRST

Dia. AB106. Mark 2D. Air conditioned (Stones equipment). 24/– 1T. B4 Bogies. 17163–17172 require at least 800 V train heat supply. ETH 5.

Lot No. 30823 Derby 1971–2. 33.5 t.

Non-Standard Livery: 17141 & 17164 are as **WV** but without lining.

Originally numbered 14141–72.

17141	**0**	CN		FK		17148		F	KN
17144		VS		DY		17151		VS	CP
17146		CN		DY		17153	**W**	CN	CS

17155		F	KN		17166		F		LT
17156		CN	DY		17167		CN		CP
17159		RV	CP		17168	M	WC ON		CS
17161		E	OM		17169		CN		CS
17163		F	KN		17170		CN		DY
17164	0	RV	CP		17171		E		KM
17165		CN	FK		17172		CN		FK

AE1G (BFO)   OPEN BRAKE FIRST

Dia. AE101. Mark 3B. Air conditioned. Fitted with hydraulic handbrake. 36/–
1T (35/– 1T w). BT10 bogies. pg. d. ETH 5X.

Lot No. 30990 Derby 1986. 35.8 t.

r Refurbished with table lamps and burgundy seat trim.

17173			P	VW	PC		17175	w		P	VW	PC
17174	r	V	P	VW	PC							

AB31 (BCK)   CORRIDOR BRAKE COMPOSITE

Dia. AB301 (AB302*). Mark 1. There are two variants depending upon whether
the standard class compartments have armrests. Each vehicle has two first
class and three standard class compartments. 12/18 2T (12/24 2T *). ETH 2.

21096. Lot No. 30185. Metro-Cammell 1956. BR Mark 1 bogies. Steam heat
only. 32.5 t.
21224. Lot No. 30245. Metro-Cammell 1958. B4 bogies. 33 t.
21236–21246. Lot No. 30669 Swindon 1961–2. Commonwealth bogies. 36 t.
21256. Lot No. 30731 Derby 1963. Commonwealth bogies. 37 t.
21265–21272. Lot No. 30732 Derby 1964. Commonwealth bogies. 37 t.

21096	x	M	O	OS	BQ		21256	x	M	WC ON		CS
21224		RB	VS	ON	CP		21265	*	BG	WC		KM
21236	v	M	RV	OS	ZG		21266	*		FS		SZ
21241	x		SP		BT		21268	*		FS		SZ
21245	x	CC	RS	ON	BN		21269	*	WV	RS	ON	BN
21246		BG	RS	ON	BN		21272	x*	CH	RV		CP

AA21 (SK)   CORRIDOR STANDARD

Dia. AA201 (AA202*). Mark 1. There are two variants depending upon whether
the standard class compartments have armrests. Each vehicle has eight compartments. All remaining vehicles have metal window frames and melamine
interior panelling. Commonwealth bogies. –/48 2T (–/64 2T *). ETH 4.

25729–25893. Lot No. 30685 Derby 1961–2. 36 t.
25955. Lot No. 30686 Derby 1962. 36 t.
26013. Lot No. 30719 Derby 1962. 37 t.

Non-Standard Livery: 25767, 25837, 25893 & 26013 are Pilkington's K (green with white red chevron and light blue block).

f Facelifted with fluorescent lighting.

† Rebuilt internally as TSO using components from 4936. –/64 2T.

These coaches were renumbered 18729–19013 for a time.

25729	x*f	**M**	WC	*ON*	CS	25837	x	**O**	WC *ON*	CS
25756	x	**M**	WC	*ON*	CS	25862	x	**M**	WC *ON*	CS
25767	x	**O**	WC	*ON*	CS	25893	x	**O**	WC *ON*	CS
25806	x†	**M**	WC	*ON*	CS	25955	x*f	**M**	WC *ON*	CS
25808	x	**M**	WC	*ON*	CS	26013	x	**O**	WC *ON*	CS

AB21 (BSK)   CORRIDOR BRAKE STANDARD

Dia. AB201 (AB202*). Mark 1. There are two variants depending upon whether the standard class compartments have armrests. Each variant has four compartments. Lots 30699, 30721 and 30728 have metal window frames and melamine interior panelling Commonwealth bogies. –/24 1T (* –/32 1T). ETH2.

g Converted to a generator vehicle for electric train supply.

34525–34556. Lot No. 30095 Wolverton 1955. BR Mark 1 bogies. 34 t. (34525 C 36 t.).
34952–34991. Lot No. 30229 Metro-Cammell 1956–7. BR Mark 1 bogies. 34 t. (34991 C 36 t.).
35073. Lot No. 30233 Gloucester 1956–7. BR Mark 1 bogies. 35 t.
35185–35207. Lot No. 30427 Wolverton 1959. B4 bogies. 33 t.
35290. Lot No. 30573 Gloucester 1960. B4 bogies. 33 t.
35317–35333. Lot No. 30699 Wolverton 1962–3. Commonwealth bogies. 37 t.
35407, 35452–35486. Lot No. 30721 Wolverton 1963. Commonwealth bogies. 37 t.
35449. Lot No. 30728 Wolverton 1963. Commonwealth bogies. 37 t.

Non-Standard Liveries: 35290 is black. 35407 is in London & North Western Railway livery.

34525	g	**M**	GS		CS	35449	v	**CH**	O	*OS*	SZ
34556	v	**BG**	VS		SL	35452	x	**RR**	F	*NW*	OY
34952	v*	**BG**	VS		SL	35453	x	**CH**	RV	*ON*	CP
34991	*	**PC**	VS	*ON*	SL	35457	v	**M**	O	*OS*	BQ
35073	v	**M**	WC		CS	35459	x	**M**	WC *ON*	CS
35185	x	**M**	SP		BT	35461	x	**CH**	RV		CP
35204	v	**M**	VS		SL	35463	v	**M**	WC *OS*	CS
35207	x*	**CC**	VS	*OS*	SL	35465	x	**WV**	LW	*OS*	CQ
35290	v	**O**	CN		CQ	35467	v	**M**	RV	*OS*	KR
35317	v	**M**	WT	*ON*	CS	35468	v	**M**	NR	*OS*	YM
35329	v	**G**	MH	*ON*	RL	35469	xg	**CC**	RS	*ON*	BN
35333	x	**CH**	O	*OS*	DI	35470	v	**CH**	O	*OS*	TM
35407	xg	**O**	SH	*ON*	CJ	35486	v	**M**	O	*OS*	KR

AB2A/AB2C (BSK)   CORRIDOR BRAKE STANDARD

Dia. AB204. Mark 2A (2C*). Pressure ventilated. Renumbered from BFK. –/24 1T. B4 bogies. ETH 4.

35507–9/11. Lot No. 30796 Derby 1969–70. 32.5 t.
35510/12–14. Lot No. 30775 Derby 1967–68. 32 t.
35515–18. Lot No. 30786 Derby 1968. 32 t.

§ Cage removed from brake compartment. Now used as first class again (24/– 1T)

35507	(14123, 17123)	*	**RR**	F		LM
35508	(14128, 17128)	*	**RR**	CN		CP
35509	(14138, 17138)	*	**RR**	F		ZH
35510	(14075, 17075)		**RR**	F		LM
35511	(14130, 17130)	*	**RR**	F		KN
35512	(14057, 17057)	§	**RR**	F	NW	OY
35513	(14063, 17063)	§	**RR**	F	NW	OY
35514	(14069, 17069)	§	**RR**	F	NW	OY
35515	(14079, 17079)	§	**RR**	F	NW	OY
35516	(14080, 17080)	§	**RR**	F	NW	OY
35517	(14088, 17088)	§	**RR**	F	NW	OY
35518	(14097, 17097)	§	**RR**	F	NW	OY

NAMED COACHES

The following miscellaneous coaches carry names:

1659	CAMELOT	5212	CAPERKAILZIE
1683	CAROL	5275	Wendy
1953	LANCASTRIAN	5350	Dawn
3065	ORCHID	5364	Andrea
3105	Julia	5365	Deborah
3125	LOCH SHIEL	5373	Felicity
3130	BERYL	5376	Michaela
3181	MONARCH	5378	Sarah
3188	SOVEREIGN	9385	BALMACARA
3240	PENDENNIS	9388	BAILECHAUL
3267	TREGENNA	9417	Ellen
3273	RESTORMEL	10569	LEVIATHAN
5132	CLAN MUNRO	17007	MERCATOR
5154	CLAN FRASER	17077	Catherine
5166	CLAN MACKENZIE	17086	Georgina
5191	CLAN DONALD	34991	BAGGAGE CAR No. 9
5193	CLAN MACLEOD	35449	ELIZABETH

2.2. HIGH SPEED TRAIN TRAILER CARS

GENERAL INFORMATION

HSTs normally run in formations of 7 or 8 trailer cars with a Class 43 locomotive at each end. All trailer vehicles are classified Mark 3 and have BT10 bogies with disc brakes. Heating is by a three-phase electric supply and all trailer vehicles have air conditioning. Maximum speed is 125 m.p.h.

All vehicles underwent a mid-life refurbishment in the 1980s, and they are at present undergoing further refurbishment. Each train operating company (TOC) has adopted a different scheme:

First Great Western: Green seat covers and extra partitions between seat bays.

Great North Eastern Railway: New ceiling lighting panels and brown seat covers. First class vehicles have table lamps and imitation walnut plastic end panels.

Virgin Cross-Country: Green seat covers and standard class vehicles have four seats in the centre of each carriage replaced with a luggage stack.

Midland Mainline: Grey seat covers, redesigned seat squabs, side carpeting and two seats in the centre of each carriage replaced with a luggage stack. All vehicles re-liveried in TOC colours have been refurbished.

Tops Type Codes

TOPS type codes for HST trailer cars are made up as follows:

(1) Two letters denoting the layout of the vehicle as follows:

GH	Open
GJ	Open with Guard's compartment.
GK	Buffet
GL	Kitchen
GN	Buffet

(2) A digit denoting the class of passenger accommodation

1	First
2	Standard (formerly second)
4	Unclassified

(3) A suffix relating to the build of coach.

G	Mark 3

Operating Codes

Normal operating codes are given in parentheses after TOPS type codes. These are as follows:

TCSD	Trailer Conductor's Standard	TRFK	Trailer Kitchen First
TF	Trailer First	TRFM	Trailer Modular Buffet First
TGS	Trailer Guard's Standard	TRSB	Trailer Buffet Standard
TRB	Trailer Buffet First (ex-TRSB)	TS	Trailer Standard
TRFB	Trailer Buffet First		

GN4G (TRB)   TRAILER BUFFET FIRST

Dia. GN401. Converted from TRSB by fitting first class seats. Renumbered from 404xx series by subtracting 200. d p q. 23/– (w 22/– 1W).

40204–40228. Lot No. 30883 BREL Derby 1976–7. 36.12 t.
40231. Lot No. 30899 BREL Derby 1978–9. 36.12 t.

40204	**GW**	A	*GW*	LA	40210	**GW**	A	*GW*	PM
40205	**GW**	A	*GW*	PM	40212 w		P	*VX*	LA
40206	**GW**	A	*GW*	PM	40213	**GW**	A	*GW*	PM
40207	**GW**	A	*GW*	PM	40221	**GW**	A	*GW*	PM
40208	**GW**	A	*GW*	LA	40228	**GW**	A	*GW*	PM
40209	**GW**	A	*GW*	PM	40231	**GW**	A	*GW*	PM

GK2G (TRSB)   TRAILER BUFFET STANDARD

Dia. GK202. Renumbered from 400xx series by adding 400. d p q. –/33 1W.

40401–40427. Lot No. 30883 BREL Derby 1976–7. 36.12 t.
40429–40437. Lot No. 30899 BREL Derby 1978–9. 36.12 t.

40411/32–4 were numbered 40211/32–4 for a time when fitted with first class seats.

40401	**V**	P	*VX*	LA	40424		P	*VX*	LA
40402	**V**	P	*VX*	LA	40425		P	*VX*	LA
40403		P	*VX*	LA	40426		P	*VX*	LA
40411	**V**	P	*VX*	LA	40427	**V**	P	*VX*	LA
40414		P	*VX*	LA	40429	**V**	P	*VX*	LA
40415	**V**	P	*VX*	LA	40430		P	*VX*	LA
40416		P	*VX*	LA	40432	**V**	P	*VX*	LA
40417		P	*VX*	LA	40433	**V**	P	*VX*	LA
40418	**V**	P	*VX*	LA	40434	**V**	P	*VX*	LA
40419		P	*VX*	LA	40435	**V**	P	*VX*	LA
40420	**V**	P	*VX*	LA	40436	**V**	P	*VX*	LA
40422	**V**	P	*VX*	LA	40437	**V**	P	*VX*	LA
40423	**V**	P	*VX*	LA					

GL1G (TRFK)   TRAILER KITCHEN FIRST

Dia. GL101. Reclassified from TRUK. d p q. 24/–.

Lot No. 30884 BREL Derby 1976–7. 37 t.

40501		P		ZD	40513 d		P	ZD

GK1G (TRFM)   TRAILER MODULAR BUFFET FIRST

Dia. GK102. Conversion of TRFB 40719 to modular catering. d p q. 17/–.

Lot No. 30921 BREL Derby 1978–9. 38.16 t.

40619	P	*VX*	LA

GK1G (TRFB)   TRAILER BUFFET FIRST

Dia. GK101. These vehicles have larger kitchens than 402xx and 404xx series vehicles, and are used in trains where full meal service is required. They were renumbered from the 403xx series (in which the seats were unclassified) by adding 400 to previous number. d p q. 17/–.

40700–40721. Lot No. 30921 BREL Derby 1978–9. 38.16 t.
40722–40735. Lot No. 30940 BREL Derby 1979–80. 38.16 t.
40736–40753. Lot No. 30948 BREL Derby 1980–1. 38.16 t.
40754–40757. Lot No. 30966 BREL Derby 1982. 38.16 t.

40700	**MM**	P	*MM*	NL	40730	**MM**	P	*MM*	NL
40701	**MM**	P	*MM*	NL	40731	**GW**	A	*GW*	LA
40702	**MM**	P	*MM*	NL	40732		A	*VW*	LA
40703	**GW**	A	*GW*	LA	40733	**GW**	A	*GW*	LA
40704	**GN**	A	*GN*	EC	40734	**GW**	A	*GW*	LA
40705	**GN**	A	*GN*	EC	40735	**GN**	A	*GN*	EC
40706	**GN**	A	*GN*	EC	40736	**GW**	A	*GW*	LA
40707	**GW**	A	*GW*	LA	40737	**GN**	A	*GN*	EC
40708	**MM**	P	*MM*	NL	40738	**GW**	A	*GW*	LA
40709	**GW**	A	*GW*	LA	40739	**GW**	A	*GW*	PM
40710		A	*GW*	LA	40740	**GN**	A	*GN*	EC
40711	**GN**	A	*GN*	EC	40741	**MM**	P	*MM*	NL
40712	**GW**	A	*GW*	LA	40742		A	*VW*	LA
40713	**GW**	A	*GW*	LA	40743	**GW**	A	*GW*	LA
40714	**GW**	A	*GW*	PM	40744	**GW**	A	*GW*	PM
40715	**GW**	A	*GW*	PM	40745	**GW**	A	*GW*	LA
40716	**GW**	A	*GW*	PM	40746	**MM**	P	*MM*	NL
40717	**GW**	A	*GW*	PM	40747		A	*GW*	PM
40718	**GW**	A	*GW*	LA	40748	**GN**	A	*GN*	EC
40720	**GN**	A	*GN*	EC	40749	**MM**	P	*MM*	NL
40721	**GW**	A	*GW*	LA	40750	**GN**	A	*GN*	EC
40722	**GW**	A	*GW*	LA	40751	**MM**	P	*MM*	NL
40723		A	*VW*	LA	40752	**GW**	A	*GW*	PM
40724	**GW**	A	*GW*	PM	40753	**MM**	P	*MM*	NL
40725	**GW**	A	*GW*	LA	40754	**MM**	P	*MM*	NL
40726	**GW**	A	*GW*	LA	40755	**GW**	A	*GW*	LA
40727	**GW**	A	*GW*	LA	40756	**MM**	P	*MM*	NL
40728	**MM**	P	*MM*	NL	40757	**GW**	A	*GW*	LA
40729	**MM**	P	*MM*	NL					

GH1G (TF)   TRAILER FIRST

Dia. GH102. d. 48/– 2T (w 47/– 2T 1W).

41003–41056. Lot No. 30881 BREL Derby 1976–7. 33.66 t.
41057–41120. Lot No. 30896 BREL Derby 1977–8. 33.66 t.
41121–41148. Lot No. 30938 BREL Derby 1979–80. 33.66 t.
41149–41166. Lot No. 30947 BREL Derby 1980. 33.66 t.
41167–41169. Lot No. 30963 BREL Derby 1982. 33.66 t.

41170. Lot No. 30967 BREL Derby 1982. Former prototype vehicle. 33.66 t.
41178. Lot No. 30882 BREL Derby 1976–7. 33.60 t.
41179/80. Lot No. 30884 BREL Derby 1976–7. 33.60 t.

§ Centre luggage stack. 46/– 1T 1TD 1W.

41170 was converted from 41001. 41178 is a prototype refurbished vehicle converted from 42011 which was damaged by fire. 41179/80 have been converted from 40505 and 40511 respectively.

41003 p	**GW**	A	*GW*	PM		41042 w	**GW**	A	*GW*	PM
41004 w	**GW**	A	*GW*	PM		41043 w	**GN**	A	*GN*	EC
41005 p	**GW**	A	*GW*	PM		41044	**GN**	A	*GN*	EC
41006 w	**GW**	A	*GW*	PM		41045 w		P	*VX*	LA
41007 p		A	*GW*	PM		41046 §	**MM**	P	*MM*	NL
41008 w		A	*GW*	PM		41049		A		ZD
41009 p	**GW**	A	*GW*	LA		41051 w		A	*GW*	LA
41010 w	**GW**	A	*GW*	LA		41052		A	*GW*	LA
41011 p	**GW**	A	*GW*	PM		41055 w	**GW**	A	*GW*	LA
41012 w	**GW**	A	*GW*	PM		41056 w	**GW**	A	*GW*	LA
41013 p	**GW**	A	*GW*	PM		41057	**MM**	P	*MM*	NL
41014 w	**GW**	A	*GW*	PM		41058 §	**MM**	P	*MM*	NL
41015 p	**GW**	A	*GW*	PM		41059 w		P	*VX*	LA
41016 w	**GW**	A	*GW*	PM		41060 w	**GW**	A	*GW*	LA
41017 p		A	*GW*	LA		41061	**MM**	P	*MM*	NL
41018	**GW**	A	*GW*	PM		41062 w	**MM**	P	*MM*	NL
41019 p	**GW**	A	*GW*	PM		41063	**MM**	P	*MM*	EC
41020 w	**GW**	A	*GW*	PM		41064 §	**MM**	P	*MM*	NL
41021 p	**GW**	A	*GW*	PM		41065 w	**GW**	A	*GW*	LA
41022	**GW**	A	*GW*	PM		41066 pw		A	*VW*	LA
41023 p	**GW**	A	*GW*	LA		41067 §	**MM**	P	*MM*	NL
41024 w	**GW**	A	*GW*	LA		41068 §	**MM**	P	*MM*	NL
41025 p		A	*VW*	LA		41069 §	**MM**	P	*MM*	NL
41026		A	*VW*	LA		41070 §	**MM**	P	*MM*	NL
41027 pw	**GW**	A	*GW*	LA		41071	**MM**	P	*MM*	NL
41028 w	**GW**	A	*GW*	LA		41072 §	**MM**	P	*MM*	NL
41029 pw	**GW**	A	*GW*	LA		41075	**MM**	P	*MM*	NL
41030 w	**GW**	A	*GW*	LA		41076 §	**MM**	P	*MM*	NL
41031 p	**GW**	A	*GW*	LA		41077	**MM**	P	*MM*	NL
41032 w	**GW**	A	*GW*	LA		41078	**MM**	P	*MM*	NL
41033 p	**GW**	A	*GW*	LA		41079	**MM**	P	*MM*	NL
41034	**GW**	A	*GW*	LA		41080 §	**MM**	P	*MM*	NL
41035 p		A	*VW*	LA		41081 w	**V**	P	*VX*	LA
41036		A	*VW*	LA		41082 w		P	*VX*	LA
41037 p	**GW**	A	*GW*	LA		41083	**MM**	P	*MM*	NL
41038	**GW**	A	*GW*	LA		41084 §	**MM**	P	*MM*	NL
41039	**GN**	A	*GN*	EC		41085 w	**V**	P	*VX*	LA
41040	**GN**	A	*GN*	EC		41086 w	**V**	P	*VX*	LA
41041 p§	**MM**	P	*MM*	NL		41087	**GN**	A	*GN*	EC

41088	w	**GN**	A	*GN*	EC	41131	p	**GW**	A	*GW*	LA
41089		**GW**	A	*GW*	LA	41132	w	**GW**	A	*GW*	LA
41090	w	**GN**	A	*GN*	EC	41133	p	**GW**	A	*GW*	LA
41091		**GN**	A	*GN*	EC	41134	w	**GW**	A	*GW*	LA
41092	w	**GN**	A	*GN*	EC	41135	p	**GW**	A	*GW*	LA
41093		**GW**	A	*GW*	LA	41136	w	**GW**	A	*GW*	PM
41094		**GW**	A	*GW*	LA	41137	pw	**GW**	A	*GW*	PM
41095	w	**V**	P	*VX*	LA	41138	w	**GW**	A	*GW*	PM
41096			P	*VX*	LA	41139	p	**GW**	A	*GW*	LA
41097	w	**GN**	A	*GN*	EC	41140	w	**GW**	A	*GW*	LA
41098	w	**GN**	A	*GN*	EC	41141	pw	**GW**	A	*GW*	LA
41099		**GN**	A	*GN*	EC	41142	w	**GW**	A	*GW*	LA
41100	w	**GN**	A	*GN*	EC	41143	p	**GW**	A	*GW*	LA
41101		**GW**	A	*GW*	LA	41144	w	**GW**	A	*GW*	LA
41102	w	**GW**	A	*GW*	LA	41145	p	**GW**	A	*GW*	PM
41103	w	**GW**	A	*GW*	LA	41146	w	**GW**	A	*GW*	PM
41104	w	**GW**	A	*GW*	LA	41147	w	**V**	P	*VX*	LA
41105		**GW**	A	*GW*	PM	41148	w	**V**	P	*VX*	LA
41106	w	**GW**	A	*GW*	PM	41149	w	**V**	P	*VX*	LA
41107	w	**V**	P	*VX*	LA	41150	w	**GN**	A	*GN*	EC
41108	w	**V**	P	*VX*	LA	41151		**GN**	A	*GN*	EC
41109	w	**V**	P	*VX*	LA	41152		**GN**	A	*GN*	EC
41110		**GW**	A	*GW*	PM	41153		**MM**	P	*MM*	NL
41111		**MM**	P	*MM*	NL	41154	§	**MM**	P	*MM*	NL
41112		**MM**	P	*MM*	NL	41155		**MM**	P	*MM*	NL
41113	§	**MM**	P	*MM*	NL	41156		**MM**	P	*MM*	NL
41114	w		P	*VX*	LA	41157		**GW**	A	*GW*	LA
41115			P	*VX*	LA	41158	w	**GW**	A	*GW*	LA
41116		**GW**	A	*GW*	LA	41159	w		P	*VX*	LA
41117		**MM**	P	*MM*	NL	41160	w	**V**	P	*VX*	LA
41118	w	**GN**	A	*GN*	EC	41161	w		P	*VX*	LA
41119	w	**V**	P	*VX*	LA	41162	w		P	*VX*	LA
41120		**GN**	A	*GN*	EC	41163	w		P	*VX*	LA
41121	p	**GW**	A	*GW*	LA	41164	p		A	*VW*	LA
41122	w	**GW**	A	*GW*	LA	41165	w		P	*VX*	LA
41123	p	**GW**	A	*GW*	PM	41166	w		P	*VX*	LA
41124	w	**GW**	A	*GW*	PM	41167	w	**V**	P	*VX*	LA
41125		**GW**	A	*GW*	PM	41168	w	**V**	P	*VX*	LA
41126	p	**GW**	A	*GW*	PM	41169	w	**V**	P	*VX*	LA
41127	p	**GW**	A	*GW*	PM	41170		**GN**	A	*GN*	EC
41128	w	**GW**	A	*GW*	PM	41178		**GW**	A	*GW*	PM
41129	pw	**GW**	A	*GW*	PM	41179		**GW**	A	*GW*	LA
41130	w	**GW**	A	*GW*	PM	41180		**GW**	A	*GW*	LA

GH2G (TS)   TRAILER STANDARD

Dia. GH203. d. –/76 2T.

42003–42090/42362. Lot No. 30882 BREL Derby 1976–7. 33.60 t.
42091–42250. Lot No. 30897 BREL Derby 1977–9. 33.60 t.
42251–42305. Lot No. 30939 BREL Derby 1979–80. 33.60 t.

42306–42322. Lot No. 30969 BREL Derby 1982. 33.60 t.
42323–42341. Lot No. 30983 BREL Derby 1984–5. 33.60 t.
42342/60. Lot No. 30949 BREL Derby 1982. 33.47 t. Converted from TGS.
42343/5. Lot No. 30970 BREL Derby 1982. 33.47 t. Converted from TGS.
42344/61. Lot No. 30964 BREL Derby 1982. 33.47 t. Converted from TGS.
42346/7/50/1. Lot No. 30881 BREL Derby 1976–7. 33.66 t. Converted from TF.
42348/9. Lot No. 30896 BREL Derby 1977–8. 33.66 t. Converted from TF.
42353/5–7. Lot No. 30967 BREL Derby 1982. Ex prototype vehicles. 33.66 t.
42352/4. Lot No. 30897 BREL Derby 1977. Were TF from 1983 to 1992. 33.66 t.

§ Centre luggage stack –/74 2T (w –72 2T 1W).
† Centre luggage stack –/72 2T.
• Centre luggage stack –/72 2T. pt.
* 5 'Priority' tip-up seats. –/65 1T 1TD.

42158 was also numbered 41177 for a time when fitted with first class seats.

42003		GW	A	GW	PM	42040	GW	A	GW	LA

42003		GW	A	GW	PM	42040		GW	A	GW	LA
42004	*	GW	A	GW	LA	42041		GW	A	GW	LA
42005		GW	A	GW	PM	42042		GW	A	GW	LA
42006	*	GW	A	GW	PM	42043		GW	A	GW	LA
42007	*	GW	A	GW	LA	42044		GW	A	GW	LA
42008	*	GW	A	GW	PM	42045		GW	A	GW	LA
42009		GW	A	GW	PM	42046		GW	A	GW	LA
42010		GW	A	GW	PM	42047		GW	A	GW	LA
42012	*	GW	A	GW	PM	42048		GW	A	GW	LA
42013		GW	A	GW	LA	42049		GW	A	GW	LA
42014		GW	A	GW	LA	42050		GW	A	GW	LA
42015	*	GW	A	GW	PM	42051			A	VW	LA
42016		GW	A	GW	PM	42052			A	VW	LA
42017		GW	A	GW	PM	42053			A	VW	LA
42018	*	GW	A	GW	PM	42054		GW	A	GW	PM
42019		GW	A	GW	PM	42055		GW	A	GW	LA
42020		GW	A	GW	PM	42056		GW	A	GW	LA
42021	*	GW	A	GW	PM	42057		GN	A	GN	EC
42022		GW	A	GW	PM	42058		GN	A	GN	EC
42023		GW	A	GW	PM	42059		GN	A	GN	EC
42024	*	GW	A	GW	LA	42060		GW	A	GW	PM
42025		GW	A	GW	LA	42061		GW	A	GW	PM
42026		GW	A	GW	LA	42062	*	GW	A	GW	LA
42027		GW	A	GW	PM	42063		GN	A	GN	EC
42028		GW	A	GW	PM	42064		GN	A	GN	EC
42029		GW	A	GW	PM	42065		GN	A	GN	EC
42030	*	GW	A	GW	PM	42066	*	GW	A	GW	LA
42031		GW	A	GW	PM	42067	*	GW	A	GW	LA
42032		GW	A	GW	PM	42068		GW	A	GW	LA
42033		GW	A	GW	LA	42069	*	GW	A	GW	PM
42034		GW	A	GW	LA	42070	*	GW	A	GW	PM
42035		GW	A	GW	LA	42071	*	GW	A	GW	PM
42036			A	VW	LA	42072		GW	A	GW	PM
42037			A	VW	LA	42073		GW	A	GW	PM
42038			A	VW	LA	42074		GW	A	GW	PM
42039		GW	A	GW	LA	42075			A	GW	LA

42076			A	GW	LA	42128			P	VX	LA
42077			A	GW	LA	42129		GW	A	GW	LA
42078			A	GW	LA	42130			P	VX	LA
42079			A	GW	PM	42131 §	MM	P	MM	NL
42080			A	GW	PM	42132 §	MM	P	MM	NL
42081 *	GW	A	GW	LA	42133 §	MM	P	MM	NL
42082 *	GW	A	GW	PM	42134			A	VW	LA
42083	GW	A	GW	LA	42135 §	MM	P	MM	NL
42084			P	VX	LA	42136 §	MM	P	MM	NL
42085			P	VX	LA	42137 §	MM	P	MM	NL
42086			P	VX	LA	42138 *	GW	A	GW	PM
42087			P	VX	LA	42139 §	MM	P	MM	NL
42088			P	VX	LA	42140 §	MM	P	MM	NL
42089	GW	A	GW	PM	42141 §	MM	P	MM	NL
42090			P	VX	LA	42143		GW	A	GW	PM
42091			P	VX	LA	42144		GW	A	GW	PM
42092			P	VX	LA	42145		GW	A	GW	PM
42093			P	VX	LA	42146		GN	A	GN	EC
42094			P	VX	LA	42147 §	MM	P	MM	NL
42095			P	VX	LA	42148 §	MM	P	MM	NL
42096 *	GW	A	GW	LA	42149 §	MM	P	MM	NL
42097			A	VW	LA	42150		GN	A	GN	EC
42098 *	GW	A	GW	PM	42151 w§	MM	P	MM	NL
42099 *	GW	A	GW	LA	42152 §	MM	P	MM	NL
42100 §	MM	P	MM	NL	42153 §	MM	P	MM	NL
42101 w§	MM	P	MM	NL	42154			A	GN	EC
42102 §	MM	P	MM	NL	42155 §w	MM	P	MM	NL
42103 †	V	P	VX	LA	42156 §	MM	P	MM	NL
42104	GN	A	GN	EC	42157 §	MM	P	MM	NL
42105			P	VX	LA	42158		GN	A	GN	EC
42106	GN	A	GN	EC	42159			P	VX	LA
42107	GW	A	GW	LA	42160			P	VX	LA
42108			P	VX	LA	42161			P	VX	LA
42109			P	VX	LA	42162 †	V	P	VX	LA
42110			P	VX	LA	42163 §w	MM	P	MM	NL
42111 §	MM	P	MM	NL	42164 §	MM	P	MM	NL
42112 §	MM	P	MM	NL	42165 §	MM	P	MM	NL
42113 §	MM	P	MM	NL	42166 •	V	P	VX	LA
42115			P	VX	LA	42167 †	V	P	VX	LA
42116			P	VX	LA	42168 •	V	P	VX	LA
42117			P	VX	LA	42169 †	V	P	VX	LA
42118	GW	A	GW	PM	42170 †	V	P	VX	LA
42119 §	MM	P	MM	NL	42171		GN	A	GN	EC
42120 §	MM	P	MM	NL	42172		GN	A	GN	EC
42121 §	MM	P	MM	NL	42173 †	V	P	VX	LA
42122			A	VW	LA	42174 †	V	P	VX	LA
42123 §	MM	P	MM	NL	42175			P	VX	LA
42124 §	MM	P	MM	NL	42176			P	VX	LA
42125 §	MM	P	MM	NL	42177			P	VX	LA
42126	GW	A	GW	LA	42178			P	VX	LA
42127			P	VX	LA	42179		GN	A	GN	EC

42180		GN	A	GN	EC	42231		P	VX	LA

Number	Mark	Code1	Code2	Code3	Code4	Number	Mark	Code1	Code2	Code3	Code4
42180		GN	A	GN	EC	42231		P	VX	LA
42181		GN	A	GN	EC	42232		P	VX	LA
42182		GN	A	GN	EC	42233		P	VX	LA
42183 *	GW	A	GW	LA	42234		P	VX	LA
42184	GW	A	GW	LA	42235	GN	A	GN	EC
42185	GW	A	GW	LA	42236		A	GW	PM
42186	GN	A	GN	EC	42237	V	P	VX	LA
42187 †	V	P	VX	LA	42238	V	P	VX	LA
42188 †	V	P	VX	LA	42239	V	P	VX	LA
42189 †	V	P	VX	LA	42240	GN	A	GN	EC
42190	GN	A	GN	EC	42241	GN	A	GN	EC
42191	GN	A	GN	EC	42242	GN	A	GN	EC
42192	GN	A	GN	EC	42243	GN	A	GN	EC
42193	GN	A	GN	EC	42244	GN	A	GN	EC
42194 w§	MM	P	MM	NL	42245	GW	A	GW	LA
42195 †	V	P	VX	LA	42246 †	V	P	VX	LA
42196 *	GW	A	GW	LA	42247 •	V	P	VX	LA
42197	GW	A	GW	PM	42248 †	V	P	VX	LA
42198	GN	A	GN	EC	42249 †	V	P	VX	LA
42199	GN	A	GN	EC	42250	GW	A	GW	LA
42200 *	GW	A	GW	LA	42251 *	GW	A	GW	PM
42201 *	GW	A	GW	LA	42252	GW	A	GW	LA
42202 *	GW	A	GW	LA	42253	GW	A	GW	LA
42203	GW	A	GW	LA	42254 †	V	P	VX	LA
42204	GW	A	GW	LA	42255 *	GW	A	GW	PM
42205 §	MM	P	MM	NL	42256	GW	A	GW	PM
42206 *	GW	A	GW	LA	42257	GW	A	GW	PM
42207 *	GW	A	GW	LA	42258 †	V	P	VX	LA
42208 *	GW	A	GW	LA	42259 *	GW	A	GW	PM
42209	GW	A	GW	LA	42260	GW	A	GW	PM
42210 §	MM	P	MM	NL	42261	GW	A	GW	PM
42211 *	GW	A	GW	PM	42262 †	V	P	VX	LA
42212	GW	A	GW	PM	42263	GW	A	GW	PM
42213	GW	A	GW	PM	42264 *	GW	A	GW	PM
42214	GW	A	GW	PM	42265	GW	A	GW	LA
42215	GN	A	GN	EC	42266 †	V	P	VX	LA
42216	GW	A	GW	LA	42267 *	GW	A	GW	PM
42217 •	V	P	VX	LA	42268 *	GW	A	GW	LA
42218 †	V	P	VX	LA	42269	GW	A	GW	PM
42219	GN	A	GN	EC	42270 †	V	P	VX	LA
42220 w§	MM	P	MM	NL	42271 *	GW	A	GW	LA
42221	GW	A	GW	LA	42272	GW	A	GW	LA
42222 •	V	P	VX	LA	42273	GW	A	GW	LA
42223 †	V	P	VX	LA	42274 •	V	P	VX	LA
42224 †	V	P	VX	LA	42275 *	GW	A	GW	LA
42225 §	MM	P	MM	NL	42276	GW	A	GW	LA
42226	GN	A	GN	EC	42277	GW	A	GW	LA
42227 §	MM	P	MM	NL	42278 †	V	P	VX	LA
42228 §	MM	P	MM	NL	42279 *	GW	A	GW	LA
42229 §	MM	P	MM	NL	42280	GW	A	GW	LA
42230 §	MM	P	MM	NL	42281	GW	A	GW	LA

42282	†	**V**	P	*VX*	LA
42283		**GW**	A	*GW*	LA
42284		**GW**	A	*GW*	PM
42285		**GW**	A	*GW*	PM
42286			P	*VX*	LA
42287	*	**GW**	A	*GW*	LA
42288		**GW**	A	*GW*	LA
42289		**GW**	A	*GW*	LA
42290			P	*VX*	LA
42291	*	**GW**	A	*GW*	LA
42292	*	**GW**	A	*GW*	LA
42293		**GW**	A	*GW*	LA
42294			P	*VX*	LA
42295	*	**GW**	A	*GW*	LA
42296		**GW**	A	*GW*	LA
42297		**GW**	A	*GW*	LA
42298			P	*VX*	LA
42299	*	**GW**	A	*GW*	PM
42300		**GW**	A	*GW*	PM
42301		**GW**	A	*GW*	PM
42302	†	**V**	P	*VX*	LA
42303	•	**V**	P	*VX*	LA
42304	†	**V**	P	*VX*	LA
42305	†	**V**	P	*VX*	LA
42306			P	*VX*	LA
42307			P	*VX*	LA
42308			P	*VX*	LA
42309			P	*VX*	LA
42310	†	**V**	P	*VX*	LA
42311	•	**V**	P	*VX*	LA

42312	†	**V**	P	*VX*	LA
42313	†	**V**	P	*VX*	LA
42314	†	**V**	P	*VX*	LA
42315	•	**V**	P	*VX*	LA
42316	†	**V**	P	*VX*	LA
42317	†	**V**	P	*VX*	LA
42318	†	**V**	P	*VX*	LA
42319	†	**V**	P	*VX*	LA
42320	†	**V**	P	*VX*	LA
42321	†	**V**	P	*VX*	LA
42322			P	*VX*	LA
42323		**GN**	A	*GN*	EC
42324	w§	**MM**	P	*MM*	NL
42325		**GW**	A	*GW*	PM
42326	†	**V**	P	*VX*	LA
42327	w§	**MM**	P	*MM*	NL
42328	w§	**MM**	P	*MM*	NL
42329	w§	**MM**	P	*MM*	NL
42330		**V**	P	*VX*	LA
42331	w§	**MM**	P	*MM*	NL
42332			A	*GW*	LA
42333		**GW**	A	*GW*	LA
42334	†	**V**	P	*VX*	LA
42335	w§	**MM**	P	*MM*	NL
42336			P	*VX*	LA
42337	w§	**MM**	P	*MM*	NL
42338			P	*VX*	LA
42339	w§	**MM**	P	*MM*	NL
42340		**GN**	A	*GN*	EC
42341	§	**MM**	P	*MM*	NL

42342	(44082)			A	*VW*	LA
42343	(44095)		**GW**	A	*GW*	LA
42344	(44092)	*	**GW**	A	*GW*	PM
42345	(44096)	*	**GW**	A	*GW*	LA
42346	(41053)		**GW**	A	*GW*	PM
42347	(41054)	*	**GW**	A	*GW*	PM
42348	(41073)	*	**GW**	A	*GW*	LA
42349	(41074)		**GW**	A	*GW*	PM
42350	(41047)		**GW**	A	*GW*	LA
42351	(41048)		**GW**	A	*GW*	PM
42352	(42142, 41176)	§	**MM**	P	*MM*	NL
42353	(42001, 41171)	†	**V**	P	*VX*	LA
42354	(42114, 41175)		**GN**	A	*GN*	EC
42355	(42000, 41172)			A	*VW*	LA
42356	(42002, 41173)		**GW**	A	*GW*	PM
42357	(41002, 41174)			A	*VW*	LA
42360	(44084, 45084)			A		
42361	(44099)		**GW**	A	*GW*	PM
42362	(42011, 41178)		**GW**	A		

GJ2G (TGS)   TRAILER GUARD'S STANDARD

Dia. GJ205. d p g. –/65 1T (w –/63 1T 1W).

44000. Lot No. 30953 BREL Derby 1980. 33.47 t.
44001–44090. Lot No. 30949 BREL Derby 1980–2. 33.47 t.
44091–44094. Lot No. 30964 BREL Derby 1982. 33.47 t.
44097–44101. Lot No. 30970 BREL Derby 1982. 33.47 t.

§ Centre luggage stack –/63 1T.
† Centre luggage stack –/61 1T.

44000 †	**V**	P	*VX*	LA		44038 w	**GW**	A	*GW*	LA
44001 w	**GW**	A	*GW*	LA		44039 w	**GW**	A	*GW*	LA
44002 w	**GW**	A	*GW*	PM		44040 w	**GW**	A	*GW*	PM
44003 w	**GW**	A	*GW*	PM		44041 §	**MM**	P	*MM*	NL
44004 w	**GW**	A	*GW*	LA		44042		P	*VX*	LA
44005 w	**GW**	A	*GW*	PM		44043 w	**GW**	A	*GW*	LA
44006 w	**GW**	A	*GW*	PM		44044 §	**MM**	P	*MM*	NL
44007 w	**GW**	A	*GW*	PM		44045 w	**GN**	A	*GN*	EC
44008 w	**GW**	A	*GW*	LA		44046 §	**MM**	P	*MM*	NL
44009 w	**GW**	A	*GW*	PM		44047 §	**MM**	P	*MM*	NL
44010 w	**GW**	A	*GW*	PM		44048 §	**MM**	P	*MM*	NL
44011 w	**GW**	A	*GW*	LA		44049 w	**GW**	A	*GW*	PM
44012 w		A	*VW*	LA		44050 §	**MM**	P	*MM*	NL
44013 w	**GW**	A	*GW*	LA		44051 §	**MM**	P	*MM*	NL
44014 w	**GW**	A	*GW*	LA		44052 §	**MM**	P	*MM*	NL
44015 w	**GW**	A	*GW*	LA		44053 w		P	*VX*	LA
44016 w	**GW**	A	*GW*	LA		44054 §	**MM**	P	*MM*	NL
44017 w		A	*VW*	LA		44055 †	**V**	P	*VX*	LA
44018 w	**GW**	A	*GW*	LA		44056 w	**GN**	A	*GN*	EC
44019 w	**GN**	A	*GN*	EC		44057 †	**V**	P	*VX*	LA
44020 w	**GW**	A	*GW*	PM		44058 w	**GN**	A	*GN*	EC
44021		P	*VX*	LA		44059 w	**GW**	A	*GW*	LA
44022 w	**GW**	A	*GW*	LA		44060	**V**	P	*VX*	LA
44023 w	**GW**	A	*GW*	PM		44061 w	**GN**	A	*GN*	EC
44024 w	**GW**	A	*GW*	PM		44062 †	**V**	P	*VX*	LA
44025 w		A	*GW*	LA		44063 w	**GN**	A	*GN*	EC
44026 w		A	*GW*	PM		44064 w	**GW**	A	*GW*	LA
44027 §	**MM**	P	*MM*	NL		44065		P	*VX*	LA
44028 w	**GW**	A	*GW*	LA		44066 w	**GW**	A	*GW*	LA
44029 w	**GW**	A	*GW*	PM		44067 w	**GW**	A	*GW*	PM
44030 w	**GW**	A	*GW*	PM		44068 †	**V**	P	*VX*	LA
44031 w		A	*VW*	LA		44069		P	*VX*	LA
44032 w	**GW**	A	*GW*	PM		44070 §	**MM**	P	*MM*	NL
44033 w	**GW**	A	*GW*	LA		44071 §	**MM**	P	*MM*	NL
44034 w	**GW**	A	*GW*	LA		44072		P	*VX*	LA
44035 w	**GW**	A	*GW*	LA		44073 §	**MM**	P	*MM*	NL
44036 w	**GW**	A	*GW*	PM		44074		P	*VX*	LA
44037 w	**GW**	A	*GW*	LA		44075 †	**V**	P	*VX*	LA

44076		P	VX	LA	44088		P	VX	LA
44077 w	GN	A	GN	EC	44089 †	V	P	VX	LA
44078 †	V	P	VX	LA	44090 †	V	P	VX	LA
44079 †	V	P	VX	LA	44091 †	V	P	VX	LA
44080 w	GN	A	GN	EC	44093 w	GW	A	GW	LA
44081		P	VX	LA	44094 w	GN	A	GN	EC
44083 §	MM	P	MM	NL	44097 †	V	P	VX	LA
44085 §	MM	P	MM	NL	44098 w	GN	A	GN	EC
44086 w	GW	A	GW	LA	44100 †	V	P	VX	LA
44087		P	VX	LA	44101 †	V	P	VX	LA

GH2G (TCSD)   TRAILER CONDUCTOR STANDARD

Dia. GH201. Converted from 44084. Guard's compartment converted to walk-through conductor's compartment with a disabled persons toilet also provided. This car is normally marshalled adjacent to the buffet vehicle. d. –/63.

Lot No. 30949 BREL Derby 1982. 33.47 t.

45084		A	GW	PM

2.3. NIGHTSTAR STOCK

These coaches were designed for use on new 'Nightstar' services between Britain and Continental Europe via the Channel Tunnel. This new generation of overnight trains was to offer high quality accommodation to both business and leisure customers.

The venture was being developed by European Night Services Limited (ENS), a joint company of Eurostar (UK) Ltd., SNCF, DB and NS. It was originally intended that the trains would operate on the following routes:

London Waterloo–Amsterdam CS.
London Waterloo–Dortmund Hbf./Frankfurt Hbf.
Glasgow/Manchester–Paris Nord.
Plymouth/Swansea–Paris Nord.

Unfortunately the project has now been completely cancelled because the project has been bedevilled with both technical and commercial problems, e.g. there is no locomotive in Belgium which has enough power for the train heating and air conditioning!

Both sleeping cars and reclining seat coaches have been built. Each train was due to be formed of two half-sets, London services having two reclining seat coaches, a service vehicle and five sleeping cars in each half-set to form a sixteen coach train, whilst services from the Provinces to Paris were to be fourteen coaches long with each portion consisting of three sleeping cars, a service vehicle and three reclining seat coaches. The "regional" half-sets were to be numbered 1–9, whilst the "London" half-sets were to be numbered 10–18.

In the following lists, the UIC number for each vehicle is followed by the set number to which it was to belong. All stock is the property of Alstom, the manufacturer. Stock is stored at MoD Kineton, MoD Bicester or the Metro-Cammell works at Washwood Heath, Birmingham. Current locations are shown where known.

RECLINING SEAT CARS   SO End

Each car has 50 seats which are fully reclining, with generous leg space. A table and footrests are provided at each seat. The seats are mounted on plinths and main luggage is stored beneath the seat, while hand baggage is stored in overhead lockers. Individually controlled reading lights are provided, with different levels of ambient lighting for sleeping and non-sleeping hours. Each car has three toilet compartments with shaver sockets .

61 19 20-90 001-0	1	KN	61 19 20-90 010-1	10	
61 19 20-90 002-8	2	KN	61 19 20-90 011-9	11	
61 19 20-90 003-6	3	KN	61 19 20-90 012-7	12	
61 19 20-90 004-4	4	KN	61 19 20-90 013-5	13	
61 19 20-90 005-1	5	KN	61 19 20-90 014-3	14	
61 19 20-90 006-9	6	KN	61 19 20-90 015-0	15	
61 19 20-90 007-7	7		61 19 20-90 016-8	16	
61 19 20-90 008-5	8		61 19 20-90 017-6	17	
61 19 20-90 009-3	9		61 19 20-90 018-4	18	

RECLINING SEAT CAR   SO

Details as above, but no coupling for locomotive.

61 19 20-90 019-2	1	KN	61 19 20-90 034-1	8	
61 19 20-90 020-0	1	KN	61 19 20-90 035-8	9	
61 19 20-90 021-8	2	KN	61 19 20-90 036-6	9	
61 19 20-90 022-6	2	KN	61 19 20-90 037-4	10	
61 19 20-90 023-4	3	KN	61 19 20-90 038-2	11	
61 19 20-90 024-2	3	KN	61 19 20-90 039-0	12	
61 19 20-90 025-9	4	KN	61 19 20-90 040-8	13	
61 19 20-90 026-7	4	KN	61 19 20-90 041-6	14	
61 19 20-90 027-5	5	KN	61 19 20-90 042-4	15	
61 19 20-90 028-3	5	KN	61 19 20-90 043-2	16	
61 19 20-90 029-1	6	KN	61 19 20-90 044-0	17	
61 19 20-90 030-9	6	KN	61 19 20-90 045-7	18	
61 19 20-90 031-7	7		61 19 20-90 046-5	S	KN
61 19 20-90 032-5	7		61 19 20-90 047-3	S	KN
61 19 20-90 033-3	8				

SLEEPING CARS   SLF End

Each sleeping car has 10 cabins. Six of these have a compact en-suite shower room, with a washbasin, toilet and hairdryers. The remaining four cabins include en-suite toilet and washing facilities, but without the shower.

All cabins are convertible so that when the bunks are folded away by the attendant after passengers have got up, two comfortable armchairs with fold-out tables are revealed. The bunks themselves are generously sized one above the other and will already be made up with duvets, sheets and pillows When passengers arrive. Each cabin has a fitted wardrobe and cupboard, together with facilities for making hot drinks. Cabin telephones are provided for room service.

61 19 70-90 001-9	1	KN	61 19 70-90 010-0	10	
61 19 70-90 002-7	2	KN	61 19 70-90 011-8	11	
61 19 70-90 003-5	3	KN	61 19 70-90 012-6	12	
61 19 70-90 004-3	4	KN	61 19 70-90 013-4	13	
61 19 70-90 005-0	5	KN	61 19 70-90 014-2	14	
61 19 70-90 006-8	6	KN	61 19 70-90 015-9	15	
61 19 70-90 007-6	7		61 19 70-90 016-7	16	
61 19 70-90 008-4	8		61 19 70-90 017-5	17	
61 19 70-90 009-2	9		61 19 70-90 018-3	18	

SLEEPING CARS   SLF

Details as above, but no coupling for locomotive.

61 19 70-90 019-1	1	KN		61 19 70-90 046-4	12	
61 19 70-90 020-9	1	KN		61 19 70-90 047-2	12	
61 19 70-90 021-7	2	KN		61 19 70-90 048-0	12	
61 19 70-90 022-5	2	KN		61 19 70-90 049-8	13	
61 19 70-90 023-3	3	KN		61 19 70-90 050-6	13	
61 19 70-90 024-1	3	KN		61 19 70-90 051-4	13	
61 19 70-90 025-8	4	KN		61 19 70-90 052-2	13	
61 19 70-90 026-6	4	KN		61 19 70-90 053-0	14	
61 19 70-90 027-4	5	KN		61 19 70-90 054-8	14	
61 19 70-90 028-2	5	KN		61 19 70-90 055-5	14	
61 19 70-90 029-0	6	KN		61 19 70-90 056-3	14	
61 19 70-90 030-8	6	KN		61 19 70-90 057-1	15	
61 19 70-90 031-6	7			61 19 70-90 058-9	15	
61 19 70-90 032-4	7			61 19 70-90 059-7	15	
61 19 70-90 033-2	8			61 19 70-90 060-5	15	
61 19 70-90 034-0	8			61 19 70-90 061-3	16	
61 19 70-90 035-7	9			61 19 70-90 062-1	16	
61 19 70-90 036-5	9			61 19 70-90 063-9	16	
61 19 70-90 037-3	10	KN		61 19 70-90 064-7	16	
61 19 70-90 038-1	10			61 19 70-90 065-4	17	
61 19 70-90 039-9	10			61 19 70-90 066-2	17	
61 19 70-90 040-7	10			61 19 70-90 067-0	17	
61 19 70-90 041-5	11			61 19 70-90 068-8	17	
61 19 70-90 042-3	11			61 19 70-90 069-6	18	
61 19 70-90 043-1	11			61 19 70-90 070-4	18	
61 19 70-90 044-9	11			61 19 70-90 071-2	18	
61 19 70-90 045-6	12			61 19 70-90 072-0	18	

SERVICE VEHICLE/LOUNGE CAR   SV

Lounge cars are positioned in each half of the train, between the sleeping cars and the seated accommodation. These vehicles consist of a sleeping cabin for a disabled passenger and companion with en-suite washroom, a parcels room, offices for train manager and control authority, a lounge with bar for sleeping car passengers and public telephone and a bar for seated passengers.

The vehicle also acts as a base for the sleeping car attendants and for the trolley service which is provided for the seated passengers in the evening. There is also a seated passengers' counter so that snacks and drinks can be obtained during sleeping hours.

61 19 89-90 001-8	1	KN		61 19 89-90 011-7	11	
61 19 89-90 002-6	2	KN		61 19 89-90 012-5	12	
61 19 89-90 003-4	3	KN		61 19 89-90 013-3	13	
61 19 89-90 004-2	4	KN		61 19 89-90 014-1	14	
61 19 89-90 005-9	5	KN		61 19 89-90 015-8	15	
61 19 89-90 006-7	6	KN		61 19 89-90 016-6	16	
61 19 89-90 007-5	7			61 19 89-90 017-4	17	
61 19 89-90 008-3	8			61 19 89-90 018-2	18	
61 19 89-90 009-1	9			61 19 89-90 019-0	S	
61 19 89-90 010-9	10			61 19 89-90 020-8	S	

2.4. SALOONS

Several specialist passenger carrying vehicles, normally referred to as saloons are permitted to run on the Railtrack system. Many of these are to pre-nation-alisation designs.

LNER GENERAL MANAGERS SALOON

Built 1945 by LNER, York. Gangwayed at one end with a verandah at the other. The interior has a dining saloon seating twelve, kitchen, toilet, office and nine seat lounge. B4 bogies. ETH3.

1999   (902260)   **M**   GS   *ON*   EN

GNR FIRST CLASS SALOON

Built 1912 by GNR, Doncaster. Contains entrance vestibule, lavatory, two seperate saloons and luggage space. Gresley bogies. 19/_ 1T. 75 m.p.h.

Non-Standard Livery: Teak.

4807   (807)   x   **0**   SH   *ON*   CJ

LNWR DINING SALOON

Built 1890 by LNWR, Wolverton. Mounted on the underframe of LMS GUV 37908 in the 1980s. Contains kitchen and dining area seating 10 at two tables. Gresley bogies. 75 m.p.h.

Non-Standard Livery: London & North Western Railway.

5159   (159)   x   **0**   SH   *ON*   CJ

AZ5Z SPECIAL SALOON

Dia. AZ501. Renumbered 1989 from London Midland Region departmental series. Formerly the LMR General Manager's saloon. Rebuilt from LMS period 1 BFK M 5033 M to dia. 1654 and mounted on the underframe of BR suburban BS M 43232. B4 bogies. This vehicle has a maximum speed of 100 m.p.h. Screw couplings have been removed. ETH2.

LMS Lot No. 326 Derby 1927. 27.5 t.

Non-Standard Livery: Aircraft blue with gold lining.

6320   (5033, DM 395707) x   **0**   RV   *ON*   CP

GWR FIRST CLASS SALOON

Built 1930 by GWR, Swindon. Contains saloons at either end with body end observation windows. A seperate first class compartment and a central kitchen/

Pantry and lavatory. B5 bogies. Numbered DE321011 when in departmental service with British Railways. 25/– 1T. 100 m.p.h.

GWR Lot No. 1431 1930.

| 9004 | | x | **CH** | RA | *ON* | CP |

WCJS OBSERVATION SALOON

Built 1892 by L&NWR, Wolverton. Originally dining saloon mounted on six-wheel bogies. Rebuilt with new underframe with four-wheel bogies in 1927. Rebuilt 1960 as observation saloon with DMU end. Gangwayed at other end. The interior has a saloon, kitchen, guards vestibule and observation lounge. Gresley bogies. 19/– 1T. 28.5 t. 75 m.p.h.

Non-Standard Livery: London & North Western Railway.

| 45018 (484, 15555) | | x | **0** | SH | *ON* | CJ |

LMS INSPECTION SALOON

Built as engineers inspection saloons. Non-gangwayed. Observation windows at each end. The interior layout consists of two saloons interspersed by a central lavatory/kitchen/guards section. BR Mark 1 bogies.

45020–45026. Lot No. LMS 1356 Wolverton 1944.
45029. Lot No. LMS 1327 Wolverton 1942.
999503–999504. Lot No. BR Wagon Lot. 3093 Wolverton 1957.

45026 & 999503 are currently hired to Racal-BRT who have contracted maintenance to the Severn Valley Railway.

45020		**M**	E	*ON*	ML
45026	v	**M**	E	*ON*	KR
45029	v	**E**	E	*ON*	ML
999503	v	**M**	E	*ON*	KR
999504	v	**E**	E	*ON*	TO

ROYAL SCOTSMAN SALOONS

Mark 3A. Converted from SLEP at Carnforth Railway Restoration and Engineering Services in 1997. BT10 bogies. Attendant's and adjacent two sleeping compartments converted to generator room containing a 160 kW Volvo unit. In 99968 four sleeping compartments remain for staff use with another converted for use as a staff shower and toilet. The remaining five sleeping compartments have been replaced by two passenger cabins. In 99969 seven sleeping compartments remain for staff use. A further sleeping compartment, along with one toilet, have been converted to store rooms. The other two sleeping compartments have been combined to form a crew mess.

Lot. No. 30960 Derby 1981–3.

| 99968 (10541) | | **M** | GS | *ON* | EN | STATE CAR 5 |
| 99969 (10556) | | **M** | GS | *ON* | EN | SERVICE CAR |

RAILFILMS 'LMS CLUB CAR'

Converted from BR Mark 1 TSO at Carnforth Railway Restoration and Engineering Services in 1994. Commonwealth bogies. ETH 4.

Lot. No. 30724 York 1963. 37 t.

99993 (5067)   **M**   RA   *ON*   CP

BR INSPECTION SALOON

Mark 1. Short frames. Non-gangwayed. Observation windows at each end. The interior layout consists of two saloons interspersed by a central lavatory/kitchen/guards/luggage section. BR Mark 1 bogies.

Lot No. BR Wagon Lot. 3379 Swindon 1960.

999509   **BG**   E   *ON*   CF

2.5. PULLMAN CAR COMPANY SERIES

Pullman cars have never generally been numbered as such, although many have carried numbers, instead they have carried titles. However, a scheme of schedule numbers exists which generally lists cars in chronological order. In this section those numbers are shown followed by the cars title. Cars described as 'kitchen' contain a kitchen in addition to passenger accomodation and have gas cooking. Cars described as 'parlour' consist entirely of passenger accomodation. cars described as 'brake' contain a compartment for the use of the guard and a luggage compartment in addition to passenger accommodation.

PULLMAN PARLOUR FIRST

Built 1927 by Midland Carriage and Wagon Company. Gresley bogies. 26/–. ETH 2.

213 MINERVA   **PC** VS *ON* SL

PULLMAN BRAKE THIRD

Built 1928 by Metropolitan Carriage and Wagon Company. Gresley bogies. –/30.

232 CAR No. 79   v   **PC** NY *ON* NY

PULLMAN PARLOUR FIRST

Built 1928 by Metropolitan Carriage and Wagon Company. Gresley bogies. 24/–. ETH 4.

239 AGATHA   **PC** VS   SL
243 LUCILLE   **PC** VS *ON* SL

PULLMAN KITCHEN FIRST

Built 1925 by BRCW. Rebuilt by Midland Carriage & Wagon Company in 1928. Gresley bogies. 20/–. ETH 4.

245 IBIS   **PC** VS *ON* SL

PULLMAN PARLOUR FIRST

Built 1928 by Metropolitan Carriage and Wagon Company. Gresley bogies. 24/–. ETH 4.

254 ZENA   **PC** VS *ON* SL

PULLMAN KITCHEN FIRST

Built 1928 by Metropolitan Carriage and Wagon Company. Gresley bogies. 20/–. ETH 4.

255 IONE   **PC** VS *ON* SL

PULLMAN PARLOUR THIRD

Built 1931 by Birmingham Railway Carriage and Wagon Company. Gresley bogies. –/42.

261 CAR No. 83   **PC** VS   SL

PULLMAN KITCHEN COMPOSITE

Built 1932 by Metropolitan Carriage and Wagon Company. Originally included in 6-Pul EMU. EMU bogies. 12/16.

264 RUTH   **PC** VS   SL

PULLMAN KITCHEN FIRST

Built 1932 by Metropolitan Carriage and Wagon Company. Originally included in 'Brighton Belle' EMUs but now used as hauled stock. B5 (SR) bogies (§ EMU bogies). 20/–. ETH 2.

280 AUDREY   **PC** VS *ON* SL
281 GWEN   §   **PC** VS   SL
283 MONA   §   **PC** VS   SL
284 VERA   **PC** VS *ON* SL

PULLMAN PARLOUR THIRD

Built 1932 by Metropolitan Carriage and Wagon Company. Originally included in 'Brighton Belle' EMU. EMU bogies. –/56.

285 CAR No. 85   **PC** VS   SL
286 CAR No. 86   **PC** VS   SL

PULLMAN PARLOUR FIRST

Built 1951 by BRCW. Gresley bogies. 32/–. ETH 3.

301 PERSEUS   **PC** VS *ON* SL

Built 1952 by Pullman Car Company, Preston Park using underframe and bogies from 176 RAINBOW, the body of which had been destroyed by fire. Gresley bogies. 26/–. ETH 4.

302 PHOENIX   **PC** VS *ON* SL

PULLMAN KITCHEN FIRST

Built 1951 by Birmingham Railway Carriage & Wagon Company. Gresley bogies. 22/–.

307	CARINA	**PC** VS		SL

PULLMAN PARLOUR FIRST

Built 1951 by Birmingham Railway Carriage & Wagon Company. Gresley bogies. 32/–. ETH 3.

308	CYGNUS	**PC** VS *ON*		SL

PULLMAN KITCHEN FIRST

Built by Metro-Cammell 1960/1 for East Coast Main-line services. Commonwealth bogies. 20/– 2T. 40 t. Those vehicles used in the 'Royal Scotsman' charter train set have been modified and do not carry their names. Their current title and use is shown.

311	EAGLE	x	**PC**	NR	*ON*	NY	*(On loan to North Yorkshire Moors Rly).*	
313	FINCH	x	**M**	GS	*ON*	EN	STATE CAR 4	Sleeping Car
317	RAVEN	x	**M**	GS	*ON*	EN	DINING CAR 1	Kitchen & Dining Car
318	ROBIN	x	**PC**	NY	*ON*	NY		
319	SNIPE	x	**M**	GS	*ON*	EN	OBSERVATION CAR	Observation Car

PULLMAN PARLOUR FIRST

Built by Metro-Cammell 1960/1 for East Coast Main-line services. Commonwealth bogies. 29/– 2T. 38.5 t. Those vehicles used in the 'Royal Scotsman' charter train set have been modified and do not carry their names. Their current title and use is shown.

324	AMBER	x	**M**	GS	*ON*	EN	STATE CAR 1	Sleeping Car
325	AMETHYST	x	**PC**	FS		SZ		
328	OPAL	x	**PC**	NY	*ON*	NY		
329	PEARL	x	**M**	GS	*ON*	EN	STATE CAR 2	Sleeping Car
331	TOPAZ	x	**M**	GS	*ON*	EN	STATE CAR 3	Sleeping Car

PULLMAN KITCHEN SECOND

Built by Metro-Cammell 1960/1 for East Coast Main-line services. Commonwealth bogies. –/30 1T. 40 t.

335	CAR No. 335	x	**PC**	FS	SZ

PULLMAN PARLOUR SECOND

Built by Metro-Cammell 1960/1 for East Coast Main-line services. Commonwealth bogies. –/42 2T. 38.5 t.

347	CAR No. 347	x	**PC**	FS	SZ

348	CAR No. 348	x	**PC**	FS	SZ
349	CAR No. 349	x	**PC**	FS	On loan to Kent & East Sussex Railway
350	CAR No. 350	x	**PC**	FS	SZ
351	CAR No. 351	x	**PC**	FS	SZ
352	CAR No. 352	x	**PC**	FS	SZ
353	CAR No. 353	x	**PC**	FS	SZ

THE HADRIAN BAR

Built by Metro-Cammell 1961 for East Coast Main-line services. Commonwealth bogies. 24/– + bar seating 1T. 38.5 t.

| 354 | THE HADRIAN BAR | x | **PC** | FS | SZ |

2.6. COACHING STOCK AWAITING DISPOSAL

This list contains the last known locations of coaching stock awaiting disposal. The definition of which vehicles are "awaiting disposal" is somewhat vague, but generally speaking these are vehicles of types not now in normal service or vehicles which have been damaged by fire, vandalism or collision.

5476	Neville Hill Up Sidings
5533	Neville Hill Up Sidings
5574	Neville Hill Up Sidings
5585	Neville Hill Up Sidings
5595	Neville Hill Up Sidings
6335	LA
6339	EC
6343	HT
6345	EC
6362	LL
6363	LL
6500	Healey Mills Yard
6501	Healey Mills Yard
6521	Healey Mills Yard
6527	Healey Mills Yard
6900	Cambridge Station Yard
6901	Cambridge Station Yard
7183	Crewe Brook Sidings
9499	ZH
17054	Crewe Brook Sdgs.
17076	ZG
18416	Crewe Brook Sidings
18750	Crewe Brook Sidings
19500	Crewe Brook Sidings

2.7. 99xxx RANGE NUMBER CONVERSION TABLE

The following table is presented to help readers identify vehicles which may carry numbers in the 99xxx range, the former private owner number series which is no longer in general use.

99xxx	BR No.	99xxx	BR No.	99xxx	BR No.	99xxx	BR No.
99000	4946	99327	5044	99672	549	99824	4831
99001	4996	99328	5033	99673	550	99826	13229
99002	5008	99329	4931	99674	551	99827	3096
99052	45018	99356	21245	99675	552	99828	13230
99053	9004	99371	3128	99676	553	99829	4856
99080	21096	99405	35486	99677	586	99830	5028
99121	3105	99530	301	99678	504	99831	4836
99125	3113	99531	302	99679	506	99880	5159
99127	3117	99532	308	99680	17102	99881	4807
99131	1999	99534	245	99710	25767	99886	35407
99241	35449	99535	213	99712	25893	99887	2127
99304	21256	99536	254	99713	26013	99953	35468
99311	1882	99537	280	99716	25808	99961	324
99312	35463	99538	34991	99717	25837	99962	329
99314	25729	99539	255	99718	25862	99963	331
99315	25955	99540	3069	99721	25756	99964	313
99316	13321	99541	243	99722	25806	99965	319
99317	3766	99542	88920	99723	35459	99966	34525
99318	4912	99543	284 2	99782	17007	99967	317
99319	14168	99544	35207	99783	84025	99970	232
99321	5299	99545	80207	99792	17019	99971	311
99322	5600	99554	92904	99818	1730	99972	318
99323	5704	99566	3066	99821	9227	99973	324
99324	5714	99568	3068	99822	1859	99974	328
99325	5727	99670	546	99823	4832	99995	35457
99326	4954	99671	548				

The following table lists support coaches and the locomotives which they normally support at present. These coaches can spend considerable periods of time off the Railtrack network when the locomotives they support are not being used on that network.

17007	35028	35207	VS locos	35463	48151	35470	TM locos
17019	45407	35333	6024	35465	D 172	35486	KR locos
21096	4498	35449	34027	35467	KR locos	80217	75014
21236	30828	35457	44767	35468	YM locos	80220	34067

3. DIESEL MULTIPLE UNITS

USING THIS SECTION – LAYOUT OF INFORMATION

DMUs are listed in numerical order of class, then in numerical order of set – using current numbers as allocated by the RSL. Individual 'loose' vehicles are listed in numerical order after vehicles formed into fixed formations. Where numbers carried are differ from those officially allocated these are noted in class headings where appropriate. Where sets or vehicles have been renumbered since the previous edition of this book, former numbering detail is shown in parentheses. Each entry is laid out as in the following example:

Set No.	Detail	Livery	Owner	Operation	Depot	Formation	Name
150 257	r*	**RR**	P	*AR*	NC	5225757257	QUEEN BOADICEA

CLASS HEADINGS

Principal details and dimensions are quoted for each class in metric and/or imperial units as considered appropriate bearing in mind common usage in the UK. Abbreviations used are shown in Section 6.9.

All dimensions and weights are quoted for vehicles in an 'as new' condition with all necessary supplies (e.g. oil, water and sand) on board. Dimensions are quoted in the order Length – Width – Height. All lengths quoted are over buffers or couplings as appropriate. All width and height dimensions quoted are maxima.

DETAIL DIFFERENCES

Only detail differences which currently affect the areas and types of train which vehicles may work are shown. All other detail differences are specifically excluded. Where such differences occur within a class, these are shown alongside the individual set or vehicle number. Standard abbreviations used are:

r   Radio Electronic Token Block (RETB) equipment.
t   Tripcock equipment for working over London Underground Ltd. tracks between Harrow-on-the-Hill and Amersham.

In all cases use of the above abbreviations indicates the equipment indicated is normally operable. Meaning of non-standard abbreviations is detailed in individual class headings.

LIVERY CODES

Livery codes are used to denote the various liveries carried. Readers should note it is impossible in a publication of this size to list every livery variation which currently exists. In particular items ignored for the purposes of this book include:

•   Minor colour variations;

- All numbering, lettering and branding;
- Omission of logos.

The descriptions below are thus a general guide only and may be subject to slight variation between individual vehicles. Logos as appropriate for each livery are normally deemed to be carried. A complete list of livery codes used appears in Section 6.1.

OWNER CODES

Owner codes are used in this to denote the owners of vehicles listed. Most vehicles are leased by the TOCs from specialist leasing companies. A complete list of owner codes used appears in Section 6.4.

OPERATION CODES

Operation codes are used to denote the normal usage of the vehicles listed – i.e. A guide to the services of which train operating company any vehicle will normally be used upon. Where vehicles are used for non revenue earning purposes, an indication to the normal type of usage is given in the class heading. Where no operation code is shown, vehicles are currently not in use. A complete list of operation codes used appears in Section 6.5.

DEPOT & LOCATION CODES

Depot codes are used to denote the normal maintenance base of each operational vehicle. However, maintenance may be carried out at other locations and may also be carried out by mobile maintenance teams.

Location codes are used to denote the current actual location of stored vehicles. A location code will be followed by (S) to denote stored. A complete list of depot and location codes used appears in Section 6.6.

SET FORMATIONS

Regular set formations are shown where these are normally maintained. Readers should note set formations might be temporarily varied from time to time to suit maintenance and/or operational requirements. Vehicles shown as 'Spare' are not formed in any regular set formation.

NAMES

Only names carried with official sanction are listed. As far as possible names are shown in UPPER/lower case characters as actually shown on the name carried on the vehicle(s). Unless otherwise shown, complete units are regarded as named rather than just the individual car(s) which carry the name.

GENERAL INFORMATION

CLASSIFICATION AND NUMBERING

First generation ('Heritage') DMUs are classified in the series 100–139.
Second generation DMUs are classified in the series 140–199.
Diesel-electric multiple units are classified in the series 200–249.
Service units are classified in the series 930–999.
First and second generation individual cars are numbered in the series 50000–59999 and 79000–79999.

DEMU individual cars are numbered in the series 60000–60999, except for a few former EMU vehicles which retain their EMU numbers.

Service stock individual cars are numbered in the series 975000–975999 and 977000–977999, although this series is not exclusively used for DMU vehicles.

OPERATING CODES

These codes are used by train operating company staff to describe the various different types of vehicles and normally appear on data panels on the inner (i.e. non driving) ends of vehicles.

DM	Driving Motor.	DTCso	Driving Trailer Composite (semi-open).
DMB	Driving Motor Brake.		
DMBS	Driving Motor Brake Std.	MS	Motor Standard.
DMC	Driving Motor Composite.	T	Trailer.
DMS	Driving Motor Standard.	TC	Trailer Composite.
DT	Driving Trailer.	TCsoL	Trailer Composite (semi-open).
DTC	Driving Trailer Composite.		
DTS	Driving Trailer Standard.	TS	Trailer Standard.

All vehicles are of open configuration except where shown. A semi-open vehicle features both open and compartment accommodation, with first class accommodation usually in compartments in composite vehicles. Where two vehicles of the same type are formed within the same unit, the above codes may be suffixed by (A) and (B) to differentiate between the vehicles. The suffix 'L' denotes vehicles with a lavatory compartment.

A composite is a vehicle containing both first and standard class accommodation, although first class accommodation on first generation DMU vehicles has now all been permanently declassified. The distinction is maintained in this publication in respect of these vehicles to indicate the differing style of seating still fitted.

A brake vehicle is a vehicle containing separate specific accommodation for the conductor (as opposed to the use of rear or intermediate cabs on second generation units).

DESIGN CODES AND DIAGRAM CODES

For each type of vehicle the RSL issues a seven character 'Design Code' consisting of two letters plus four numbers and a suffix letter. (e.g. DP2010A). The first five characters of the Design Code are known as the 'Diagram Code' and these are quoted in this publication in sub-headings. The meaning of the various characters of the Design Code is as follows:

First Character
D   Diesel Multiple Unit vehicle.

Second Character
B   DEMU Driving motor passenger vehicle with brake compartment.
E   DEMU Driving trailer passenger vehicle.
H   DEMU Trailer passenger vehicle without brake compartment.
P   DMU (excl. DEMU) Driving motor passenger vehicle without brake compartment.
Q   DMU (excl. DEMU) Driving motor passenger vehicle with brake compartment.
R   DMU (excl. DEMU) Non-driving motor passenger vehicle.
S   DMU (excl. DEMU) Driving trailer passenger vehicle.
T   DMU (excl. DEMU) Trailer passenger vehicle without brake compartment.
X   DMU (excl. DEMU) Single unit railcar.
Z   All types of service vehicle.

Third Character
2   Standard class accommodation.
3   Composite accommodation.
5   No passenger accommodation.

Fourth & Fifth Characters
These distinguish between different designs of vehicle, each design being allocated a unique two digit number.

Special Note
Where vehicles have been declassified, the correct design code for a declassified vehicle is quoted in this publication, even though this may be at variance with RSL records, which do not always show the reality of the current position.

ACCOMMODATION

The information given in class headings and sub-headings is in the form F/S nT (or TD) nW. For example 12/54 1T 1W denotes 12 first class and 54 standard class seats, 1 toilet and 1 wheelchair space. In declassified vehicles the capacity is still shown in terms of first and standard class seats whilst different types of seat remain fitted.

BUILD DETAILS

Lot Numbers
Vehicles ordered under the auspices of BR were allocated a Lot (batch) number when ordered and these are quoted in class headings and sub-headings. Details of the meaning of abbreviations used to denote builders are shown in Section 6.8.

3.1 FIRST GENERATION DMUS

Very few first generation diesel multiple units remain. These are now commonly referred to as 'Heritage' units. The following features are standard unless otherwise stated:

Transmission: Mechanical. Cardan shaft and freewheel to a four-speed epicyclic gearbox with a further cardan shaft to the final drive, each engine driving the inner axle of one bogie.
Brakes: All units are equipped with twin pipe vacuum brakes.
Gangways: Within unit only.
Doors: Manually operated slam.
Couplings: Screw couplings are used on all vehicles.
Multiple Working: 'Blue Square' coupling code. All first generation vehicles may be coupled together to work in multiple to a maximum of 6 motor cars or 12 cars in total in a formation. First generation vehicles may not be coupled in multiple with second generation vehicles.
Maximum Speed: 70 mph.

CLASS 101   2- or 3-Car Unit

DMBS–DTSL (Refurbished) or DMBS–DMSL (Refurbished) or DMBS–DMCL (Facelifted).
Engines: Two Leyland 680/1 of 112 kW (150 hp) at 1800 rpm per power car.
Gangways: Midland scissors type.
Bogies: DD15 (motor) and DT11 (trailer).
Dimensions: 18.49 x 2.82 x 3.85 m.
Seating Layout: 3+2 largely unidirectional (2+2 facing in first class).
Note: Unit L842 is used in conjuction with 975010 (see page 229).

51175–51253. DMBS. Dia. DQ202. Lot No. 30467 Met-Camm. 1958–59. –/52. 32.5 t.
51426–51463 (except 51432). DMBS. Dia. DQ202. Lot No. 30500 Met-Camm. 1959. –/52. 32.5 t.
51432. DMBS. Dia. DQ232. Lot No. 30500 Met-Camm. 1959. –/49 with additional luggage racks. 32.5 t.
51800. DMBS. Dia. DQ202. Lot No. 30587 Met-Camm. 1956. –/52. 32.5 t.
53164. DMBS. Dia. DQ202. Lot No. 30254 Met-Camm. 1956. –/52. 32.5 t.
53198–53204. DMBS. Dia. DQ202. Lot No. 30259 Met-Camm. 1957. –/52. 32.5 t.
53211–53228. DMBS. Dia. DQ202. Lot No. 30261 Met-Camm. 1957. –/52. 32.5 t.
53253–53256. DMBS. Dia. DQ202. Lot No. 30266 Met-Camm. 1957. –/52. 32.5 t.
53311–53314. DMBS. Dia. DQ232. Lot No. 30275 Met-Camm. 1958. –/49 with additional luggage racks. 32.5 t.
51496–51533 (except 51498). DMSL. Dia. DP210. Lot No. 30501 Met-Camm. 1959. –/72S 1T. 32.5t.
51498. DMCL. Dia. DP317. Lot No. 30501 Met-Camm. 1959. 12/46 1T with additional luggage racks. 32.5t.
51803. DMSL. Dia. DP210. Lot No. 30588 Met-Camm. 1959. –/72 1T. 32.5 t.
53160–53163. DMSL. Dia. DP214. Lot No. 30253 Met-Camm. 1956. –/72 1T. 32.5 t.
53170–53171. DMSL. Dia. DP214. Lot No. 30255 Met-Camm. 1957. –/72 1T. 32.5 t.
53177. DMSL. Dia. DP214. Lot No. 30256 Met-Camm. 1957. –/72 1T. 32.5 t.
53266–53269. DMSL. Dia. DP210. Lot No. 30267 Met-Camm. 1957. –/72 1T. 32.5 t.

53322–53327. DMCL. Dia. DP317. Lot No. 30276 Met-Camm. 1958. 12/46 1T
with additional luggage racks. 32.5 t.
53746. DMSL. Dia. DP210. Lot No. 30271 Met-Camm. 1957. –/72 1T. 32.5 t.
54055–54061. DTSL. Dia. DS206. Lot No. 30260 Met-Camm. 1957. –/72 1T. 25.5 t.
54062–54085. DTSL. Dia. DS206. Lot No. 30262 Met-Camm. 1957. –/72 1T. 25.5 t.
54091. DTSL. Dia. DS211. Lot No. 30262 Met-Camm. 1957. –/72 1T. 25.5 t.
54343–54408. DTSL. Dia. DS206. Lot No. 30468 Met-Camm. 1958. –/72 1T. 25.5 t.
59303. TSL. Dia. DT202. Lot No. 30273 Met-Camm. 1957. –/71 1T. 25.5 t.
59539. TSL. Dia. DT202. Lot No. 30502 Met-Camm. 1959. –/71 1T. 25.5 t.

Refurbished 2-car sets. DMBS–DTSL.

101 651	**RR**	A		ZD(S)	53201	54379
101 653	**RR**	A	NW	LO	51426	54358
101 654	**RR**	A	NW	LO	51800	54408
101 655	**RR**	A	NW	LO	51428	54062
101 656	**RR**	A	NW	LO`	51230	54056
101 657	**RR**	A	NW	LO	53211	54085
101 658	**RR**	A	NW	LO	51175	54091
101 659	**RR**	A	NW	LO	51213	54352
101 660	**RR**	A	NW	LO	51189	54343
101 661	**RR**	A	NW	LO	51463	54365
101 662	**RR**	A	NW	LO	53228	54055
101 663	**RR**	A	NW	LO	51201	54347
101 664	**RR**	A	NW	LO	51442	54061
101 665	**RR**	A	NW	LO	51429	54393

Refurbished 2-car sets. DMBS–DMSL.
Non-Standard Livery:
•   101 692 is 'Caledonian' Blue with orange/yellow stripes.

101 676	**RR**	A	NW	LO	51205	51803
101 677	**RR**	A	NW	LO	51179	51496
101 678	**RR**	A	NW	LO	51210	53746
101 679	**RR**	A	NW	LO	51224	51533
101 680	**RR**	A	NW	LO	53204	53163
101 681	**RR**	A	NW	LO	51228	51506
101 682	**RR**	A	NW	LO	53256	51505
101 683	**RR**	A	NW	LO	51177	53269
101 684	**S**	A	SR	CK	51187	51509
101 685	**G**	A	NW	LO	53164	53160
101 686	**S**	A		CK(S)	51231	51500
101 687	**S**	A	SR	CK	51247	51512
101 688	**S**	A	SR	CK	51431	51501
101 689	**S**	A	SR	CK	51185	51511
101 690	**S**	A	SR	CK	51435	53177
101 691	**S**	A	SR	CK	51253	53171
101 692	**0**	A	SR	CK	53253	53170
101 693	**S**	A	SR	CK	51192	53266
101 694	**S**	A	SR	CK	51188	53268
101 695	**S**	A	SR	CK	51226	51499

Refurbished Trailers. TSL.
Note: These may be added to DMBS–DMSL formations as required.

Spare	**RR**	A		CH(S)	59303	
Spare	**G**	A		CH(S)	59539	

Facelifted 2-car sets. DMBS–DMCL (declassified).

L835	**RR**	A	*NW*	LO	51432	51498
L840	**N**	A	*NW*	LO	53311	53322
L842	**N**	A	*SO*	ZA	53314	53327

CLASS 117   2- or 3-Car Unit

DMBS–TSL–DMS or DMBS–DMS.
Engines: Two Leyland 680/1 of 112 kW (150 hp) at 1800 rpm per power car.
Gangways: GWR suspension type.
Bogies: DD10 (motor) and DT9 (trailer).
Dimensions: 20.45 x 2.82 x 3.86 m.
Seating Layout: 3+2 facing.

DMBS. Dia. DQ220. Lot No. 30546 Pressed Steel 1959–60. –/65. 36.5 t.
TSL. Dia. DT230. Lot No. 30547 Pressed Steel 1959–60. –/86 2T. 30.5 t.
DMS. Dia. DP221. Lot No. 30548 Pressed Steel 1959–60. –/89. 36.5 t.

Refurbished 3-car sets. DMBS–TSL–DMS.

117 301	**RR**	A	*SR*	HA	51353	59505	51395
117 306	**RR**	A	*SR*	HA	51369	59521	51411
117 308	**RR**	A	*SR*	HA	51371	59509	51413
117 310	**RR**	A	*SR*	HA	51373	59486	51381
117 311	**RR**	A	*SR*	HA	51352	59500	51376
117 313	**RR**	A	*SR*	HA	51339	59492	51382

Facelifted 2-car sets. DMBS–DMS.

L700	**N**	A	SL	BY		51374
117 701	**N**	A	SL	BY	51350	51392
L702	**N**	A	SL	BY	51356	51398
L704	**N**	A	SL	BY	51341	51383
L705	**N**	A	SL	BY	51358	51375
L706	**N**	A	SL	BY	51366	51408
L707	**N**	A		BY(S)	51335	51377
L708	**N**	A		BY(S)	51336	51378
117 709	**N**	A		BY(S)	51344	51386
L720	**N**	A	SL	BY	51354	51396
L721	**N**	A	SL	BY	51363	51405
117 724	**N**	A	SL	BY	51333	51400
Spare	**N**	A		BY(S)	51332	
Spare	**N**	A		BY(S)	51361	
Spare	**CH**	A		BY(S)	51368	

Name: 51358   LESLIE CRABBE

CLASS 121 — Single Car Unit

DMBS.
Engines: Two Leyland 1595 of 112 kW (150 hp) at 1800 rpm.
Gangways: Non gangwayed single cars with cabs at each end.
Bogies: DD10.
Dimensions: 20.45 x 2.82 x 3.87 m.
Seating Layout: 3+2 facing.
DMBS. Dia. DX201. Lot No. 30518 Pressed Steel 1960. –/65. 38.0 t.

L127	N	A SL	BY	55027
121 129	N	A SL	BY	55029
L131	N	A SL	BY	55031

Name:
121 129   MARSTON VALE

CLASS 122 — Route Learning Single Car Unit

DM. Converted 1995 from DMBS.
Engines: Two Leyland 1595 of 112 kW (150 hp) at 1800 rpm.
Gangways: Non gangwayed single car with cab at each end.
Bogies: DD10.
Dimensions: 20.45 x 2.82 x 3.87 m.

DM. Dia. DZ5??. Lot No. 30419 Gloucester 1958. Converted by ABB Doncaster 1995. 36.5 t.

-	LH	E E	TE	55012

3.2. SECOND GENERATION DMUS

Unit Types

Vehicles conform to one of the six basic types of vehicle as listed below unless otherwise stated:

Pacer/Railbus. Folding power operated exterior doors. Bus-type largely unidirectional 3+2 (2+2 on class 141) seating. Limited luggage space. Four-wheel chassis, wheel arrangement 1–A. Gangwayed within unit only. 75 mph.

Sprinter. Sliding power operated exterior double doors to large entrance vestibules. High backed largely unidirectional 3 + 2 seating. Limited luggage space. Bogied chassis, wheel arrangement 2–B. Gangwayed throughout (not Classes 150/0 and 150/1). 75 mph.

Super Sprinter. Sliding or sliding plug power-operated exterior doors. High backed 2+2 largely unidirectional seating with some tables. Gangwayed throughout. Bogied chassis, wheel arrangement 2–B. 75 mph.

Express. Sliding plug power-operated exterior doors. Air conditioning equipment. High backed 2+2 half-facing and half-unidirectional seating with some tables. Gangwayed throughout. Bogied chassis, wheel arrangement 2–B. 90 mph.

Network Turbo. Sliding power operated exterior double doors to large entrance vestibules. 3+2 seating. Limited luggage space. Gangwayed within unit only. Bogied chassis, wheel arrangement 2–B. 75 or 90 mph.

Clubman/Turbostar. Sliding power operated exterior double doors to large entrance vestibules. Air conditioning equipment. 2+2 facing/unidirectional seating. Limited luggage space. Gangwayed within unit only. Bogied chassis, wheel arrangement 2–B. 100 mph.

Standard Features

The following features are standard unless otherwise stated:

Public Address System: All vehicles have public address equipment, with transmission equipment in driving vehicles only.

Gangways: All vehicles have flexible diaphragm gangways.

Transmission: Hydraulic. Voith T211r with cardan shafts to Gmeinder GM190 final drive.

Couplers: Pacer/Railbus types – BSI automatic at driving ends, bar couplings at non-driving ends. Other types – BSI automatic throughout.

Brakes: All vehicles are equipped with electro-pneumatic and air brakes.

Multiple Working: Second Generation units are currently split into two groups. Vehicles may operate in multiple within a group, but not with other groups.

Group A: Classes 141–158 and 170.
Group B: Classes 165–168.

CLASS 141   2-Car Railbus

DMS–DMSL. Built from Leyland National bus components on BREL under-frame. The units leased by Serco Railtest are for conversion to track vegetation control units.
Engines: One Leyland TL11/65 of 157 kW (210 hp) at 1950 rpm (* Cummins LTA10-R of 172 kW at 2100 rpm) per car.
Transmission: Mechanical. SCG R500 4-speed epicyclic gearbox with cardan shafts to SCG RF420i final drive (* Hydraulic. Voith T211r with Gmeinder final drive).
Doors: Four-leaf folding.   **Dimensions**: 15.45 x 2.50 x 3.91 m.

55502/503/505–517/519–521. DMS, Dia. DP228. Lot No. 30977 BREL Derby 1983–84. Modified by Barclay 1988–89. –/50. 26.0 t.
55522/523/525–537/539–541. DMSL. Dia. DP229. Lot No. 30978 BREL Derby 1983–84. Modified by Barclay 1988–89. –/44 1T. 26.5 t.
55518. DM. Dia. DZ540. Lot No. 30978 BREL Derby. Converted by Serco Rail-test Derby 1998.   . t.
55538. DM. Dia. DZ541. Lot No. 30977 BREL Derby. Converted by Serco Rail-test Derby 1998.   . t.

141 101	**WY**	P		NL(S)	55521	55541
141 102	**WY**	P		HT(S)	55502	55522
141 103	**WY**	P		ZB(S)	55503	55523
141 105	**WY**	P	SO	ZA	55505	55525
141 106	**WY**	P		ZB(S)	55506	55526
141 107	**WY**	P		ZB(S)	55507	55527
141 108	**WY**	P		ZB(S)	55508	55528
141 109	**WY**	P		HT(S)	55509	55529
141 110	**WY**	P		ZB(S)	55510	55530
141 111	**WY**	P		HT(S)	55511	55531
141 112	**WY**	P	SO	ZA	55512	55532
141 113	* **WY**	P		NL(S)	55513	55533
141 114	**WY**	P		NL(S)	55514	55534
141 115	**WY**	P		HT(S)	55515	55535
141 116	**WY**	P		ZB(S)	55516	55536
141 117	**WY**	P		HT(S)	55517	55537
141 118	**WY**	P	SO	ZA	55518	55538
141 119	**WY**	P		NL(S)	55519	55539
141 120	**WY**	P		ZB(S)	55520	55540

CLASS 142   2-Car Pacer

DMS–DMSL. Development of Class 141 with wider body.
Engines: One Cummins LTA10-R of 172 kW (230 hp) at 2100 rpm († One Perkins 2006-TWH of 172 kW (230 hp) at 2100 rpm) per car.
Doors: Twin-leaf folding.   **Dimensions**: 15.55 x 2.80 x 3.86 m.

55542–55591. DMS. Dia. DP234 (* DP271) Lot No. 31003 BREL Derby 1985–86. –/62 (* –/56 Refurbished with high backed seats). 24.5 t.
55592–55641. DMSL. Dia. DP235 (* DP272) Lot No. 31004 BREL Derby 1985–86.   –/59 1T (* –/50 1T Refurbished with high backed seats). 25.0 t.

55701–55746. DMS. Dia. DP234 (* DP271) Lot No. 31013 BREL Derby 1986–87. –/62 (* –/56 Refurbished with high backed seats). 23.3 t.
55747–55792. DMSL. Dia. DP235 (*DP 272) Lot No. 31014 BREL Derby 1986–87. –/59 1T (* –/56 Refurbished with high backed seats). 25.0 t.
Non Standard Livery:
• 55709 is light blue/dark blue with white stripes.

142 001		**GM**	A	*NW*	NH	55542	55592
142 002		**GM**	A	*NW*	NH	55543	55593
142 003		**GM**	A	*NW*	NH	55544	55594
142 004		**GM**	A	*NW*	NH	55545	55595
142 005		**GM**	A	*NW*	NH	55546	55596
142 006		**GM**	A	*NW*	NH	55547	55597
142 007		**GM**	A	*NW*	NH	55548	55598
142 008		**GM**	A	*NW*	NH	55549	55599
142 009		**GM**	A	*NW*	NH	55550	55600
142 010		**GM**	A	*NW*	NH	55551	55601
142 011		**GM**	A	*NW*	NH	55552	55602
142 012		**GM**	A	*NW*	NH	55553	55603
142 013		**GM**	A	*NW*	NH	55554	55604
142 014		**GM**	A	*NW*	NH	55555	55605
142 015	*	**RR**	A	*NS*	HT	55556	55606
142 016	*	**RR**	A	*NS*	HT	55557	55607
142 017	*	**TW**	A	*NS*	HT	55558	55608
142 018		**TW**	A	*NS*	HT	55559	55609
142 019	*	**TW**	A	*NS*	HT	55560	55610
142 020	*	**TW**	A	*NS*	HT	55561	55611
142 021	*	**TW**	A	*NS*	HT	55562	55612
142 022		**TW**	A	*NS*	HT	55563	55613
142 023		**RR**	A	*NW*	NH	55564	55614
142 024	*	**RR**	A	*NS*	HT	55565	55615
142 025	*	**NS**	A	*NS*	HT	55566	55616
142 026	*	**NS**	A	*NS*	HT	55567	55617
142 027		**GM**	A	*NW*	NH	55568	55618
142 028		**GM**	A	*NW*	NH	55569	55619
142 029		**GM**	A	*NW*	NH	55570	55620
142 030		**GM**	A	*NW*	NH	55571	55621
142 031		**GM**	A	*NW*	NH	55572	55622
142 032		**GM**	A	*NW*	NH	55573	55623
142 033		**RR**	A	*NW*	NH	55574	55624
142 034		**GM**	A	*NW*	NH	55575	55625
142 035		**GM**	A	*NW*	NH	55576	55626
142 036		**RR**	A	*NW*	NH	55577	55627
142 037		**GM**	A	*NW*	NH	55578	55628
142 038		**GM**	A	*NW*	NH	55579	55629
142 039		**GM**	A	*NW*	NH	55580	55630
142 040		**GM**	A	*NW*	NH	55581	55631
142 041		**GM**	A	*NW*	NH	55582	55632
142 042		**GM**	A	*NW*	NH	55583	55633
142 043		**GM**	A	*NW*	NH	55584	55634
142 044		**RR**	A	*NW*	NH	55585	55635
142 045		**GM**	A	*NW*	NH	55586	55636

142 046		**GM**	A	*NW*	NH	55587	55637
142 047		**RR**	A	*NW*	NH	55588	55638
142 048		**RR**	A	*NW*	NH	55589	55639
142 049		**GM**	A	*NW*	NH	55590	55640
142 050	*	**NS**	A	*NS*	HT	55591	55641
142 051		**MT**	A	*NW*	NH	55701	55747
142 052		**MT**	A	*NW*	NH	55702	55748
142 053		**MT**	A	*NW*	NH	55703	55749
142 054		**MT**	A	*NW*	NH	55704	55750
142 055		**MT**	A	*NW*	NH	55705	55751
142 056		**MT**	A	*NW*	NH	55706	55752
142 057		**MT**	A	*NW*	NH	55707	55753
142 058		**MT**	A	*NW*	NH	55708	55754
142 060		**GM**	A	*NW*	NH	55710	55756
142 061		**GM**	A	*NW*	NH	55711	55757
142 062		**GM**	A	*NW*	NH	55712	55758
142 063		**GM**	A	*NW*	NH	55713	55759
142 064		**GM**	A	*NW*	NH	55714	55760
142 065	*	**NS**	A	*NS*	HT	55715	55761
142 066	*	**NS**	A	*NS*	NL	55716	55762
142 067		**GM**	A	*NW*	NH	55717	55763
142 068		**GM**	A	*NW*	NH	55718	55764
142 069		**GM**	A	*NW*	NH	55719	55765
142 070		**GM**	A	*NW*	NH	55720	55766
142 071	*	**RR**	A	*NS*	HT	55721	55767
142 072		**RR**	A	*NS*	NL	55722	55768
142 073		**RR**	A	*NS*	NL	55723	55769
142 074		**RR**	A	*NS*	NL	55724	55770
142 075		**RR**	A	*NS*	NL	55725	55771
142 076		**RR**	A	*NS*	NL	55726	55772
142 077		**RR**	A	*NS*	NL	55727	55773
142 078		**RR**	A	*NS*	NL	55728	55774
142 079		**RR**	A	*NS*	NL	55729	55775
142 080		**RR**	A	*NS*	NL	55730	55776
142 081		**RR**	A	*NS*	NL	55731	55777
142 082		**RR**	A	*NS*	NL	55732	55778
142 083		**RR**	A	*NS*	NL	55733	55779
142 084	*†	**RR**	A	*NS*	HT	55734	55780
142 085	*	**RR**	A	*CA*	CF	55735	55781
142 086	*	**RR**	A	*CA*	CF	55736	55782
142 087	*	**RR**	A	*CA*	NL	55737	55783
142 088	*	**RR**	A	*CA*	CF	55738	55784
142 089	*	**RR**	A	*CA*	CF	55739	55785
142 090	*	**RR**	A	*CA*	CF	55740	55786
142 091	*	**RR**	A	*CA*	CF	55741	55787
142 092	*	**RR**	A	*NS*	CF	55742	55788
142 093	*	**RR**	A	*NS*	NL	55743	55789
142 094	*	**RR**	A	*NS*	HT	55744	55790
142 095	*	**RR**	A	*NS*	NL	55745	55791
142 096	*	**RR**	A	*NS*	HT	55746	55792
Spare		**0**	A		NH(S)	55709	

▲ Strathclyde PTE liveried 101 695 (51226 + 51499) at Glasgow Central after arrival with a service from Paisley Canal on 5th October 1998. **Bob Sweet**

▼ 117 706 (51366 + 51408) at Bedford, forming the 14.40 Silverlink service to Bletchley on 9th October 1998. **Peter Fox**

▲ 121 029 (55029) leads L127 (55027) as the pair arrive at Bletchley with the 12.46 from Bedford on 9th October 1998. **Peter Fox**

▼ Class 142 are the only class of DMU to still appear in Tyne & Wear PTE livery. Outside the PTE area at Carlisle, 142 017 departs with the 17.26 to Sunderland on 19th April 1998. **Kevin Conkey**

▲ The first Class 142 to appear in Northern Spirit livery was 142 068, seen here at Sheffield on 21st May 1998. **Peter Fox**

▼ 143 624 and 143 617 pass Fairwood Junction, near Westbury, with a train for Bristol Temple Meads on 28th June 1998. **Hugh Ballantyne**

144 020 passes under the signal gantry at Falsgrave, Scarborough, with the 11.22 Scarborough–Leeds on 12th August 1998. **Brian Denton**

▲ 150 141, wearing Greater Manchester PTE livery, stands at Delamere whilst working the 13.01 Chester–Southport on 18th September 1996. **George Allsop**

▼ 150 216 arrives at the recently re-opened Creswell station on the 'Robin Hood Line' between Nottingham and Worksop with the 17.33 Worksop–Nottingham on 20th June 1998. **Peter Fox**

153 359 departs from Dalston (Cumbria) on May 2nd 1998 with the 06.55 Barrow-in-Furness–Carlisle.

Kevin Conkey

▲ 155 341 approaches Micklefield on the 07.47 Blackpool North–Scarborough on 13th October 1997. **John G. Teasdale**

▼ The 17.11 Barrow-in-Furness–Carlisle was unusually worked by North West Regional Railways liveried 156 441 on 28th April 1998. **Dave McAlone**

Strathclyde PTE's attractive carmine & cream livery has only been applied to a few DMU vehicles. 156 494 leaves Gretna Green on 12th June 1998 with the 12.03 Glasgow Central–Carlisle.

Kevin Conkey

Northern Spirit Trans-Pennine Express liveried 158 814 departs from Leeds with the 10.28 Manchester Airport–Middlesbrough on 19th September 1998.
Peter Fox

▲ 159 007 and 159 006 depart from Dawlish with the 09.50 Paignton–London Waterloo on 27th June 1998. **Alex Dasi-Sutton**

▼ 165 107 nears Earlswood whilst working a Reading General–Gatwick Airport service on 14th August 1998. **Hugh Ballantyne**

The 11.34 Reading General–Gatwick Airport passes the 1930's vintage former Southern Railway signal box at Reigate on 9th May 1998 worked by 166 210.

Nic Joynson

▲ Chiltern 'Clubman' 168 002 shunts into the stabling siding at Birmingham Snow Hill after arrival with the 10.40 from London Marylebone on 31st October 1998. **Peter Fox**

▼ EWS Class 114 Route Learning Unit 977775 + 977776 north of Norton Bridge on the down slow line heading towards Crewe on 17th September 1996.
Hugh Ballantyne

Unique Class 205/2 3-car DEMU 205 205 running empty stock nears Ashford (Kent) before forming the 10.52 service to Hastings on 15th May 1998. This set has now been reduced to 2-cars for the winter period. **Chris Wilson**

Serco Railtest 3-car unit 977392 + 999550 + 977391 passes Abbotswood Junction on 2nd April 1998. **Bob Sweet**

▲ Docklands Light Railway cars 82 + 63 approach Heron Quays on 9th September 1998. **Hugh Ballantyne**

▼ South Yorkshire Supertram 111, in the new Stagecoach livery, passes the Don Valley Stadium with the 15.14 Meadowhall–Herdings Park on 18th October 1998. **Peter Fox**

▲ The first Croydon Tramlink car, as yet un-numbered, on a test run near the Therapia Lane depot on 8th October 1998.   **B.J. Cross**

▼ Midland Metro car 03 on a test run at Dudley Street on 7th August 1998.
                                                                                    Mike Ballinger

CLASS 143   2-Car Pacer

DMS–DMSL. Similar design to Class 142, but bodies built by Alexander on Barclay underframe.

Engines: One Cummins LTA10-R of 172 kW (230 hp) at 2100 rpm per car.
Doors: Twin-leaf folding.   **Dimensions:** 15.55 x 2.70 x 3.73 m.
Owners: 143 601/10/14 – Mid-Glamorgan County Council; 143 609 – South Glamorgan County Council; 143 617/18/19 – West Glamorgan County Council. These units are all managed by Porterbrook Leasing Company.

DMS. Dia. DP236 Lot No. 31005 Barclay 1985–86. –/62. 24.0 t.
DMSL. Dia. DP237 Lot No. 31006 Barclay 1985–86. –/60 1T. 24.5 t.

143 601	**RR**	P	*WW*	CF	55642	55667	
143 602	**RR**	P	*CA*	CF	55651	55668	
143 603	**RR**	P	*CA*	CF	55658	55669	
143 604	**RR**	P	*CA*	CF	55645	55670	
143 605	**RR**	P	*CA*	CF	55646	55671	
143 606	**RR**	P	*CA*	CF	55647	55672	
143 607	**RR**	P	*CA*	CF	55648	55673	
143 608	**RR**	P	*CA*	CF	55649	55674	
143 609	**RR**	P	*CA*	CF	55650	55675	TOM JONES
143 610	**RR**	P	*WW*	CF	55643	55676	
143 611	**RR**	P	*CA*	CF	55652	55677	
143 612	**RR**	P	*WW*	CF	55653	55678	
143 613	**RR**	P	*CA*	CF	55654	55679	
143 614	**RR**	P	*WW*	CF	55655	55680	BEWICK'S SWAN
143 615	**RR**	P	*CA*	CF	55656	55681	MUTE SWAN
143 616	**RR**	P	*CA*	CF	55657	55682	WHOOPER SWAN
143 617	**RR**	P	*WW*	CF	55644	55683	
143 618	**RR**	P	*WW*	CF	55659	55684	
143 619	**RR**	P	*WW*	CF	55660	55685	
143 620	**RR**	P	*WW*	CF	55661	55686	
143 621	**RR**	P	*WW*	CF	55662	55687	
143 622	**RR**	P	*WW*	CF	55663	55688	
143 623	**RR**	P	*WW*	CF	55664	55689	
143 624	**RR**	P	*WW*	CF	55665	55690	
143 625	**RR**	P	*WW*	CF	55666	55691	

CLASS 144   2- or 3-Car Pacer

DMS–DMSL or DMS–MS–DMSL. Similar design to Class 143, but bodies built by Alexander on BREL underframe.

Engines: One Cummins LTA10-R of 172 kW (230 hp) at 2100 rpm per car.
Doors: Twin-leaf folding.   **Dimensions:** 15.25 x 2.70 x 3.73 m.
Owner: MS type vehicles – West Yorkshire PTE. These vehicles are managed by Porterbrook Leasing Company.

DMS. Dia. DP240 Lot No. 31015 BREL Derby 1986–87. –/62 1W. 24.0 t.
MS. Dia. DR205 Lot No. 31037 BREL Derby 1987–88. –/73. 24.0 t.
DMSL. Dia. DP241 Lot No. 31016 BREL Derby 1986–87. –/60 1T. 24.5 t.

144 001	**WY**	P	*NS*	NL	55801	55824	
144 001	**WY**	P	*NS*	NL	55801	55824	
144 002	**WY**	P	*NS*	NL	55802	55825	
144 003	**WY**	P	*NS*	NL	55803	55826	
144 004	**WY**	P	*NS*	NL	55804	55827	
144 005	**WY**	P	*NS*	NL	55805	55828	
144 006	**WY**	P	*NS*	NL	55806	55829	
144 007	**WY**	P	*NS*	NL	55807	55830	
144 008	**WY**	P	*NS*	NL	55808	55831	
144 009	**WY**	P	*NS*	NL	55809	55832	
144 010	**WY**	P	*NS*	NL	55810	55833	
144 011	**RR**	P	*NS*	NL	55811	55834	
144 012	**RR**	P	*NS*	NL	55812	55835	
144 013	**RR**	P	*NS*	NL	55813	55836	
144 014	**WY**	P	*NS*	NL	55814	55850	55837
144 015	**WY**	P	*NS*	NL	55815	55851	55838
144 016	**WY**	P	*NS*	NL	55816	55852	55839
144 017	**WY**	P	*NS*	NL	55817	55853	55840
144 018	**WY**	P	*NS*	NL	55818	55854	55841
144 019	**WY**	P	*NS*	NL	55819	55855	55842
144 020	**WY**	P	*NS*	NL	55820	55856	55843
144 021	**WY**	P	*NS*	NL	55821	55857	55844
144 022	**WY**	P	*NS*	NL	55822	55858	55845
144 023	**WY**	P	*NS*	NL	55823	55859	55846

CLASS 150/0   3-Car Sprinter

DMSL–MS–DMS. Prototype Sprinter.
Engines: One Cummins NT-855-R4 of 213 kW (285 hp) at 2100 rpm per car.
Bogies: BX8P (powered), BX8T (non-powered).
Accommodation: 3 + 2 part unidirectional and part facing seating.
Dimensions: 20.06 x 2.82 x 3.77 m (DMS & DMSL), 20.18 x 2.82 x 3.77 m (MS).

DMSL. Dia. DP238. Lot No. 30984 BREL York 1984–85. –/72 1T. 35.8 t.
MS. Dia. DR202. Lot No. 30986 BREL York 1984–85. –/92. 34.4 t.
DMS. Dia. DP239. Lot No. 30985 BREL York 1984–85. –/76. 35.6 t.

150 001	r	**CO**	A	*CT*	TS	55200	55400	55300
150 002	r	**CO**	A	*CT*	TS	55201	55401	55301

CLASS 150/1   2- or 3-Car Sprinter

DMSL–DMS or DMSL–Class 150/2 DMSL–DMS or DMSL–Class 150/2 DMS–DMS.
Engines: One Cummins NT855R5 of 213 kW (285 hp) at 2100 rpm per car.
Bogies: BP38 (powered), BT38 (non-powered).
Dimensions: 20.06 x 2.82 x 3.77 m.
Accommodation: 3+2 facing († part unidirectional and part facing seating).
Note: For details of centre cars of 3-car units, see Class 150/2 vehicle data.

DMSL. Dia. DP238. Lot No. 31011 BREL York 1985–86. –/72 (* –/64; § –/68) 1T.
37.6 t.
DMS. Dia. DP239. Lot No. 31012 BREL York 1985–86. –/76 (* –/70; § –/66). 36.7 t.

150 010	r†	**CO**	A	*CT*	TS	52110	57226	57110
150 011	r†	**CO**	A	*CT*	TS	52111	57206	57111
150 012	r†	**CO**	A	*CT*	TS	52112	52204	57112
150 013	r†	**CO**	A	*CT*	TS	52113	52226	57113
150 014	r†	**CO**	A	*CT*	TS	52114	57204	57114
150 015	r†	**CO**	A	*CT*	TS	52115	52206	57115
150 016	r†	**CO**	A	*CT*	TS	52116	57212	57116
150 017	r†	**CO**	A	*CT*	TS	52117	57209	57117
150 101	r†	**CO**	A	*CT*	TS	52101	57101	
150 102	r†	**CO**	A	*CT*	TS	52102	57102	
150 103	r†	**CO**	A	*CT*	TS	52103	57103	
150 104	r†	**CO**	A	*CT*	TS	52104	57104	
150 105	r†	**CO**	A	*CT*	TS	52105	57105	
150 106	r†	**CO**	A	*CT*	TS	52106	57106	
150 107	r†	**CO**	A	*CT*	TS	52107	57107	
150 108	r†	**CO**	A	*CT*	TS	52108	57108	
150 109	r†	**CO**	A	*CT*	TS	52109	57109	
150 118	r†	**CO**	A	*CT*	TS	52118	57118	
150 119	r†	**CO**	A	*CT*	TS	52119	57119	
150 120	r†	**CO**	A	*CT*	TS	52120	57120	
150 121	r†	**CO**	A	*CT*	TS	52121	57121	
150 122	r†	**CO**	A	*CT*	TS	52122	57122	
150 123	r†	**CO**	A	*CT*	TS	52123	57123	
150 124	r†	**CO**	A	*CT*	TS	52124	57124	
150 125	r†	**CO**	A	*CT*	TS	52125	57125	
150 126	r†	**CO**	A	*CT*	TS	52126	57126	
150 127	r†	**CO**	A	*CT*	TS	52127	57127	
150 128	r†	**CO**	A	*CT*	TS	52128	57128	
150 129	r†	**CO**	A	*CT*	TS	52129	57129	
150 130	r†	**CO**	A	*CT*	TS	52130	57130	
150 131	r†	**CO**	A	*CT*	TS	52131	57131	
150 132	r†	**CO**	A	*CT*	TS	52132	57132	
150 133	*	**GM**	A	*NW*	NH	52133	57133	
150 134	*	**NW**	A	*NW*	NH	52134	57134	
150 135	*	**GM**	A	*NW*	NH	52135	57135	
150 136	*	**GM**	A	*NW*	NH	52136	57136	
150 137	§ *	**GM**	A	*NW*	NH	52137	57137	
150 138	*	**GM**	A	*NW*	NH	52138	57138	
150 139	*	**GM**	A	*NW*	NH	52139	57139	
150 140	*	**GM**	A	*NW*	NH	52140	57140	
150 141	*	**GM**	A	*NW*	NH	52141	57141	
150 142	§	**GM**	A	*NW*	NH	52142	57142	
150 143	*	**PS**	A	*NW*	NH	52143	57143	
150 144	§	**PS**	A	*NW*	NH	52144	57144	
150 145	§	**PS**	A	*NW*	NH	52145	57145	
150 146	§	**RR**	A	*NW*	NH	52146	57146	
150 147	§	**PS**	A	*NW*	NH	52147	57147	
150 148	§	**PS**	A	*NW*	NH	52148	57148	
150 149	§	**PS**	A	*NW*	NH	52149	57149	
150 150	§	**PS**	A	*NW*	NH	52150	57150	

CLASS 150/2   2-Car Sprinter

DMSL–DMS.
Engines: One Cummins NT855R5 of 213 kW (285 hp) at 2100 rpm per car.
Bogies: BP38 (powered), BT38 (non-powered).
Dimensions: 20.06 x 2.82 x 3.77 m.

DMSL. Dia. DP242. Lot No. 31017 York 1987. –/73 (†§ –/70)1T. 37.5 t.
DMS. Dia. DP243. Lot No. 31018 York 1987. –/76 (* –/68; ‡§ –/73). 36.5 t.

150 201	†	**MT**	A	*NW*	NH	52201	57201
150 202		**CO**	A	*CT*	TS	52202	57202
150 203	†	**MT**	A	*NW*	NH	52203	57203
150 205	†	**MT**	A	*NW*	NH	52205	57205
150 207	‡	**MT**	A	*NW*	NH	52207	57207
150 208		**RR**	P	*SR*	HA	52208	57208
150 210		**CO**	A	*CT*	TS	52210	57210
150 211	‡	**MT**	A	*NW*	NH	52211	57211
150 213	r*	**RR**	P	*AR*	NC	52213	57213	LORD NELSON
150 214		**CO**	A	*CT*	TS	52214	57214
150 215		**GM**	A	*NW*	NH	52215	57215
150 216		**CO**	A	*CT*	TS	52216	57216
150 217	r*	**RR**	P	*AR*	NC	52217	57217	OLIVER CROMWELL
150 218	§	**GM**	A	*NW*	NH	52218	57218
150 219	r	**RR**	P	*WW*	CF	52219	57219
150 220		**CO**	A	*CT*	TS	52220	57220
150 221	r	**RR**	P	*WW*	CF	52221	57221
150 222	§	**GM**	A	*NW*	NH	52222	57222
150 223	†	**GM**	A	*NW*	NH	52223	57223
150 224	†	**GM**	A	*NW*	NH	52224	57224
150 225	‡	**GM**	A	*NW*	NH	52225	57225
150 227	r*	**RR**	P	*AR*	NC	52227	57227	SIR ALF RAMSEY
150 228		**RR**	P	*SR*	HA	52228	57228
150 229	r*	**RR**	P	*AR*	NC	52229	57229	GEORGE BORROW
150 230	r	**RR**	P	*WW*	CF	52230	57230
150 231	r*	**RR**	P	*AR*	NC	52231	57231	KING EDMUND
150 232	r	**RR**	P	*WW*	CF	52232	57232
150 233	r	**RR**	P	*WW*	CF	52233	57233
150 234	r	**RR**	P	*WW*	CF	52234	57234
150 235	r*	**RR**	P	*AR*	NC	52235	57235	CARDINAL WOLSEY
150 236	r	**RR**	P	*WW*	CF	52236	57236
150 237	r*	**RR**	P	*AR*	NC	52237	57237	HEREWARD THE WAKE
150 238	r	**RR**	P	*WW*	CF	52238	57238
150 239	r	**RR**	P	*WW*	CF	52239	57239
150 240	r	**RR**	P	*WW*	CF	52240	57240
150 241	r	**RR**	P	*WW*	CF	52241	57241
150 242	r	**RR**	P	*WW*	CF	52242	57242
150 243	r	**RR**	P	*WW*	CF	52243	57243
150 244	r	**RR**	P	*WW*	CF	52244	57244
150 245	r	**RR**	P	*SR*	HA	52245	57245
150 246	r	**RR**	P	*WW*	CF	52246	57246

150 247	r	**RR**	P	*WW*	CF	52247	57247
150 248	r	**RR**	P	*WW*	CF	52248	57248
150 249	r	**RR**	P	*WW*	CF	52249	57249
150 250		**RR**	P	*SR*	HA	52250	57250
150 251	r	**RR**	P	*WW*	CF	52251	57251
150 252		**RR**	P	*SR*	HA	52252	57252
150 253	r	**RR**	P	*WW*	CF	52253	57253
150 254	r	**RR**	P	*WW*	CF	52254	57254
150 255	r*	**RR**	P	*AR*	NC	52255	57255	HENRY BLOGG
150 256		**RR**	P	*SR*	HA	52256	57256
150 257	r*	**RR**	P	*AR*	NC	52257	57257	QUEEN BOADICEA
150 258		**RR**	P	*SR*	HA	52258	57258
150 259		**RR**	P	*SR*	HA	52259	57259
150 260		**RR**	P	*SR*	HA	52260	57260
150 261	r	**RR**	P	*WW*	CF	52261	57261
150 262		**RR**	P	*SR*	HA	52262	57262
150 263	r	**RR**	P	*WW*	CF	52263	57263
150 264		**RR**	P	*SR*	HA	52264	57264
150 265	r	**RR**	P	*WW*	CF	52265	57265
150 266	r	**RR**	P	*WW*	CF	52266	57266
150 267	r	**RR**	P	*WW*	CF	52267	57267
150 268		**RR**	P	*NS*	NL	52268	57268
150 269		**RR**	P	*NS*	NL	52269	57269
150 270		**RR**	P	*NS*	NL	52270	57270
150 271		**RR**	P	*NS*	NL	52271	57271
150 272		**RR**	P	*NS*	NL	52272	57272
150 273		**RR**	P	*NS*	NL	52273	57273
150 274		**RR**	P	*NS*	NL	52274	57274
150 275		**RR**	P	*CA*	CF	52275	57275
150 276		**RR**	P	*CA*	CF	52276	57276
150 277		**RR**	P	*CA*	CF	52277	57277
150 278		**RR**	P	*CA*	CF	52278	57278
150 279		**RR**	P	*CA*	CF	52279	57279
150 280		**RR**	P	*CA*	CF	52280	57280
150 281		**RR**	P	*CA*	CF	52281	57281
150 282		**RR**	P	*CA*	CF	52282	57282
150 283		**RR**	P	*SR*	HA	52283	57283
150 284		**RR**	P	*SR*	HA	52284	57284
150 285		**RR**	P	*SR*	HA	52285	57285	EDINBURGH-BATHGATE 1986-1996

CLASS 153   Single Car Super Sprinter

DMSL. Converted from Class 155/0 2-car units.
Engine: One Cummins NT855R5 of 213 kW (285 hp) at 2100 rpm.
Bogies: P3-10 (powered), BT38 (non-powered).
Dimensions: 23.29 x 2.69 x 3.75 m.   **Doors:** Sliding plug.

DMSL. Dia. DX203. Lot No. 31115 Leyland Bus 1987–88. Converted by Hunslet-Barclay 1991–92. –/72 (* –/66) 1TD. 41.2 t.

153 301		**RR**	A	*NS*	HT	52301	
153 302	r	**RR**	A	*WW*	CF	52302	
153 303	r	**RR**	A	*WW*	CF	52303	
153 304		**RR**	A	*NS*	HT	52304	
153 305	r	**RR**	A	*WW*	CF	52305	
153 306	r*	**RR**	P	*AR*	NC	52306	EDITH CAVELL
153 307		**RR**	A	*NS*	HT	52307	
153 308	r	**RR**	A	*WW*	CF	52308	
153 309	r*	**RR**	P	*AR*	NC	52309	GERARD FIENNES
153 310		**RR**	P	*NW*	NH	52310	
153 311	r*	**RR**	P	*AR*	NC	52311	JOHN CONSTABLE
153 312	r	**RR**	A	*WW*	CF	52312	
153 313		**RR**	P	*NW*	NH	52313	
153 314	r*	**RR**	P	*AR*	NC	52314	DELIA SMITH
153 315		**RR**	A	*NS*	HT	52315	
153 316		**RR**	P	*NW*	NH	52316	
153 317		**RR**	A	*NS*	HT	52317	
153 318	r	**RR**	A	*WW*	CF	52318	
153 319		**RR**	A	*NS*	HT	52319	
153 320	r	**RR**	P	*CT*	TS	52320	
153 321	r	**RR**	P	*CT*	TS	52321	
153 322	r*	**RR**	P	*AR*	NC	52322	BENJAMIN BRITTEN
153 323	r	**RR**	P	*CT*	TS	52323	
153 324		**RR**	P	*NW*	NH	52324	
153 325	r	**RR**	P	*CT*	TS	52325	
153 326	r*	**RR**	P	*AR*	NC	52326	TED ELLIS
153 327	r	**RR**	A	*WW*	CF	52327	
153 328		**RR**	A	*NS*	HT	52328	
153 329	r	**RR**	P	*CT*	TS	52329	
153 330		**RR**	P	*NW*	NH	52330	
153 331		**RR**	A	*NS*	HT	52331	
153 332		**RR**	P	*NW*	NH	52332	
153 333	r	**RR**	P	*CT*	TS	52333	
153 334	r	**RR**	P	*CT*	TS	52334	
153 335	r*	**RR**	P	*AR*	NC	52335	MICHAEL PALIN
153 351		**RR**	A	*NS*	HT	57351	
153 352		**RR**	A	*NS*	HT	57352	
153 353	r	**RR**	A	*WW*	CF	57353	
153 354	r	**RR**	P	*CT*	TS	57354	
153 355	r	**RR**	A	*WW*	CF	57355	
153 356	r	**RR**	P	*CT*	TS	57356	
153 357		**RR**	A	*NS*	HT	57357	
153 358		**RR**	P	*NW*	NH	57358	
153 359		**RR**	P	*NW*	NH	57359	
153 360		**RR**	P	*NW*	NH	57360	
153 361		**RR**	P	*NW*	NH	57361	
153 362	r	**RR**	A	*WW*	CF	57362	
153 363		**RR**	P	*NW*	NH	57363	
153 364	r	**RR**	P	*CT*	TS	57364	
153 365	r	**RR**	P	*CT*	TS	57365	
153 366	r	**RR**	P	*CT*	TS	57366	

153 367		**RR**	P	*NW*	NH	57367
153 368	r	**RR**	A	*WW*	CF	57368
153 369	r	**RR**	P	*CT*	TS	57369
153 370	r	**RR**	A	*WW*	CF	57370
153 371	r	**RR**	P	*CT*	TS	57371
153 372	r	**RR**	A	*WW*	CF	57372
153 373	r	**RR**	A	*WW*	CF	57373
153 374	r	**RR**	A	*WW*	CF	57374
153 375	r	**RR**	P	*CT*	TS	57375
153 376	r	**RR**	P	*CT*	TS	57376
153 377	r	**RR**	A	*WW*	CF	57377
153 378		**RR**	A	*NS*	HT	57378
153 379	r	**RR**	P	*CT*	TS	57379
153 380	r	**RR**	A	*WW*	CF	57380
153 381	r	**RR**	P	*CT*	TS	57381
153 382	r	**RR**	A	*WW*	CF	57382
153 383	r	**RR**	P	*CT*	TS	57383
153 384	r	**RR**	P	*CT*	TS	57384
153 385	r	**RR**	P	*CT*	TS	57385

CLASS 155/1   2-Car Super Sprinter

DMSL–DMS.
Engines: One Cummins NT855R5 of 213 kW (285 hp) at 2100 rpm per car.
Bogies: P3-10 (powered), BT38 (non-powered).
Dimensions: 23.21 x 2.69 x 3.75 m.   **Doors:** Sliding plug.
Owner: These units are owned by West Yorkshire PTE but are managed by Porterbrook Leasing Company.

DMSL. Dia. DP248. Lot No. 31057 Leyland Bus 1988. –/80 1TD. 39.0 t.
DMS. Dia. DP249. Lot No. 31058 Leyland Bus 1988. –/80. 38.6 t.

155 341	**WY**	P	*NS*	NL	52341	57341
155 342	**WY**	P	*NS*	NL	52342	57342
155 343	**WY**	P	*NS*	NL	52343	57343
155 344	**WY**	P	*NS*	NL	52344	57344
155 345	**WY**	P	*NS*	NL	52345	57345
155 346	**WY**	P	*NS*	NL	52346	57346
155 347	**WY**	P	*NS*	NL	52347	57347

CLASS 156   2-Car Super Sprinter

DMSL–DMS.
Engines: One Cummins NT855R5 of 213 kW (285 hp) at 2100 rpm per car.
Bogies: P3-10 (powered), BT38 (non-powered).
Dimensions: 23.03 x 2.73 x 3.81 m.   **Doors:** Sliding.
Owner: 156 500–514 are owned by Strathclyde PTE, but are managed by Angel Trains Contracts.

DMSL. Dia. DP244. Lot No. 31028 Met-Camm. 1987–89. –/74 (*† –/72; § –/70) 1TD. 35.8 t.
DMS. Dia. DP245. Lot No. 31029 Met-Camm. 1987–89. –/76 (* 72). 35.8 t.

156 401	r†	**RR**	P	*CT*	TS	52401	57401	
156 401	r†	**RR**	P	*CT*	TS	52401	57401	
156 402	r†	**RR**	P	*CT*	TS	52402	57402	
156 403	r†	**RR**	P	*CT*	TS	52403	57403	
156 404	r†	**RR**	P	*CT*	TS	52404	57404	
156 405	r†	**RR**	P	*CT*	TS	52405	57405	
156 406	r†	**RR**	P	*CT*	TS	52406	57406	
156 407	r†	**RR**	P	*CT*	TS	52407	57407	
156 408	r†	**RR**	P	*CT*	TS	52408	57408	
156 409	r†	**RR**	P	*CT*	TS	52409	57409	
156 410	r†	**RR**	P	*CT*	TS	52410	57410	
156 411	r†	**RR**	P	*CT*	TS	52411	57411	
156 412	r†	**RR**	P	*CT*	TS	52412	57412	
156 413	r†	**RR**	P	*CT*	TS	52413	57413	
156 414	r†	**RR**	P	*CT*	TS	52414	57414	
156 415	r†	**RR**	P	*CT*	TS	52415	57415	
156 416	r†	**RR**	P	*CT*	TS	52416	57416	
156 417	r†	**RR**	P	*CT*	TS	52417	57417	
156 418	r†	**RR**	P	*CT*	TS	52418	57418	
156 419	r†	**RR**	P	*CT*	TS	52419	57419	
156 420	§	**RN**	P	*NW*	NH	52420	57420	
156 421	§	**RN**	P	*NW*	NH	52421	57421	
156 422	r†	**RR**	P	*CT*	TS	52422	57422	
156 423	§	**RN**	P	*NW*	NH	52423	57423	
156 424	§	**RN**	P	*NW*	NH	52424	57424	
156 425	§	**RN**	P	*NW*	NH	52425	57425	
156 426	§	**RN**	P	*NW*	NH	52426	57426	
156 427	§	**RN**	P	*NW*	NH	52427	57427	
156 428	§	**RN**	P	*NW*	NH	52428	57428	
156 429	§	**RN**	P	*NW*	NH	52429	57429	
156 430	r*	**RR**	A	*SR*	CK	52430	57430	
156 431	r*	**RR**	A	*SR*	CK	52431	57431	
156 432	r*	**RR**	A	*SR*	CK	52432	57432	
156 433	r*	**CC**	A	*SR*	CK	52433	57433	The Kilmarnock Edition
156 434	r*	**RR**	A	*SR*	CK	52434	57434	
156 435	r*	**RR**	A	*SR*	CK	52435	57435	
156 436	*	**RR**	A	*SR*	CK	52436	57436	
156 437	*	**RR**	A	*SR*	CK	52437	57437	
156 438		**PS**	A	*NS*	NL	52438	57438	
156 439	r*	**RR**	A	*SR*	CK	52439	57439	
156 440	§	**RN**	P	*NW*	NH	52440	57440	
156 441	§	**RN**	P	*NW*	NH	52441	57441	
156 442	*	**RR**	A	*SR*	CK	52442	57442	
156 443		**PS**	A	*NS*	HT	52443	57443	
156 444		**PS**	A	*NS*	HT	52444	57444	
156 445	r*	**RR**	A	*SR*	CK	52445	57445	
156 446	r*	**RR**	A	*SR*	IS	52446	57446	
156 447	r*	**PS**	A	*SR*	CK	52447	57447	
156 448		**PS**	A	*NS*	HT	52448	57448	
156 449	r*	**PS**	A	*SR*	CK	52449	57449	saint columba
156 450	r*	**RR**	A	*SR*	CK	52450	57450	
156 451		**PS**	A	*NS*	HT	52451	57451	

156 452	§	**RN**	A	*NW*	NH	52452	57452
156 453	r*	**RR**	A	*SR*	CK	52453	57453
156 454		**PS**	A	*NS*	HT	52454	57454	Whitby Endeavour
156 455	§	**RN**	P	*NW*	NH	52455	57455
156 456	r*	**RR**	A	*SR*	CK	52456	57456
156 457	r*	**RR**	A	*SR*	IS	52457	57457
156 458	r*	**RR**	A	*SR*	IS	52458	57458
156 459	§	**RN**	P	*NW*	NH	52459	57459
156 460	§	**RN**	P	*NW*	NH	52460	57460
156 461	§	**RN**	P	*NW*	NH	52461	57461
156 462	r*	**RR**	A	*SR*	CK	52462	57462
156 463		**PS**	A	*NS*	HT	52463	57463
156 464	§	**RN**	P	*NW*	NH	52464	57464
156 465	r*	**RR**	A	*SR*	CK	52465	57465	Bonny Prince Charlie
156 466	§	**RN**	P	*NW*	NH	52466	57466
156 467	r*	**RR**	A	*SR*	CK	52467	57467
156 468		**PS**	A	*NS*	NL	52468	57468
156 469		**PS**	A	*NS*	HT	52469	57469
156 470		**PS**	A	*NS*	NL	52470	57470
156 471		**PS**	A	*NS*	NL	52471	57471
156 472		**PS**	A	*NS*	NL	52472	57472
156 473		**PS**	A	*NS*	NL	52473	57473
156 474	r*	**RR**	A	*SR*	IS	52474	57474
156 475		**PS**	A	*NS*	NL	52475	57475
156 476	*	**RR**	A	*SR*	CK	52476	57476
156 477	r*	**RR**	A	*SR*	IS	52477	57477	HIGHLAND FESTIVAL
156 478	r*	**PS**	A	*SR*	IS	52478	57478
156 479		**PS**	A	*NS*	NL	52479	57479
156 480		**PS**	A	*NS*	NL	52480	57480
156 481		**PS**	A	*NS*	NL	52481	57481
156 482		**PS**	A	*NS*	NL	52482	57482
156 483		**PS**	A	*NS*	NL	52483	57483
156 484		**PS**	A	*NS*	NL	52484	57484
156 485	r*	**RR**	A	*SR*	CK	52485	57485
156 486		**PS**	A	*NS*	NL	52486	57486
156 487		**PS**	A	*NS*	NL	52487	57487
156 488		**PS**	A	*NS*	NL	52488	57488
156 489		**PS**	A	*NS*	NL	52489	57489
156 490		**PS**	A	*NS*	NL	52490	57490
156 491		**PS**	A	*NS*	NL	52491	57491
156 492	r*	**RR**	A	*SR*	CK	52492	57492
156 493	r*	**RR**	A	*SR*	CK	52493	57493
156 494	r*	**CC**	A	*SR*	CK	52494	57494
156 495	r*	**RR**	A	*SR*	CK	52495	57495
156 496	r*	**RR**	A	*SR*	CK	52496	57496
156 497		**PS**	A	*NS*	NL	52497	57497
156 498		**PS**	A	*NS*	NL	52498	57498
156 499	r*	**PS**	A	*SR*	IS	52499	57499
156 500	r*	**RR**	A	*SR*	CK	52500	57500
156 501		**S**	A	*SR*	CK	52501	57501
156 502		**S**	A	*SR*	CK	52502	57502

156 503		S	A	*SR*	CK	52503	57503
156 504	r*	S	A	*SR*	CK	52504	57504
156 505	r*	S	A	*SR*	CK	52506	57506
156 507		S	A	*SR*	CK	52507	57507
156 508		S	A	*SR*	CK	52508	57508
156 509		CC	A	*SR*	CK	52509	57509
156 510		S	A	*SR*	CK	52510	57510
156 511		S	A	*SR*	CK	52511	57511
156 512		S	A	*SR*	CK	52512	57512
156 513		S	A	*SR*	CK	52513	57513
156 514		S	A	*SR*	CK	52514	57514

CLASS 158/0   2- or 3-Car Express Unit

DMSL(B)–DMSL(A), * DMCL–DMSL, DMSL(B)–MSL–DMSL(A), or § DMSL–MSL–DMCL.
Engines: One Cummins NTA855R1 of 261 kW (350 hp) at 1900 rpm (‡ One Cummins NTA855R3 of 298 kW (400 hp) at 1900 rpm; † One Perkins 2006-TWH of 261 kW (350 hp) at 2100 rpm) per car.
Bogies: BREL P4-4 (powered), BREL T4-4 (non-powered).
Dimensions: 23.21 x 2.82 x ?.?? m.

52701–52746. DMCL. Dia. DP252. Lot No. 31051 BREL Derby 1989–90. 15/51 1TD 1W. 38.1 t.
52747–52751. DMCL. Dia. DP323. Lot No. 31051 BREL Derby 1989–90. 9/51 1TD 1W. 38.1 t.
52752–756/760–764/766–768/770–772/774–872. DMSL(B). Dia. DP252. Lot No. 31051 BREL Derby 1989–92. –/68 (• –/66)1TD 1W. 38.1 t.
52757–52759. DMCL. Dia. DP333. Lot No. 31051 BREL Derby 1989–90. 16/51 1TD 1W. 38.1 t.
52765/769/773. DMCL. Dia. DP3??. Lot No. 31051 BREL Derby 1989–90. 16/48 1TD 1W. 38.1 t.
MSL. Dia. DR207. Lot No. 31050 BREL Derby 1991. 37.1 t. –/70 2T.
DMSL (A) (§ DMCL). Dia. DP251 (§ DP3??). Lot No. 31052 BREL Derby 1989–92. –/70 (• –/68; § 32/32) 1T. 38.1 t.

158 701	*	SR	P	*SR*	HA	52701	57701	
158 702	*	RE	P	*SR*	HA	52702	57702	BBC Scotland - 75 Years
158 703	*	RE	P	*SR*	HA	52703	57703	
158 704	*	RE	P	*SR*	HA	52704	57704	
158 705	*	RE	P	*SR*	HA	52705	57705	
158 706	*	RE	P	*SR*	HA	52706	57706	
158 707	*	RE	P	*SR*	HA	52707	57707	
158 708	*	RE	P	*SR*	HA	52708	57708	
158 709	*	RE	P	*SR*	HA	52709	57709	
158 710	*	RE	P	*SR*	HA	52710	57710	
158 711	*	RE	P	*SR*	HA	52711	57711	
158 712	*	RE	P	*SR*	HA	52712	57712	
158 713	*	RE	P	*SR*	HA	52713	57713	
158 714	*	RE	P	*SR*	HA	52714	57714	
158 715	*	RE	P	*SR*	HA	52715	57715	Haymarket
158 716	*	RE	P	*SR*	HA	52716	57716	

158 717	*	**RE**	P	*SR*	HA	52717	57717
158 718	*	**RE**	P	*SR*	HA	52718	57718
158 719	*	**RE**	P	*SR*	HA	52719	57719
158 720	*	**RE**	P	*SR*	HA	52720	57720
158 721	*	**RE**	P	*SR*	HA	52721	57721
158 722	*	**RE**	P	*SR*	HA	52722	57722
158 723	*	**RE**	P	*SR*	HA	52723	57723
158 724	*	**RE**	P	*SR*	HA	52724	57724
158 725	*	**RE**	P	*SR*	HA	52725	57725
158 726	*	**RE**	P	*SR*	HA	52726	57726
158 727	*	**RE**	P	*SR*	HA	52727	57727
158 728	*	**RE**	P	*SR*	HA	52728	57728
158 729	*	**RE**	P	*SR*	HA	52729	57729
158 730	*	**RE**	P	*SR*	HA	52730	57730
158 731	*	**RE**	P	*SR*	HA	52731	57731
158 732	*	**RE**	P	*SR*	HA	52732	57732
158 733	*	**RE**	P	*SR*	HA	52733	57733
158 734	*	**RE**	P	*SR*	HA	52734	57734
158 735	*	**RE**	P	*SR*	HA	52735	57735
158 736	*	**RE**	P	*SR*	HA	52736	57736
158 737	*	**RE**	P	*SR*	HA	52737	57737
158 738	*	**RE**	P	*SR*	HA	52738	57738
158 739	*	**RE**	P	*SR*	HA	52739	57739
158 740	*	**RE**	P	*SR*	HA	52740	57740
158 741	*	**RE**	P	*SR*	HA	52741	57741
158 742	*	**RE**	P	*SR*	HA	52742	57742
158 743	*	**RE**	P	*SR*	HA	52743	57743
158 744	*	**RE**	P	*SR*	HA	52744	57744
158 745	*	**RE**	P	*SR*	HA	52745	57745
158 746	*	**RE**	P	*SR*	HA	52746	57746
158 747	*	**RE**	P	VX	NH	52747	57747
158 748	*	**RE**	P	VX	NH	52748	57748
158 749	*	**RE**	P	VX	NH	52749	57749
158 750	*	**RE**	P	VX	NH	52750	57750
158 751	*	**RE**	P	VX	NH	52751	57751
158 752		**RE**	P	*NW*	NH	52752	57752
158 753		**RE**	P	*NW*	NH	52753	57753
158 754		**RE**	P	*NW*	NH	52754	57754
158 755		**RE**	P	*NW*	NH	52755	57755
158 756		**RE**	P	*NW*	NH	52756	57756
158 757	*	**NW**	P	*NW*	NH	52757	57757
158 758	*	**NW**	P	*NW*	NH	52758	57758
158 759	*	**NW**	P	*NW*	NH	52759	57759
158 760		**TX**	P	*NS*	NL	52760	57760
158 761		**TX**	P	*NS*	NL	52761	57761
158 762		**TX**	P	*NS*	NL	52762	57762
158 763		**TX**	P	*NS*	NL	52763	57763
158 764		**RE**	P	*NS*	NL	52764	57764
158 765	*	**TX**	P	*NS*	NL	52765	57765
158 766		**TX**	P	*NS*	NL	52766	57766
158 767		**RE**	P	*NS*	NL	52767	57767

158 768		**TX**	P	*NS*	NL	52768	57768	
158 769	*	**TX**	P	*NS*	NL	52769	57769	
158 770		**TX**	P	*NS*	NL	52770	57770	
158 771		**RE**	P	*NS*	HT	52771	57771	
158 772		**TX**	P	*NS*	NL	52772	57772	
158 773	*	**TX**	P	*NS*	NL	52773	57773	
158 774		**RE**	P	*NS*	HT	52774	57774	
158 775		**RE**	P	*NS*	HT	52775	57775	
158 776		**RE**	P	*NS*	HT	52776	57776	
158 777		**RE**	P	*NS*	HT	52777	57777	
158 778		**RE**	P	*NS*	HT	52778	57778	
158 779		**RE**	P	*NS*	HT	52779	57779	
158 780	r	**RE**	A	*CT*	TS	52780	57780	
158 781		**RE**	P	*NS*	HT	52781	57781	
158 782	r	**RE**	A	*CT*	TS	52782	57782	
158 783	r	**RE**	A	*CT*	TS	52783	57783	
158 784	r	**RE**	A	*CT*	TS	52784	57784	
158 785	r	**RE**	A	*CT*	TS	52785	57785	
158 786	r	**RE**	A	*CT*	TS	52786	57786	
158 787	r	**RE**	A	*CT*	TS	52787	57787	
158 788	r	**RE**	A	*CT*	TS	52788	57788	
158 789	r	**RE**	A	*CT*	TS	52789	57789	
158 790	r	**RE**	A	*CT*	TS	52790	57790	
158 791	r	**RE**	A	*CT*	TS	52791	57791	
158 792	r	**RE**	A	*CT*	TS	52792	57792	
158 793	r	**RE**	A	*CT*	TS	52793	57793	
158 794	r	**RE**	A	*CT*	TS	52794	57794	
158 795	r	**RE**	A	*CT*	TS	52795	57795	
158 796	r	**RE**	A	*CT*	TS	52796	·57796	
158 797	r	**RE**	A	*CT*	TS	52797	57797	
158 798		**TX**	P	*NS*	HT	52798	58715	57798
158 799		**TX**	P	*NS*	HT	52799	58716	57799
158 800		**TX**	P	*NS*	HT	52800	58717	57800
158 801		**RE**	P	*NS*	HT	52801	58701	57801
158 802		**TX**	P	*NS*	HT	52802	58702	57802
158 803		**TX**	P	*NS*	HT	52803	58703	57803
158 804		**TX**	P	*NS*	HT	52804	58704	57804
158 805		**TX**	P	*NS*	HT	52805	58705	57805
158 806		**TX**	P	*NS*	HT	52806	58706	57806
158 807		**RE**	P	*NS*	HT	52807	58707	57807
158 808		**RE**	P	*NS*	HT	52808	58708	57808
158 809		**TX**	P	*NS*	HT	52809	58709	57809
158 810		**TX**	P	*NS*	HT	52810	58710	57810
158 811	§	**TX**	P	*NS*	HT	52811	58711	57811
158 812		**RE**	P	*NS*	HT	52812	58712	57812
158 813		**TX**	P	*NS*	HT	52813	58713	57813
158 814		**TX**	P	*NS*	HT	52814	58714	57814
158 815	†	**RE**	A	*WW*	CF	52815	57815	
158 816	†•	**RE**	A	*WW*	CF	52816	57816	
158 817	†	**RE**	A	*WW*	CF	52817	57817	
158 818	†	**RE**	A	*WW*	CF	52818	57818	

158 819	†	**RE**	A	*WW*	CF	52819	57819
158 820	†•	**RE**	A	*WW*	CF	52820	57820
158 821	†•	**RE**	A	*WW*	CF	52821	57821
158 822	†•	**RE**	A	*WW*	CF	52822	57822
158 823	†	**RE**	A	*WW*	CF	52823	57823
158 824	†•	**RE**	A	*WW*	CF	52824	57824
158 825	†•	**RE**	A	*WW*	CF	52825	57825
158 826	†•	**RE**	A	*WW*	CF	52826	57826
158 827	†•	**RE**	A	*WW*	CF	52827	57827
158 828	†•	**RE**	A	*WW*	CF	52828	57828
158 829	†	**RE**	A	*WW*	CF	52829	57829
158 830	†•	**RE**	A	*WW*	CF	52830	57830
158 831	†•	**RE**	A	*WW*	CF	52831	57831
158 832	†•	**RE**	A	*WW*	CF	52832	57832
158 833	†•	**RE**	A	*WW*	CF	52833	57833
158 834	†•	**RE**	A	*WW*	CF	52834	57834
158 835	†	**RE**	A	*WW*	CF	52835	57835
158 836	†	**RE**	A	*WW*	CF	52836	57836
158 837	†•	**RE**	A	*WW*	CF	52837	57837
158 838	†•	**RE**	A	*WW*	CF	52838	57838
158 839	†•	**RE**	A	*WW*	CF	52839	57839
158 840	†•	**RE**	A	*WW*	CF	52840	57840
158 841	†•	**RE**	A	*WW*	CF	52841	57841
158 842	†	**RE**	A	*WW*	CF	52842	57842
158 843	†	**RE**	A	*WW*	CF	52843	57843
158 844	r†	**RE**	A	*CT*	TS	52844	57844
158 845	r†	**RE**	A	*CT*	TS	52845	57845
158 846	r†	**RE**	A	*CT*	TS	52846	57846
158 847	r†	**RE**	A	*CT*	TS	52847	57847
158 848	r†	**RE**	A	*CT*	TS	52848	57848
158 849	r†	**RE**	A	*CT*	TS	52849	57849
158 850	r†	**RE**	A	*CT*	TS	52850	57850
158 851	r†	**RE**	A	*CT*	TS	52851	57851
158 852	r†	**RE**	A	*CT*	TS	52852	57852
158 853	r†	**RE**	A	*CT*	TS	52853	57853
158 854	r†	**RE**	A	*CT*	TS	52854	57854
158 855	r†	**RE**	A	*CT*	TS	52855	57855
158 856	r†	**RE**	A	*CT*	TS	52856	57856
158 857	r†	**RE**	A	*CT*	TS	52857	57857
158 858	r†	**RE**	A	*CT*	TS	52858	57858
158 859	r†	**RE**	A	*CT*	TS	52859	57859
158 860	r†	**RE**	A	*CT*	TS	52860	57860
158 861	r†	**RE**	A	*CT*	TS	52861	57861
158 862	r†	**RE**	A	*CT*	TS	52862	57862
158 863	‡•	**RE**	A	*WW*	CF	52863	57863
158 864	‡•	**RE**	A	*WW*	CF	52864	57864
158 865	‡•	**RE**	A	*WW*	CF	52865	57865
158 866	‡•	**RE**	A	*WW*	CF	52866	57866
158 867	‡•	**RE**	A	*WW*	CF	52867	57867
158 868	‡•	**RE**	A	*WW*	CF	52868	57868
158 869	‡•	**RE**	A	*WW*	CF	52869	57869

158 870	‡• **RE**	A	*WW*	CF		52870	57870
158 871	‡• **RE**	A	*WW*	CF		52871	57871
158 872	‡ **RE**	A	*WW*	CF	′	52872	57872

CLASS 158/9   2-Car Express Unit

DMSL–DMS.
Details as Class 158/0 except:
Owner: These units are owned by West Yorkshire PTE, but are managed by
Porterbrook Leasing Company.

DMSL. Dia. DP252. Lot No. 31051 BREL Derby 1991. –/70 1TD 1W. 38.1 t.
DMS. Dia. DP251. Lot No. 31052 BREL Derby 1991. –/72. 37.8 t.

158 901	**WY**	P	*NS*	NL	52901	57901
158 902	**WY**	P	*NS*	NL	52902	57902
158 903	**WY**	P	*NS*	NL	52903	57903
158 904	**WY**	P	*NS*	NL	52904	57904
158 905	**WY**	P	*NS*	NL	52905	57905
158 906	**WY**	P	*NS*	NL	52906	57906
158 907	**WY**	P	*NS*	NL	52907	57907
158 908	**WY**	P	*NS*	NL	52908	57908
158 909	**YN**	P	*NS*	NL	52909	57909
158 910	**WY**	P	*NS*	NL	52910	57910

CLASS 159   3-Car Express Unit

DMCL–MSL–DMSL. Built to Class 158 specification but converted before en-
tering passenger service.
Engines: One Cummins NTA855R3 of 298 kW (400 hp) at 1900 rpm per car.
Bogies: BREL P4-4 (powered), BREL T4-4 (non-powered).
Dimensions: 23.21 x 2.82 x ?.?? m.

DMCL. Dia. DP322. Lot No. 31051 BREL Derby 1992–93. Converted by Rosyth
Dockyard 1992–93. 24/28 1TD 1W. 38.1 t.
MSL. Dia. DR209. Lot No. 31050 BREL Derby 1992–93. Converted by Rosyth
Dockyard 1992–93. 37.1 t. –/72 2T.
DMSL. Dia. DP260. Lot No. 31052 BREL Derby 1992–93. Converted by Rosyth
Dockyard 1992–93. –/72 1T. 37.8 t.

159 001	**NT**	P	*SW*	SA	52873	58718	57873	CITY OF EXETER
159 002	**NT**	P	*SW*	SA	52874	58719	57874	CITY OF SALISBURY
159 003	**NT**	P	*SW*	SA	52875	58720	57875	TEMPLECOMBE
159 004	**NT**	P	*SW*	SA	52876	58721	57876	BASINGSTOKE AND DEANE
159 005	**NT**	P	*SW*	SA	52877	58722	57877	
159 006	**NT**	P	*SW*	SA	52878	58723	57878	
159 007	**NT**	P	*SW*	SA	52879	58724	57879	
159 008	**NT**	P	*SW*	SA	52880	58725	57880	
159 009	**NT**	P	*SW*	SA	52881	58726	57881	
159 010	**NT**	P	*SW*	SA	52882	58727	57882	
159 011	**NT**	P	*SW*	SA	52883	58728	57883	

159 012		**NT**	P	*SW*	SA	52884	58729	57884
159 013		**NT**	P	*SW*	SA	52885	58730	57885
159 014		**NT**	P	*SW*	SA	52886	58731	57886
159 015		**NT**	P	*SW*	SA	52887	58732	57887
159 016		**NT**	P	*SW*	SA	52888	58733	57888
159 017		**NT**	P	*SW*	SA	52889	58734	57889
159 018		**NT**	P	*SW*	SA	52890	58735	57890
159 019		**NT**	P	*SW*	SA	52891	58736	57891
159 020		**NT**	P	*SW*	SA	52892	58737	57892
159 021		**NT**	P	*SW*	SA	52893	58738	57893
159 022		**NT**	P	*SW*	SA	52894	58739	57894

CLASS 165/0   2- or 3-Car Network Turbo

DMCL–DMS or DMCL–MS–DMS.
Engines: One Perkins 2006-TWH of 261 kW (350 hp) at 2100 rpm per car.
Bogies: BREL P3-17 (powered), BREL T3-17 (non-powered).
Dimensions: 22.91 (driving cars) or 22.72 (non-driving cars) x 2.81 x ?.?? m.
Maximum Speed: 75 mph

58801–58822, 58873–58878. DMCL. Dia. DP319. Lot No. 31087 BREL York 1991.
16/72 1T. 37.0 t.
58823–58833. DMCL. Dia. DP320. Lot No. 31089 BREL York 1991–92. 24/60
1T. 37.0 t.
MS. Dia. DR208. Lot No. 31090 BREL York 1991–92. 106S. 37.0 t.
DMS. Dia. DP253. Lot No. 31088 BREL York 1991–92. 98S. 37.0 t.

165 001		**NT**	A	*TT*	RG	58801	58834
165 002		**NT**	A	*TT*	RG	58802	58835
165 003		**NT**	A	*TT*	RG	58803	58836
165 004		**NT**	A	*TT*	RG	58804	58837
165 005		**NT**	A	*TT*	RG	58805	58838
165 006	t	**NT**	A	*CR*	AL	58806	58839
165 007	t	**NT**	A	*CR*	AL	58807	58840
165 008	t	**NT**	A	*CR*	AL	58808	58841
165 009	t	**NT**	A	*CR*	AL	58809	58842
165 010	t	**NT**	A	*CR*	AL	58810	58843
165 011	t	**NT**	A	*CR*	AL	58811	58844
165 012	t	**NT**	A	*CR*	AL	58812	58845
165 013	t	**NT**	A	*CR*	AL	58813	58846
165 014	t	**NT**	A	*CR*	AL	58814	58847
165 015	t	**NT**	A	*CR*	AL	58815	58848
165 016	t	**NT**	A	*CR*	AL	58816	58849
165 017	t	**NT**	A	*CR*	AL	58817	58850
165 018	t	**NT**	A	*CR*	AL	58818	58851
165 019	t	**NT**	A	*CR*	AL	58819	58852
165 020	t	**NT**	A	*CR*	AL	58820	58853
165 021	t	**NT**	A	*CR*	AL	58821	58854
165 022	t	**NT**	A	*CR*	AL	58822	58855
165 023	t	**NT**	A	*CR*	AL	58873	58867
165 024	t	**NT**	A	*CR*	AL	58874	58868
165 025	t	**NT**	A	*CR*	AL	58875	58869

165 026	t	**NT**	A	*CR*	AL	58876	58870
165 027	t	**NT**	A	*CR*	AL	58877	58871
165 028	t	**NT**	A	*CR*	AL	58878	58872
165 029	t	**NT**	A	*CR*	AL	58823	55404	58856
165 030	t	**NT**	A	*CR*	AL	58824	55405	58857
165 031	t	**NT**	A	*CR*	AL	58825	55406	58858
165 032	t	**NT**	A	*CR*	AL	58826	55407	58859
165 033	t	**NT**	A	*CR*	AL	58827	55408	58860
165 034	t	**NT**	A	*CR*	AL	58828	55409	58861
165 035	t	**NT**	A	*CR*	AL	58829	55410	58862
165 036	t	**NT**	A	*CR*	AL	58830	55411	58863
165 037	t	**NT**	A	*CR*	AL	58831	55412	58864
165 038	t	**NT**	A	*CR*	AL	58832	55413	58865
165 039	t	**NT**	A	*CR*	AL	58833	55414	58866

CLASS 165/1   2- or 3-Car Network Turbo

DMCL–DMS or DMCL–MS–DMS.
Engines: One Perkins 2006-TWH of 261 kW (350 hp) at 2100 rpm per car.
Bogies: BREL P3-17 (powered), BREL T3-17 (non-powered).
Dimensions: 22.91 (driving cars) or 22.72 (non-driving cars) x 2.81 x ?.?? m.
Maximum Speed: 90 mph.

58953–58969. DMCL. Dia. DP320. Lot No. 31098 BREL York 1992. 24/58 1T. 37.0 t.
58879–58898. DMCL. Dia. DP319. Lot No. 31096 BREL/ABB York 1992–3. 16/72 1T. 37.0 t.
MS. Dia. DR208. Lot No. 31099 BREL/ABB York 1992–3. –/106. 37.0 t.
DMS. Dia. DP253. Lot No. 31097 BREL/ABB York 1992–3. –/98. 37.0 t.

165 101	**NT**	A	*TT*	RG	58953	55415	58916
165 102	**NT**	A	*TT*	RG	58954	55416	58917
165 103	**NT**	A	*TT*	RG	58955	55417	58918
165 104	**NT**	A	*TT*	RG	58956	55418	58919
165 105	**NT**	A	*TT*	RG	58957	55419	58920
165 106	**NT**	A	*TT*	RG	58958	55420	58921
165 107	**NT**	A	*TT*	RG	58959	55421	58922
165 108	**NT**	A	*TT*	RG	58960	55422	58923
165 109	**NT**	A	*TT*	RG	58961	55423	58924
165 110	**NT**	A	*TT*	RG	58962	55424	58925
165 111	**NT**	A	*TT*	RG	58963	55425	58926
165 112	**NT**	A	*TT*	RG	58964	55426	58927
165 113	**NT**	A	*TT*	RG	58965	55427	58928
165 114	**NT**	A	*TT*	RG	58966	55428	58929
165 115	**NT**	A	*TT*	RG	58967	55429	58930
165 116	**NT**	A	*TT*	RG	58968	55430	58931
165 117	**NT**	A	*TT*	RG	58969	55431	58932
165 118	**NT**	A	*TT*	RG	58879	58933
165 119	**NT**	A	*TT*	RG	58880	58934
165 120	**NT**	A	*TT*	RG	58881	58935
165 121	**NT**	A	*TT*	RG	58882	58936
165 122	**NT**	A	*TT*	RG	58883	58937
165 123	**NT**	A	*TT*	RG	58884	58938

165 124	**NT**	A	*TT*	RG	58885	58939
165 125	**NT**	A	*TT*	RG	58886	58940
165 126	**NT**	A	*TT*	RG	58887	58941
165 127	**NT**	A	*TT*	RG	58888	58942
165 128	**NT**	A	*TT*	RG	58889	58943
165 129	**NT**	A	*TT*	RG	58890	58944
165 130	**NT**	A	*TT*	RG	58891	58945
165 131	**NT**	A	*TT*	RG	58892	58946
165 132	**NT**	A	*TT*	RG	58893	58947
165 133	**NT**	A	*TT*	RG	58894	58948
165 134	**NT**	A	*TT*	RG	58895	58950
165 135	**NT**	A	*TT*	RG	58896	58950
165 136	**NT**	A	*TT*	RG	58897	58951
165 137	**NT**	A	*TT*	RG	58898	58952

CLASS 166   3-Car Network Express Turbo

DMCL(A)–MS–DMCL(B).
Engines: One Perkins 2006-TWH of 261 kW (350 hp) at 2100 rpm per car.
Bogies: BREL P3-17 (powered), BREL T3-17 (non-powered).
Gangways: Within unit only.   **Doors:** Sliding plug.
Dimensions: 22.91 (driving cars) or 22.72 (non-driving cars) x 2.81 x ?.?? m.

DMCL(A). Dia. DP321. Lot No. 31116 ABB York 1993. 16/68 1T. 40.6 t.
MS. Dia. DR210. Lot No. 31117 ABB York 1993. –/88. 38.4 t.
DMCL(B). Dia. DP321. Lot No. 31116 ABB York 1993. 16/68 1T. 40.6 t.

166 201	**NT**	A	*TT*	RG	58101	58601	58122
166 202	**NT**	A	*TT*	RG	58102	58602	58123
166 203	**NT**	A	*TT*	RG	58103	58603	58124
166 204	**NT**	A	*TT*	RG	58104	58604	58125
166 205	**NT**	A	*TT*	RG	58105	58605	58126
166 206	**NT**	A	*TT*	RG	58106	58606	58127
166 207	**NT**	A	*TT*	RG	58107	58607	58128
166 208	**NT**	A	*TT*	RG	58108	58608	58129
166 209	**NT**	A	*TT*	RG	58109	58609	58130
166 210	**NT**	A	*TT*	RG	58110	58610	58131
166 211	**NT**	A	*TT*	RG	58111	58611	58132
166 212	**NT**	A	*TT*	RG	58112	58612	58133
166 213	**NT**	A	*TT*	RG	58113	58613	58134
166 214	**NT**	A	*TT*	RG	58114	58614	58135
166 215	**NT**	A	*TT*	RG	58115	58615	58136
166 216	**NT**	A	*TT*	RG	58116	58616	58137
166 217	**NT**	A	*TT*	RG	58117	58617	58138
166 218	**NT**	A	*TT*	RG	58118	58618	58139
166 219	**NT**	A	*TT*	RG	58119	58619	58140
166 220	**NT**	A	*TT*	RG	58120	58620	58141
166 221	**NT**	A	*TT*	RG	58121	58621	58142

CLASS 168   4-Car Chiltern Clubman

DMSL(A)–MSL–MS–DMSL(B).
Engines: One MTU 6R183TD13H of 315 kW (422 hp) at 1900 rpm per car.
Bogies: BREL P3-23 (powered), BREL T3-23 (non-powered).
Transmission: Hydraulic. Voith T211rzze to ZF final drive.
Dimensions: 22.93 x 2.69 x ?.?? m (DMSL), 22.80 x 2.69 x ??.?? m (MS).

DMSL(A). Dia. DP270. Adtranz Derby 1997–8. –/60 1TD 1W. 43.7 t.
MSL. Dia. DR211. Adtranz Derby 1998. –/73 1T. 41.0 t.
MS. Dia. DR211. Adtranz Derby 1998. –/77. 40.5 t.
DMSL(B). Dia. DP270. Adtranz Derby 1998. –/66 1T. 43.6 t.

168 001	t	**CR**	P	*CR*	AL	58151	58651	58451	58251
168 002	t	**CR**	P	*CR*	AL	58152	58652	58452	58252
168 003	t	**CR**	P	*CR*	AL	58153	58653	58453	58253
168 004	t	**CR**	P	*CR*	AL	58154	58654	58454	58254
168 005	t	**CR**	P	*CR*	AL	58155	58655	58455	58255

CLASS 170   2- or 3-Car Turbostar

Various formations (see below).
Engines: One MTU 6R183TD13H of 315 kW (422 hp) at 1900 rpm per car.
Bogies: BREL P3-23 (powered), BREL T3-23 (non-powered).
Transmission: Hydraulic. Voith T211rzze to ZF final drive.
Dimensions: 23.62 x 2.69 x 3.77 m. (Driving Cars), 23.61 x 2.69 x 3.77 m. (Other cars).
Maximum Speed: 100 mph.

Class 170/1. Vehicles for Midland Mainline. DMCL(A)–DMCL(B).
DMCL(A). Dia. DP324. Adtranz Derby 1998–99. 12/45 1TD 2W. 45.2 t.
DMCL(B). Dia. DP325. Adtranz Derby 1998–99. 12/52 1T. 44.8 t.

170 101	**MM**	P	*MM*	DY	50101	79101
170 102	**MM**	P	*MM*	DY	50102	79102
170 103	**MM**	P	*MM*	DY	50103	79103
170 104	**MM**	P	*MM*		50104	79104
170 105	**MM**	P	*MM*		50105	79105
170 106	**MM**	P	*MM*		50106	79106
170 107	**MM**	P	*MM*		50107	79107
170 108	**MM**	P	*MM*		50108	79108
170 109	**MM**	P	*MM*		50109	79109
170 110	**MM**	P	*MM*		50110	79110
170 111	**MM**	P	*MM*		50111	79111
170 112	**MM**	P	*MM*		50112	79112
170 113	**MM**	P	*MM*		50113	79113
170 114	**MM**	P	*MM*		50114	79114
170 115	**MM**	P	*MM*		50115	79115
170 116	**MM**	P	*MM*		50116	79116
170 117	**MM**	P	*MM*		50117	79117

Class 170/2. Vehicles on order for Anglia Railways. DMCL–MS–DMSL.
DMCL. Dia. DP326. Adtranz Derby 1999. 29/3 1TD 2W.
MSLRMB. Dia. DR212. Adtranz Derby 1999. –/58 1T.
DMSL. Dia. DP274. Adtranz Derby 1999. –/66 1T.

170 201	**AR**	P	*AR*	50201	56201	79201
170 202	**AR**	P	*AR*	50202	56202	79202
170 203	**AR**	P	*AR*	50203	56203	79203
170 204	**AR**	P	*AR*	50204	56204	79204
170 205	**AR**	P	*AR*	50205	56205	79205
170 206	**AR**	P	*AR*	50206	56206	79206
170 207	**AR**	P	*AR*	50207	56207	79207
170 208	**AR**	P	*AR*	50208	56208	79208

Class 170/4. Vehicles on order for ScotRail. DMCL(A)–MS–DMCL(B).
DMCL. Dia. DP329. Adtranz Derby 1999. 9/38 1TD 2W.
MS. Dia. DR213. Adtranz Derby 1999. –/80 1T.
DMCL. Dia. DP330. Adtranz Derby 1999. 9/54 1T.

170 401	**SR**	P	*SR*	50401	56401	79401
170 402	**SR**	P	*SR*	50402	56402	79402
170 403	**SR**	P	*SR*	50403	56403	79403
170 404	**SR**	P	*SR*	50404	56404	79404
170 405	**SR**	P	*SR*	50405	56405	79405
170 406	**SR**	P	*SR*	50406	56406	79406
170 407	**SR**	P	*SR*	50407	56407	79407
170 408	**SR**	P	*SR*	50408	56408	79408
170 409	**SR**	P	*SR*	50409	56409	79409
170 410	**SR**	P	*SR*	50410	56410	79410
170 411	**SR**	P	*SR*	50411	56411	79411
170 412	**SR**	P	*SR*	50412	56412	79412
170 413	**SR**	P	*SR*	50413	56413	79413
170 414	**SR**	P	*SR*	50414	56414	79414
170 415	**SR**	P	*SR*	50415	56415	79415

Class 170/5. Vehicles on order for Central Trains. DMSL(A)–DMSL(B).
DMSL(A). Dia. DP275. Adtranz Derby 1999. –/55 1TD 2W.
DMSL(B). Dia. DP273. Adtranz Derby 1999. –/69 1T.

170 501	**CT**	P	*CT*	50501	79501
170 502	**CT**	P	*CT*	50502	79502
170 503	**CT**	P	*CT*	50503	79503
170 504	**CT**	P	*CT*	50504	79504
170 505	**CT**	P	*CT*	50505	79505
170 506	**CT**	P	*CT*	50506	79506
170 507	**CT**	P	*CT*	50507	79507
170 508	**CT**	P	*CT*	50508	79508
170 509	**CT**	P	*CT*	50509	79509
170 510	**CT**	P	*CT*	50510	79510
170 511	**CT**	P	*CT*	50511	79511
170 512	**CT**	P	*CT*	50512	79512
170 513	**CT**	P	*CT*	50513	79513
170 514	**CT**	P	*CT*	50514	79514

170 515	**CT**	P	*CT*	50515	79515
170 516	**CT**	P	*CT*	50516	79516
170 517	**CT**	P	*CT*	50517	79517
170 518	**CT**	P	*CT*	50518	79518
170 519	**CT**	P	*CT*	50519	79519
170 520	**CT**	P	*CT*	50520	79520
170 521	**CT**	P	*CT*	50521	79521
170 522	**CT**	P	*CT*	50522	79522
170 523	**CT**	P	*CT*	50523	79523

Class 170/6. Vehicles on order for Central Trains. DMSL–MS–DMSL.
DMSL(A). Dia. DP275. Adtranz Derby 1999. –/55 1TD 2W.
MS. Dia. DR214. Adtranz Derby 1999. –/80.
DMSL(B). Dia. DP273. Adtranz Derby 1999. –/69 1T.

170 630	**CT**	P	*CT*	50630	56630	79630
170 631	**CT**	P	*CT*	50631	56631	79631
170 632	**CT**	P	*CT*	50632	56632	79632
170 633	**CT**	P	*CT*	50633	56633	79633
170 634	**CT**	P	*CT*	50634	56634	79634
170 635	**CT**	P	*CT*	50635	56635	79635
170 636	**CT**	P	*CT*	50636	56636	79636
170 637	**CT**	P	*CT*	50637	56637	79637
170 638	**CT**	P	*CT*	50638	56638	79638
170 639	**CT**	P	*CT*	50639	56639	79639

CLASS 180/1   5-Car Unit

Further details awaited. Vehicles on order for First Great Western.
Engines: Cummins.
Bogies:
Transmission: Hydraulic. Voith.
Dimensions:
Maximum Speed: 125 mph.

180 101	**GW**	FB	*GW*
180 102	**GW**	FB	*GW*
180 103	**GW**	FB	*GW*
180 104	**GW**	FB	*GW*
180 105	**GW**	FB	*GW*
180 106	**GW**	FB	*GW*
180 107	**GW**	FB	*GW*
180 108	**GW**	FB	*GW*

3.3. DIESEL ELECTRIC MULTIPLE UNITS

The following features are standard to all diesel-electric multiple unit power cars:

Engine: One English Electric 4SRKT Mk. 2 of 450 kW (600 hp) at 850 rpm.
Main Generator: English Electric EE824.
Traction Motors: Two English Electric EE507 mounted on the inner bogie.

The following features are standard to all diesel-electric multiple unit cars unless otherwise stated:

Couplings: Drophead buckeye.   **Doors:** Manually operated slam.
Brakes: Electro-pneumatic and automatic air.
Bogies: SR Mk. 4. (Former EMU TSOL vehicles have Commonwealth bogies).
Maximum Speed: 75 mph.   **Multiple Working:** Other DEMU vehicles.

CLASS 201/202 (5H)   5-Car 'Hastings' Unit

DMBSO–3TSOL–DMBSO.
Gangways: Within unit only.
Dimensions: 18.36 x 2.50 x 3.83 m (60000/60501), 20.34 x 2.50 x 3.83 m. (60118/60529) 20.34 x 2.82 x 3.83 m (70262).

60000. DMBSO. Dia. DB203. Lot No. 30329 Eastleigh 1957. –/22. 54.0 t.
60118. DMBSO. Dia. DB203. Lot No. 30395 Eastleigh 1957. –/30. 55.0 t.
60501. TSOL. Dia. DB204. Lot No. 30331 Eastleigh 1957. –/52 2T. 29.0 t.
60529. TSOL. Dia. DH203. Lot No. 30397 Eastleigh 1957. –/60 2T. 30.0 t.
70262. TSOL. Dia. DH208. Previously a Class 411/5 vehicle. Lot No. 30455 Eastleigh 1959. –/64 2T. 33.8 t.

| 1001 | G | HD | AR | NC | | 60000 | 60501 | 70262 | 60529 | 60118 |

Names:
60000   Hastings | 60118   Tunbridge Wells

CLASS 205/0 (3H)   3-Car Unit

DMBSO–TSO–DTCsoL.
Gangways: Non-gangwayed.
Dimensions: 20.33 (DMBSO), 20.28 (TSO), 20.36 (DTCsoL) x 2.82 x 3.86 (DMBSO), 3.77 (TSO), 3.82 (DTCsoL) m.

60108–60117/154. DMBSO. Dia. DB203. Lot No. 30332 Eastleigh 1957. –/52. 56.0 t.
60122–60124. DMBSO. Dia. DB203. Lot No. 30540 Eastleigh 1958–59. –/52. 56.0 t.
60146–60151. DMBSO. Dia. DB204. Lot No. 30671 Eastleigh 1960–62. –/42. 56.0 t.
60650–60670. TSO. Dia. DH203. Lot No. 30542 Eastleigh 1958–59. –/104. 30.0 t.
60673–60678. TSO. Dia. DH203. Lot No. 30672 Eastleigh 1960–62. –/104. 30.0 t.
60800 DTCsoL. Dia. DE301. Lot No. 30333 Eastleigh 1956–57. 13/50 2T. 32.0 t.
60808–60811. DTCsoL. Dia. DE302. Lot No. 30333 Eastleigh 1956–57. 19/50 2T. 32.0 t.
60822. DTCsoL. Dia. DE302. Lot No. 30541 Eastleigh 1958–59. 19/50 2T. 32.0 t.
60823–60824. DTCsoL. Dia. DE301. Lot No. 30541 Eastleigh 1958–59. 13/50 2T. 32.0 t.
60827–60832. DTCsoL. Dia. DE303. Lot No. 30673 Eastleigh 1960–62. 13/62 2T. 32.0 t.

205 001	*	N	P	SC	SU	60154	60650	60800
205 009		CX	P	SC	SU	60108	60658	60808
205 012		N	P	SC	SU	60111	60661	60811
205 018		N	P	SC	SU	60117	60674	60828
205 024	*	N	P	SC	SU	60123	60669	60823
205 025	*	N	P	SC	SU	60124	60670	60824
205 028		CX	P	SC	SU	60146	60673	60827
205 032		N	P	SC	SU	60150	60677	60831
205 033	*	CX	P	SC	SU	60151	60678	60832
Spare		N	P		ZG(S)		60822	

CLASS 205/2 (3H(M))   2- or 3-Car Unit

DMBSO–DTSOL or DMBSO–TSOL–DTSOL. Refurbished 1980. Operates as a
3-car unit in summer, 2-car unit in winter.
Gangways: Within unit only.
Dimensions: 20.33 (DMBSO), 20.34 (TSOL), 20.36 m x 2.82 x 3.86 (DMBSO),
3.83 (TSOL), 3.82 (DTSOL) m.

DMBSO. Dia. DB203. Lot No. 30332 Eastleigh 1957. –/39. 57.0 t.
TSOL. Dia. DH207. Previously a Class 411/5 vehicle, but originally built as a
loco-hauled TSO. Lot No. 30149 Swindon 1956. –/64 2T. 33.8 t.
DTSOL. Dia. DE204. Lot No. 30333 Eastleigh 1957. –/76 2T. 32.0 t.

205 205	CX	P	SC	SU	60110		60810
Spare	N	P	SC	ZG(S)		71634	

CLASS 207/0 (2D)   2-Car Unit

DMBSO–DTSO. Formerly 3-car unit DMBSO–TCsoL–DTSO.
Gangways: Non-gangwayed.
Dimensions: 20.33 x 2.74 x 3.82 m. (DMBSO), 20.32 x 2.74 x 3.73 m. (DTSO),
20.33 x 2.74 x 3.73 m.(TCsoL).

DMBSO. Dia. DB205. Lot No. 30625 Eastleigh 1962. –/42. 56.0 t.
TCsoL. Dia. DH301. Lot No. 30626 Eastleigh 1962. 24/42 1T. 31.0 t.
DTSO. Dia. DE201. Lot No. 30627 Eastleigh 1962. –/76. 32.0 t.

207 017	N	P	SC	SU	60142		60916
Spare	N	P		SE(S)		60616	

CLASS 207/2 (3D)   2- or 3-Car Unit

DMBSO–DTSO or DMBSO–TSOL–DTSO. Operate as 3-car units in summer,
2-car units in winter.
Gangways: Within unit.
Dimensions: 20.33 x 2.74 x 3.82 m. (DMBSO), 20.34 x 2.82 x 3.83 m. (TSOL),
20.32 x 2.74 x 3.73 m. (DTSO).

DMBSO. Dia. DB205. Lot No. 30625 Eastleigh 1962. –/40. 56.0 t.
70286. TSOL. Dia. DH206. Previously a Class 411/5 vehicle. Lot No. 30455
Eastleigh 1958. –/64 2T. 33.8 t.

70547/9. TSOL. Dia. DH206. Previously a Class 411/5 vehicle.Lot No. 30620
Eastleigh 1961 –/64 2T. 33.8 t.
DTSO. Dia. DE201. Lot No. 30627 Eastleigh 1962. –/75. 32.0 t.

207 201	**CX**	P	*SC*	SU	60129	60901
207 202	**CX**	P	*SC*	SU	60130	60904
207 203	**N**	P	*SC*	SU(S)	60127	60903
Spare	**N**	P	*SC*	SU(S)	70286	
Spare	**N**	P	*SC*	SU(S)	70547	
Spare	**N**	P	*SC*	SU(S)	70549	

Names (Carried on DMBSO):
207 201   Ashford Fayre | 207 202   Brighton Royal Pavillion

3.4 SERVICE DMUS

This section lists vehicles not used for revenue earning purposes which are numbered in the special service stock number series or in the internal user series (An internal user vehicle is a vehicle specifically for use in one location/area which is not otherwise permitted over the Railtrack network without special authority).

CLASS 101   Internal User Office Vehicle

Converted 1990 from Class 101 DTCL. Gangwayed.
Maximum Speed: 70 mph.
Bogies: DT11.   **Couplings:** Screw.
Brakes: Twin pipe vacuum.   **Multiple Working:** Blue Square.
Doors: Manually operated slam.   **Dimensions:** 18.49 x 2.82 x 3.85 m.
Note: Allocated Internal User number 042222, but this is not carried.

DT. Dia. DZ5??. Lot No. 30468 Met-Camm. 1958. 22.5 t.

Spare   **BG**   NS   NL(S)   54342

CLASS 114/1   Route Learning Unit

DMB–DT. Converted 1992 from Class 114/1. Gangwayed within unit.
Engines: Two Leyland TL11/40 of 153 kW (205 hp) at 1950 rpm per car.
Transmission: Mechanical. Cardan shaft and freewheel to a four-speed epicyclic gearbox with a further cardan shaft to the final drive, each engine driving the inner axle of one bogie.
Maximum Speed: 70 mph.   **Couplings:** Screw.
Bogies: DD9 + DT9.   **Multiple Working:** Blue Square.
Brakes: Twin pipe vacuum.   **Dimensions:** 20.45 x 2.82 x 3.87 m.
Doors: Manually operated slam/roller shutter.
Non-Standard Livery: Grey, red and yellow.

DMB. Dia. DZ518. Lot No. 30209 Derby 1957. 39.0 t.
DT. Dia. DZ516. Lot No. 30210 Derby 1957. 29.2 t.

-                  **0**   E   MG(S) 977775 977776

CLASS 210   2-Car Track Inspection Unit

DM–DMB*. Prototype second generation DEMU currently undergoing conversion.
Engines: One MTU 12V396TC12 of 914 kW (1225 hp) at 1500 rpm (* One
Paxman Valenta 6RP200 of 842 kW (1129 hp) at 1500 rpm.
Main Alternator: GEC G563AZ (* Brush BA1002A).
Transmission: Electric. Four GEC (* Brush) traction motors.
Maximum Speed: 90 mph.   **Bogies:** BP20.
Brakes: Electro-pneumatic.   **Doors:** Power operated sliding.
Couplers: Tightlock (outer), bar (inner) end.
Multiple Working: Within class only. **Dimensions:** 20.52 x 2.82 x 3.77 m.

DM. Dia. DZ5??. Lot No. 30931 BREL Derby 1982.
DMB. Dia. DZ5??. Lot No. 30930 BREL Derby 1982.

210 001   **N**   AY   ZG(S)   60200   60201*

CLASS 930   Sandite/De-icing Unit

DMB–T–DMB. Converted 1993 from Class 205. Gangwayed within unit. Sandite
trailer 977870 is replaced by de-icing trailer 977364 as required.
Engine: One English Electric 4SRKT Mk. 2 of 450 kW (600 hp) at 850 rpm per
power car.
Transmission: Electric. Two English Electric EE507 traction motors mounted
on the inner bogie of each power car.
Maximum Speed: 75 mph.   **Bogies:** SR Mk. 4.
Brakes: Electro-pneumatic and automatic air.
Doors: Manually operated slam.   **Couplings:** Drophead buckeye.
Multiple Working: DEMU vehicles (except Class 210).
Dimensions: 20.33 x 2.82 x 3.87 m. (DMB); 20.28 x 2.82 x 3.87 m. (T).

DMB. Dia. DZ537. Lot No. 30671 Eastleigh 1962. 56.0 t.
T. Dia. DZ533. Lot No. 30542 Eastleigh 1960. 30.5 t.

930 301   **RK**   RT *RT*   SU   977939 977870 977940

CLASS 960   Ultrasonic Test Train/Tractor Unit

DM–DM. Converted 1986 from Class 101. Gangwayed within unit. Often works
with 975091, 999550 or 999602.
Engines: Two Leyland 680/1 of 112 kW (150 hp) at 1800 rpm per car.
Transmission: Mechanical. Cardan shaft and freewheel to a four-speed
epicyclic gearbox with a further cardan shaft to the final drive, each engine
driving the inner axle of one bogie.   **Dimensions:** 18.49 x 2.82 x 3.85 m.
Maximum Speed: 70 mph.   **Doors:** Manually operated slam.
Bogies: DD15.   **Couplings:** Screw.
Brakes: Twin pipe vacuum.   **Multiple Working:** Blue Square.

977391. DM. Dia. DZ503. Lot No. 30500 Met-Camm. 1959. 32.5 t.
977392. DM. Dia. DZ503. Lot No. 30254 Met-Camm. 1956. 32.5 t.

-            **S0**   SO *SO*   RG   977391 977392

CLASS 960   Test Unit

DM–DM. Converted 1991 from Class 101. Gangwayed within unit.
Engines: Two Leyland 680/1 of 112 kW (150 hp) at 1800 rpm per car.
Transmission: Mechanical. Cardan shaft and freewheel to a four-speed
epicyclic gearbox with a further cardan shaft to the final drive, each engine
driving the inner axle of one bogie.   **Maximum Speed:** 70 mph.
Bogies: DD15.   **Couplings:** Screw.
Brakes: Twin pipe vacuum.   **Multiple Working:** Blue Square.
Doors: Manually operated slam.   **Dimensions:** 18.49 x 2.82 x 3.85 m.

977693. DM. Dia. DZ503. Lot No. 30261 Met-Camm. 1957. 32.5 t.
977694. DM. Dia. DZ503. Lot No. 30276 Met-Camm. 1958. 32.5 t.

-		**SO**	SO	*SO*	BY	977693	977694	Iris 2

CLASS 960   Sandite Unit

DMB. Converted 1991/93 from Class 121. Non gangwayed.
Engines: Two Leyland 1595 of 112 kW (150 hp) at 1800 rpm.
Transmission: Mechanical. Cardan shaft and freewheel to a four-speed
epicyclic gearbox with a further cardan shaft to the final drive, each engine
driving the inner axle of one bogie.
Maximum Speed: 70 mph.
Bogies: DD10.   **Couplings:** Screw.
Brakes: Twin pipe vacuum.   **Multiple Working:** Blue Square.
Doors: Manually operated slam.   **Dimensions:** 20.45 x 2.82 x 3.87 m.

977722-23. DMB. Dia. DZ515. Lot No. 30518 Pressed Steel 1960. 38.0 t.
977858–60/66/73. DMB. Dia. DZ526. Lot No. 30518 Pressed Steel 1960. 38.0 t.

960 002	**N**	RT	*RT*	RG	977722
121 121	**RK**	RT	*RT*	BY	977723
55024	**M**	RT	*RT*	AL	977858
960 011	**N**	RT	*RT*	LO	977859
960 012	**N**	RT	*RT*	RG	977860
960 013	**RK**	RT	*RT*	NC	977866
960 014	**N**	RT	*RT*	RG	977873

CLASS 960   Sandite Unit

DMB. Converted 1991 from Class 122 vehicle. Non gangwayed.
Engines: Two Leyland 1595 of 112 kW (150 hp) at 1800 rpm.
Transmission: Mechanical. Cardan shaft and freewheel to a four-speed
epicyclic gearbox with a further cardan shaft to the final drive, each engine
driving the inner axle of one bogie.   **Maximum Speed:** 70 mph.
Bogies: DD10.   **Couplings:** Screw.
Brakes: Twin pipe vacuum.   **Multiple Working:** Blue Square.
Doors: Manually operated slam.   **Dimensions:** 20.45 x 2.82 x 3.87 m.

DM. Dia. DZ516. Lot No. 30419 Gloucester 1958. 36.5 t.

960 015	**RK**	RT	*RT*	BY	975042

CLASS 960/9   Sandite & Route Learning Unit

DM–DM. Converted 1993 from Class 101 vehicles. Gangwayed within unit.
Engines: Two Leyland 680/1 of 112 kW (150 hp) at 1800 rpm per car.
Transmission: Mechanical. Cardan shaft and freewheel to a four-speed epicyclic gearbox with a further cardan shaft to the final drive, each engine driving the inner axle of one bogie.   **Maximum Speed:** 70 mph.
Bogies: DD15.   **Couplings:** Screw.
Brakes: Twin pipe vacuum.   **Multiple Working:** Blue Square.
Doors: Manually operated slam.   **Dimensions:** 18.49 x 2.82 x 3.85 m.

977895. DM. Dia. DZ503. Lot No. 30275 Met-Camm. 1958. 32.5 t.
977896/900. DM. Dia. DZ504. Lot No. 30276 Met-Camm. 1958. 32.5 t.
977897/901/903. DM. Dia. DZ503. Lot No. 30259 Met-Camm. 1957. 32.5 t.
977898. DM. Dia. DZ515. Lot No. 30256 Met-Camm. 1957. 32.5 t.
977899. DM. Dia. DZ503. Lot No. 30500 Met-Camm. 1959. 32.5 t.
977902. DM. Dia. DZ503. Lot No. 30270 Met-Camm. 1957. 32.5 t.
977904. DM. Dia. DZ503. Lot No. 30270 Met-Camm. 1957. 32.5 t.

960 991	**N**	RT	*RT*	LO	977895	977896
960 992	**BG**	RT	*RT*	LO	977897	977898
960 993	**BG**	RT	*RT*	LO	977899	977900
960 994	**BG**	RT	*RT*	LO	977901	977902
960 995	**BG**	RT	*RT*	LO	977903	977904

UNCLASSIFIED   Test Unit

DMB. Converted 1968 from Unclassified DMBS. Non gangwayed.
Engines: Two Leyland 680/1 of 112 kW (150 hp) at 1800 rpm.
Transmission: Mechanical. Cardan shaft and freewheel to a four-speed epicyclic gearbox with a further cardan shaft to the final drive, each engine driving the inner axle of one bogie.   **Maximum Speed:** 70 mph.
Bogies: **Couplings:** Screw.
Brakes: Twin pipe vacuum.   **Dimensions:** 18.49 x 2.79 x 3.87 m.
Doors: Manually operated slam.   **Note:** Also carries former number 79900.
Multiple Working: Obsolete Yellow Diamond system/Blue Square.

DMB. Dia. DZ530. Lot No. 30380 Derby 1956. 27.2 t.

| - | **G** | SO | *SO* | BY | 975010 | | Iris |

UNCLASSIFIED   Overhead Line Test Car

T. Converted 1972 from hauled stock BSK. Wired for DMU working 1998. Non gangwayed. Used with 977391/2 or loco-hauled.
Maximum Speed: 70 mph.
Bogies: B5.   **Couplings:** Drophead buckeye.
Brakes: Air and Vacuum.   **Dimensions:**
Doors: Manually operated slam.   **Multiple Working:** Blue Square.

T. Dia. DZ538. Lot No. 30142 Gloucester 1955. 39.0 t.

| - | **SO** | SO | *SO* | ZA | 975091 | | Mentor |

UNCLASSIFIED   De-icing Trailer

T. Converted 1960 from 4-Sub EMU vehicle. Non gangwayed. Operates as
required with the power cars from 930 301.
Maximum Speed: 70 mph.   **Couplings:** Drophead buckeye.
Bogies: Central 43 inch.   **Multiple Working:** SR system.
Brakes: Electro-pneumatic and automatic air.
Doors: Manually operated slam.   **Dimensions:**
T. Dia. EZ520. Lancing/Eastleigh 1946. 29.0 t.

-              **RK**   RT   *RT*   SU   977364

UNCLASSIFIED   Track Recording Coach

T. Purpose built service vehicle. Wired for DMU working 1998. Gangwayed.
Used with 977391/2 or loco-hauled.   **Maximum Speed:** 70 mph.
Bogies: B4.   **Couplings:** Drophead buckeye.
Brakes: Air and vacuum.   **Multiple Working:** Blue square.
Doors: Manually operated slam.   **Dimensions:**

T. Dia. DZ539. Lot No. 3830 BREL Derby 1976. 45.0 t.

-              **SO**   SO   *SO*   ZA   999550

UNCLASSIFIED   Track Assessment Unit

DM–DM. Purpose built service unit. Gangwayed within unit.
Engine: One Cummins NT-855-RT5 of 213 kW (285 hp) at 2100 rpm per power car.
Transmission: Hydraulic. Voith T211r with cardan shafts to Gmeinder GM190
final drive.
Maximum Speed: 75 mph.   **Couplers:** BSI automatic.
Bogies: BP38 (powered), BT38 (non-powered).
Brakes: Electro-pneumatic.   **Dimensions:** 20.06 x 2.82 x 3.77 m.
Doors: Manually operated slam & power operated sliding.
Multiple Working: With classes 141–158 and 170 only.
Non-Standard Livery: Grey, red and blue.

999600. DM. Dia. DZ536. Lot No. 4060 BREL York 1987. 36.5 t.
999601. DM. Dia. DZ536. Lot No. 4061 BREL York 1987. 36.5 t.

-              **0**   SO   *SO*   NC   999600 999601

UNCLASSIFIED   Ultrasonic Test Car

T. Converted 1986 from Class 432 EMU. Gangwayed. Used with 977391/2.
Maximum Speed: 70 mph.
Bogies: SR Mk. 6.   **Couplings:** Screw.
Brakes: Twin pipe vacuum.   **Multiple Working:** Blue Square.
Doors: Manually operated slam.   **Dimensions:** 19.66 x 2.82 x 3.90 m.

T. Dia. DZ531. Lot No. 30862 York 1974. 55.5 t.

-              **0**   SO   *SO*   ZA   999602

3.5 VEHICLES AWAITING DISPOSAL

This section lists vehicles awaiting disposal of classes or types not otherwise represented in this publication (except as Internal User vehicles). Notes regarding common detail applicable to first and second generation units also apply to this section as appropriate.

CLASS 151   3-Car Sprinter

DMSL–MS († MSL)–DMS. Prototype Met-Camm. Sprinter.
Engines: One Cummins NT-855-R4 of 213 kW (285 hp) at 2100 rpm per car.
Transmission: Hydraulic. Twin Disc TA-33-1316 with cardan shafts to Gmeinder GM190 final drive.
Bogies: BX9P (powered), BX9T(non-powered).
Gangways: Within unit only.
Dimensions: 19.98 x 2.81 x 3.89 m.
Non-Standard Livery:
• 151 103/104 are unpainted.

DMSL. Dia. DP233. Lot No. 30987 Met-Camm. 1985. –/72 1T. 32.4 t.
MS. Dia. DR204. Lot No. 30989 Met-Camm. 1985. –/76. 36.5 t.
MSL. Dia. DR2??. Lot No. 30989 Met-Camm. 1985. –/73. 37.50 t.
DMS. Dia. DP232. Lot No. 30988 Met-Camm. 1985. –/76. 36.70 t.

| 151 103 | **0** | A | ZA(S) | 55202 | 55302 | 55402 |
| 151 104 | **0** | A | ZA(S) | 55203 | 55303 | 55403 |

MISCELLANEOUS VEHICLES

Class 101	DTCL	54350		CB(S)
Class 117	TCL	59518		OM(S)
Class 100	QXV	977191	(56106)	CB(S)
Class 951	T	977696	(60522)	ZG(S)

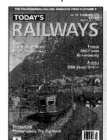

4. ELECTRIC MULTIPLE UNITS

USING THIS SECTION – LAYOUT OF INFORMATION

25 kV a.c. 50 Hz overhead EMUs and 'Versatile' EMUs (units with one type of electric supply but with provision for ther types) are listed in numerical order of class number, then in numerical order of set number – using official numbers as allocated by the RSL. Individual 'loose' vehicles are listed in numerical order after vehicles formed into fixed formations. Where numbers carried are different to those officially allocated (e.g. former numbers), these are noted in class headings where appropriate.

750 V d.c. third rail EMUs are listed in numerical order of the set numbers actually carried. Some of these may vary from the six digit numbers allocated by the RSL.

Where sets or vehicles have been renumbered since the previous edition of this book, former numbering detail is shown in parentheses.

Each entry is laid out as in the following example:

Set No.	Detail	Livery	Owner	Operation	Depot	Formation			
1706	†	**N**	A	*SC*	Bl	76094	63035	70713	76040

CLASS HEADINGS

Principal details and dimensions are quoted for each class in metric and/or imperial units as considered appropriate bearing in mind common usage in the UK. Abbreviations used are shown in Section 6.9.

All dimensions and weights are quoted for vehicles in an 'as new' condition with all necessary supplies on board. Dimensions are quoted in the order Length – Width – Height. All lengths quoted are over buffers or couplings as appropriate. All width and height dimensions quoted are maxima.

DETAIL DIFFERENCES

Only detail differences which currently affect the areas and types of train which vehicles may work are shown. All other detail differences are specifically excluded – details of these may be found in more specialist publications. Where such differences occur within a class or part class, these are shown alongside the individual set or vehicle number. Meaning of abbreviations used in this context is detailed in individual class headings.

LIVERY CODES

Livery codes are used to denote the various liveries carried. Readers should note it is impossible in a publication of this size to list every livery variation currently extant. In particular items ignored for the purposes of this book include:

- •   Minor colour variations;
- •   All numbering, lettering and branding;
- •   Omission of logos.

The descriptions quoted are thus a general guide only and may be subject to slight variation between individual vehicles. Logos as appropriate for each livery are normally deemed to be carried.

A complete list of livery codes used appears in Section 6.5.

OWNER CODES

Owner codes are used to denote the owners of vehicles listed. Most vehicles are leased by the TOCs from specialist leasing companies.

A complete list of owner codes used appears in Section 6.4.

OPERATION CODES

Operation codes are used to denote the normal usage of the vehicles listed – i.e. A guide to the services of which train operating company any vehicle will normally be used upon. Where vehicles are used for non revenue earning purposes, an indication to the normal type of usage is given in the class heading. Where no operation code is shown, vehicles are currently not in use.

A complete list of operation codes used appears in Section 6.5.

DEPOT & LOCATION CODES

Depot codes are used to denote the normal maintenance base of each operational vehicle. However, maintenance may be carried out at other locations and may also be carried out by mobile maintenance teams.

Location codes are used to denote the current actual location of stored vehicles. A location code will be followed by (S) to denote stored.

A complete list of depot and location codes used appears in Section 6.6.

SET FORMATIONS

Set formations shown are those normally maintained. Readers should note some set formations may be temporarily varied from time to time to suit maintenance and/or operational requirements. Vehicles shown as 'Spare' are not formed in any regular set formation.

NAMES

Only names carried with official sanction are listed in this publication. As far as possible names are shown in UPPER/lower case characters as actually shown on the name carried on the vehicle(s). Unless otherwise shown, officially complete units are regarded as named rather than just the individual car(s) which carry the name.

GENERAL INFORMATION

CLASSIFICATION AND NUMBERING

25 kV a.c. 50 Hz overhead and 'Versatile' EMUs are classified in the series 300–399.

750 V d.c. third rail EMUs (excluding Merseyrail) are classified in the series 400–499.

750 V d.c. third rail Merseyrail EMUs are classified in the series 500–599.

Service units are classified in the series 900–949.

EMU individual cars are numbered in the series 61000–78999, except for vehicles used on the Isle of Wight – which are numbered in a separate series.

Service stock individual cars are numbered in the series 975000–975999 and 977000–977999, although this series is not exclusively used for EMU vehicles.

DESIGN CONSIDERATIONS

Unless otherwise stated all vehicles listed have bar couplings at non-driving ends and tread brakes. In all types of vehicle except 'Express' stock, seating is 3 + 2 in standard class open vehicles, 2 + 2 in first class open vehicles, 8 per compartment in standard class and 6 per compartment in first class. In Express stock, seating is 2 + 2 in standard class open vehicles and 2 + 1 in first class open vehicles.

OPERATING CODES

These codes are used by train operating company staff to describe the various different types of vehicles and normally appear on data panels on the inner (i.e. non driving) ends of vehicles.

BDMSO	Battery Driving Motor Standard Open
BDT	Battery Driving Trailer
BDTCO	Battery Driving Trailer Composite Open
BDTCso	Battery Driving Trailer Composite Semi-Open
DM	Driving Motor
DMCO	Driving Motor Composite Open
DMFO	Driving Motor First Open
DMLFO	Driving Motor Lounge First Open
DMLV	Driving Motor Luggage Van
DMSO	Driving Motor Standard Open
DT	Driving Trailer
DTB	Driving Trailer Brake
DTCO	Driving Trailer Composite Open
DTCso	Driving Trailer Composite Semi-Open
DTFso	Driving Trailer First Semi-Open
DTPMV	Driving Trailer Parcels & Miscellaneous Van
DTSO	Driving Trailer Standard Open

DTSso	Driving Trailer Standard Semi-Open
M	Motor
MB	Motor Brake
MBRSM	Motor Brake Buffet Standard Modular
MBSO	Motor Brake Standard Open
MPMV	Motor Parcels & Miscellaneous Van
MSO	Motor Standard Open
PBDTB	Pantograph Battery Driving Trailer Brake
PBDTBSO	Pantograph Battery Driving Trailer Brake Standard Open
PTSO	Pantograph Trailer Standard Open
RB	Buffet Car
TB	Trailer Brake
TBCK	Trailer Brake Composite Corridor
TBFO	Trailer Brake First Open
TBSK	Trailer Brake Standard Corridor
TCO	Trailer Composite Open
TFK	Trailer First Corridor
TFO	Trailer First Open
TFOH	Trailer First Open with Handbrake
TPMV	Trailer Parcels & Miscellaneous Van
TSO	Trailer Standard Open
TSRB	Trailer Standard Buffet Car

A semi open vehicle features both open and compartment accommodation, with first class accommodation in compartments in composite vehicles. Where two vehicles of the same type are formed within the same unit, the above codes may be suffixed by (A) and (B) to differentiate between the vehicles. The suffix 'L' denotes vehicles with a lavatory compartment. A suffix (T) denotes a vehicle with a catering trolley counter.

A composite is a vehicle containing both first and standard class accommodation, although first class accommodation on some EMU vehicles has now all been permanently declassified. A brake vehicle is a vehicle containing separate specific accommodation for the conductor (as opposed to the use of rear or intermediate cabs on some units).

Single motor coach overhead supply EMUs (except Class 306) all have the pantograph mounted on the motor coach. Units with more than one motor coach have the pantograph mounted on a trailer car denoted as shown above.

DESIGN CODES AND DIAGRAM CODES

For each type of vehicle the RSL issues a seven character 'Design Code' consisting of 2 letters plus 4 numbers and a suffix letter. (e.g. EF2110A). The first 5 characters of the Design Code are known as the 'Diagram Code', and these are quoted in this publication in sub-headings. The meaning of the various characters of the Design Code is as follows:

First Character
| E | Electric Multiple Unit vehicle |
| L | Eurostar vehicle |

Second Character (EMU vehicles)
| A | Driving motor vehicle |

B	Driving motor vehicle with brake compartment
C	Non-driving motor vehicle
D	Non-driving motor vehicle with a brake compartment
E	Driving trailer vehicle
F	Battery driving trailer vehicle
G	Driving trailer vehicle with a brake compartment
H	Trailer vehicle
I	Battery driving motor vehicle
J	Trailer vehicle with a brake compartment
N	Trailer vehicle with a buffet area
O	Battery driving trailer vehicle with a brake compartment
P	Trailer vehicle with a handbrake
X	Driving motor luggage vans
Z	All types of service vehicle

Second Character (Eurostar vehicles)

A	Driving motor vehicle
B	Non-driving motor vehicle
C	Trailer vehicle with train manager's compartment
D, F or H	Trailer vehicle
E	Trailer vehicle with public telephone
G	Kitchen/Bar vehicle
J	Trailer vehicle with public telephone
K	Trailer vehicle with staff compartment

Third Character

1	First class accommodation
2	Standard class accommodation
3	Composite accommodation
5	No passenger accommodation

Fourth & Fifth Characters

These distinguish between different designs of vehicle, each design being allocated a unique two digit number.

Special Note

Where vehicles have been declassified, the correct design code for a declassified vehicle is quoted in this publication, even though this may be at variance with RSL records, which do not always show the reality of the current position.

ACCOMMODATION

The information given in class headings and sub-headings is in the form F/S nT (or TD) nW. For example 12/54 1T 1W denotes 12 first class and 54 standard class seats, 1 toilet and 1 wheelchair space.

BUILD DETAILS

Lot Numbers

Vehicles ordered under the auspices of BR were allocated a Lot (batch) number when ordered and these are quoted in class headings and sub-headings. Details of the meaning of abbreviations used to denote builders are shown in Section 6.8.

4.1 25 kV a.c. 50 Hz OVERHEAD & 'VERSATILE' EMUS

Note: All units operate on 25 kV a.c. 50 Hz overhead only except where otherwise stated.

CLASS 303   3-Car Unit

DTSO–MBSO–BDTSO. Gangwayed within unit.
Traction Motors: Four Metropolitan Vickers of 155 kW each.
Dimensions: 20.18 x 2.82 x 3.86 m.
Maximum Speed: 75 mph.   **Doors:** Power operated sliding.
Couplings: Buckeye.   **Bogies:** Gresley.
Multiple Working: Classes 303–312 only.

75566–75599. DTSO. Dia. EE241. Lot No. 30579 Pressed Steel 1959–60. –/56. 34.4 t.
75747–75801. DTSO. Dia. EE241. Lot No. 30629 Pressed Steel 1960–61. –/56. 34.4 t.
61481–61514. MBSO. Dia. ED220. Lot No. 30580 Pressed Steel 1959–60. –/48. 56.4 t.
61813–61867. MBSO. Dia. ED220. Lot No. 30630 Pressed Steel 1960–61. –/48. 56.4 t.
75601–75635. BDTSO. Dia. EF217. Lot No. 30581 Pressed Steel 1959–60. –/56. 38.4 t.
75803–75857. BDTSO. Dia. EF217. Lot No. 30631 Pressed Steel 1960–61. –/56. 38.4 t.

303 001	S	A	SR	GW	75566	61481	75601
303 003	S	A	SR	GW	75568	61483	75603
303 004	S	A	SR	GW	75569	61484	75604
303 006	S	A	SR	GW	75571	61486	75606
303 008	S	A	SR	GW	75573	61488	75608
303 009	S	A	SR	GW	75574	61489	75609
303 010	S	A	SR	GW	75575	61490	75610
303 011	S	A	SR	GW	75576	61491	75611
303 012	S	A	SR	GW	75577	61492	75612
303 013	S	A	SR	GW	75578	61493	75613
303 014	S	A	SR	GW	75579	61494	75614
303 016	S	A	SR	GW	75750	61496	75616
303 019	CC	A	SR	GW	75584	61499	75619
303 020	S	A	SR	GW	75585	61500	75620
303 021	CC	A	SR	GW	75586	61501	75621
303 023	CC	A	SR	GW	75588	61503	75623
303 024	S	A		LT(S)	75589	61504	75624
303 025	S	A	SR	GW	75590	61505	75625
303 027	S	A	SR	GW	75592	61507	75627
303 028	S	A		LT(S)	75600	61508	75635
303 032	S	A	SR	GW	75597	61512	75632
303 033	S	A	SR	GW	75595	61860	75817
303 034	S	A	SR	GW	75599	61514	75634
303 037	S	A	SR	GW	75781	61813	75803
303 040	S	A	SR	GW	75581	61816	75806
303 043	S	A	SR	GW	75572	61819	75809

303 045	S	A	SR	GW	75755	61821	75811
303 047	S	A	SR	GW	75757	61823	75813
303 054	S	A	SR	GW	75764	61830	75820
303 055	S	A	SR	GW	75765	61831	75821
303 056	S	A	SR	GW	75766	61832	75822
303 058	S	A	SR	GW	75768	61834	75824
303 061	S	A	SR	GW	75771	61837	75827
303 065	S	A	SR	GW	75775	61841	75831
303 070	S	A	SR	GW	75780	61846	75836
303 077	S	A	SR	GW	75787	61853	75843
303 079	S	A	SR	GW	75789	61855	75845
303 080	S	A	SR	GW	75790	61856	75846
303 083	S	A	SR	GW	75793	61859	75849
303 085	S	A	SR	GW	75795	61861	75851
303 087	CC	A	SR	GW	75797	61863	75853
303 088	S	A	SR	GW	75798	61864	75854
303 089	S	A	SR	GW	75799	61865	75855
303 090	S	A	SR	GW	75800	61866	75856
303 091	S	A	SR	GW	75801	61867	75857
Spare	BG	A		YO(S)	75773		

Name (carried on MBSO):

303 089   COWAL HIGHLAND GATHERING 1894–1994

CLASS 305   3- or 4-Car Unit

BDTCOL (declassified)–MBSO–DTSO or BDTCOL (declassified)–MBSO–DTSO.
Gangwayed within unit.
Traction Motors: Four GEC WT380 of 153 kW each.
Dimensions: 20.35 x 2.82 x 3.84 m (BDTCOL), 20.29 x 2.82 x 3.84 m (other cars).
Maximum Speed: 75 mph.   **Doors:** Manually operated slam.
Couplings: Buckeye.   **Bogies:** Gresley.
Multiple Working: Classes 303–312 only.

BDTCOL. Dia. EF304. Lot No. 30566 Doncaster 1960. 24/52 (* 20/40) 1T. 36.5 t.
MBSO. Dia. ED216. Lot No. 30567 Doncaster 1960. –/76 (* –/58). 56.5 t.
TSOL. Dia. EH223. Lot No. 30568 Doncaster 1960. –/86 1T. 31.5 t.
DTSO. Dia. EE220. Lot No. 30569 Doncaster 1960. –/88 (* –/70). 32.7 t.

305 501		RR	A	SR	GW	75424	61410	70356	75443
305 502		RR	A	SR	GW	75425	61421	70357	75444
305 503	*	GM	A		MA(S)	75426	61412		75445
305 506		GM	A	NW	LG	75429	61415		75448
305 507		RR	A		MA(S)	75430	61416		75449
305 508		RR	A	SR	GW	75431	61417	70363	75450
305 510		GM	A	NW	LG	75433	61419		75452
305 511	*	GM	A	NW	LG	75434	61420		75453
305 515	*	GM	A		MA(S)	75438	61424		75457
305 516		GM	A	NW	LG	75439	61425		75458
305 517		RR	A	SR	GW	75440	61426	70372	75459
305 519		RR	A	SR	GW	75442	61428	70374	75461

CLASS 306   3-Car Unit

DMSO–PTBSO–DTSO. Non gangwayed.
Traction Motors: Four Crompton Parkinson of 155 kW each.
Dimensions: 19.24 x 2.89 x 3.84 m (outer cars), 17.40 x 2.89 x 3.84 m (PTBSO).
Maximum Speed: 70 mph.   **Doors:** Power operated sliding.
Couplings: Screw.   **Bogies:** LNER design.
Multiple Working: Classes 303–312 only.

DMSO. Dia. EA203. Lot No. 363 Met-Camm. 1949. –/62. 51.7 t.
PTBSO. Dia. EJ201. Lot No. 365 BRCW 1949. –/46. 26.4 t.
DTSO. Dia. EE211. Lot No. 364 Met-Camm. 1949. –/60. 27.9 t.

| 306 017 | **G** | F | | IL(S) | 65217 | 65417 | 65617 |

CLASS 308   3-Car Unit

BDTCOL (declassified)–MBSO–DTSO. Gangwayed within unit.
Traction Motors: Four English Electric EE536A of 143.5 kW each.
Dimensions: 19.88 x 2.82 x 3.86 m (outer cars), 19.35 x 2.82 x 3.86 m (inner cars).
Maximum Speed: 75 mph.   **Doors:** Manually operated slam.
Couplings: Buckeye.   **Bogies:** Gresley.
Multiple Working: Classes 303–312 only.

75879–75886. BDTCOL. Dia. EF304. Lot No. 30652 York 1961–62. 24/52 1T. 36.3 t.
75897–75919. BDTCOL. Dia. EF304. Lot No. 30656 York 1961–62. 24/52 1T. 36.3 t.
61884–61891. MBSO. Dia. ED216. Lot No. 30653 York 1961–62. –/76. 55.0 t.
61893–61915. MBSO. Dia. ED216. Lot No. 30657 York 1961–62. –/76. 55.0 t.
75888–75895. DTSO. Dia. EE220. Lot No. 30655 York 1961–62. –/88. 33.0 t.
75930–75952. DTSO. Dia. EE220. Lot No. 30659 York 1961–62. –/88. 33.0 t.

308 134	**WY**	A	*NS*	NL(S)	75879	61884	75888
308 136	**WY**	A	*NS*	NL	75881	61886	75890
308 137	**WY**	A	*NS*	NL	75882	61887	75891
308 138	**WY**	A	*NS*	NL	75883	61888	75892
308 141	**WY**	A	*NS*	NL	75886	61891	75895
308 143	**WY**	A	*NS*	NL	75897	61893	75930
308 144	**WY**	A	*NS*	NL	75880	61894	75931
308 145	**WY**	A	*NS*	NL	75899	61895	75932
308 147	**WY**	A	*NS*	NL	75901	61897	75934
308 152	**WY**	A	*NS*	NL	75913	61902	75939
308 153	**WY**	A	*NS*	NL	75907	61903	75940
308 154	**WY**	A	*NS*	NL	75908	61904	75941
308 155	**WY**	A	*NS*	NL	75909	61905	75942
308 157	**WY**	A	*NS*	NL	75915	61907	75944
308 158	**WY**	A	*NS*	NL	75912	61908	75945
308 159	**WY**	A	*NS*	NL	75906	61909	75946
308 161	**WY**	A	*NS*	NL	75911	61911	75948
308 162	**WY**	A	*NS*	NL	75916	61912	75949
308 163	**WY**	A	*NS*	NL	75917	61913	75950
308 164	**WY**	A	*NS*	NL	75918	61914	75951
308 165	**WY**	A	*NS*	NL	75919	61915	75952

CLASS 309   'CLACTON'   4-Car Express Unit

BDTCsoL–MBSOL(T)–TSO–DTSOL. Gangwayed throughout.
Traction Motors: Four GEC of 210 kW each.
Dimensions: 20.18 x 2.82 x 3.90 m.
Maximum Speed: 100 mph.   **Doors:** Manually operated slam.
Couplings: Buckeye.   **Bogies:** Commonwealth.
Multiple Working: Classes 303–312 only.
Non-standard Livery:
• 309 624 is in 'Manchester Airport Air Express' livery (blue & white).

75639–75644. BDTCsoL. Dia. EF305. Lot No. 30679 York 1962. 18/32 2T. 37.5 t.
75965. BDTCsoL. Dia. EF305. Lot No. 30675 York 1962. 18/32 2T. 37.5 t.
61927–61931. MBSOL(T). Dia. ED218. Lot No. 30676 York 1962. –/48 2T. 58.0 t.
61934–61938. MBSOL(T). Dia. ED218. Lot No. 30680 York 1962. –/48 2T. 58.0 t.
70256–70259. TSO. Dia. EH229. Lot No. 30677 York 1962. –/68 35.0 t.
71756–71760. TSO. Dia. EH228. Built as loco-hauled vehicles to Lot No. 30724
York 1962–63. Converted to Lot No. 31001 BREL Wolverton 1984–87. –/68. 35.0 t.
75972–75975. DTSOL. Dia. EE229. Lot No. 30678 York 1962. –/56 2T 37.0 t.
75978–75982. DTSOL. Dia. EE229. Lot No. 30682 York 1962–63. –/56 2T. 37.0 t.

309 613	**RN**	A	*NW*	LG	75639	61934	71756	75978
309 616	**RN**	A	*NW*	LG	75642	61937	71759	75981
309 617	**RN**	A	*NW*	LG	75643	61938	71760	75982
309 623	**RN**	A	*NW*	LG	75641	61927	71758	75980
309 624	**0**	A	*NW*	LG	75965	61928	70256	75972
309 627	**RN**	A	*NW*	LG	75644	61931	70259	75975

CLASS 310   3- or 4-Car Unit

Various formations (see below). Gangwayed within unit. Disc brakes.
Traction Motors: Four English Electric EE546 of 201.5 kW each.
Dimensions: 20.18 x 2.82 x 3.86 m.
Maximum Speed: 75 mph.   **Doors:** Manually operated slam.
Couplings: Buckeye.   **Bogies:** B4.
Multiple Working: Classes 303–312 only.
Non Standard Livery:
• Spare TSO are 'Provincial Midline' livery (Dark blue/grey with dark blue
  and grey stripes and 'Midline' logo.

76130–76179. BDTSOL. Dia. EF211. Lot No. 30745 Derby 1965–67. –/80 2T. 37.3 t.
76228. BDTSOL (ex-DTCOL). Dia. EF210. Lot No. 30748 Derby 1967. –/68 2T. 34.5 t.
76998. BDTSOL (ex-TSO). Dia. EF214. Lot No. 30747 Derby 1965–67. –/75 2T. 35.0 t.
MBSO. Dia. ED219. Lot No. 30746 Derby 1965–67. –/68. 57.2 t.
TSO. Dia. EH232. Lot No. 30747 Derby 1965–67. –/98. 31.7 t.
DTCOL. Dia. EE306. Lot No. 30748 Derby 1965–67. 25/43 2T. 34.4 t.
DTSOL. Dia. EE237. Lot No. 30748 Derby 1965–67. –/75 2T. 34.4 t.

Class 310/0. 4-car units. BDTSOL–MBSO–TSO–DTCOL (declassified).

| 310 046 | **N** | F | *LS* | EM | 76130 | 62071 | 70731 | 76180 |
| 310 047 | **N** | F | *LS* | EM | 76131 | 62072 | 70732 | 76181 |

310 049	**N**	F	*LS*	EM	76133	62074	70734	76183
310 050	**N**	F	*LS*	EM	76134	62075	70735	76184
310 051	**N**	F	*LS*	EM	76135	62076	70736	76185
310 052	**N**	F	*LS*	EM	76136	62077	70737	76186
310 057	**N**	F	*LS*	EM	76141	62082	70742	76191
310 058	**N**	F	*LS*	EM	76142	62083	70743	76192
310 059	**N**	F	*LS*	EM	76143	62084	70744	76205
310 060	**N**	F	*LS*	EM	76144	62085	70745	76194
310 064	**N**	F	*LS*	EM	76148	62089	70749	76198
310 066	**N**	F	*LS*	EM	76228	62091	70751	76200
310 067	**N**	F	*LS*	EM	76151	62092	70752	76201
310 068	**N**	F	*LS*	EM	76152	62093	70753	76202
310 069	**N**	F	*LS*	EM	76153	62094	70754	76203
310 070	**N**	F	*LS*	EM	76154	62095	70755	76204
310 074	**N**	F	*LS*	EM	76145	62099	70759	76208
310 075	**N**	F	*LS*	EM	76159	62100	70760	76209
310 077	**N**	F	*LS*	EM	76161	62102	70762	76211
310 079	**N**	F	*LS*	EM	76163	62104	70764	76222
310 080	**N**	F	*LS*	EM	76164	62105	70765	76214
310 081	**N**	F	*LS*	EM	76165	62106	70766	76215
310 082	**N**	F	*LS*	EM	76166	62107	70767	76216
310 083	**N**	F	*LS*	EM	76167	62108	70768	76217
310 084	**N**	F	*LS*	EM	76168	62109	70769	76218
310 085	**N**	F	*LS*	EM	76169	62110	70770	76219
310 086	**N**	F	*LS*	EM	76170	62111	70771	76220
310 087	**N**	F	*LS*	EM	76171	62112	70772	76221
310 088	**N**	F	*LS*	EM	76172	62113	70773	76213
310 089	**N**	F	*LS*	EM	76173	62114	70774	76223
310 091	**N**	F	*LS*	EM	76175	62116	70776	76225
310 092	**N**	F	*LS*	EM	76176	62117	70777	76226
310 093	**N**	F	*LS*	EM	76177	62118	70778	76190
310 094	**N**	F	*LS*	EM	76998	62119	70780	76193
310 095	**N**	F	*LS*	EM	76179	62120	70779	76229

Name (carried on MBSO): 310 058   Chafford Hundred.

Class 310/1. 3-car units. BDTSOL–MBSO–DTSOL (* DTCOL declassified).

310 101	**RR**	F	CT	BY	76157	62098	76207	
310 102	**RR**	F	CT	BY	76139	62080	76189	
310 103	**RR**	F	CT	BY	76160	62101	76210	
310 104	**RR**	F	CT	BY	76162	62103	76212	
310 105	**RR**	F	CT	BY	76174	62115	76224	
310 106	**RR**	F	CT	BY	76156	62097	76206	
310 107	**RR**	F	CT	BY	76146	62087	76196	
310 108	**RR**	F	CT	BY	76132	62073	76182	
310 109	**RR**	F	CT	BY	76137	62078	76187	
310 110	**RR**	F	CT	BY	76138	62079	76188	
310 111	**RR**	F	CT	BY	76147	62088	76197	
310 112 *	**RR**	F	CT	BY	76140	62086	76227	
310 113 *	**RR**	F	CT	BY	76158	62090	76195	
Spare	**0**	F		KN(S)	70733	70747	70748	70757
					70763			

CLASS 312   4-Car Unit

BDTSOL–MBSO–TSO–DTCOL (declassified*). Gangwayed within unit. Disc brakes.
Traction Motors: Four English Electric EE546 of 201.5 kW each.
Dimensions: 20.18 x 2.82 x 3.86 m.
Maximum Speed: 90 mph.   **Doors:** Manually operated slam.
Couplings: Buckeye.   **Bogies:** B4.
Multiple Working: Classes 303–312 only.

Class 312/0. Built to operate on 25 kV 50 Hz a.c. overhead only.

76949–76974 BDTSOL. Dia. EF213. Lot No. 30863 BREL York 1977–78. –/84 1T. 34.9 t.
76994–76997 BDTSOL. Dia. EF213. Lot No. 30891 BREL York 1976. –/84 1T. 34.9 t.
62484–62509 MBSO. Dia. ED212. Lot No. 30864 BREL York 1977–78. –/68. 56.0 t.
62657–62560 MBSO. Dia. ED214. Lot No. 30892 BREL York 1976. –/68. 56.0 t.
71168–71193 TSO. Dia. EH209. Lot No. 30865 BREL York 1977–78. –/98. 30.5 t.
71277–71280 TSO. Dia. EH209. Lot No. 30893 BREL York 1976. –/98. 30.5 t.
78045–78048 DTCOL. Dia. EE305. Lot No. 30894 BREL York 1976. 25/47 2T. 33.0 t.
78000–25 DTCOL. Dia. EE305. Lot No. 30866 BREL York 1977–78. 25/47 2T. 33.0 t.

312 701	GE	A	GE	IL	76949	62484	71168	78000
312 702	N	A	GE	IL	76950	62485	71169	78001
312 703	GE	A	GE	IL	76951	62486	71170	78002
312 704	GE	A	GE	IL	76952	62487	71171	78003
312 705	GE	A	GE	IL	76953	62488	71172	78004
312 706	GE	A	GE	IL	76954	62489	71173	78005
312 707	GE	A	GE	IL	76955	62490	71174	78006
312 708	GE	A	GE	IL	76956	62491	71175	78007
312 709	GE	A	GE	IL	76957	62492	71176	78008
312 710	GE	A	GE	IL	76958	62493	71177	78009
312 711	GE	A	GE	IL	76959	62494	71178	78010
312 712	GE	A	GE	IL	76960	62495	71179	78011
312 713	N	A	GE	IL	76961	62496	71180	78012
312 714	GE	A	GE	IL	76962	62497	71181	78013
312 715	GE	A	GE	IL	76963	62498	71182	78014
312 716	GE	A	GE	IL	76964	62499	71183	78015
312 717	N	A	GE	IL	76965	62500	71184	78016
312 718	GE	A	GE	IL	76966	62501	71185	78017
312 719	GE	A	GE	IL	76967	62502	71186	78018
312 720	GE	A	GE	IL	76968	62503	71187	78019
312 721	N	A	GE	IL	76969	62504	71188	78020
312 722	N	A	GE	IL	76970	62505	71189	78021
312 723	N	A	GE	IL	76971	62506	71190	78022
312 724	N	A	GE	IL	76972	62507	71191	78023
312 725 *	N	A	LS	EM	76973	62509	71193	78025
312 726 *	N	A	LS	EM	76974	62508	71192	78024
312 727 *	N	A	LS	EM	76994	62657	71277	78045
312 728 *	N	A	LS	EM	76995	62658	71278	78046
312 729 *	N	A	LS	EM	76996	62659	71279	78047
312 730 *	N	A	LS	EM	76997	62660	71280	78048

Class 312/1. Built to operate on 25 kV 50 Hz a.c. or 6.25 kV 50 Hz a.c. overhead.

BDTSOL. Dia. EF213. Lot No. 30867 BREL York 1975–76. –/84 2T. 34.9 t.
MBSO. Dia. ED213. Lot No. 30868 BREL York 1975–76. –/68. 56.0 t.
TSO. Dia. EH209. Lot No. 30869 BREL York 1975–76. –/98. 30.5 t.
DTCOL. Dia. EE305. Lot No. 30870 BREL York 1975–76. 25/47 2T. 33.0 t.

312 781	*	**N**	A	*LS*	EM	76975	62510	71194	78026
312 782	*	**N**	A	*LS*	EM	76976	62511	71195	78027
312 783	*	**N**	A	*LS*	EM	76977	62512	71196	78028
312 784	*	**N**	A	*LS*	EM	76978	62513	71197	78029
312 785	*	**N**	A	*LS*	EM	76979	62514	71198	78030
312 786	*	**N**	A	*LS*	EM	76980	62515	71199	78031
312 787	*	**N**	A	*LS*	EM	76981	62516	71200	78032
312 788	*	**N**	A	*LS*	EM	76982	62517	71201	78033
312 789	*	**N**	A	*LS*	EM	76983	62518	71202	78034
312 790	*	**N**	A	*LS*	EM	76984	62519	71203	78035
312 791	*	**N**	A	*LS*	EM	76985	62520	71204	78036
312 792	*	**N**	A	*LS*	EM	76986	62521	71205	78037
312 793	*	**N**	A	*LS*	EM	76987	62522	71206	78038
312 794	*	**N**	A	*LS*	EM	76988	62523	71207	78039
312 795	*	**N**	A	*LS*	EM	76989	62524	71208	78040
312 796	*	**N**	A	*LS*	EM	76990	62525	71209	78041
312 797	*	**N**	A	*LS*	EM	76991	62526	71210	78042
312 798	*	**N**	A	*LS*	EM	76992	62527	71211	78043
312 799	*	**N**	A	*LS*	EM	76993	62528	71212	78044

CLASS 313   3-Car Unit

DMSO–PTSO–BDMSO. Gangwayed within unit. End doors. Disc and rheo-static brakes.
Supply System: 25 kV 50 Hz a.c. overhead or 750 V d.c. third rail.
Traction Motors: Four GEC G310AZ of 82.125 kW each.
Dimensions: 19.80 x 2.82 x 3.58 m (outer cars), 19.92 x 2.82 x 3.58 m (inner cars).
Maximum Speed: 75 mph.   **Doors:** Power operated sliding.
Couplers: Tightlock.   **Bogies:** BX1.
Multiple Working: Classes 313–323.

DMSO. Dia. EA204. Lot No. 30879 BREL York 1976–77. –/74. 36.4 t.
PTSO. Dia. EH210. Lot No. 30880 BREL York 1976–77. –/84 (* –/80). 30.5 t.
BDMSO. Dia. EI201. Lot No. 30885 BREL York 1976–77. –/74. 37.6 t.

Class 313/0 and 313/1*. Silverlink Train Services units. Equipped with additional shoegear for working on London Underground 750 V d.c. 4-rail system. These units are being renumbered and reclassified to 313/1 as they are modernised.

313 101	*	(313 001)	**SL**	F	*SL*	BY	62529	71213	62593
313 102	*	(313 002)	**SL**	F	*SL*	BY	62530	71214	62594
313 103	*	(313 003)	**SL**	F	*SL*	BY	62531	71215	62595
		313 004	**N**	F	*SL*	BY	62532	71216	62596
313 105	*	(313 005)	**SL**	F	*SL*	BY	62533	71217	62597
		313 006	**N**	F	*SL*	BY	62534	71218	62598

313 107 * (313 007)	**SL**	F	*SL*	BY	62535	71219	62599
313 008	**N**	F	*SL*	BY	62536	71220	62600
313 009	**N**	F	*SL*	BY	62537	71221	62601
313 010	**N**	F	*SL*	BY	62538	71222	62602
313 011	**N**	F	*SL*	BY	62539	71223	62603
313 112 * (313 112)	**SL**	F	*SL*	BY	62540	71224	62604
313 013	**N**	F	*SL*	BY	62541	71225	62605
313 014	**N**	F	*SL*	BY	62542	71226	62606
313 115 * (313 115)	**SL**	F	*SL*	BY	62543	71227	62607
313 016	**N**	F	*SL*	BY	62544	71228	62608
313 017	**SL**	F	*SL*	BY	62545	71229	62609
313 018	**N**	F	*WN*	HE	62546	71230	62610
313 019	**N**	F	*SL*	BY	62547	71231	62611
313 020	**N**	F	*SL*	BY	62548	71232	62612
313 121 * (313 021)	**SL**	F	*SL*	BY	62549	71233	62613
313 022	**SL**	F	*SL*	BY	62550	71234	62614
313 023	**N**	F	*SL*	BY	62551	71235	62615
313 024	**N**	F	*WN*	HE	62552	71236	62616
313 025	**N**	F	*WN*	HE	62553	71237	62617
313 026	**N**	F	*WN*	HE	62554	71238	62618
313 027	**N**	F	*WN*	HE	62555	71239	62619
313 028	**N**	F	*WN*	HE	62556	71240	62620
313 029	**N**	F	*WN*	HE	62557	71241	62621
313 030	**N**	F	*WN*	HE	62558	71242	62622
313 031	**N**	F	*WN*	HE	62559	71243	62623
313 032	**N**	F	*WN*	HE	62560	71244	62643
313 033	**N**	F	*WN*	HE	62561	71245	62625
313 134 * (313 034)	**SL**	F	*SL*	BY	62562	71246	62626

Name (carried on PTSO): 313 020   PARLIAMENT HILL

Class 313/0. West Anglia Great Northern Railway units.

313 035	**N**	F	*WN*	HE	62563	71247	62627
313 036	**N**	F	*WN*	HE	62564	71248	62628
313 037	**N**	F	*WN*	HE	62565	71249	62629
313 038	**N**	F	*WN*	HE	62566	71250	62630
313 039	**N**	F	*WN*	HE	62567	71251	62631
313 040	**N**	F	*WN*	HE	62568	71252	62632
313 041	**N**	F	*WN*	HE	62569	71253	62633
313 042	**N**	F	*WN*	HE	62570	71254	62634
313 043	**N**	F	*WN*	HE	62571	71255	62635
313 044	**N**	F	*WN*	HE	62572	71256	62636
313 045	**N**	F	*WN*	HE	62573	71257	62637
313 046	**N**	F	*WN*	HE	62574	71258	62638
313 047	**N**	F	*WN*	HE	62575	71259	62639
313 048	**N**	F	*WN*	HE	62576	71260	62640
313 049	**N**	F	*WN*	HE	62577	71261	62641
313 050	**N**	F	*WN*	HE	62578	71262	62649
313 051	**N**	F	*WN*	HE	62579	71263	62624
313 052	**N**	F	*WN*	HE	62580	71264	62644
313 053	**N**	F	*WN*	HE	62581	71265	62645
313 054	**N**	F	*WN*	HE	62582	71266	62646

313 055	N	F	*WN*	HE	62583	71267	62647
313 056	N	F	*WN*	HE	62584	71268	62648
313 057	N	F	*WN*	HE	62585	71269	62642
313 058	N	F	*WN*	HE	62586	71270	62650
313 059	N	F	*WN*	HE	62587	71271	62651
313 060	N	F	*WN*	HE	62588	71272	62652
313 061	N	F	*WN*	HE	62589	71273	62653
313 062	N	F	*WN*	HE	62590	71274	62654
313 063	N	F	*WN*	HE	62591	71275	62655
313 064	N	F	*WN*	HE	62592	71276	62656

CLASS 314   3-Car Unit

DMSO–PTSO–DMSO. Gangwayed within unit. End doors. Disc and rheostatic brakes.
Traction Motors: Four Brush TM61-53 (* GEC G310AZ) of 82.125 kW each.
Dimensions: 19.80 x 2.82 x 3.58 m (outer cars), 19.92 x 2.82 x 3.58 m (inner cars).
Maximum Speed: 75 mph.   **Doors:** Power operated sliding.
Couplers: Tightlock.   **Bogies:** BX1.
Multiple Working: Classes 313–323.

64583–64614. DMSO. Dia. EA206. Lot No. 30912 BREL York 1979. –/68. 34.5 t.
64588ᴵᴵ. DMSO (ex-Class 507 DMSO). Dia. EA206. Lot No. 30908 BREL York 1978–80. Rebuilt Railcare Glasgow 1996. –/74. 35.6 t.
PTSO. Dia. EH211. Lot No. 30913 BREL York 1979. –/76. 33.0 t.

314 201	S	A	*SR*	GW	64583	71450	64584
314 202	S	A	*SR*	GW	64585	71451	64586
314 203	S	A	*SR*	GW	64587	71452	64588ᴵᴵ
314 204	S	A	*SR*	GW	64589	71453	64590
314 205	CC	A	*SR*	GW	64591	71454	64592
314 206	CC	A	*SR*	GW	64593	71455	64594
314 207 *	S	A	*SR*	GW	64595	71456	64596
314 208 *	S	A	*SR*	GW	64597	71457	64598
314 209 *	S	A	*SR*	GW	64599	71458	64600
314 210 *	S	A	*SR*	GW	64601	71459	64602
314 211 *	S	A	*SR*	GW	64603	71460	64604
314 212 *	S	A	*SR*	GW	64605	71461	64606
314 213 *	S	A	*SR*	GW	64607	71462	64608
314 214 *	S	A	*SR*	GW	64609	71463	64610
314 215 *	CC	A	*SR*	GW	64611	71464	64612
314 216 *	CC	A	*SR*	GW	64613	71465	64614

Name (carried on PTSO): 314 203   European Union

CLASS 315   4-Car Unit

DMSO–TSO–PTSO–DMSO. Gangwayed within unit. End doors. Disc and rheostatic brakes.
Traction Motors: Four GEC G310AZ (* Brush TM61-53) of 82.125 kW each.
Dimensions: 19.80 x 2.82 x 3.58 m (outer cars), 19.92 x 2.82 x 3.58 m (inner cars).
Maximum Speed: 75 mph.   **Doors:** Power operated sliding.
Couplers: Tightlock.   **Bogies:** BX1.
Multiple Working: Classes 313–323.

64461–64582. DMSO. Dia. EA207. Lot No. 30902 BRELYork 1980–81. –/74. 35.0 t.
71281–71341. TSO. Dia. EH216. Lot No. 30904 BREL York 1980–81. –/86. 25.5 t.
71389–71449. PTSO. Dia. EH217. Lot No. 30903 BREL York 1980–81. –/84. 32.0 t.

315 801	**GE**	F	*GE*	IL	64461	71281	71389	64462
315 802	**GE**	F	*GE*	IL	64463	71282	71390	64464
315 803	**GE**	F	*GE*	IL	64465	71283	71391	64466
315 804	**GE**	F	*GE*	IL	64467	71284	71392	64468
315 805	**GE**	F	*GE*	IL	64469	71285	71393	64470
315 806	**GE**	F	*GE*	IL	64471	71286	71394	64472
315 807	**GE**	F	*GE*	IL	64473	71287	71395	64474
315 808	**GE**	F	*GE*	IL	64475	71288	71396	64476
315 809	**GE**	F	*GE*	IL	64477	71289	71397	64478
315 810	**GE**	F	*GE*	IL	64479	71290	71398	64480
315 811	**GE**	F	*GE*	IL	64481	71291	71399	64482
315 812	**GE**	F	*GE*	IL	64483	71292	71400	64484
315 813	**GE**	F	*GE*	IL	64485	71293	71401	64486
315 814	**N**	F	*GE*	IL	64487	71294	71402	64488
315 815	**GE**	F	*GE*	IL	64489	71295	71403	64490
315 816	**GE**	F	*GE*	IL	64491	71296	71404	64492
315 817	**GE**	F	*GE*	IL	64493	71297	71405	64494
315 818	**GE**	F	*GE*	IL	64495	71298	71406	64496
315 819	**GE**	F	*GE*	IL	64497	71299	71407	64498
315 820	**GE**	F	*GE*	IL	64499	71300	71408	64500
315 821	**GE**	F	*GE*	IL	64501	71301	71409	64502
315 822	**GE**	F	*GE*	IL	64503	71302	71410	64504
315 823	**GE**	F	*GE*	IL	64505	71303	71411	64506
315 824	**GE**	F	*GE*	IL	64507	71304	71412	64508
315 825	**N**	F	*GE*	IL	64509	71305	71413	64510
315 826	**GE**	F	*GE*	IL	64511	71306	71414	64512
315 827	**GE**	F	*GE*	IL	64513	71307	71415	64514
315 828	**N**	F	*GE*	IL	64515	71308	71416	64516
315 829	**GE**	F	*GE*	IL	64517	71309	71417	64518
315 830	**N**	F	*GE*	IL	64519	71310	71418	64520
315 831	**GE**	F	*GE*	IL	64521	71311	71419	64522
315 832	**N**	F	*GE*	IL	64523	71312	71420	64524
315 833	**N**	F	*GE*	IL	64525	71313	71421	64526
315 834	**N**	F	*GE*	IL	64527	71314	71422	64528
315 835	**N**	F	*GE*	IL	64529	71315	71423	64530
315 836	**N**	F	*GE*	IL	64531	71316	71424	64532
315 837	**N**	F	*GE*	IL	64533	71317	71425	64534
315 838	**N**	F	*GE*	IL	64535	71318	71426	64536
315 839	**N**	F	*GE*	IL	64537	71319	71427	64538
315 840	**N**	F	*GE*	IL	64539	71320	71428	64540
315 841	**N**	F	*GE*	IL	64541	71321	71429	64542
315 842 *	**N**	F	*GE*	IL	64543	71322	71430	64544
315 843 *	**N**	F	*GE*	IL	64545	71323	71431	64546
315 844 *	**N**	F	*WN*	HE	64547	71324	71432	64548
315 845 *	**N**	F	*WN*	HE	64549	71325	71433	64550
315 846 *	**N**	F	*WN*	HE	64551	71326	71434	64552
315 847 *	**N**	F	*WN*	HE	64553	71327	71435	64554
315 848 *	**N**	F	*WN*	HE	64555	71328	71436	64556

315 849	*	N	F	WN	HE	64557	71329	71437	64558
315 850	*	N	F	WN	HE	64559	71330	71438	64560
315 851	*	N	F	WN	HE	64561	71331	71439	64562
315 852	*	N	F	WN	HE	64563	71332	71440	64564
315 853	*	N	F	WN	HE	64565	71333	71441	64566
315 854	*	N	F	WN	HE	64567	71334	71442	64568
315 855	*	N	F	WN	HE	64569	71335	71443	64570
315 856	*	N	F	WN	HE	64571	71336	71444	64572
315 857	*	N	F	WN	HE	64573	71337	71445	64574
315 858	*	N	F	WN	HE	64579	71338	71446	64580
315 859	*	N	F	WN	HE	64577	71339	71447	64578
315 860	*	N	F	WN	HE	64575	71340	71448	64576
315 861	*	N	F	WN	HE	64581	71341	71449	64582

CLASS 317   4-Car Unit

Various formations (see below). Gangwayed throughout. Disc brakes.
Traction Motors: Four GEC G315BZ of 247.5 kW each.
Dimensions: 20.13 x 2.82 x 3.58 m (outer cars), 20.18 x 2.82 x 3.58 m (inner cars).
Maximum Speed: 100 mph.   **Doors:** Power operated sliding.
Couplers: Tightlock.   **Bogies:** BP20 (MSO), BT13 (others).
Multiple Working: Classes 313–323.

Class 317/1. Pressure heating & ventilation. DTSO(A)–MSO–TCOL († declassified)–DTSO(B).

DTSO(A). Dia. EE216. Lot No. 30955 BREL York 1981–82. –/74. 29.4 t.
MSO. Dia. EC208. Lot No. 30958 BREL York 1981–82. –/79. 49.8 t.
TCOL. Dia. EH307 († EH242). Lot No. 30957 BREL Derby 1981–82. 22/46 2T. 28.8 t.
DTSO(B). Dia. EE235 (*EE232). Lot No. 30956 York 1981–82. –/70. (* –/71). 29.3 t.

317 301	†	LS	A	LS	EM	77024	62661	71577	77048
317 302	†	LS	A	LS	EM	77001	62662	71578	77049
317 303	†	LS	A	LS	EM	77002	62663	71579	77050
317 304	†	LS	A	LS	EM	77003	62664	71580	77051
317 305	†	LS	A	LS	EM	77004	62665	71581	77052
317 306	†	LS	A	LS	EM	77005	62666	71582	77053
317 307	†	LS	A	LS	EM	77006	62667	71583	77054
317 308		N	A	WN	HE	77007	62668	71584	77055
317 309		N	A	WN	HE	77008	62669	71585	77056
317 310		N	A	WN	HE	77009	62670	71586	77057
317 311	†	LS	A	LS	EM	77010	62697	71587	77058
317 312	†	LS	A	LS	EM	77011	62672	71588	77059
317 313	†	LS	A	LS	EM	77012	62673	71589	77060
317 314	†	N	A	LS	EM	77013	62674	71590	77061
317 315		N	A	WN	HE	77014	62675	71591	77062
317 316		N	A	WN	HE	77015	62676	71592	77063
317 317	†	LS	A	LS	EM	77016	62677	71593	77064
317 318		N	A	WN	HE	77017	62678	71594	77065
317 319	†	LS	A	LS	EM	77018	62679	71595	77066
317 320		N	A	WN	HE	77019	62680	71596	77067
317 321		N	A	WN	HE	77020	62681	71597	77068

317 323 †	**LS**	A	*LS*	EM	77022	62683	71599	77070
317 324	**N**	A	*WN*	HE	77023	62684	71600	77071
317 325	**N**	A	*WN*	HE	77000	62685	71601	77072
317 326	**N**	A	*WN*	HE	77025	62686	71602	77073
317 327	**N**	A	*WN*	HE	77026	62687	71603	77074
317 328	**N**	A	*WN*	HE	77027	62688	71604	77075
317 329 †	**LS**	A	*LS*	EM	77028	62689	71605	77076
317 330	**N**	A	*WN*	HE	77043	62704	71606	77077
317 331	**N**	A	*WN*	HE	77030	62691	71607	77078
317 332 †	**LS**	A	*LS*	EM	77031	62692	71608	77079
317 333	**N**	A	*WN*	HE	77032	62693	71609	77080
317 334	**N**	A	*WN*	HE	77033	62694	71610	77081
317 335	**N**	A	*WN*	HE	77034	62695	71611	77082
317 336	**N**	A	*WN*	HE	77035	62696	71612	77083
317 337 *	**N**	A	*WN*	HE	77036	62671	71613	77084
317 338 *	**N**	A	*WN*	HE	77037	62698	71614	77085
317 339 *	**N**	A	*WN*	HE	77038	62699	71615	77086
317 340 *	**N**	A	*WN*	HE	77039	62700	71616	77087
317 341 *	**N**	A	*WN*	HE	77040	62701	71617	77088
317 342 *	**N**	A	*WN*	HE	77041	62702	71618	77089
317 343 *	**N**	A	*WN*	HE	77042	62703	71619	77090
317 344 *	**N**	A	*WN*	HE	77029	62690	71620	77091
317 345 *	**N**	A	*WN*	HE	77044	62705	71621	77092
317 346 *	**N**	A	*WN*	HE	77045	62706	71622	77093
317 347 *	**N**	A	*WN*	HE	77046	62707	71623	77094
317 348 *	**N**	A	*WN*	HE	77047	62708	71624	77095

Class 317/2. Convection heating. DTSO(A)–MSO–TCOL–DTSO(B). These units are being renumbered and reclassified to 317/6 as they are refurbished.

77200–19. DTSO(A). Dia. EE224. Lot No. 30994 BREL York 1985–86. –/74. 29.3 t.
77280–83. DTSO(A). Dia. EE224. Lot No. 31007 BREL York 1987. –/74. 29.3 t.
62846–65. MSO. Dia. EC205. Lot No. 30996 BREL York 1985–86. –/79. 50.1 t.
62886–89. MSO. Dia. EC205. Lot No. 31009 BREL York 1987. –/79. 50.1 t.
71734–53. TCOL. Dia. EH308. Lot No. 30997 BREL York 1985–86. 22/46 2T. 28.3 t.
71762–65. TCOL. Dia. EH308. Lot No. 31010 BREL York 1987. 22/46 2T. 28.3 t.
77220–39. DTSO(B). Dia. EE225. Lot No. 30995 BREL York 1985–86. –/71. 29.3 t.
77284–87. DTSO(B). Dia. EE225. Lot No. 31008 BREL York 1987. –/71. 29.3 t.

Class 317/6. Convection heating. DTSO–MSO–TSOL–DTCO.

77200–77219. DTSO. Dia. EE247. Lot No. 30994 BREL York 1985–86. Refurbished Railcare Wolverton 1998–99. –/64. 29.3 t.
77280–77283. DTSO. Dia. EE247. Lot No. 31007 BREL York 1987. Refurbished Railcare Wolverton 1998–99. –/64. 29.3 t.
62846–62865. MSO. Dia. EC222. Lot No. 30996 BREL York 1985–86. Refurbished Railcare Wolverton 1998–99. –/71. 50.1 t.
62886–62889. MSO. Dia. EC222. Lot No. 31009 BREL York 1987. Refurbished Railcare Wolverton 1998–99. –/71. 50.1 t.
71734–71753. TSOL. Dia. EH247. Lot No. 30997 BREL York 1985–86. Refurbished Railcare Wolverton 1998–99. 22/46 2T. 28.3 t.
71762–71765. TSOL. Dia. EH247. Lot No. 31010 BREL York 1987. Refurbished Railcare Wolverton 1998–99. 22/46 2T. 28.3 t.

77220–77239. DTCO. Dia. EE375. Lot No. 30995 BREL York 1985–86. Refurbished Railcare Wolverton 1998–99. –/71. 29.3 t.
77284–77287. DTCO. Dia. EE375. Lot No. 31008 BREL York 1987. Refurbished Railcare Wolverton 1998–99. –/71. 29.3 t.

317 649	(317 349)	**WN**	A	*WN*	HE	77200	62846	71734	77220
317 650	(317 350)	**WN**	A	*WN*	HE	77201	62847	71735	77221
317 651	(317 351)	**WN**	A	*WN*	HE	77202	62848	71736	77222
317 652	(317 352)	**WN**	A	*WN*	HE	77203	62849	71739	77223
317 653	(317 353)	**WN**	A	*WN*	HE	77204	62850	71738	77224
317 654	(317 354)	**WN**	A	*WN*	HE	77205	62851	71737	77225
317 655	(317 355)	**WN**	A	*WN*	HE	77206	62852	71740	77226
317 656	(317 356)	**WN**	A	*WN*	HE	77207	62853	71742	77227
317 657	(317 357)	**WN**	A	*WN*	HE	77208	62854	71741	77228
317 658	(317 358)	**WN**	A	*WN*	HE	77209	62855	71743	77229
317 659	(317 359)	**WN**	A	*WN*	HE	77210	62856	71744	77230
317 660	(317 360)	**WN**	A	*WN*	HE	77211	62857	71745	77231
317 661	(317 361)	**WN**	A	*WN*	HE	77212	62858	71746	77232
317 662	(317 362)	**WN**	A	*WN*	HE	77213	62859	71747	77233
	317 363	**N**	A	*WN*	HE	77214	62860	71748	77234
	317 364	**N**	A	*WN*	HE	77215	62861	71749	77235
	317 365	**N**	A	*WN*	HE	77216	62862	71750	77236
	317 366	**N**	A	*WN*	HE	77217	62863	71752	77237
	317 367	**N**	A	*WN*	HE	77218	62864	71751	77238
	317 368	**N**	A	*WN*	HE	77219	62865	71753	77239
	317 369	**N**	A	*WN*	HE	77280	62886	71762	77284
	317 370	**N**	A	*WN*	HE	77281	62887	71763	77285
	317 371	**N**	A	*WN*	HE	77282	62888	71764	77286
	317 372	**N**	A	*WN*	HE	77283	62889	71765	77287

Names (carried on TCOL):

317 363	THE HATFIELD COMET
317 366	LETCHWORTH GARDEN CITY.
317 371	STEVENAGE new town 50 years – 1946 – 1996.
317 372	WELWYN GARDEN CITY Seventy five years.
317 650	HARLOW 50 years 1947 – 1997.
317 661	KINGS LYNN FESTIVAL

Class 317/3. Pressure heating & ventilation. DTSO(A)–MSO–TCOL (declassified)–DTSO(B).

DTSO(A). Dia. EE216. Lot No. 30955 BREL York 1981–82. –/74. 29.4 t.
MSO. Dia. EC208. Lot No. 30958 BREL York 1981–82. –/79. 49.8 t.
TCOL. Dia. EH242. Lot No. 30957 BREL Derby 1981–82. 22/46 2T. 28.8 t.
DTSO(B). Dia. EE235. Lot No. 30956 BREL York 1981–82. –/70. 29.3 t.

317 392		**LS**	A	*LS*	EM	77021	62682	71598	77069

CLASS 318   3-Car Unit

DTSOL–MSO–DTSO. Gangwayed throughout. Disc brakes.
Traction Motors: Four Brush TM 2141 of 268 kW each.
Dimensions: 20.13 x 2.82 x 3.77 m (outer cars), 20.18 x 2.82 x 3.77 m (inner cars).

Maximum Speed: 90 mph.   **Doors:** Power operated sliding.
Couplers: Tightlock.   **Bogies:** BP20 (MSO), BT13 (others).
Multiple Working: Classes 313–323.

77240–59. DTSOL. Dia. EE227. Lot No. 30999 BREL York 1985–86. –/66 1T. 30.0 t.
77288. DTSOL. Dia. EE227. Lot No. 31020 BREL York 1986–87. –/66 1T. 30.0 t.
62866–85. MSO. Dia. EC207. Lot No. 30998 BREL York 1985–86. –/79. 50.9 t.
62890. MSO. Dia. EC207. Lot No. 31019 BREL York 1987. –/79. 50.9 t.
77260–79. DTSO. Dia. EE228. Lot No. 31000 BREL York 1985–86. –/71. 26.6 t.
77289. DTSO. Dia. EE228. Lot No. 31021 BREL York 1987. –/71. 26.6 t.

318 250	S	F	*SR*	GW	77260	62866	77240
318 251	S	F	*SR*	GW	77261	62867	77241
318 252	S	F	*SR*	GW	77262	62868	77242
318 253	S	F	*SR*	GW	77263	62869	77243
318 254	CC	F	*SR*	GW	77264	62870	77244
318 255	S	F	*SR*	GW	77265	62871	77245
318 256	S	F	*SR*	GW	77266	62872	77246
318 257	CC	F	*SR*	GW	77267	62873	77247
318 258	CC	F	*SR*	GW	77268	62874	77248
318 259	CC	F	*SR*	GW	77269	62875	77249
318 260	S	F	*SR*	GW	77270	62876	77250
318 261	S	F	*SR*	GW	77271	62877	77251
318 262	S	F	*SR*	GW	77272	62878	77252
318 263	S	F	*SR*	GW	77273	62879	77253
318 264	S	F	*SR*	GW	77274	62880	77254
318 265	S	F	*SR*	GW	77275	62881	77255
318 266	CC	F	*SR*	GW	77276	62882	77256
318 267	S	F	*SR*	GW	77277	62883	77257
318 268	S	F	*SR*	GW	77278	62884	77258
318 269	S	F	*SR*	GW	77279	62885	77259
318 270	CC	F	*SR*	GW	77289	62890	77288

Names (carried on/inside DTSOL):

318 250	GEOFF SHAW	318 260	STRATHCLYDER
318 259	CITIZENS NETWORK		

CLASS 319   4-Car Unit

Various formations (see below). Gangwayed within unit. End doors. Disc brakes.
Supply System: 25 kV 50 Hz a.c. overhead or 750 V d.c. third rail.
Traction Motors: Four GEC G315BZ of 247.5 kW each.
Dimensions: 20.13 x 2.82 x 3.77 m (outer cars), 20.18 x 2.82 x 3.77 m (inner cars).
Maximum Speed: 100 mph.   **Doors:** Power operated sliding.
Couplers: Tightlock.   **Bogies:** P7-4 (MSO), T3-7 (others).
Multiple Working: Classes 313–323.

Class 319/0. DTSO–MSO–TSOL–DTSO. Connex South Central units.

DTSO. Dia. EE233. Lot No. 31022 (odd nos.) BREL York 1987–8. –/82. 30.1 t.
MSO. Dia. EC209. Lot No. 31023 BREL York 1987–8. –/82. 51.0 t.
TSOL. Dia. EH234. Lot No. 31024 BREL York 1987–8. –/77 2T. 30.0 t.
DTSO. Dia. EE234. Lot No. 31025 (even nos.) BREL York 1987–8. –/78. 30.0 t.

319 001	**CX**	P	*SC*	SU	77291	62891	71772	77290
319 002	**CX**	P	*SC*	SU	77293	62892	71773	77292
319 003	**CX**	P	*SC*	SU	77295	62893	71774	77294
319 004	**CX**	P	*SC*	SU	77297	62894	71775	77296
319 005	**CX**	P	*SC*	SU	77299	62895	71776	77298
319 006	**CX**	P	*SC*	SU	77301	62896	71777	77300
319 007	**CX**	P	*SC*	SU	77303	62897	71778	77302
319 008	**CX**	P	*SC*	SU	77305	62898	71779	77304
319 009	**CX**	P	*SC*	SU	77307	62899	71780	77306
319 010	**CX**	P	*SC*	SU	77309	62900	71781	77308
319 011	**CX**	P	*SC*	SU	77311	62901	71782	77310
319 012	**CX**	P	*SC*	SU	77313	62902	71783	77312
319 013	**CX**	P	*SC*	SU	77315	62903	71784	77314

Names (carried on TSOL):

| 319 005 | Partnership For Progress | 319 009 | Coquelles |
| 319 008 | Cheriton | 319 011 | John Ruskin College |

Class 319/2. DTSO–MSO–TSOL–DTCO. Refurbished units for Connex South Central London Victoria–Brighton route.

DTSO. Dia. EE244. Lot No. 31022 (odd nos.) BREL York 1987–8. Refurbished Railcare Wolverton 1996. –/64. 29.7 t.
MSO. Dia. EC262. Lot No. 31023 BREL York 1987–8. Refurbished Railcare Wolverton 1996. –/60. 51.0 t.
TSOL. Dia. EH212. Lot No. 31024 BREL York 1987–8. Refurbished Railcare Wolverton 1996. –/52 1T 1TD. 31.0 t.
DTCO. Dia. EE374. Lot No. 31025 (even nos.) BREL York 1987–8. Refurbished Railcare Wolverton 1996. 18/36. 29.0 t.

319 214	**CX**	P	*SC*	SU	77317	62904	71785	77316
319 215	**CX**	P	*SC*	SU	77319	62905	71786	77318
319 216	**CX**	P	*SC*	SU	77321	62906	71787	77320
319 217	**CX**	P	*SC*	SU	77323	62907	71788	77322
319 218	**CX**	P	*SC*	SU	77325	62908	71789	77324
319 219	**CX**	P	*SC*	SU	77327	62909	71790	77326
319 220	**CX**	P	*SC*	SU	77329	62910	71791	77328

Names (carried on TSOL):

| 319 215 | London | 319 218 | Croydon |
| 319 217 | Brighton | | |

Class 319/1. DTCO–MSO–TSOL–DTSO.
Class 319/3. DTSO(A)–MSO–TSOL–DTSO(B).

Thameslink Rail units for 'City Metro' Luton–Sutton route. These units are being renumbered and reclassified from 319/1 to 319/3 as they are reconfigured.

DTCO. Dia. EE310. Lot No. 31063 BREL York 1990. 16/54. 29.0 t.
DTSO(A). Dia. EE240. Lot No. 31063 BREL York 1990. –/70. 29.0 t.
MSO. Dia. EC214. Lot No. 31064 BREL York 1990. –/79. 50.6 t.
TSOL. Dia. EH238. Lot No. 31065 BREL York 1990. –/74 2T. 31.0 t.
DTSO(B). Dia. EE240. Lot No. 31066 BREL York 1990. –/78. 29.7 t.

319 361	(319 161)	**TR**	P	*TR*	SU	77459	63043	71929	77458
319 362	(319 162)	**TR**	P	*TR*	SU	77461	63044	71930	77460
319 363	(319 163)	**TR**	P	*TR*	SU	77463	63045	71931	77462
319 364	(319 164)	**TR**	P	*TR*	SU	77465	63046	71932	77464
319 365	(319 165)	**TR**	P	*TR*	SU	77467	63047	71933	77466
319 366	(319 166)	**TR**	P	*TR*	SU	77469	63048	71934	77468
319 367	(319 167)	**TR**	P	*TR*	SU	77471	63049	71935	77470
319 368	(319 168)	**TR**	P	*TR*	SU	77473	63050	71936	77472
319 369	(319 169)	**TR**	P	*TR*	SU	77475	63051	71937	77474
319 370	(319 170)	**TR**	P	*TR*	SU	77477	63052	71938	77476
319 371	(319 171)	**TR**	P	*TR*	SU	77479	63053	71939	77478
319 372	(319 172)	**TR**	P	*TR*	SU	77481	63054	71940	77480
	319 173	**N**	P	*TR*	SU	77483	63055	71941	77482
	319 174	**N**	P	*TR*	SU	77485	63056	71942	77484
	319 175	**N**	P	*TR*	SU	77487	63057	71943	77486
	319 176	**N**	P	*TR*	SU	77489	63058	71944	77488
319 377	(319 177)	**TR**	P	*TR*	SU	77491	63059	71945	77490
	319 178	**N**	P	*TR*	SU	77493	63060	71946	77492
	319 179	**N**	P	*TR*	SU	77495	63061	71947	77494
	319 180	**N**	P	*TR*	SU	77497	63062	71948	77496
	319 181	**N**	P	*TR*	SU	77973	63093	71979	77974
	319 182	**N**	P	*TR*	SU	77975	63094	71980	77976
319 383	(319 183)	**TR**	P	*TR*	SU	77977	63095	71981	77978
319 384	(319 184)	**TR**	P	*TR*	SU	77979	63096	71982	77980
319 385	(319 185)	**TR**	P	*TR*	SU	77981	63097	71983	77982
	319 186	**N**	P	*TR*	SU	77983	63098	71984	77984

Class 319/4. DTCO–MSO–TSOL–DTSO(B). Facelifted units for Thameslink Rail 'City Flyer' Bedford–Gatwick Airport–Brighton route.

77331–77381. DTCO. Dia. EE314. Lot No. 31022 (odd nos.) BREL York 1987–88. 12/54. 30.0 t.
77431–77457. DTCO. Dia. EE314. Lot No. 31038 (odd nos.) BREL York 1988. 12/54. 30.0 t.
62911–62936. MSO. Dia. EC209. Lot No. 31023 BREL York 1987–88. –/82. 51.0 t.
62961–62974. MSO. Dia. EC209. Lot No. 31039 BREL York 1988. –/82. 51.0 t.
71792–71817. TSOL. Dia. EH234. Lot No. 31024 BREL York 1987–88. –/77 2T. 31.0 t.
71866–71879. TSOL. Dia. EH234. Lot No. 31040 BREL York 1988. –/77 2T. 31.0 t.
77330–77380. DTSO. Dia. EE234. Lot No. 31025 (even nos.) BREL York 1987-88. –/78. 30.0 t.
77430–77456. DTSO. Dia. EE234. Lot No. 31041 (even nos.) BREL York 1988. –/78. 30.0 t.

319 421	**TR**	P	*TR*	SU	77331	62911	71792	77330
319 422	**TR**	P	*TR*	SU	77333	62912	71793	77332
319 423	**TR**	P	*TR*	SU	77335	62913	71794	77334
319 424	**TR**	P	*TR*	SU	77337	62914	71795	77336
319 425	**TR**	P	*TR*	SU	77339	62915	71796	77338
319 426	**TR**	P	*TR*	SU	77341	62916	71797	77340
319 427	**TR**	P	*TR*	SU	77343	62917	71798	77342
319 428	**TR**	P	*TR*	SU	77345	62918	71799	77344
319 429	**TR**	P	*TR*	SU	77347	62919	71800	77346

319 430	**TR**	P	*TR*	SU	77349	62920	71801	77348
319 431	**TR**	P	*TR*	SU	77351	62921	71802	77350
319 432	**TR**	P	*TR*	SU	77353	62922	71803	77352
319 433	**TR**	P	*TR*	SU	77355	62923	71804	77354
319 434	**TR**	P	*TR*	SU	77357	62924	71805	77356
319 435	**TR**	P	*TR*	SU	77359	62925	71806	77358
319 436	**TR**	P	*TR*	SU	77361	62926	71807	77360
319 437	**TR**	P	*TR*	SU	77363	62927	71808	77362
319 438	**TR**	P	*TR*	SU	77365	62928	71809	77364
319 439	**TR**	P	*TR*	SU	77367	62929	71810	77366
319 440	**TR**	P	*TR*	SU	77369	62930	71811	77368
319 441	**TR**	P	*TR*	SU	77371	62931	71812	77370
319 442	**TR**	P	*TR*	SU	77373	62932	71813	77372
319 443	**TR**	P	*TR*	SU	77375	62933	71814	77374
319 444	**TR**	P	*TR*	SU	77377	62934	71815	77376
319 445	**TR**	P	*TR*	SU	77379	62935	71816	77378
319 446	**TR**	P	*TR*	SU	77381	62936	71817	77380
319 447	**TR**	P	*TR*	SU	77431	62961	71866	77430
319 448	**TR**	P	*TR*	SU	77433	62962	71867	77432
319 449	**TR**	P	*TR*	SU	77435	62963	71868	77434
319 450	**TR**	P	*TR*	SU	77437	62964	71869	77436
319 451	**TR**	P	*TR*	SU	77439	62965	71870	77438
319 452	**TR**	P	*TR*	SU	77441	62966	71871	77440
319 453	**TR**	P	*TR*	SU	77443	62967	71872	77442
319 454	**TR**	P	*TR*	SU	77445	62968	71873	77444
319 455	**TR**	P	*TR*	SU	77447	62969	71874	77446
319 456	**TR**	P	*TR*	SU	77449	62970	71875	77448
319 457	**TR**	P	*TR*	SU	77451	62971	71876	77450
319 458	**TR**	P	*TR*	SU	77453	62972	71877	77452
319 459	**TR**	P	*TR*	SU	77455	62973	71878	77454
319 460	**TR**	P	*TR*	SU	77457	62974	71879	77456

CLASS 320   3-Car Unit

DTSO–MSO–DTSO. Gangwayed within unit. Disc brakes.
Traction Motors: Four Brush TM2141B of 268 kW each.
Dimensions: 19.95 x 2.82 x 3.78 m (outer cars), 19.92 x 2.82 x 3.78 m (inner car).
Maximum Speed: 75 mph.   **Doors:** Power operated sliding.
Couplers: Tightlock.   **Bogies:** P7-4 (MSO), T3-7 (others).
Multiple Working: Classes 313–323.

DTSO (A). Dia. EE238. Lot No. 31060 BREL York 1990. –/77. 30.7 t.
MSO. Dia. EC212. Lot No. 31062 BREL York 1990. –/77. 52.1 t.
DTSO (B). Dia. EE239. Lot No. 31061 BREL York 1990. –/76 31.7 t.

320 301	**S**	F	*SR*	GW	77899	63021	77921
320 302	**S**	F	*SR*	GW	77900	63022	77922
320 303	**S**	F	*SR*	GW	77901	63023	77923
320 304	**S**	F	*SR*	GW	77902	63024	77924
320 305	**S**	F	*SR*	GW	77903	63025	77925
320 306	**CC**	F	*SR*	GW	77904	63026	77926
320 307	**CC**	F	*SR*	GW	77905	63027	77927

320 308	**CC**	F	*SR*	GW	77906	63028	77928
320 309	**CC**	F	*SR*	GW	77907	63029	77929
320 310	**CC**	F	*SR*	GW	77908	63030	77930
320 311	**CC**	F	*SR*	GW	77909	63031	77931
320 312	**CC**	F	*SR*	GW	77910	63032	77932
320 313	**CC**	F	*SR*	GW	77911	63033	77933
320 314	**CC**	F	*SR*	GW	77912	63034	77934
320 315	**CC**	F	*SR*	GW	77913	63035	77935
320 316	**CC**	F	*SR*	GW	77914	63036	77936
320 317	**CC**	F	*SR*	GW	77915	63037	77937
320 318	**CC**	F	*SR*	GW	77916	63038	77938
320 319	**CC**	F	*SR*	GW	77917	63039	77939
320 320	**CC**	F	*SR*	GW	77918	63040	77940
320 321	**CC**	F	*SR*	GW	77919	63041	77941
320 322	**CC**	F	*SR*	GW	77920	63042	77942

Names (carried on MSO):

320 305	GLASGOW SCHOOL OF ART 1844–150–1994
320 306	MODEL RAIL SCOTLAND
320 309	Radio Clyde 25th Anniversary
320 321	The Rt. Hon. John Smith, QC, MP
320 322	FESTIVE GLASGOW ORCHID

CLASS 321 4-Car Unit

DTCO (DTSO on Class 321/9)–MSO–TSOL–DTSO. Gangwayed within unit. Disc brakes.
Traction Motors: Four Brush TM2141B of 268 kW each.
Dimensions: 19.95 x 2.82 x 3.78 m (outer cars), 19.92 x 2.82 m (inner cars).
Maximum Speed: 100 mph. **Doors:** Power operated sliding.
Couplers: Tightlock. **Bogies:** P7-4 (MSO), T3-7 (others).
Multiple Working: Classes 313–323.

Class 321/3. Small first class area.

DTCO. Dia. EE308. Lot No. 31053 BREL York 1988–90. 12/56. 29.3 t.
MSO. Dia. EC210. Lot No. 31054 BREL York 1988–90. –/79. 51.5 t.
TSOL. Dia. EH235. Lot No. 31055 BREL York 1988–90. –/74 2T. 28 t.
DTSO. Dia. EE236. Lot No. 31056 BREL York 1988–90. –/78. 29.1 t.

321 301	**GE**	F	*GE*	IL	78049	62975	71880	77853
321 302	**GE**	F	*GE*	IL	78050	62976	71881	77854
321 303	**GE**	F	*GE*	IL	78051	62977	71882	77855
321 304	**GE**	F	*GE*	IL	78052	62978	71883	77856
321 305	**GE**	F	*GE*	IL	78053	62979	71884	77857
321 306	**GE**	F	*GE*	IL	78054	62980	71885	77858
321 307	**GE**	F	*GE*	IL	78055	62981	71886	77859
321 308	**GE**	F	*GE*	IL	78056	62982	71887	77860
321 309	**GE**	F	*GE*	IL	78057	62983	71888	77861
321 310	**GE**	F	*GE*	IL	78058	62984	71889	77862
321 311	**GE**	F	*GE*	IL	78059	62985	71890	77863
321 312	**GE**	F	*GE*	IL	78060	62986	71891	77864
321 313	**GE**	F	*GE*	IL	78061	62987	71892	77865

321 314	GE	F	GE	IL	78062	62988	71893	77866
321 315	GE	F	GE	IL	78063	62989	71894	77867
321 316	GE	F	GE	IL	78064	62990	71895	77868
321 317	GE	F	GE	IL	78065	62991	71896	77869
321 318	GE	F	GE	IL	78066	62992	71897	77870
321 319	GE	F	GE	IL	78067	62993	71898	77871
321 320	GE	F	GE	IL	78068	62994	71899	77872
321 321	GE	F	GE	IL	78069	62995	71900	77873
321 322	GE	F	GE	IL	78070	62996	71901	77874
321 323	GE	F	GE	IL	78071	62997	71902	77875
321 324	GE	F	GE	IL	78072	62998	71903	77876
321 325	GE	F	GE	IL	78073	62999	71904	77877
321 326	GE	F	GE	IL	78074	63000	71905	77878
321 327	GE	F	GE	IL	78075	63001	71906	77879
321 328	GE	F	GE	IL	78076	63002	71907	77880
321 329	GE	F	GE	IL	78077	63003	71908	77881
321 330	GE	F	GE	IL	78078	63004	71909	77882
321 331	GE	F	GE	IL	78079	63005	71910	77883
321 332	GE	F	GE	IL	78080	63006	71911	77884
321 333	GE	F	GE	IL	78081	63007	71912	77885
321 334	GE	F	GE	IL	78082	63008	71913	77886
321 335	GE	F	GE	IL	78083	63009	71914	77887
321 336	GE	F	GE	IL	78084	63010	71915	77888
321 337	GE	F	GE	IL	78085	63011	71916	77889
321 338	GE	F	GE	IL	78086	63012	71917	77890
321 339	GE	F	GE	IL	78087	63013	71918	77891
321 340	GE	F	GE	IL	78088	63014	71919	77892
321 341	GE	F	GE	IL	78089	63015	71920	77893
321 342	GE	F	GE	IL	78090	63016	71921	77894
321 343	GE	F	GE	IL	78091	63017	71922	77895
321 344	GE	F	GE	IL	78092	63018	71923	77896
321 345	GE	F	GE	IL	78093	63019	71924	77897
321 346	GE	F	GE	IL	78094	63020	71925	77898
321 347	GE	F	GE	IL	78131	63105	71991	78280
321 348	GE	F	GE	IL	78132	63106	71992	78281
321 349	GE	F	GE	IL	78133	63107	71993	78282
321 350	GE	F	GE	IL	78134	63108	71994	78283
321 351	GE	F	GE	IL	78135	63109	71995	78284
321 352	GE	F	GE	IL	78136	63110	71996	78285
321 353	GE	F	GE	IL	78137	63111	71997	78286
321 354	GE	F	GE	IL	78138	63112	71998	78287
321 355	GE	F	GE	IL	78139	63113	71999	78288
321 356	GE	F	GE	IL	78140	63114	72000	78289
321 357	GE	F	GE	IL	78141	63115	72001	78290
321 358	GE	F	GE	IL	78142	63116	72002	78291
321 359	GE	F	GE	IL	78143	63117	72003	78292
321 360	GE	F	GE	IL	78144	63118	72004	78293
321 361	GE	F	GE	IL	78145	63119	72005	78294
321 362	GE	F	GE	IL	78146	63120	72006	78295
321 363	GE	F	GE	IL	78147	63121	72007	78296
321 364	GE	F	GE	IL	78148	63122	72008	78297

| 321 365 | **GE** | F | *GE* | IL | 78149 | 63123 | 72009 | 78298 |
| 321 366 | **GE** | F | *GE* | IL | 78150 | 63124 | 72010 | 78299 |

Names (carried on TSOL):

| 321 312 | Southend-on-Sea | 321 336 | GEOFFREY FREEMAN ALLEN |
| 321 334 | Amsterdam | 321 351 | GURKHA |

Class 321/4. Larger first class area.
Advertising Livery:
• 321 428 advertises Silverlink Train Services.

DTCO. Dia. EE309. Lot No. 31067 BREL York 1989–90. 28/40. 29.3 t. First Great Eastern units have 12 first class seats declassified.
MSO. Dia. EC210. Lot No. 31068 BREL York 1989–90. –/79. 51.5 t.
TSOL. Dia. EH235. Lot No. 31069 BREL York 1989–90. –/74 2T. 28.0 t.
DTSO. Dia. EE236. Lot No. 31070 BREL York 1989–90. –/78. 29.1 t.

321 401	**N**	F	*SL*	BY	78095	63063	71949	77943
321 402	**N**	F	*SL*	BY	78096	63064	71950	77944
321 403	**N**	F	*SL*	BY	78097	63065	71951	77945
321 404	**N**	F	*SL*	BY	78098	63066	71952	77946
321 405	**N**	F	*SL*	BY	78099	63067	71953	77947
321 406	**N**	F	*SL*	BY	78100	63068	71954	77948
321 407	**N**	F	*SL*	BY	78101	63069	71955	77949
321 408	**N**	F	*SL*	BY	78102	63070	71956	77950
321 409	**N**	F	*SL*	BY	78103	63071	71957	77951
321 410	**N**	F	*SL*	BY	78104	63072	71958	77952
321 411	**N**	F	*SL*	BY	78105	63073	71959	77953
321 412	**N**	F	*SL*	BY	78106	63074	71960	77954
321 413	**N**	F	*SL*	BY	78107	63075	71961	77955
321 414	**N**	F	*SL*	BY	78108	63076	71962	77956
321 415	**N**	F	*SL*	BY	78109	63077	71963	77957
321 416	**N**	F	*SL*	BY	78110	63078	71964	77958
321 417	**N**	F	*SL*	BY	78111	63079	71965	77959
321 418	**N**	F	*SL*	BY	78112	63080	71968	77962
321 419	**N**	F	*SL*	BY	78113	63081	71967	77961
321 420	**SL**	F	*SL*	BY	78114	63082	71966	77960
321 421	**N**	F	*SL*	BY	78115	63083	71969	77963
321 422	**SL**	F	*SL*	BY	78116	63084	71970	77964
321 423	**N**	F	*SL*	BY	78117	63085	71971	77965
321 424	**N**	F	*SL*	BY	78118	63086	71972	77966
321 425	**N**	F	*SL*	BY	78119	63087	71973	77967
321 426	**N**	F	*SL*	BY	78120	63088	71974	77968
321 427	**N**	F	*SL*	BY	78121	63089	71975	77969
321 428	**AL**	F	*SL*	BY	78122	63090	71976	77970
321 429	**SL**	F	*SL*	BY	78123	63091	71977	77971
321 430	**SL**	F	*SL*	BY	78124	63092	71978	77972
321 431	**SL**	F	*SL*	BY	78151	63125	72011	78300
321 432	**SL**	F	*SL*	BY	78152	63126	72012	78301
321 433	**SL**	F	*SL*	BY	78153	63127	72013	78302
321 434	**SL**	F	*SL*	BY	78154	63128	72014	78303
321 435	**SL**	F	*SL*	BY	78155	63129	72015	78304
321 436	**SL**	F	*SL*	BY	78156	63130	72016	78305

321 437	**SL**	F	*SL*	BY	78157	63131	72017	78306
321 438	**GE**	F	*GE*	IL	78158	63132	72018	78307
321 439	**GE**	F	*GE*	IL	78159	63133	72019	78308
321 440	**GE**	F	*GE*	IL	78160	63134	72020	78309
321 441	**GE**	F	*GE*	IL	78161	63135	72021	78310
321 442	**GE**	F	*GE*	IL	78162	63136	72022	78311
321 443	**GE**	F	*GE*	IL	78125	63099	71985	78274
321 444	**GE**	F	*GE*	IL	78126	63100	71986	78275
321 445	**GE**	F	*GE*	IL	78127	63101	71987	78276
321 446	**GE**	F	*GE*	IL	78128	63102	71988	78277
321 447	**GE**	F	*GE*	IL	78129	63103	71989	78278
321 448	**N**	F	*GE*	IL	78130	63104	71990	78279

Names (carried on TSOL):
321 407   HERTFORDSHIRE WRVS | 321 439 Chelmsford Cathedral Festival

Class 321/9. Leased by West Yorkshire PTE from International Bank of Scotland, but managed by Porterbrook Leasing Company. DTSO(A)–MSO–TSOL–DTSO(B).

DTSO (A). Dia. EE277. Lot No. 31108 BREL York 1991. –/78. 29.3 t.
MSO. Dia. EC216. Lot No. 31109 BREL York 1991. –/79. 51.5 t.
TSOL. Dia. EH240. Lot No. 31110 BREL York 1991. –/74 2T. 28.0 t.
DTSO (B). Dia. EE277. Lot No. 31111 BREL York 1991. –/78. 29.1 t.

321 901	**WY**	P	*NS*	NL	77990	63153	72128	77993
321 902	**WY**	P	*NS*	NL	77991	63154	72129	77994
321 903	**WY**	P	*NS*	NL	77992	63155	72130	77995

CLASS 322   4-Car Unit

DTCO–MSO–TSOL–DTSO. Gangwayed within unit. Disc brakes.
Traction Motors: Four Brush TM2141C of 268 kW each.
Dimensions: 19.95 x 2.82 x 3.78 m (outer cars), 19.92 x 2.82 x 3.78 m (inner cars).
Maximum Speed: 100 mph.   **Doors:** Power operated sliding.
Couplers: Tightlock.   **Bogies:** P7-4 (MSO), T3-7 (others).
Multiple Working: Classes 313–323.
Note: Two Class 322 units are hired to First North Western on a day-to-day basis for use on Manchester Airport–London Euston workings. 323 484/485, are normally the units hired, but others may be substituted as necessary.
Non-Standard Livery:
•   'Stansted Skytrain' livery (grey with a yellow stripe).

DTCO. Dia. EE313. Lot No. 31094 BREL York 1990. 35/22. 30.4 t.
MSO. Dia. EC215. Lot No. 31092 BREL York 1990. –/70. 52.3 t.
TSOL. Dia. EH239. Lot No. 31093 BREL York 1990. –/60 2T. 29.5 t.
DTSO. Dia. EE242. Lot No. 31091 BREL York 1990. –/65. 29.8 t.

322 481	**0**	F	*WN*	HE	78163	72023	63137	77985
322 482	**0**	F	*WN*	HE	78164	72024	63138	77986
322 483	**0**	F	*WN*	HE	78165	72025	63139	77987
322 484	**NW**	F	*WN*	HE	78166	72026	63140	77988
322 485	**NW**	F	*WN*	HE	78167	72027	63141	77989

CLASS 323   3-Car Unit

DMSO(A)–PTSOL–DMSO(B). Gangwayed within unit. Disc brakes.
Traction Motors: Four Holec DMKT 52/24 of 146 kW per power car.
Dimensions: 23.37 x 2.80 x   . m (DMSO), 23.44 x 2.80 x   . m (TSOL).
Maximum Speed: 90 mph.   **Doors:** Power operated sliding plug.
Couplers: Tightlock.
Bogies: RFS BP62 (DMSO), BT52 (TSOL).
Multiple Working: Classes 313–323.
Notes: Two numbers are duplicated. 65003^{II} is actually 65005. 65021^{II} is actually 65019.

DMSO(A). Dia. EA272. Lot No. 31112 Hunslet TPL 1992–93. –/98 (* –/82). 41.0 t.
PTSOL. Dia. EH296. Lot No. 31113 Hunslet TPL 1992–93. –/88 (* –/80) 1T. 39.4 t.
DMSO(B). Dia. EA272. Lot No. 31114 Hunslet TPL 1992–93. –/98 (* –/82). 41.0 t.

323 201		CO	P	CT	LC	64001	72201	65001
323 202		CO	P	CT	LC	64002	72202	65002
323 203		CO	P	CT	LC	64003	72203	65003^{II}
323 204		CO	P	CT	LC	64004	72204	65004
323 205		CO	P	CT	LC	64005	72205	65003
323 206		CO	P	CT	LC	64006	72206	65006
323 207		CO	P	CT	LC	64007	72207	65007
323 208		CO	P	CT	LC	64008	72208	65008
323 209		CO	P	CT	LC	64009	72209	65009
323 210		CO	P	CT	LC	64010	72210	65010
323 211		CO	P	CT	LC	64011	72211	65011
323 212		CO	P	CT	LC	64012	72212	65012
323 213		CO	P	CT	LC	64013	72213	65013
323 214		CO	P	CT	LC	64014	72214	65014
323 215		CO	P	CT	LC	64015	72215	65015
323 216		CO	P	CT	LC	64016	72216	65016
323 217		CO	P	CT	LC	64017	72217	65017
323 218		CO	P	CT	LC	64018	72218	65018
323 219		CO	P	CT	LC	64019	72219	65021
323 220		CO	P	CT	LC	64020	72220	65020
323 221		CO	P	CT	LC	64021	72221	65021^{II}
323 222		CO	P	CT	LC	64022	72222	65022
323 223	*	GM	P	NW	LG	64023	72223	65023
323 224	*	NW	P	NW	LG	64024	72224	65024
323 225	*	GM	P	NW	LG	64025	72225	65025
323 226		GM	P	NW	LG	64026	72226	65026
323 227		GM	P	NW	LG	64027	72227	65027
323 228		GM	P	NW	LG	64028	72228	65028
323 229		GM	P	NW	LG	64029	72229	65029
323 230		GM	P	NW	LG	64030	72230	65030
323 231		GM	P	NW	LG	64031	72231	65031
323 232		GM	P	NW	LG	64032	72232	65032
323 233		NW	P	NW	LG	64033	72233	65033
323 234		GM	P	NW	LG	64034	72234	65034
323 235		GM	P	NW	LG	64035	72235	65035

323 236	**GM**	P	*NW*	LG	64036	72236	65036
323 237	**GM**	P	*NW*	LG	64037	72237	65037
323 238	**GM**	P	*NW*	LG	64038	72238	65038
323 239	**GM**	P	*NW*	LG	64039	72239	65039
323 240	**CO**	P	*CT*	LC	64040	72340	65040
323 241	**CO**	P	*CT*	LC	64041	72341	65041
323 242	**CO**	P	*CT*	LC	64042	72342	65042
323 243	**CO**	P	*CT*	LC	64043	72343	65043

CLASS 325   4-Car Royal Mail Unit

DTPMV(A)–MPMV–TPMV–DTPMV(B). Non gangwayed. Disc brakes.
Supply System: 25 kV 50 Hz a.c. overhead or 750 V d.c. third rail.
Traction Motors: Four GEC G315BZ of 247.5 kW each.
Dimensions: 20.35 x 2.82 x . m.
Maximum Speed: 100 mph.   **Doors:** Roller shutter.
Couplers: Buckeye.   **Bogies:** P7-4 (MSO), T3-7 (others).
Multiple Working: Within class only.

68300–68330 (Even Nos.). DTPMV(A). Dia. EE503. Lot No. 31144 ABB Derby 1995. Load capacity 12.0 t. 29.2 t.
MPMV. Dia. EC501. Lot No. 31145 ABB Derby 1995. Load 12.0 tonnes. 49.5 t.
TPMV. Dia. EH501. Lot No. 31146 ABB Derby 1995. Load 12.0 tonnes. 30.7 t.
68301–68331 (Odd Nos.). DTPMV(B). Dia. EE503. Lot No. 31144 ABB Derby 1995. Load 12.0 tonnes. 29.1 t.

325 001	**RM**	RM	*E*	CE	68300	68340	68360	68301
325 002	**RM**	RM	*E*	CE	68302	68341	68361	68303
325 003	**RM**	RM	*E*	CE	68304	68342	68362	68305
325 004	**RM**	RM	*E*	CE	68306	68343	68363	68307
325 005	**RM**	RM	*E*	CE	68308	68344	68364	68309
325 006	**RM**	RM	*E*	CE	68310	68345	68365	68311
325 007	**RM**	RM	*E*	CE	68312	68346	68366	68313
325 008	**RM**	RM	*E*	CE	68314	68347	68367	68315
325 009	**RM**	RM	*E*	CE	68316	68348	68368	68317
325 010	**RM**	RM	*E*	CE	68318	68349	68369	68319
325 011	**RM**	RM	*E*	CE	68320	68350	68370	68321
325 012	**RM**	RM	*E*	CE	68322	68351	68371	68323
325 013	**RM**	RM	*E*	CE	68324	68352	68372	68325
325 014	**RM**	RM	*E*	CE	68326	68353	68373	68327
325 015	**RM**	RM	*E*	CE	68328	68354	68374	68329
325 016	**RM**	RM	*E*	CE	68330	68355	68375	68331

Names (carried on one DTPMV per side):

325 002	Royal Mail North Wales and North West
325 006	John Grierson
325 008	Peter Howarth C.B.E.

CLASS 332   4-Car Express Unit

DMFO–TSO–PTSOL–DMSO or DMSO–TSO–PTSOL–DMLFO. Gangwayed within unit. Disc brakes. Air conditioned.

Traction Motors: Four Siemens of 175 kW each per power car.
Dimensions: 23.74 x 2.75 x . m.
Maximum Speed: 160 km/h.   **Doors:** Power operated sliding plug.
Couplers: Scharfenberg.   **Bogies:** CAF.
Multiple Working: Within Class only.

Sets 001–007. DMFO–TSO–PTSOL–DMSO.

DMFO (ex-DMSO). CAF 1997–98. 26/–. . t.
TSO. Dia. EH245. CAF 1997–98. –/56. 45.2 t.
PTSOL. Dia. EH243. CAF 1997–98. –/44. 45.6 t.
DMSO(A). Dia. EA243. CAF 1997–98. –/48. 48.8 t.

332 001	**HX**	HX	*HX*	OH	78400	72412	63400	78401
332 002	**HX**	HX	*HX*	OH	78402	72409	63401	78403
332 003	**HX**	HX	*HX*	OH	78404	72407	63402	78405
332 004	**HX**	HX	*HX*	OH	78406	72405	63403	78407
332 005	**HX**	HX	*HX*	OH	78408	72411	63404	78409
332 006	**HX**	HX	*HX*	OH	78410	72410	63405	78411
332 007	**HX**	HX	*HX*	OH	78412	72401	63406	78413

Sets 008–014. DMSO–TSO–PTSOL–DMLFO.

DMSO(B). Dia. EA244. CAF 1997–98. –/48. 48.8 t.
TSO. Dia. EH245. CAF 1997–98. –/56. 45.2 t.
PTSOL. Dia. EH243. CAF 1997–98. –/44. 45.6 t.
DMLFO (ex DMSO). CAF 1997–98. 14/–. . t.

332 008	**HX**	HX	*HX*	OH	78414	72413	63407	78415
332 009	**HX**	HX	*HX*	OH	78416	72400	63408	78417
332 010	**HX**	HX	*HX*	OH	78418	72402	63409	78419
332 011	**HX**	HX	*HX*	OH	78420	72403	63410	78421
332 012	**HX**	HX	*HX*	OH	78422	72404	63411	78423
332 013	**HX**	HX	*HX*	OH	78424	72408	63412	78425
332 014	**HX**	HX	*HX*	OH	78426	72406	63413	78427

CLASS 334   'Juniper'   3-Car Unit

DMSO(A)–PTSO–DMSO(B). Gangwayed within unit. Disc brakes. Air conditioned.
Traction Motors: Two Alstom of 270 kW each per power car.
Dimensions: **Doors:** Power operated sliding plug.
Maximum Speed: 100 mph.   **Bogies:** ACR.
Couplers: Scharfenberg.   **Multiple Working:** Within Class only.
Notes: Set numbers may be subject to alteration.

DMSO (A). Dia. EA2??. Alstom Birmingham 1999–2000.
PTSO. Dia.EH2??. Alstom Birmingham 1999–2000.
DMSO (B). Dia. EA2??. Alstom Birmingham 1999–2000.

334 001	**SN**	F	*SR*	64101	74301	65101
334 002	**SN**	F	*SR*	64102	74302	65102
334 003	**SN**	F	*SR*	64103	74303	65103
334 004	**SN**	F	*SR*	64104	74304	65104
334 005	**SN**	F	*SR*	64105	74305	65105
334 006	**SN**	F	*SR*	64106	74306	65106

334 007	**SN**	F	*SR*		64107	74307	65107
334 008	**SN**	F	*SR*		64108	74308	65108
334 009	**SN**	F	*SR*		64109	74309	65109
334 010	**SN**	F	*SR*		64110	74310	65110
334 011	**SN**	F	*SR*		64111	74311	65111
334 012	**SN**	F	*SR*		64112	74312	65112
334 013	**SN**	F	*SR*		64113	74313	65113
334 014	**SN**	F	*SR*		64114	74314	65114
334 015	**SN**	F	*SR*		64115	74315	65115
334 016	**SN**	F	*SR*		64116	74316	65116
334 017	**SN**	F	*SR*		64117	74317	65117
334 018	**SN**	F	*SR*		64118	74318	65118
334 019	**SN**	F	*SR*		64119	74319	65119
334 020	**SN**	F	*SR*		64120	74320	65120
334 021	**SN**	F	*SR*		64121	74321	65121
334 022	**SN**	F	*SR*		64122	74322	65122
334 023	**SN**	F	*SR*		64123	74323	65123
334 024	**SN**	F	*SR*		64124	74324	65124
334 025	**SN**	F	*SR*		64125	74325	65125
334 026	**SN**	F	*SR*		64126	74326	65126
334 027	**SN**	F	*SR*		64127	74327	65127
334 028	**SN**	F	*SR*		64128	74328	65128
334 029	**SN**	F	*SR*		64129	74329	65129
334 030	**SN**	F	*SR*		64130	74330	65130
334 031	**SN**	F	*SR*		64131	74331	65131
334 032	**SN**	F	*SR*		64132	74332	65132
334 033	**SN**	F	*SR*		64133	74333	65133
334 034	**SN**	F	*SR*		64134	74334	65134
334 035	**SN**	F	*SR*		64135	74335	65135
334 036	**SN**	F	*SR*		64136	74336	65136
334 037	**SN**	F	*SR*		64137	74337	65137
334 038	**SN**	F	*SR*		64138	74338	65138
334 039	**SN**	F	*SR*		64139	74339	65139
334 040	**SN**	F	*SR*		64140	74340	65140

CLASS 357   'Electrostar'   4-Car Unit

DMSO(A)–PTSOL–MSO–DMSO(B). Gangwayed within unit. Disc and regenerative brakes. Air conditioning.
Supply System: 25 kV a.c. 50Hz overhead (with provision for 750 V d.c. third rail supply).
Traction Motors: Two Adtranz of 250 kW each per motor car.
Dimensions: 20.40 m x 2.80 x 3.78 m (outer cars), 19.99 x 2.80 x 3.78 m (inner cars).
Maximum Speed: 100 mph.   **Doors:** Power operated sliding plug.
Bogies: Adtranz P3-25 (motor), T3-25 (PTSOL).
Multiple Working: Within class.   **Couplers:** Tightlock.

DMSO(A). Dia. EA273. Adtranz Derby 1998–99. –/71. . t.
PTSOL. Dia. EH215. Adtranz Derby 1998–99. –/62 1TD 2W . t.
MSO. Dia. EC225. Adtranz Derby 1998–99. –/78 . . t.
DMSO(B). Dia. EA214. Adtranz Derby 1998–99. –/71. . t.

357 001	**LS**	P	*LS*	67651	74051	74151	67751
357 002	**LS**	P	*LS*	67652	74052	74152	67752
357 003	**LS**	P	*LS*	67653	74053	74153	67753
357 004	**LS**	P	*LS*	67654	74054	74154	67754
357 005	**LS**	P	*LS*	67655	74055	74155	67755
357 006	**LS**	P	*LS*	67656	74056	74156	67756
357 007	**LS**	P	*LS*	67657	74057	74157	67757
357 008	**LS**	P	*LS*	67658	74058	74158	67758
357 009	**LS**	P	*LS*	67659	74059	74159	67759
357 010	**LS**	P	*LS*	67660	74060	74160	67760
357 011	**LS**	P	*LS*	67661	74061	74161	67761
357 012	**LS**	P	*LS*	67662	74062	74162	67762
357 013	**LS**	P	*LS*	67663	74063	74163	67763
357 014	**LS**	P	*LS*	67664	74064	74164	67764
357 015	**LS**	P	*LS*	67665	74065	74165	67765
357 016	**LS**	P	*LS*	67666	74066	74166	67766
357 017	**LS**	P	*LS*	67667	74067	74167	67767
357 018	**LS**	P	*LS*	67668	74068	74168	67768
357 019	**LS**	P	*LS*	67669	74069	74169	67769
357 020	**LS**	P	*LS*	67670	74070	74170	67770
357 021	**LS**	P	*LS*	67671	74071	74171	67771
357 022	**LS**	P	*LS*	67672	74072	74172	67772
357 023	**LS**	P	*LS*	67673	74073	74173	67773
357 024	**LS**	P	*LS*	67674	74074	74174	67774
357 025	**LS**	P	*LS*	67675	74075	74175	67775
357 026	**LS**	P	*LS*	67676	74076	74176	67776
357 027	**LS**	P	*LS*	67677	74077	74177	67777
357 028	**LS**	P	*LS*	67678	74078	74178	67778
357 029	**LS**	P	*LS*	67679	74079	74179	67779
357 030	**LS**	P	*LS*	67680	74080	74180	67780
357 031	**LS**	P	*LS*	67681	74081	74181	67781
357 032	**LS**	P	*LS*	67682	74082	74182	67782
357 033	**LS**	P	*LS*	67683	74083	74183	67783
357 034	**LS**	P	*LS*	67684	74084	74184	67784
357 035	**LS**	P	*LS*	67685	74085	74185	67785
357 036	**LS**	P	*LS*	67686	74086	74186	67786
357 037	**LS**	P	*LS*	67687	74087	74187	67787
357 038	**LS**	P	*LS*	67688	74088	74188	67788
357 039	**LS**	P	*LS*	67689	74089	74189	67789
357 040	**LS**	P	*LS*	67690	74090	74190	67790
357 041	**LS**	P	*LS*	67691	74091	74191	67791
357 042	**LS**	P	*LS*	67692	74092	74192	67792
357 043	**LS**	P	*LS*	67693	74093	74193	67793
357 044	**LS**	P	*LS*	67694	74094	74194	67794

CLASS 365   'Networker'   4-Car Express Unit

DMCO–TSOL–PTSOL–DMCO. Gangwayed within unit. Disc, rheostatic and regenerative braking.

Supply System: 25 kV a.c. 50 Hz overhead (with provision for 750 V d.c. third rail supply) or * 750 V d.c. third rail (with provision for 25 kV a.c. 50 Hz overhead supply).

Traction Motors: Four GEC Alsthom G354CX of 157 kW each per power car.

Dimensions: 20.89 x 2.81 x . m (outer cars), 20.06 x 2.81 x . m (inner cars).

Maximum Speed: 100 mph.   **Doors:** Power operated sliding plug.

Couplers: Tightlock.   **Bogies:** P7 (DMCO), T3 (trailers).

Multiple Working: Classes 365, 465 and 466.

DMCO. Dia. EA301. Lot No. 31133 ABB York 1994–95. 12/56. 41.7 t.
TSOL. Dia. EH298. Lot No. 31134 ABB York 1994–95. –/65 1TD. 32.9 t.
PTSOL. Dia. EH298. Lot No. 31135 ABB York 1994–95. –/68 1T. 34.6 t.
DMCO. Dia. EA301. Lot No. 31136 ABB York 1994–95. 12/56. 41.7 t.

365 501 *	**CS**	F	*SE*	SG	65894	72241	72240	65935
365 502 *	**CS**	F	*SE*	SG	65895	72243	72242	65936
365 503 *	**CS**	F	*SE*	SG	65896	72245	72244	65937
365 504 *	**CS**	F	*SE*	SG	65897	72247	72246	65938
365 505 *	**CS**	F	*SE*	SG	65898	72249	72248	65939
365 506 *	**CS**	F	*SE*	SG	65899	72251	72250	65940
365 507 *	**CS**	F	*SE*	SG	65900	72253	72252	65941
365 508 *	**CS**	F	*SE*	SG	65901	72255	72254	65942
365 509 *	**CS**	F	*SE*	SG	65902	72257	72256	65943
365 510 *	**CS**	F	*SE*	SG	65903	72259	72258	65944
365 511 *	**CS**	F	*SE*	SG	65904	72261	72260	65945
365 512 *	**CS**	F	*SE*	SG	65905	72263	72262	65946
365 513 *	**CS**	F	*SE*	SG	65906	72265	72264	65947
365 514 *	**CS**	F	*SE*	SG	65907	72267	72266	65948
365 515 *	**CS**	F	*SE*	SG	65908	72269	72268	65949
365 516 *	**CS**	F	*SE*	SG	65909	72271	72270	65950
365 517	**NT**	F	*WN*	HE	65910	72273	72272	65951
365 518	**NT**	F	*WN*	HE	65911	72275	72274	65952
365 519	**NT**	F	*WN*	HE	65912	72277	72276	65953
365 520	**NT**	F	*WN*	HE	65913	72279	72278	65954
365 521	**NT**	F	*WN*	HE	65914	72281	72280	65955
365 522	**NT**	F	*WN*	HE	65915	72283	72282	65956
365 523	**NT**	F	*WN*	HE	65916	72285	72284	65957
365 524	**NT**	F	*WN*	HE	65917	72287	72286	65958
365 525	**NT**	F	*WN*	HE	65918	72289	72288	65959
365 526	**NT**	F	*WN*	HE	65919	72291	72290	65960
365 527	**NT**	F	*WN*	HE	65920	72293	72292	65961
365 528	**NT**	F	*WN*	HE	65921	72295	72294	65962
365 529	**NT**	F	*WN*	HE	65922	72297	72296	65963
365 530	**NT**	F	*WN*	HE	65923	72299	72298	65964
365 531	**NT**	F	*WN*	HE	65924	72301	72300	65965
365 532	**NT**	F	*WN*	HE	65925	72303	72302	65966
365 533	**NT**	F	*WN*	HE	65926	72305	72304	65967

365 534	**NT**	F	*WN*	HE	65927	72307	72306	65968
365 535	**NT**	F	*WN*	HE	65928	72309	72308	65969
365 536	**NT**	F	*WN*	HE	65929	72311	72310	65970
365 537	**NT**	F	*WN*	HE	65930	72313	72312	65971
365 538	**NT**	F	*WN*	HE	65931	72315	72314	65972
365 539	**NT**	F	*WN*	HE	65932	72317	72316	65973
365 540	**NT**	F	*WN*	HE	65933	72319	72318	65974
365 541	**NT**	F	*WN*	HE	65934	72321	72320	65975

CLASS 375   'Electrostar'   4-Car Unit

DMSO(A)–PTSOL–MSOL–DMSO(B). Gangwayed throughout. Disc and regenerative braking. Air conditioned.
System: 750 V d.c. third rail (with provision for 25 kV a.c. 50Hz overhead supply).
Traction Motors:
Dimensions:
Maximum Speed: 100 mph.   **Doors:** Power operated sliding plug.
Couplers: Tightlock.   **Bogies:**
Multiple Working: Within class.

DMSO(A). Dia. EA2??. Adtranz Derby 1998–2000. . . t.
PTSOL. Dia. EH2??. Adtranz Derby 1998–2000. . . t.
MSOL. Dia. EC2??. Adtranz Derby 1998–2000. . . t.
DMSO(B). Dia. EA2??. Adtranz Derby 1998–2000. . t.

375 601	**CX**	F	*SE*	67801	74201	74251	67851
375 602	**CX**	F	*SE*	67802	74202	74252	67852
375 603	**CX**	F	*SE*	67803	74203	74253	67853
375 604	**CX**	F	*SE*	67804	74204	74254	67854
375 605	**CX**	F	*SE*	67805	74205	74255	67855
375 606	**CX**	F	*SE*	67806	74206	74256	67856
375 607	**CX**	F	*SE*	67807	74207	74257	67857
375 608	**CX**	F	*SE*	67808	74208	74258	67858
375 609	**CX**	F	*SE*	67809	74209	74259	67859
375 610	**CX**	F	*SE*	67810	74210	74260	67860
375 611	**CX**	F	*SE*	67811	74211	74261	67861
375 612	**CX**	F	*SE*	67812	74212	74262	67862
375 613	**CX**	F	*SE*	67813	74213	74263	67863
375 614	**CX**	F	*SE*	67814	74214	74264	67864
375 615	**CX**	F	*SE*	67815	74215	74265	67865
375 616	**CX**	F	*SE*	67816	74216	74266	67866
375 617	**CX**	F	*SE*	67817	74217	74267	67867
375 618	**CX**	F	*SE*	67818	74218	74268	67868
375 619	**CX**	F	*SE*	67819	74219	74269	67869
375 620	**CX**	F	*SE*	67820	74220	74270	67870
375 621	**CX**	F	*SE*	67821	74221	74271	67871
375 622	**CX**	F	*SE*	67822	74222	74272	67872
375 623	**CX**	F	*SE*	67823	74223	74273	67873
375 624	**CX**	F	*SE*	67824	74224	74274	67874
375 625	**CX**	F	*SE*	67825	74225	74275	67875
375 626	**CX**	F	*SE*	67826	74226	74276	67876
375 627	**CX**	F	*SE*	67827	74227	74277	67877

375 628	**CX**	F	*SE*	67828	74228	74278	67878
375 629	**CX**	F	*SE*	67829	74229	74279	67879
375 630	**CX**	F	*SE*	67830	74230	74280	67880

HIGH SPEED IN EUROPE

by David Haydock

Today's Railways editior David Haydock examines the development of European high speed railways over the past 20 years, and looks at the new trains and new lines which will be making international travel easier in the next 20. First published in 1995, the book includes the following:

- **The Channel Tunnel Rail Link**
- **Eurostar: A Truly International Train**
- **Development of the TGV**
- **Les Lignes à Grand Vitesse**
- **TGV Duplex & Thalys Trainsets**
- **The German ICE & Swedish X 2000**
- **Pendolino: Tilting Through Italy**
- **High Speed Lines in Belgium, Netherlands, Germany, Sweden, Italy and Spain.**

High Speed in Europe also includes an index of European High Speed Line Statistics, and details of European High Speed Train Numbering. 80 pages including 38 in full colour. Thread Sewn. **£9.95.**

Available from the Platform 5 Mail Order Department.
To place an order, please follow the instructions on the last page of this book.

▲ 305 515 heads for Dinting with the 16.08 Hadfield–Manchester Piccadilly on 24th September 1997. This route is now operated by Class 323. **Nic Joynson**

▼ A solitary Class 306 unit is retained for special workings only. 306 017 is seen here at Harwich Town on 22nd June 1997 prior to working the 14.07 to Manningtree. **Michael J. Collins**

▲ 308 141 at Ben Rhydding whilst working the 10.21 Ilkley–Leeds on 23rd April 1997. This class are used on suburban services in Airedale and Wharfedale.
John G. Teasdale

▼ North West Regional Railways liveried 309 623 passes Madeley signal box working the 17.16 Manchester Piccadilly–Birmingham New Street on 19th May 1998.
Nic Joynson

▲ 310 058 near Chalkwell with the 14.05 Shoeburyness–London Fenchurch Street on 4th July 1998. **Chris Wilson**

▼ With Docklands Light Railway tracks in the foreground, 312 783 approaches Shadwell with the 10.40 London Fenchurch Street–Grays LTS Rail service on 30th May 1998. **Kevin Conkey**

▲ Sporting recently applied Silverlink 'Metro' livery, 313 112 runs into the newly lengthened down platform at Kensington Olympia with the 13.27 Willesden Junction–Clapham Junction on 25th August 1998. **David Brown**

▼ First Great Eastern liveried 315 817 enters Stratford station with the 13.40 London Liverpool Street–Shenfield on 19th September 1998. **Kevin Conkey**

▲ Thameslink Rail are applying their revised livery to units as they are over-hauled. 319 421 pauses at Cricklewood on 22nd April 1998 with the 12.56 Luton–Brighton service. **Kevin Conkey**

▼ Class 317 units have replaced Class 302 on LTS Rail services. 317 304 is seen here at Westcliff on 4th July 1998 working the 12.10 London Fenchurch Street–Shoeburyness. **Chris Wilson**

▲ 320 301 and 320 316 at Helensburgh Central forming the 15.27 departure for Airdrie on 5th October 1998. **Bob Sweet**

▼ 321 438 approaches Stratford with the 12.30 London Liverpool Street–Colchester Town service on 17th September 1998. **Brian Denton**

▲ The 13.04 Coventry–Wolverhampton arrives at Birmingham International on 19th January 1998 worked by 323 218.　　　　**Stephen Widdowson**

▼ Royal Mail's 325 008 leads a 12-car Class 325 formation forming the 16.00 Willesden Royal Mail Terminal–Shieldmuir RMT past Madeley signal box on 19th May 1998.　　　　**Nic Joynson**

▲ Heathrow Express unit 332 006 at London Paddington forming the 17.40 departure for Heathrow Airport on 6th August 1998. **Hugh Ballantyne**

▼ West Anglia Great Northern's 365 532 near Offord with the 09.16 Peterborough–London King's Cross on 29th October 1997. **Michael J. Collins**

▲ Island Line Class 483 unit 006 forms the rear section of a 4-car unit working the 16.35 Shanklin–Ryde Pier Head on 24th July 1998. Now withdrawn unit 001 is in the background. **Martyn Hilbert**

▼ Class 421/7 '3-Cop' unit 1404 departs from Lewes with the 09.04 West Worthing–Seaford on 8th August 1998. **David Brown**

▲ Class 411 '4-Cep' unit 1539 departs from St. Denys with the 17.33 Portsmouth Harbour–Southampton Central on 6th August 1998. **Nic Joynson**

▼ Class 421 '4-Cig' unit 1808 passes Northam Yard, on the eastern outskirts of Southampton with a local service on 16th September 1998. **Nic Joynson**

▲ Class 412 '4-Bep' 2304 wears the South West Trains livery carried by older units. It is seen here approaching Guildford with the 14.20 London Waterloo–Portsmouth Harbour on 20th July 1998. **David Brown**

▼ Class 442 '5-Wes' 2405 carries the more recent variety of South West Trains livery. It is seen here passing Wimbledon depot working the 12.30 London Waterloo–Weymouth Town on 19th August 1998. **David Brown**

▲ Connex liveried Class 423 '4-Vep' 3515 departs from Redhill with a London-bound service on 14th August 1998. **Hugh Ballantyne**

▼ Class 455/8 5827 near Redhill with the 17.34 London Victoria–Horsham on 28th June 1998. **Alex Dasi-Sutton**

▲ The prototype Class 424 ADtranz 'Classic' vehicle 76112 was displayed at London Victoria for a short period during March 1998. It is seen at the London terminus on 10th March 1998. **Bob Sweet**

▼ 465 002 heads an 8-car formation on a London Charing Cross–Sevenoaks working on 20th July 1998. **Rodney Lissenden**

▲ A side view showing the advertising livery applied to Class 488/2 unit 8208 as it departs from Gatwick Airport as part of the 10.50 to London Victoria on 20th July 1998. **David Brown**

▼ Class 489 luggage van 9104 forms the rear vehicle on the 17.45 London Victoria–Gatwick Airport on 10th July 1998. **Hugh Ballantyne**

4.2. 750 V d.c. THIRD RAIL EMUS

Supply System: 660–850 V d.c. third rail unless otherwise stated.

CLASS 460   'Juniper'   8-Gat Express Unit

DMLFO–TFOL–TCOL–MSO (A)–MSO(B)–TSOL–MSO(C)–DMSO. Gangwayed within unit. Disc and regenerative brakes.
Traction Motors: Two Alstom of 270 kW each per power car.
Dimensions: 21.01 x 2.80 x . m (driving cars), 19.94 x 2.80 x . m.
Maximum Speed: 100 mph.   **Doors:** Power operated sliding plug.
Couplers: Scharfenberg.   **Bogies:** ACR.
Multiple Working:

DMLFO. Dia. EA101. Alstom Birmingham. 1999. 10/–. 42.6 t.
TFOL. Dia. EH161. Alstom Birmingham 1999. –/– 1TD 1W. 33.5 t.
TCOL. Dia. EH364. Alstom Birmingham 1999. 9/42 1T. 34.9 t.
MSO(A). Dia. EC227. Alstom Birmingham 1999. –/60. 42.5 t.
MSO(B). Dia. EC228. Alstom Birmingham 1999. –/60. 42.5 t.
TSOL. Dia. EH251. Alstom Birmingham 1999. –/38 1TD 1W. 35.2 t.
MSO(C). Dia. EC229 . Alstom Birmingham 1999. –/60. 40.5 t.
DMSO. Dia. EA274. Alstom Birmingham 1999. –/56. 45.3 t.

01	**U**	P	*GX*	67901	74401	74411	74421	74431	74441	74451	67911
02	**GX**	P	*GX*	67902	74402	74412	74422	74432	74442	74452	67912
03	**GX**	P	*GX*	67903	74403	74413	74423	74433	74443	74453	67913
04	**GX**	P	*GX*	67904	74404	74414	74424	74434	74444	74454	67914
05	**GX**	P	*GX*	67905	74405	74415	74425	74435	74445	74455	67915
06	**GX**	P	*GX*	67906	74406	74416	74426	74436	74446	74456	67916
07	**GX**	P	*GX*	67907	74407	74417	74427	74437	74447	74457	67917
08	**GX**	P	*GX*	67908	74408	74418	74428	74438	74448	74458	67918

CLASS 483   2-Car Unit

DMSO(A)–DMSO(B). Non gangwayed. End doors. Converted from vehicles purchased from London Transport in 1988.
Traction Motors: Two Crompton Parkinson/GEC/BTH LT100 of 125 kW each per power car.
Dimensions: 15.94 x 2.65 x 2.88 m.   **Doors:** Power operated sliding.
Maximum Speed: 45 mph.   **Bogies:** London Transport design.
Couplings: Buckeye.   **Multiple Working:** Within class.

DMSO (A). Dia. EA265. Lot No. 31071. Met-Camm. 1938. Rebuilt BRML Eastleigh 1989–92. –/42. 27.5 t.
DMSO (B). Dia. EA266. Lot No. 31072. Met-Camm. 1938. Rebuilt BRML Eastleigh 1989–92. –/42. 27.5 t.

002	**N**	F	*IL*	RY	122	225
003	**N**	F		RY(S)	123	221
004	**N**	F	*IL*	RY	124	224

006	N	F	*IL*	RY	126	226
007	N	F	*IL*	RY	127	227
008	N	F	*IL*	RY	128	228
009	N	F	*IL*	RY	129	229

CLASS 411   3- or 4-Cep Express Unit

DMSO (A)–TBCK–TSOL–DMSO (B) or DMSO(A)–TBCK–DMSO(B). Gangwayed throughout.
Traction Motors: Two English Elecric EE507 of 185 kW each per power car.
Dimensions: 20.34 x 2.82 x 3.83 m.
Maximum Speed: 90 mph.   **Doors:** Manually operated slam.
Couplings: Buckeye.   **Multiple Working:** SR type.
Bogies: Mk. 4 (* Mk. 3B; †‡ Mk. 6) motor, Commonwealth (†‡ B5 (SR)) unpowered.

61229–61239 (odd nos). DMSO (A). Dia. EA263. Lot No. 30449 Eastleigh 1958. –/64. 44.2 t.
61307–61409 (odd nos). DMSO (A). Dia. EA263. Lot No. 30454 Eastleigh 1958–59. –/64. 44.2 t.
61697–61811 (odd nos). DMSO (A). Dia. EA263. Lot No. 30619 Eastleigh 1960–61. –/64. 44.2 t.
61868. DMSO (A). Dia. EA263. Lot No. 30638 Eastleigh 1960–61. –/64. 44.2 t.
61948–61958 (even nos). DMSO (A). Dia. EA263. Lot No. 30708 Eastleigh 1963. –/64. 44.2 t.
70043–70044. TBCK. Dia. EJ361. Lot No. 30639 Eastleigh 1961. 24/6 2T. 36.2 t.
70235–70239. TBCK. Dia. EJ361. Lot No. 30451 Eastleigh 1958. 24/6 2T. 36.2 t.
61696–61810 (even nos). DMSO (B). Dia. EA264. Lot No. 30619 Eastleigh 1960–61. –/64. 43.5 t.
61869. DMSO (B). Dia. EA263. Lot No. 30638 Eastleigh 1960–61. –/64. 43.5 t.
61949–61959 (odd nos). DMSO (B). Dia. EA264. Lot No. 30708 Eastleigh 1963. –/64. 43.5 t.

Class 411/9. 3-car units used for peak hour strengthening.

1101		N	P	*SE*	RE	61331	70316	61330
1102		N	P	*SE*	RE	61231	70604	61232
1103	*	N	P	*SE*	RE	61750	70580	61751
1104	*	N	P	*SE*	RE	61760	70585	61761
1105	*	N	P	*SE*	RE	61952	70655	61953

(Class continued with 1501)

CLASS 421   4-Cig or 3-Cop (Phase 2) Express Unit

DTCsoL (A) or DTSsoL–MBSO–TSO–DTCsoL (B) or DTSOL(A)–MBSO–DTSOL(B). Gangwayed throughout.
Traction Motors: Four English Electric EE507 of 185 kW each.
Dimensions: 20.19 x 2.82 x 3.86 m.
Maximum Speed: 90 mph.   **Doors:** Manually operated slam.
Couplings: Buckeye.   **Multiple Working:** SR type.
Bogies: Mk. 6 (MBSO), B5 (SR) (other cars).

76561–76570. DTCsoL(A) (†‡ DTSsoL; § DTSOL(A)). Dia. EE369 (§ EE245). Lot No. 30802 York 1970 (§ Rebuilt Wessex Traincare/Alstom Eastleigh 1997–98). 18/36 (* 12/42; † –/54; ‡§ –/60) 2(§ 1)T. 35.5 t.
76581–76610. DTCsoL(A) (†‡ DTSsoL; § DTSOL(A)). Dia. EE369 (§ EE245). Lot No. 30806 York 1970 (§ Rebuilt Wessex Traincare/Alstom Eastleigh 1997–98). 18/36 (* 12/42; † –/54; ‡§ –/60) 2(§ 1)T. 35.5 t.
76717–76787. DTCsoL(A) (†‡ DTSsoL; § DTSOL(A)). Dia. EE369 (§ EE245). Lot No. 30814 York 1970–72 (§ Rebuilt Wessex Traincare/Alstom Eastleigh 1997–98). 18/36 (* 12/42; † –/54; ‡§ –/60) 2(§ 1)T. 35.5 t.
76859. DTCsoL(A). Dia. EE369. Lot No. 30827 York 1972. 12/42 2T. 35.5 t.
62277–62286. MBSO. Dia. ED264. Lot No. 30804 York 1970. –/56. 49.0 t.
62287–62316. MBSO. Dia. ED 264. Lot No. 30808 York 1970. –/56. 49.0 t.
62355–62425. MBSO. Dia. ED264. Lot No. 30816 York 1970. –/56. 49.0 t.
62430. MBSO. Dia. ED264. Lot No. 30829 York 1972. –/56. 49.0 t.
70967–70996 (excl. 70995). TSO. Dia. EH287. Lot No. 30809 York 1970–71. –/72. 31.5t. This vehicle remains in original condition (i.e. not refurbished).
70995. TSO. Dia. EH275. Lot No. 30809 York 1970–71. –/72. 31.5 t.
71035–71105. TSO. Dia. EH287. Lot No. 30817 York 1970. –/72. 31.5t.
71106. TSO. Dia. EH287. Lot No. 30830 York 1972. –/72. 31.5t.
71926. TSO. Dia. EH287. Built as EMU TSORB to Lot No. 30744 York 1963–66. Converted BRML Eastleigh 1988. –/72. 31.5t.
71927/28. TSO. Dia. EH287. Built as EMU TSORB to Lot No. 30805 York 1970. Converted BRML Eastleigh 1988. –/72. 31.5t.
76571–76580. DTCsoL(B) (§ DTSOL(B)). Dia. EE369 (§ EE246). Lot No. 30802 York 1970 (§ Rebuilt Wessex Traincare/Alstom Eastleigh 1997–98). 18/36 2(§ 1)T. 35.5 t.
76611–76640. DTCsoL(B) (§ DTSOL(B)). Dia. EE369 (§ EE246). Lot No. 30807 York 1970 (§ Rebuilt Wessex Traincare/Alstom Eastleigh 1997–98). 18/36 2(§1)T. 35.5 t.
76788–76858 (excl. 76824). DTCsoL(B) (§ DTSOL(B)). Dia. EE369 (§ EE246). Lot No. 30815 York 1970–72. (§ Rebuilt Wessex Traincare/Alstom Eastleigh 1997–98). 18/36 2T. 35.5 t.
76824. DTCsoL(B). Dia. EE363. Lot No. 30815 York 1970–72. 24/28 2T. 35.5 t.
76859. DTCsoL(B). Dia. EE369. Lot No. 30828 York 1972. 18/36 2(§ 1)T. 35.5 t.

Class 421/5. 'Greyhound' units with additional stage of field weakening to improve the maximum attainable speed.

1301	**ST**	F	*SW*	FR	76595	62301	70981	76625
1302	**ST**	F	*SW*	FR	76584	62290	70970	76614
1303	**ST**	F	*SW*	FR	76581	62287	70967	76611
1304	**ST**	F	*SW*	FR	76583	62289	70969	76613
1305	**ST**	F	*SW*	FR	76717	62355	71035	76788
1306	**ST**	F	*SW*	FR	76723	62361	71041	76794
1307	**ST**	F	*SW*	FR	76586	62292	70972	76616
1308	**ST**	F	*SW*	FR	76627	62298	70978	76622
1309	**N**	F	*SW*	FR	76594	62300	70980	76624
1310	**N**	F	*SW*	FR	76567	62283	71926	76577
1311	**N**	F	*SW*	FR	76561	62277	71927	76571
1312	**N**	F	*SW*	FR	76562	62278	71928	76572
1313	**ST**	F	*SW*	FR	76596	62302	70982	76626
1314	**ST**	F	*SW*	FR	76588	62294	70974	76618

1315		**ST**	F	*SW*	FR	76608	62314	70994	76638
1316		**ST**	F	*SW*	FR	76585	62291	70971	76615
1317		**ST**	F	*SW*	FR	76597	62303	70983	76592
1318		**ST**	F	*SW*	FR	76590	62296	70976	76620
1319		**ST**	F	*SW*	FR	76591	62297	70977	76621
1320		**ST**	F	*SW*	FR	76593	62299	70979	76623
1321		**ST**	F	*SW*	FR	76589	62295	70975	76619
1322		**ST**	F	*SW*	FR	76587	62293	70973	76617

Class 421/7. 3-car units for Brighton–Portsmouth 'Coastway' route.

1401	§	**CX**	P	*SC*	BI	76568	62284	76578
1402	§	**CX**	P	*SC*	BI	76564	62280	76574
1403	§	**CX**	P	*SC*	BI	76563	62279	76573
1404	§	**CX**	P	*SC*	BI	76602	62308	76632
1405	§	**CX**	P	*SC*	BI	76565	62281	76575
1406	§	**CX**	P	*SC*	BI	76728	62366	76799
1407	§	**CX**	P	*SC*	BI	76729	62367	76800
1408	§	**CX**	P	*SC*	BI	76750	62388	76821
1409	§	**CX**	P	*SC*	BI	76569	62285	76579
1410	§	**CX**	P	*SC*	BI	76734	62372	76805
1411	§	**CX**	P	*SC*	BI	76570	62286	76580

Name (Carried on MBSO):
1409   Operation Perseus

(Class continued with 1701)

CLASS 411   4-Cep Express Unit

For details see page 268.

Class 411/5. 4-car units

1507	**ST**	P	*SW*	FR	61363	70332	70289	61362
1509	**N**	P	*SE*	RE	61335	70318	70275	61334
1510	**N**	P	*SE*	RE	61365	70333	70290	61364
1511	**N**	P	*SE*	RE	61367	70334	70291	61366
1512	**ST**	P	*SW*	FR	61321	70311	70268	61320
1517	**N**	P	*SW*	FR	61317	70309	70266	61316
1518	**N**	P		ZG(S)	61333	70317	70274	61332
1519	**ST**	P	*SW*	FR	61403	70352	70516	61402
1520	**N**	P	*SE*	RE	61343	70327	70284	61380
1527	**N**	P	*SE*	RE	61237	70239	70233	61238
1531	**ST**	P	*SW*	FR	61233	70237	70231	61234
1532	**N**	P		FR(S)	61391	70346	71628	61390
1533	**ST**	P	*SW*	FR	61393	70347	71627	61385
1534	**ST**	P	*SW*	FR	61405	70353	71626	61404
1535	**ST**	P	*SW*	FR	61397	70349	71629	61396
1536	**N**	P	*SE*	RE	61399	70350	71631	61398
1537	**ST**	P	*SW*	FR	61229	70235	70229	61230
1538	**ST**	P	*SW*	FR	61307	70304	70261	61306
1539	**ST**	P	*SW*	FR	61401	70351	71632	61400
1541	**N**	P	*SE*	RE	61409	70355	71633	61408

1543		**N**	P	*SE*	RE	61323	70312	70297	61322
1544		**ST**	P	*SW*	FR	61315	70308	70265	61349
1547		**ST**	P	*SW*	FR	61329	70578	70272	61328
1548		**ST**	P	*SW*	FR	61375	70338	70295	61374
1549		**N**	P	*SE*	RE	61339	70320	70277	61338
1550		**N**	P	*SW*	FR	61313	70307	70264	61312
1551		**N**	P	*SE*	RE	61325	70313	70270	61324
1553		**N**	P	*SW*	FR	61728	70306	70263	61350
1554		**N**	P	*SE*	RE	61369	70335	70292	61368
1555		**N**	P	*SW*	FR	61311	70326	70283	61310
1556		**N**	P	*SE*	RE	61371	70336	70293	61370
1557		**N**	P	*SE*	RE	61337	70331	70288	61360
1559		**N**	P	*SE*	RE	61377	70339	70296	61376
1560		**N**	P	*SE*	RE	61387	70344	70301	61386
1562		**N**	P	*SE*	RE	61407	70236	70241	61406
1563		**N**	P	*SE*	RE(S)	61740	70575	70526	61741
1564	*	**N**	P	*SE*	RE	61788	70599	70550	61789
1565	*	**ST**	P	*SW*	FR	61762	70586	71711	61763
1566	*	**ST**	P	*SW*	FR	61722	70566	70517	61723
1568	*	**ST**	P	*SW*	FR	61766	70588	70539	61767
1570	*	**N**	P	*SE*	RE	61738	70574	70525	61739
1571	*	**N**	P	*SW*	FR	61806	70608	71636	61807
1572	*	**N**	P	*SE*	RE(S)	61734	70572	70523	61735
1573	*	**ST**	P	*SW*	FR	61726	70568	70519	61727
1574	*	**N**	P	*SE*	RE	61792	70601	71635	61793
1575	*	**N**	P	*SE*	RE	61768	70583	70540	61769
1576	*	**N**	P	*SE*	RE	61770	70590	70541	61771
1577	*	**N**	P	*SE*	RE	61718	70564	70515	61719
1578	*	**ST**	P	*SW*	FR	61700	70555	70506	61701
1580	*	**N**	P	*SE*	RE	61756	70589	70534	61757
1581	*	**ST**	P	*SW*	FR	61784	70597	70548	61785
1582	*	**N**	P	*SE*	RE	61748	70603	71630	61797
1584	*	**N**	P	*SE*	RE	61752	70581	70532	61753
1585	*	**N**	P	*SE*	RE	61710	70560	70511	61711
1586	*	**N**	P	*SE*	RE	61714	70562	70513	61715
1587	*	**N**	P	*SE*	RE	61764	70587	71625	61765
1588	*	**N**	P	*SE*	RE	61720	70044	70520	61721
1589	*	**N**	P		AF(S)	61742	70576	70527	61743
1590	*	**N**	P	*SE*	RE	61696	70553	70504	61697
1591	*	**N**	P	*SE*	RE	61790	70600	70551	61791
1592	*	**N**	P	*SE*	RE	61778	70594	70545	61779
1593	*	**N**	P	*SE*	RE	61730	70570	70521	61731
1594	*	**N**	P	*SE*	RE	61754	70582	70533	61755
1595	*	**N**	P	*SE*	RE	61704	70557	70508	61705
1597	*	**N**	P	*SE*	RE	61708	70559	70510	61709
1599	*	**N**	P	*SE*	RE	61706	70558	70509	61707
1602	*	**N**	P	*SE*	RE	61958	70565	70279	61959
1606	*	**N**	P		AF(S)	61694	70552		61695
1607	*	**N**	P	*SE*	RE	61698	70554	70505	61699
1609	*	**N**	P	*SE*	RE	61744	70577	70528	61745
1611	*	**N**	P	*SE*	RE	61758	70584	70537	61759

1612	*	ST	P	SW	FR	61794	70602	70535	61795
1614	*	N	P	SE	RE	61702	70556	70507	61703
1615	*	N	P	SE	RE	61956	70657	70664	61957
1616	*	N	P	SE	RE	61950	70654	70543	61951
1617	*	N	P	SE	RE(S)	61800	70605	70661	61801
1618	*	N	P		RE(S)	61868	70043	70230	61869
1697	‡	N	P	SW	FR	61373	70337	70294	61372
1698	‡	N	P	SW	FR	61355	70343	70300	61384
1699	†	N	P	SW	FR	61712	70561	70512	61713

Spare TSO.

Spare		N	P		ZD(S)	61383			
Spare		N	P		SU(S)		70035		
Spare		N	P		ZG(S)		70262	70503	
Spare		N	P		ZC(S)		70287		
Spare		N	P		ZA(S)		70660		
Spare		N	P		RE(S)		70273	70531	
Spare		N	P		RE(S)		70536	70662	
Spare		N	P		??(S)		70663		

CLASS 421   4-Cig (Phase 1) Express Unit

DTCsoL(A) or DTSsoL–MBSO–TSO–DTCsoL(B). Gangwayed throughout.
Traction Motors: Four English Elecric EE507 of 185 kW each.
Dimensions: 20.19 x 2.82 x 3.86 m.
Maximum Speed: 90 mph.   **Doors:** Manually operated slam.
Couplings: Buckeye.   **Multiple Working:** SR type.
Bogies: Mk. 4 or Mk. 6 (MBSO). B5 (SR) (other cars).

DTCsoL(A) (†‡ DTSsoL). Dia. EE369 (‡ EE3??). Lot No. 30741 York 1964–65.
18/36(† –/54; ‡ –/60) 2T. 35.5 t.
MBSO. Dia. ED264. Lot No. 30742 York 1964–65. –/56. 49 t.
70695–70730. TSO. Dia. EH287. Lot No. 30730 York 1964–65. –/72. 31.5 t.
71044–71097. TSO. Dia. EH287. Lot No. 30817 York 1970. –/72. 31.5 t.
71766–71770. TSO. Dia. EH287. Built as EMU TSORB to Lot No. 30744 York
1963–66. Converted BRML Eastleigh 1985–87. –/72. 31.5 t.
DTCsoL(B). Dia. EE369. Lot No. 30740 York 1964–65. 18/36 2T.

Class 421/3. Mark 4 motor bogies.

1701		U	A	SE	RE	76087	62028	70706	76033
1702		N	A	SC	BI	76101	62042	70720	76047
1703	†	N	A	SC	BI	76097	62038	70716	76043
1704		CX	A	SC	BI	76092	62033	70711	76038
1705	†	N	A	SC	BI	76076	62017	70695	76022
1706	†	N	A	SC	BI	76094	62035	70713	76040
1707	†	N	A	SC	BI	76084	62025	70703	76030
1708	†	N	A	SC	BI	76110	62051	70729	76056
1709	†	N	A	SC	BI	76103	62044	70722	76049
1710	†	CX	A	SC	BI	76078	62019	70697	76024
1711	‡	N	A	SC	BI	76114	62055	71766	76060
1712	†	N	A	SC	BI	76079	62020	70698	76025

1713	†	N	A	SC	BI	76128	62069	71767	76074
1714	†	N	A	SC	BI	76077	62018	70696	76023
1717	†	N	A	SC	BI	76083	62024	70702	76029
1719	†	CX	A	SC	BI	76116	62057	70719	76062
1720	†	N	A	SC	BI	76098	62039	71769	76044
1721	†	CX	A	SC	BI	76090	62031	70709	76036
1722	‡	CX	A	SC	BI	76106	62047	70725	76052
1724	†	CX	A	SC	BI	76120	62061	71770	76066
1725		CX	A	SC	BI	76088	62029	70707	76034
1726	†	CX	A	SC	BI	76109	62050	70728	76055
1727	†	CX	A	SC	BI	76111	62052	70730	76057
1731	†	CX	A	SC	BI	76095	62036	70714	76041
1733	†	CX	A	SC	BI	76122	62063	71047	76068
1734	†	CX	A	SC	BI	76063	62054	71044	76059
1735	†	CX	A	SC	BI	76117	62058	71050	76051
1736	†	U	A	SC	BI	76124	62065	71052	76070
1737		U	A	SC	BI	76121	62062	71058	76067
1738	†	CX	A	SC	BI	76129	62064	71046	76069
1739	†	CX	A	SC	BI	76123	62070	71066	76075
1740	†	CX	A	SC	BI	76126	62067	71097	76072
1741	†	CX	A	SC	BI	76089	62030	70708	76035
1742		U	A	SE	RE	76086	62027	70705	76032
1743	†	CX	A	SC	BI	76118	62059	71065	76064
1744	†	CX	A	SC	BI	76127	62068	71064	76073
1745	†	N	A	SC	BI	76085	62026	70704	76031
1746	‡	N	A	SC	BI	76091	62032	70710	76037
1747	†	N	A	SC	BI	76093	62034	70712	76026
1748		U	A	SE	RE	76115	62056	71067	76061
1749		N	A		AF(S)		62053	71068	76058
1750	†	N	A	SC	BI	76080	62021	70699	76039
1751	†	N	A	SC	BI	76125	62066	71051	76071
1752	†	N	A	SC	BI	76119	62060	70717	76065
1753	†	N	A	SC	BI	76102	62043	70721	76048

CLASS 421   4-Cig (Phase 2) Express Unit

For details see page 268.

Class 421/4.

1801	†	N	P	*SC*	BI	76848	71095	62415	76777
1802	†	N	P	*SC*	BI	76754	62392	71072	76825
1803	†	N	A	*SC*	BI	76780	62418	71098	76851
1804	†	N	A	*SC*	BI	76778	62416	71096	76849
1805	†	N	A	*SC*	BI	76782	62420	71100	76853
1806	*	N	F	*SE*	RE	76783	62421	71101	76854
1807	*	N	F	*SE*	RE	76784	62422	71102	76855
1808	*	N	F	*SE*	RE	76785	62423	71103	76856
1809	*	N	F	*SE*	RE	76786	62424	71104	76857
1810	*	N	F	*SE*	RE	76787	62425	71105	76858
1811	*	N	F	*SE*	RE	76781	62419	71099	76852
1812	*	N	F	*SE*	RE(S)	76757	62395	71075	76828

1813	*	N	F	*SE*	RE	76859	62430	71106	76860
1831	†	**CX**	A	*SC*	BI	76598	62304	70984	76628
1832	†	**CX**	A	*SC*	BI	76719	62357	71037	76790
1833	†	**CX**	A	*SC*	BI	76582	62288	70968	76612
1834	†	**CX**	A	*SC*	BI	76566	62282	70988	76576
1835	†	**CX**	A	*SC*	BI	76601	62307	70987	76631
1837		**CX**	A	*SC*	BI	76722	62360	71040	76793
1839	*	N	F	*SE*	RE	76607	62313	70993	76637
1840	*	N	F	*SE*	RE	76724	62362	71042	76795
1841	*	N	F	*SE*	RE	76603	62309	70989	76633
1842	*	N	F	*SE*	RE	76725	62363	71043	76796
1843	*	N	F	*SE*	RE	76731	62369	71049	76802
1845	†	**CX**	A	*SC*	BI	76599	62305	70985	76629
1846	†	**CX**	A	*SC*	BI	76737	62375	71055	76808
1847	†	**CX**	A	*SC*	BI	76600	62306	70986	76630
1848	†	**CX**	A	*SC*	BI	76605	62311	70991	76635
1850	†	**CX**	A	*SC*	BI	76718	62356	71036	76789
1851	†	**CX**	A	*SC*	BI	76721	62359	71039	76792
1853	†	**CX**	A	*SC*	BI	76606	62312	70992	76636
1854	†	**CX**	A	*SC*	BI	76738	62376	71056	76809
1855	†	**CX**	A	*SC*	BI	76720	62358	71038	76791
1856	†	**CX**	A	*SC*	BI	76739	62377	71057	76810
1857		**CX**	A	*SC*	BI	76610	62316	70996	76640
1858	‡	**CX**	A	*SC*	BI	76604	62310	70990	76634
1859	‡	**CX**	A	*SC*	BI	76727	62365	71045	76798
1860	‡	**CX**	A	*SC*	BI	76752	62390	71070	76823
1861	‡	**CX**	A	*SC*	BI	76735	62373	71053	76806
1862	†	**CX**	A	*SC*	BI	76736	62374	71054	76807
1863	†	**CX**	A	*SC*	BI	76742	62380	71060	76813
1864	†	**CX**	A	*SC*	BI	76741	62379	71059	76812
1865	†	**CX**	A	*SC*	BI	76745	62383	71063	76639
1866	†	**CX**	A	*SC*	BI	76743	62381	71061	76814
1867	†	N	A	*SC*	BI	76744	62382	71062	76815
1868	†	N	A	*SC*	BI	76751	62389	71069	76822
1869	†	N	A	*SC*	BI	76753	62391	71071	76804
1870	*	N	F	*SE*	RE	76108	62409	71089	76842
1871	*	N	F	*SE*	RE	76756	62394	71074	76827
1872	*	N	F	*SE*	RE	76771	62396	71076	76829
1873	*	N	F	*SE*	RE	76759	62397	71077	76830
1874	†	N	A	*SC*	BI	76755	62393	71073	76826
1876	*	N	F	*SE*	RE	76761	62399	71079	76832
1877	*	N	F	*SE*	RE	76763	62401	71081	76834
1878	*	N	F	*SE*	RE	76768	62406	71086	76828
1879	*	N	F	*SE*	RE	76760	62398	71078	76831
1880		N	F	*SW*	FR	76770	62408	71088	76841
1881		N	F	*SW*	FR	76762	62400	71080	76833
1882		N	F	*SW*	FR	76765	62403	71083	76836
1883		N	F	*SW*	FR	76764	62402	71082	76835
1884		N	F	*SW*	FR	76767	62405	71085	76838
1885		N	F	*SW*	FR	76769	62407	71087	76840
1886		N	F	*SW*	FR	76772	62410	71090	76843

1887	**N**	F	*SW*	FR	76766	62404	71084	76837
1888	**N**	F	*SW*	FR	76773	62411	71091	76844
1889	**N**	F	*SW*	FR	76774	62412	71092	76845
1890	**N**	F	*SW*	FR	76775	62413	71093	76846
1891	**N**	F	*SW*	FR	76776	62414	71094	76847
Spare	**BG**	A		ZG(S)			70995	

CLASS 421   4-Cig (Phase 1) Express Unit

For details see page 272.

Class 421/6. Mark 6 motor bogies.

1901		**N**	P	*SC*	BI	76082	62023	70701	76028
1902	†	**N**	P	*SC*	BI	76100	62041	71768	76046
1903	†	**CX**	A	*SC*	BI	76081	62022	70700	76027
1904	†	**CX**	A	*SC*	BI	76107	62048	70726	76053
1905	‡	**CX**	A	*SC*	BI	76099	62040	70718	76045
1906	†	**CX**	A	*SC*	BI	76105	62046	70724	76113
1907	†	**CX**	A	*SC*	BI	76104	62045	70723	76050
1908	†	**CX**	A	*SC*	BI	76096	62037	70715	76042

CLASS 422/3   4-Big (Phases 1 & 2) Express Unit

DTCsoL (A)–MBSO–TSRB–DTCsoL (B). Phase 2 units with Phase 1 TSRB (69333 is phase 2). For details see page 268.

69301–69318. TSRB. Dia. EN260. Lot No. 30744 York 1966. –/40. 35.0 t.
69333–69339. TSRB. Dia. EN260. Lot No. 30805 York 1970. –/40. 35.0 t.

2251	**N**	P	*SW*	BM	76726	62364	69302	76797
2254	**N**	P	*SW*	FR	76803	62370	69306	76732
2255	**N**	P	*SW*	FR	76811	62378	69310	76740
2256	**N**	P	*SW*	FR	76747	62385	69307	76818
2258	**N**	P	*SW*	FR	76746	62384	69316	76817
2259	**N**	P	*SW*	FR	76819	62386	69318	76748
2260	**N**	P	*SC*	BI	76749	62387	69304	76820
2262	**N**	P	*SW*	FR	76850	62417	69333	76779

Spare TSRB (Phase 1).

| Spare | **N** | P | | ZG(S) | 69312 | | | |

Spare TSRB (Phase 2).

| Spare | **N** | P | | ZG(S) | 69335 | | | |

CLASS 412   4-Bep Express Unit

DMSO (A)–TBCK–TSRB–DMSO (B). Gangwayed throughout.
Traction Motors: Four English Electric EE507 of 185 kW each.
Dimensions: 20.34 x 2.82 x 3.83 m.
Maximum Speed: 90 mph.   **Doors:** Manually operated slam.
Couplings: Buckeye.   **Multiple Working:** SR type.
Bogies: Mk 6 (motor), B5(SR) (unpowered).

61736–61808 (even numbers). DMSO (A). Dia. EA264. Lot No. 30619 Eastleigh 1960–61. –/64. 44.2 t.
61954. DMSO (A). Dia. EA264. Lot No. 30708 Eastleigh 1963.–/64. 44.2 t.
70354. TBCK. Dia. EJ361. Lot No. 30456 Eastleigh 1959. 24/6 2T. 36.2 t.
70573–70609. TBCK. Dia. EJ361. Lot No. 30621 Eastleigh 1960-61. 24/6 2T. 36.2 t.
70656. TBCK. Dia. EJ361. Lot No. 30709 Eastleigh 1963. 24/6 2T. 36.2 t.
69341–69347. TSRB. Dia. EN261. Built as TRB to Lot No. 30622 Eastleigh 1961. Converted BREL Swindon 1982–84. –/24 plus 9 chairs 1T. 35.5 t.
61737–61809 (odd numbers). DMSO (B). Dia. EA264. Lot No. 30619 Eastleigh 1960–61. –/64. 43.5 t.
61955. DMSO (B). Dia. EA264. Lot No. 30708 Eastleigh 1963.–/64. 43.5 t.

2301	N	P	*SW*	FR	61804	70607	69341	61805
2302	ST	P	*SW*	FR	61774	70592	69342	61809
2303	ST	P	*SW*	FR	61954	70656	69343	61955
2304	ST	P	*SW*	FR	61736	70573	69344	61737
2305	ST	P	*SW*	FR	61798	70354	69345	61799
2306	ST	P	*SW*	FR	61808	70609	69346	61775
2307	ST	P	*SW*	FR	61802	70606	69347	61803

CLASS 442   5-Wes Express Unit

DTFsoL–TSOL(A)–MBRSM–TSOL(B)–DTSOL. Gangwayed throughout. Air conditioned.
Traction Motors: Four English Electric EE546 of 300 kW each.
Dimensions: 22.57 x 2.74 x 3.81m.   **Doors:** Power operated sliding plug.
Maximum Speed: 100 mph.   **Bogies:** Mk 6 (MBRSM). T4 (other cars).
Couplings: Buckeye.   **Multiple Working:** SR type.

DTFsoL. Dia. EE160. Lot No. 31030 BREL Derby 1988–89. 50/– 1T. 39.1 t.
TSOL (A). Dia. EH288. Lot No. 31032 BREL Derby 1988–89. –/80 2T. 35.3 t.
MBRSM. Dia. ED268. Lot No. 31034 BREL Derby 1988–89. Modified Adtranz Crewe 1998. –/30). 54.1 t.
TSOL (B). Dia. EH289. Lot No. 31033 BREL Derby 1988–89. –/76 1W 2T. 35.4 t.
DTSOL. Dia. EE273. Lot No. 31031 BREL Derby 1988–89. –/78 1T. 39.1 t.

2401	SW	A	*SW*	BM	77382	71818	62937	71842	77406
2402	SW	A	*SW*	BM	77383	71819	62938	71843	77407
2403	SW	A	*SW*	BM	77384	71820	62941	71844	77408
2404	SW	A	*SW*	BM	77385	71821	62939	71845	77409
2405	SW	A	*SW*	BM	77386	71822	62944	71846	77410
2406	SW	A	*SW*	BM	77389	71823	62942	71847	77411
2407	SW	A	*SW*	BM	77388	71824	62943	71848	77412
2408	SW	A	*SW*	BM	77387	71825	62945	71849	77413
2409	SW	A	*SW*	BM	77390	71826	62946	71850	77414
2410	SW	A	*SW*	BM	77391	71827	62948	71851	77415
2411	SW	A	*SW*	BM	77392	71828	62940	71858	77422
2412	SW	A	*SW*	BM	77393	71829	62947	71853	77417
2413	SW	A	*SW*	BM	77394	71830	62949	71854	77418
2414	SW	A	*SW*	BM	77395	71831	62950	71855	77419
2415	SW	A	*SW*	BM	77396	71832	62951	71856	77420
2416	SW	A	*SW*	BM	77397	71833	62952	71857	77421
2417	SW	A	*SW*	BM	77398	71834	62953	71852	77416

2418	**SW**	A	*SW*	BM	77399 71835 62954 71859 77423
2419	**SW**	A	*SW*	BM	77400 71836 62955 71860 77424
2420	**SW**	A	*SW*	BM	77401 71837 62956 71861 77425
2421	**SW**	A	*SW*	BM	77402 71838 62957 71862 77426
2422	**SW**	A	*SW*	BM	77403 71839 62958 71863 77427
2423	**SW**	A	*SW*	BM	77404 71840 62959 71864 77428
2424	**SW**	A	*SW*	BM	77405 71841 62960 71865 77429

Names (carried on MBRSM):

2401	Beaulieu	2409	Bournemouth Orchestras
2402	County Of Hampshire	2410	Meridian Tonight
2403	The New Forest	2412	Special Olympics
2404	Borough Of Woking	2415	Mary Rose
2405	City Of Portsmouth	2416	Mum in a Million 1997 –
2406	Victory		Doreen Scanlon
2407	Thomas Hardy	2418	Wessex Cancer Trust
2408	County Of Dorset	2419	BBC South Today
2420	City Southampton	2423	County Of Surrey
2422	OPERATION OVERLORD		

CLASS 423/1   4-Vep Unit

DTCsoL–MBSO–TSO–DTCsoL. Gangwayed throughout.
Traction Motors: Four English Electric EE507 of 185 kW each.
Dimensions: 20.18 x 2.82 x 3.84 m.
Maximum Speed: 90 mph.   **Doors:** Manually operated slam.
Couplings: Buckeye.   **Multiple Working:** SR type.
Bogies: Mk. 4 (MBSO), B5 (SR) (other cars).

62121–62140. MBSO. Dia. ED266. Lot No. 30760 Derby 1967. –/76. 49.0 t.
62182–62216. MBSO. Dia. ED266. Lot No. 30773 York 1967–68. –/76. 49.0 t.
62217–62266. MBSO. Dia. ED266. Lot No. 30794 York 1968–69. –/76. 49.0 t.
62267–62276. MBSO. Dia. ED266. Lot No. 30800 York 1970. –/76. 49.0 t.
62317–62354. MBSO. Dia. ED266. Lot No. 30813 York 1970–73. –/76. 49.0 t.
62435–62475. MBSO. Dia. ED266. Lot No. 30851 York 1973–74. –/76. 49.0 t.
70781–70800. TSO. Dia. EH291. Lot No. 30759 Derby 1967. –/98. 31.5 t.
70872–70906. TSO. Dia. EH291. Lot No. 30772 York 1967–68. –/98. 31.5 t.
70907–70956. TSO. Dia. EH291. Lot No. 30793 York 1968–69. –/98. 31.5 t.
70957–70966. TSO. Dia. EH291. Lot No. 30801 York 1970. –/98. 31.5 t.
70997–71034. TSO. Dia. EH291. Lot No. 30812 York 1970–73. –/98. 31.5 t.
71115–71155. TSO. Dia. EH291. Lot No. 30852 York 1973–74. –/98. 31.5 t.
76230–76269. DTCsoL. Dia. EE373. Lot No. 30758 York 1967. 18/46 (†§ 12/52)1T. 35 t.
76275. DTSO. Dia. EE266. Built as loco-hauled vehicle to Lot No. 30086 Eastleigh 1953–55. Converted to Lot No. 30764 York 1966. –/64. 32.0 t.
76333–76400. DTCsoL (‡ DTSO). Dia. EE373 (‡ EE278). Lot No. 30771 York 1967–68. 18/46 († 12/52)1T ; (‡ –/88 0T). 32.5 t.
76441–76540. DTCsoL. Dia. EE373. Lot No. 30792 York 1968–69. 18/46 (†‡ 12/52) 1T. 32.5 t.
76541–76560. DTCsoL. Dia. EE373. Lot No. 30799 York 1970. 18/46 († 12/52) 1T. 32.5 t.

76641–76716. DTCsoL. Dia. EE373. Lot No. 30811 York 1970–73. 18/46 († 12/52) 1T. 32.5 t.
76861–76942. DTCsoL. Dia. EE368. Lot No. 30853 York 1973–74. 18/46 († 12/52) 1T. 32.5 t.

3401		ST	F	*SW*	WD	76230	62276	70781	76231
3402		N	F	*SW*	WD	76233	62123	70782	76232
3403		CX	F	*SC*	BI	76234	62254	70783	76235
3404		N	F	*SW*	WD	76378	62261	70894	76236
3405		N	F	*SW*	WD	76239	62271	70785	76238
3406		ST	F	*SW*	WD	76241	62130	70786	76240
3407		ST	F	*SW*	WD	76243	62348	70787	76242
3408		N	F	*SW*	WD	76244	62435	70788	76245
3409		ST	F	*SW*	WD	76246	62239	70789	76247
3410		ST	F	*SW*	WD	76369	62442	70790	76249
3411		ST	F	*SW*	WD	76250	62342	70791	76251
3412	†	N	A	*SE*	RE	76252	62340	70792	76253
3413		ST	F	*SW*	WD	76255	62441	70793	76254
3414		ST	F	*SW*	WD	76257	62446	70794	76248
3415		N	F	*SW*	WD	76258	62462	70795	76259
3416	†	N	A	*SE*	RE	76261	62451	70796	76260
3417		ST	F	*SW*	WD	76262	62236	70797	76263
3418		ST	F	*SW*	WD	76265	62133	70875	76264
3419		ST	F	*SW*	WD	76267	62354	70799	76266
3420		ST	F	*SW*	WD	76269	62349	70800	76268
3421	†	CX	A	*SE*	RE	76889	62449	71129	76890
3422	†	CX	A	*SE*	RE	76372	62201	70891	76371
3423	†	CX	A	*SE*	RE	76452	62222	70912	76451
3424	†	CX	A	*SE*	RE	76354	62185	70882	76353
3425		ST	F	*SW*	WD	76338	62192	70874	76358
3426		ST	F	*SW*	WD	76386	62208	70898	76385
3427		ST	F	*SW*	WD	76374	62184	70892	76373
3428		ST	F	*SW*	WD	76454	62223	70913	76453
3429		ST	F	*SW*	WD	76334	62202	70872	76333
3430		ST	F	*SW*	WD	76348	62189	70879	76347
3431		N	F	*SW*	WD	76458	62182	70915	76457
3432		N	F	*SW*	WD	76400	62225	70905	76399
3433		N	F	*SW*	WD	76444	62215	70908	76443
3434		N	F	*SW*	WD	76462	62218	70917	76461
3435		CX	P	*SC*	BI	76342	62228	70876	76341
3436		CX	P	*SC*	BI	76350	62190	70880	76349
3437		CX	P	*SC*	BI	76346	62186	70878	76345
3438		N	P	*SC*	BI	76530	62262	70951	76529
3442		N	P	*SC*	BI	76492	62216	70932	76491
3445	†	N	A	*SE*	RE	76450	62242	70911	76449
3446	†	N	A	*SE*	RE	76532	62243	70952	76531
3447	†	CX	A	*SE*	RE	76380	62199	70895	76379
3448	†	N	A	*SE*	RE	76376	62221	70886	76375
3449	†	N	A	*SE*	RE	76336	62205	70873	76335
3450	†	N	A	*SE*	RE	76460	62203	70916	76459
3451	†	N	A	*SE*	RE	76488	62240	70930	76487

3452	†	**N**	A	*SE*	RE	76340	62183	71021	76690
3453	†	**N**	A	*SE*	RE	76382	62226	70896	76381
3454	†	**N**	A	*SE*	RE	76390	62200	70798	76389
3455		**N**	F	*SW*	WD	76388	62206	70899	76387
3456		**N**	F	*SW*	WD	76456	62210	70914	76455
3457		**N**	F	*SW*	WD	76392	62197	70901	76391
3458		**N**	F	*SW*	WD	76394	62209	70902	76393
3459		**N**	F	*SW*	WD	76396	62224	70903	76395
3462		**N**	P	*SC*	BI	76536	62213	70954	76535
3463		**CX**	P	*SC*	BI	76398	62266	70904	76397
3464		**N**	P	*SC*	BI	76442	62265	70907	76441
3466		**N**	F	*SW*	WD	76464	62214	70918	76463
3467		**N**	F	*SW*	WD	76446	62217	70909	76445
3468		**N**	F	*SW*	WD	76448	62267	70910	76447
3469		**N**	F	*SW*	WD	76546	62219	70959	76545
3470		**N**	F	*SW*	WD	76496	62220	70934	76495
3471	†	**N**	A	*SE*	RE	76498	62269	70935	76497
3472	†	**N**	A	*SE*	RE	76500	62244	70936	76499
3473	‡	**N**	A	*SE*	RE	76502	62245	70937	76339
3474	†	**N**	A	*SE*	RE	76504	62246	70938	76503
3475	†	**N**	A	*SE*	RE	76552	62270	70962	76551
3476		**N**	P	*SC*	BI	76548	62247	70960	76547
3478		**N**	P	*SC*	BI	76653	62125	71003	76654
3479		**CX**	F	*SC*	BI	76655	62272	71004	76656
3480		**N**	F	*SC*	BI	76474	62323	70923	76473
3481		**N**	F	*SW*	WD	76647	62324	70900	76648
3482		**CX**	F	*SC*	BI	76657	62320	71005	76658
3483		**CX**	F	*SC*	BI	76661	62233	71007	76662
3484		**CX**	F	*SC*	BI	76476	62325	70924	76475
3485		**N**	F	*SC*	BI	76508	62327	70940	76507
3486		**N**	F	*SC*	BI	76478	62234	70925	76477
3487	†	**N**	A	*SE*	RE	76645	62250	70941	76509
3488		**CX**	F	*SC*	BI	76663	62235	71008	76664
3489		**CX**	F	*SC*	BI	76665	62251	71009	76666
3490		**N**	F	*SC*	BI	76695	62328	71024	76696
3491	†	**N**	A	*SE*	RE	76337	62436	70927	76481
3492	†	**N**	A	*SE*	RE	76667	62344	71010	76668
3493	†	**N**	A	*SE*	RE	76669	62237	71011	76670
3494	†	**N**	A	*SE*	RE	76675	62330	71014	76676
3495	†	**N**	A	*SE*	RE	76699	62331	71026	76700
3496	†	**N**	A	*SE*	RE	76673	62334	71013	76674
3497	†	**N**	A	*SE*	RE	76671	62346	71012	76672
3498	†	**N**	A	*SE*	RE	76701	62333	71027	76702
3499	†	**N**	A	*SE*	RE	76901	62347	71135	76902
3500	†	**N**	A	*SE*	RE	76470	62455	70921	76469
3501		**CX**	P	*SC*	BI	76512	62332	70942	76511
3503		**CX**	P	*SC*	BI	76681	62231	71017	76682
3504		**CX**	P	*SC*	BI	76711	62351	71032	76712
3505		**CX**	P	*SC*	BI	76472	62352	70922	76471
3506		**N**	P	*SC*	BI	76554	62317	70963	76553
3507		**N**	P	*SC*	BI	76558	62232	70965	76557

3508		ST	F	SW	WD	76643	62273	70998	76644
3509		ST	F	SW	WD	76560	62275	70966	76559
3510		ST	F	SW	WD	76641	62318	70997	76642
3511	†	CX	A	SE	RE	76893	62135	70999	76646
3512		CX	P	SC	BI	76679	62337	71016	76680
3513		N	P	SC	BI	76691	62336	71022	76692
3514		CX	P	SC	BI	76683	62136	71018	76684
3515		CX	P	SC	BI	76544	62319	70958	76543
3516		ST	F	SW	WD	76693	62268	71023	76694
3517		CX	P	SC	BI	76685	62338	71019	76686
3518		CX	P	SC	BI	76689	62343	70887	76363
3519		ST	F	SW	WD	76556	62274	70964	76555
3520		ST	F	SW	WD	76697	62131	71025	76698
3521	†	N	A	SE	RE	76484	62345	70928	76483
3522		CX	P	SC	BI	76705	62341	71029	76706
3523		CX	F	SC	BI	76651	62139	71002	76652
3524		CX	F	SC	BI	76466	62322	70919	76370
3526		N	P	SC	BI	76524	62255	70948	76523
3527		N	P	SC	BI	76520	62326	70946	76519
3528		N	P	SC	BI	76518	62258	70945	76517
3529		N	F	SC	BI	76659	62257	71006	76660
3530		N	F	SC	BI	76468	62256	70920	76467
3531		N	F	SC	BI	76649	62230	71001	76650
3532		N	P	SC	BI	76528	62321	70950	76527
3533		N	P	SC	BI	76364	62260	70949	76525
3534		N	P	SC	BI	76506	62259	70939	76505
3535		CX	P	SC	BI	76677	62335	71015	76678
3536		N	F	SW	WD	76384	62207	70897	76383
3539		N	F	SW	WD	76861	62122	71115	76862
3540		N	F	SW	WD	76863	62128	71116	76864
3542		ST	F	SW	WD	76480	62127	70926	76479
3543	†	N	A	SE	RE	76899	62137	71134	76900
3544	†	N	A	SE	RE	76892	62454	71131	76894
3545	†	N	A	SE	RE	76875	62121	71122	76876
3546		CX	P	SC	BI	76687	62339	71020	76688
3547	†	N	A	SE	RE	76895	62126	71132	76896
3548	†	N	A	SE	RE	76903	62452	71136	76904
3549		CX	P	SC	BI	76707	62132	71030	76708
3550		CX	P	SC	BI	76490	62350	70931	76489
3551		CX	P	SC	BI	76465	62456	71033	76714
3552		ST	F	SW	WD	76715	62353	71034	76716
3553	†	N	A	SE	RE	76913	62241	71141	76914
3554	†	CX	A	SE	RE	76905	62461	71137	76906
3555		ST	F	SW	WD	76865	62140	71117	76866
3556	†	CX	A	SE	RE	76885	62457	71127	76886
3557		ST	F	SW	WD	76869	62437	71119	76870
3558		ST	F	SW	WD	76352	62447	70881	76351
3559		ST	F	SW	WD	76486	62439	70929	76485
3560	†	CX	A	SE	RE	76897	62191	71133	76898
3561		ST	F	SW	WD	76867	62453	71118	76868
3562	†	CX	A	SE	RE	76907	62129	71138	76908

3563		ST	F	SW	WD	76873	62438	71121	76874
3564	†	CX	A	SE	RE	76883	62458	71126	76884
3565	†	CX	A	SE	RE	76877	62134	71123	76878
3566	†	CX	A	SE	RE	76915	62443	71142	76916
3567		ST	F	SW	WD	76871	62138	71120	76872
3568	†	CX	A	SE	RE	76887	62440	71128	76888
3569		ST	F	SW	WD	76344	62448	70877	76343
3570	†	CX	A	SE	RE	76909	62187	71139	76910
3571	†	CX	A	SE	RE	76927	62463	71148	76928
3572	†	CX	A	SE	RE	76879	62468	71124	76880
3573	†	CX	A	SE	RE	76919	62444	71144	76920
3574	†	CX	A	SE	RE	76929	62464	71149	76930
3575	†	CX	A	SE	RE	76931	62469	71150	76932
3576		ST	F	SW	WD	76362	62196	70890	76361
3577	†	CX	A	SE	RE	76933	62459	71151	76934
3578		ST	F	SW	WD	76356	62193	70883	76355
3579	†	CX	A	SE	RE	76935	62471	71152	76936
3580		ST	F	SW	WD	76360	62195	70885	76359
3581		ST	F	SW	WD	76366	62198	70888	76365
3582	†	CX	A	SE	RE	76891	62472	71130	76275
3583	†	N	A	SE	RE	76937	62450	71153	76938
3584	†	CX	A	SE	RE	76881	62473	71125	76882
3585	†	CX	A	SE	RE	76939	62445	71154	76940
3586	†	CX	A	SE	RE	76921	62474	71145	76922
3587	†	CX	A	SE	RE	76925	62465	71147	76926
3588	†	N	A	SE	RE	76923	62467	71146	76924
3589	†	CX	A	SE	RE	76911	62466	71140	76912
3590	†	N	A	SE	RE	76941	62460	71155	76942
3591	†	N	A	SE	RE	76917	62475	71143	76918
3801	†	CX	P	SE	RE	76522	62229	70947	76521
3802	†	CX	P	SE	RE	76534	62188	70953	76533
3803	†	N	P	SE	RE	76494	62263	70933	76493
3804	†	N	P	SE	RE	76368	62204	70889	76367
3805	†	N	P	SE	RE	76540	62211	70956	76539
3806	†	N	P	SE	RE	76538	62212	70955	76537
3807	†	N	P	SE	RE	76542	62264	70957	76541
3808	†	N	P	SE	RE	76550	62248	70961	76549
3809		N	P	SW	WD	76516	62253	70944	76515
3810		N	P	SW	WD	76709	62252	71031	76710
3811		N	P	SW	WD	76514	62249	70943	76513
3812		ST	P	SW	WD	76703	62238	71028	76704
Spare		N	F		WD(S)		62470		

CLASS 423/2   4-Vop Unit

DTSOL–MBSO–TSO–DTSOL. Gangwayed throughout. 19 Class 423/1 units de-classified 1998 onwards for South London 'Metro' services.
Details as Class 423/1 except:

76401–76402. DTSOL. Dia. EE281. Lot No. 30771 York 1967–68. –/70. 32.5 t.

3901	(3439)	CX	P	SC	BI	76402	62227	70906	76401

3902
3903
3904
3905
3906
3907
3908
3909
3910
3911
3912
3913
3914
3915
3916
3917
3918
3919

CLASS 455   4-Car Unit

DTSO–MSO–TSO–DTSO. Gangwayed throughout. Disc brakes (5913–15 have tread brakes).
Traction Motors: Four GEC507-20J of 185 kW each.
Dimensions: 19.92 x 2.82 x 3.58 m. (Class 455/7 TSO), 19.92 x 2.82 x 3.77 m (other cars).
Maximum Speed: 75 mph.   **Couplers:** Tightlock.
Doors: Power operated sliding (* Power operated sliding plug).
Bogies: BT13 (DTSO & Cl. 455/8 and 455/9 TSO), BP27 (MSO), BX1 (Cl. 455/7 TSO).
Multiple Working: Classes 455–457, 507 and 508.

Class 455/7. Built as 3-car units, augmented with ex-Class 507 TSOs. Pressure heating & ventilation.

DTSO. Dia. EE218. Lot No. 30976 BREL York 1984–85. –/74. 29.5 t.
MSO. Dia. EC203. Lot No. 30975 BREL York 1984–85. –/84. 45.0 t.
TSO. Dia. EH219. Lot No. 30944 BREL York 1977–80. –/86. 25.5 t.

5701	**N**	P	*SW*	WD	77727	62783	71545	77728
5702	**N**	P	*SW*	WD	77729	62784	71547	77730
5703	**N**	P	*SW*	WD	77731	62785	71540	77732
5704	**N**	P	*SW*	WD	77733	62786	71548	77734
5705	**N**	P	*SW*	WD	77735	62787	71565	77736
5706	**N**	P	*SW*	WD	77737	62788	71534	77738
5707	**N**	P	*SW*	WD	77739	62789	71536	77740
5708	**N**	P	*SW*	WD	77741	62790	71560	77742
5709	**N**	P	*SW*	WD	77743	62791	71532	77744
5710	**N**	P	*SW*	WD	77745	62792	71566	77746
5711	**N**	P	*SW*	WD	77747	62793	71542	77748
5712	**N**	P	*SW*	WD	77749	62794	71546	77750
5713	**N**	P	*SW*	WD	77751	62795	71567	77752
5714	**ST**	P	*SW*	WD	77753	62796	71539	77754

5715	**ST**	P	*SW*	WD	77755	62797	71535	77756
5716	**ST**	P	*SW*	WD	77757	62798	71564	77758
5717	**N**	P	*SW*	WD	77759	62799	71528	77760
5718	**ST**	P	*SW*	WD	77761	62800	71557	77762
5719	**ST**	P	*SW*	WD	77763	62801	71558	77764
5720	**ST**	P	*SW*	WD	77765	62802	71568	77766
5721	**ST**	P	*SW*	WD	77767	62803	71553	77768
5722	**ST**	P	*SW*	WD	77769	62804	71533	77770
5723	**ST**	P	*SW*	WD	77771	62805	71526	77772
5724	**ST**	P	*SW*	WD	77773	62806	71561	77774
5725	**ST**	P	*SW*	WD	77775	62807	71541	77776
5726	**ST**	P	*SW*	WD	77777	62808	71556	77778
5727	**ST**	P	*SW*	WD	77779	62809	71562	77780
5728	**ST**	P	*SW*	WD	77781	62810	71527	77782
5729	**ST**	P	*SW*	WD	77783	62811	71550	77784
5730	**ST**	P	*SW*	WD	77785	62812	71551	77786
5731	**ST**	P	*SW*	WD	77787	62813	71555	77788
5732	**ST**	P	*SW*	WD	77789	62814	71552	77790
5733	**ST**	P	*SW*	WD	77791	62815	71549	77792
5734	**ST**	P	*SW*	WD	77793	62816	71531	77794
5735	**ST**	P	*SW*	WD	77795	62817	71563	77796
5736	**ST**	P	*SW*	WD	77797	62818	71554	77798
5737	**ST**	P	*SW*	WD	77799	62819	71544	77800
5738	**ST**	P	*SW*	WD	77801	62820	71529	77802
5739	**ST**	P	*SW*	WD	77803	62821	71537	77804
5740	**ST**	P	*SW*	WD	77805	62822	71530	77806
5741	**ST**	P	*SW*	WD	77807	62823	71559	77808
5742	**ST**	P	*SW*	WD	77809	62824	71543	77810
5750	**ST**	P	*SW*	WD	77811	62825	71538	77812

Names:

5711	SPIRIT OF RUGBY		5735	The Royal Borough of Kingston
5731	VARIETY CLUB		5750	Wimbledon Train Care

Class 455/8. Pressure heating & ventilation.

DTSO. Dia. EE218. Lot No. 30972 BREL York 1982–84. –/74. 29.5 t.
MSO. Dia. EC203. Lot No. 30973 BREL York 1982–84. –/84. 45.6 t.
TSO. Dia. EH221. Lot No. 30974 BREL York 1982–84. –/84. 27.1 t.

5801	**N**	F	*SC*	SU	77579	62709	71637	77580
5802	**N**	F	*SC*	SU	77581	62710	71664	77582
5803	**N**	F	*SC*	SU	77583	62711	71639	77584
5804	**CX**	F	*SC*	SU	77585	62712	71640	77586
5805	**N**	F	*SC*	SU	77587	62713	71641	77588
5806	**N**	F	*SC*	SU	77589	62714	71642	77590
5807	**N**	F	*SC*	SU	77591	62715	71643	77592
5808	**N**	F	*SC*	SU	77593	62716	71644	77594
5809	**N**	F	*SC*	SU	77595	62717	71645	77596
5810	**N**	F	*SC*	SU	77597	62718	71646	77598
5811	**N**	F	*SC*	SU	77599	62719	71647	77600
5812	**N**	F	*SC*	SU	77601	62720	71648	77602
5813	**N**	F	*SC*	SU	77603	62721	71649	77604

5814	N	F	*SC*	SU	77605	62722	71650	77606
5815	N	F	*SC*	SU	77607	62723	71651	77608
5816	N	F	*SC*	SU	77609	62724	71652	77633
5817	N	F	*SC*	SU	77611	62725	71653	77612
5818	N	F	*SC*	SU	77613	62726	71654	77614
5819	N	F	*SC*	SU	77615	62727	71655	77616
5820	N	F	*SC*	SU	77617	62728	71656	77618
5821	N	F	*SC*	SU	77619	62729	71657	77620
5822	N	F	*SC*	SU	77621	62730	71658	77622
5823	N	F	*SC*	SU	77623	62731	71659	77624
5824	N	F	*SC*	SU	77637	62732	71660	77626
5825	N	F	*SC*	SU	77627	62733	71661	77628
5826	N	F	*SC*	SU	77629	62734	71662	77630
5827	N	F	*SC*	SU	77610	62735	71663	77632
5828	N	F	*SC*	SU	77631	62736	71638	77634
5829	N	F	*SC*	SU	77635	62737	71665	77636
5830	N	F	*SC*	SU	77625	62743	71666	77638
5831	N	F	*SC*	SU	77639	62739	71667	77640
5832	N	F	*SC*	SU	77641	62740	71668	77642
5833	N	F	*SC*	SU	77643	62741	71669	77644
5834	N	F	*SC*	SU	77645	62742	71670	77646
5835	N	F	*SC*	SU	77647	62738	71671	77648
5836	N	F	*SC*	SU	77649	62744	71672	77650
5837	N	F	*SC*	SU	77651	62745	71673	77652
5838	N	F	*SC*	SU	77653	62746	71674	77654
5839	N	F	*SC*	SU	77655	62747	71675	77656
5840	N	F	*SC*	SU	77657	62748	71676	77658
5841	N	F	*SC*	SU	77659	62749	71677	77660
5842	N	F	*SC*	SU	77661	62750	71678	77662
5843	N	F	*SC*	SU	77663	62751	71679	77664
5844	N	F	*SC*	SU	77665	62752	71680	77666
5845	N	F	*SC*	SU	77667	62753	71681	77668
5846	N	F	*SC*	SU	77669	62754	71682	77670
5847	N	P	*SW*	WD	77671	62755	71683	77672
5848	N	P	*SW*	WD	77673	62756	71684	77674
5849	N	P	*SW*	WD	77675	62757	71685	77676
5850	N	P	*SW*	WD	77677	62758	71686	77678
5851	N	P	*SW*	WD	77679	62759	71687	77680
5852	N	P	*SW*	WD	77681	62760	71688	77682
5853	N	P	*SW*	WD	77683	62761	71689	77684
5854	N	P	*SW*	WD	77685	62762	71690	77686
5855	N	P	*SW*	WD	77687	62763	71691	77688
5856	N	P	*SW*	WD	77689	62764	71692	77690
5857	N	P	*SW*	WD	77691	62765	71693	77692
5858	N	P	*SW*	WD	77693	62766	71694	77694
5859	N	P	*SW*	WD	77695	62767	71695	77696
5860	N	P	*SW*	WD	77697	62768	71696	77698
5861	N	P	*SW*	WD	77699	62769	71697	77700
5862	N	P	*SW*	WD	77701	62770	71698	77702
5863	N	P	*SW*	WD	77703	62771	71699	77704
5864	N	P	*SW*	WD	77705	62772	71700	77706

5865	**N**	P	*SW*	WD	77707	62773	71701	77708
5866	**N**	P	*SW*	WD	77709	62774	71702	77710
5867	**N**	P	*SW*	WD	77711	62775	71703	77712
5868	**N**	P	*SW*	WD	77713	62776	71704	77714
5869	**N**	P	*SW*	WD	77715	62777	71705	77716
5870	**N**	P	*SW*	WD	77717	62778	71706	77718
5871	**N**	P	*SW*	WD	77719	62779	71707	77720
5872	**N**	P	*SW*	WD	77721	62780	71708	77722
5873	**N**	P	*SW*	WD	77723	62781	71709	77724
5874	**N**	P	*SW*	WD	77725	62782	71710	77726

Class 455/9. Convection heating.

DTSO. Dia. EE226. Lot No. 30991 BREL York 1985. –/74. 29.5 t.
MSO. Dia. EC206. Lot No. 30992 BREL York 1985. –/84. 45.6 († 48.0) t.
71714–71733. TSO. Dia. EH224. Lot No. 30993 BREL York 1985. –/84. 27.1 t.
67400. TSO. Dia. EH236. Built as a DEMU vehicle to Lot No. 30932 BREL Derby 1981. Subsequently converted to EMU vehicle. –/84. 26.8 t.

5901		**ST**	P	*SW*	WD	77813	62826	71714	77814
5902		**ST**	P	*SW*	WD	77815	62827	71715	77816
5903		**ST**	P	*SW*	WD	77817	62828	71716	77818
5904		**ST**	P	*SW*	WD	77819	62829	71717	77820
5905		**ST**	P	*SW*	WD	77821	62830	71725	77822
5906		**ST**	P	*SW*	WD	77823	62831	71719	77824
5907		**ST**	P	*SW*	WD	77825	62832	71720	77826
5908		**ST**	P	*SW*	WD	77827	62833	71721	77828
5909		**ST**	P	*SW*	WD	77829	62834	71722	77830
5910		**ST**	P	*SW*	WD	77831	62835	71723	77832
5911		**ST**	P	*SW*	WD	77833	62836	71724	77834
5912	†	**N**	P		ZG(S)	77835	62837	71731*	77836
5913		**ST**	P	*SW*	WD	77837	62838	71726	77838
5914		**ST**	P	*SW*	WD	77839	62839	71727	77840
5915		**N**	P	*SW*	WD	77841	62840	71728	77842
5916		**ST**	P	*SW*	WD	77843	62841	71729	77844
5917		**N**	P	*SW*	WD	77845	62842	71730	77846
5918		**N**	P	*SW*	WD	77847	62843	71732*	77848
5919		**ST**	P	*SW*	WD	77849	62844	71718	77850
5920		**N**	P	*SW*	WD	77851	62845	71733	77852
Spare		**N**	P		WD(S)			67400	

CLASS 458   'Juniper'   4-Jop

DMCO(A)–PTSOL–MSOL–DMCO(B). Gangwayed throughout. Disc and regenerative brakes. Air conditioned.
Supply System: 750 V dc third rail (Provision for 25 kV a.c. 50 Hz overhead).
Traction Motors: Two Alstom of 270 kW each per power car.
Dimensions: 21.16 x 2.80 x   . m (DMCO), 19.94 x 2.80 x   . m (other cars).
Maximum Speed: 100 mph.   **Doors:** Power operated sliding plug.
Couplers: Tightlock.   **Bogies:** ACR.
Multiple Working:

DMCO(A). Dia. EA302. Alstom Birmingham 1998–2000. 12/63. 45.2 t.
PTSOL. Dia. EH250. Alstom Birmingham 1998–2000. –/49 1TD 2W. 33.3 t.
MSOL. Dia. EC226. Alstom Birmingham 1998–2000. –/75 1T. 40.6 t.
DMCO(B). Dia. EA303. Alstom Birmingham 1998–2000. 12/63. 45.2 t.

8001	U	P	*SW*	WD	67601	74001	74101	67701
8002	**SW**	P	*SW*		67602	74002	74102	67702
8003	**SW**	P	*SW*		67603	74003	74103	67703
8004	**SW**	P	*SW*		67604	74004	74104	67704
8005	**SW**	P	*SW*		67605	74005	74105	67705
8006	**SW**	P	*SW*		67606	74006	74106	67706
8007	**SW**	P	*SW*		67607	74007	74107	67707
8008	**SW**	P	*SW*		67608	74008	74108	67708
8009	**SW**	P	*SW*		67609	74009	74109	67709
8010	**SW**	P	*SW*		67610	74010	74110	67710
8011	**SW**	P	*SW*		67611	74011	74111	67711
8012	**SW**	P	*SW*		67612	74012	74112	67712
8013	**SW**	P	*SW*		67613	74013	74113	67713
8014	**SW**	P	*SW*		67614	74014	74114	67714
8015	**SW**	P	*SW*		67615	74015	74115	67715
8016	**SW**	P	*SW*		67616	74016	74116	67716
8017	**SW**	P	*SW*		67617	74017	74117	67717
8018	**SW**	P	*SW*		67618	74018	74118	67718
8019	**SW**	P	*SW*		67619	74019	74119	67719
8020	**SW**	P	*SW*		67620	74020	74120	67720
8021	**SW**	P	*SW*		67621	74021	74121	67721
8022	**SW**	P	*SW*		67622	74022	74122	67722
8023	**SW**	P	*SW*		67623	74023	74123	67723
8024	**SW**	P	*SW*		67624	74024	74124	67724
8025	**SW**	P	*SW*		67625	74025	74125	67724
8026	**SW**	P	*SW*		67626	74026	74126	67726
8027	**SW**	P	*SW*		67627	74027	74127	67727
8028	**SW**	P	*SW*		67628	74028	74128	67728
8029	**SW**	P	*SW*		67629	74029	74129	67729
8030	**SW**	P	*SW*		67630	74030	74130	67730

CLASS 488   2- or 3-Car Express Trailer Unit

TFOLH–TSOLH or TFOLH–TSOL–TSOLH. Gangwayed throughout. Air conditioned.

Dimensions: 20.38 x 2.84 x 3.79 m.
Maximum Speed: 90 mph.   **Doors:** Manually operated slam.
Couplings: Buckeye.   **Bogies:** B4.
Multiple Working: SR type.
Advertising Livery:
• Continental Airlines.

72500–72509. TFOLH. Dia. EP101. Built as loco-hauled vehicles to Lot No. 30859 Derby 1973–74. Converted BREL Eastleigh 1983–84. 41/– 1T. 35.0 t.
72602–14/6–8/20–44/6/7. TSOLH. Dia. EP201. Built as loco-hauled vehicles to Lot No. 30860 Derby 1973–74. Converted BREL Eastleigh 1983–84. –/48 1T. 35.0 t.
72615/19/45. TSOLH. Dia. EP201. Built as loco-hauled vehicles to Lot No. 30846 Derby 1973. Converted BREL Eastleigh 1983–84. –/48 1T. 35.0 t.

72701–72718. TSOL. Dia. EH290. Built as loco-hauled vehicles to Lot No. 30860 Derby 1973–74. Converted BREL Eastleigh 1983–84. –/48 1T. 35.0 t.

CLASS 488/2. 2-car units.

8201	**GX**	P	*GX*	SL	72500	72638
8202	**AL**	P	*GX*	SL	72501	72617
8203	**AL**	P	*GX*	SL	72502	72640
8204	**AL**	P	*GX*	SL	72503	72641
8205	**GX**	P	*GX*	SL	72504	72628
8206	**GX**	P	*GX*	SL	72505	72629
8207	**AL**	P	*GX*	SL	72506	72642
8208	**AL**	P	*GX*	SL	72507	72643
8209	**GX**	P	*GX*	SL	72508	72644
8210	**GX**	P	*GX*	SL	72509	72635

CLASS 488/3. 3-car units.

8302	**GX**	P	*GX*	SL	72602	72701	72604
8303	**GX**	P	*GX*	SL	72603	72702	72608
8304	**AL**	P	*GX*	SL	72606	72703	72611
8305	**AL**	P	*GX*	SL	72605	72704	72609
8306	**GX**	P	*GX*	SL	72607	72705	72610
8307	**GX**	P	*GX*	SL	72612	72706	72613
8308	**GX**	P	*GX*	SL	72614	72707	72615
8309	**GX**	P	*GX*	SL	72616	72708	72639
8310	**GX**	P	*GX*	SL	72618	72709	72619
8311	**GX**	P	*GX*	SL	72620	72710	72621
8312	**GX**	P	*GX*	SL	72622	72711	72623
8313	**GX**	P	*GX*	SL	72624	72712	72625
8314	**AL**	P	*GX*	SL	72626	72713	72627
8315	**GX**	P	*GX*	SL	72636	72714	72645
8316	**GX**	P	*GX*	SL	72630	72715	72631
8317	**GX**	P	*GX*	SL	72632	72716	72633
8318	**GX**	P	*GX*	SL	72634	72717	72637
8319	**AL**	P	*GX*	SL	72646	72718	72647

CLASS 489   Gatwick Luggage Van

DMLV. Gangwayed at non-driving end only. Operate with Class 488.
Traction Motors: Two English Electric EE507 of 185 kW each.
Dimensions: 20.45 x 2.82 x 3.86 m.
Maximum Speed: 90 mph.   **Doors:** Manually operated slam.
Couplings: Buckeye.   **Bogies:** B4.
Multiple Working: SR type.

DMLV. Dia. EB501. Built as DMBSO to Lot No. 30452 Eastleigh 1959. Converted BREL Eastleigh 1983–84. 40.5 t.

9101	**GX**	P	*GX*	SL	68500
9102	**GX**	P	*GX*	SL	68501
9103	**GX**	P	*GX*	SL	68502
9104	**GX**	P	*GX*	SL	68503
9105	**GX**	P	*GX*	SL	68504

9106	**GX**	P	*GX*	SL	68505
9107	**GX**	P	*GX*	SL	68506
9108	**GX**	P	*GX*	SL	68507
9109	**GX**	P	*GX*	SL	68508
9110	**GX**	P	*GX*	SL	68509

CLASS 424   Adtranz Classic Prototype

DTSO. Gangwayed within unit.

Dimensions: **Doors:** Power operated sliding.
Maximum Speed: 90 mph.   **Bogies:** B5 (SR).
Couplers: Tightlock.   **Multiple Working:**
Non Standard Livery:
• Silver with black window surrounds.

DTSO. Dia. EE280. Built as DTCsoL to Lot No. 30741 York 1963–66. Rebuilt Adtranz Derby 1997. –/77. 34.0 t.

| 424 001 | **0** | A | | ZD(S) | 76112 |

CLASS 456   2-Car Unit

DMSO–DTSO. Gangwayed within unit. Disc brakes.
Traction Motors: Two GEC507-20J of 185 kW each.
Dimensions: 19.95 x 2.82 x . m.
Maximum Speed: 75 mph.   **Doors:** Power operated sliding.
Couplers: Tightlock.   **Bogies:** P7 (DMSO), T3 (DTSO).
Multiple Working: Classes 455–457, 507 & 508.

DMSO. Dia. EA267. Lot No. 31073 BREL York 1990–91. –/79. 41.1 t.
DTSO. Dia. EE276. Lot No. 31074 BREL York 1990–91. –/73. 31.4 t.

456 001	**N**	P	*SC*	SU	64735	78250
456 002	**N**	P	*SC*	SU	64736	78251
456 003	**N**	P	*SC*	SU	64737	78252
456 004	**N**	P	*SC*	SU	64738	78253
456 005	**N**	P	*SC*	SU	64739	78254
456 006	**N**	P	*SC*	SU	64740	78255
456 007	**N**	P	*SC*	SU	64741	78256
456 008	**N**	P	*SC*	SU	64742	78257
456 009	**N**	P	*SC*	SU	64743	78258
456 010	**N**	P	*SC*	SU	64744	78259
456 011	**N**	P	*SC*	SU	64745	78260
456 012	**N**	P	*SC*	SU	64746	78261
456 013	**N**	P	*SC*	SU	64747	78262
456 014	**N**	P	*SC*	SU	64748	78263
456 015	**N**	P	*SC*	SU	64749	78264
456 016	**N**	P	*SC*	SU	64750	78265
456 017	**N**	P	*SC*	SU	64751	78266
456 018	**N**	P	*SC*	SU	64752	78267
456 019	**N**	P	*SC*	SU	64753	78268
456 020	**N**	P	*SC*	SU	64754	78269

456 021	N	P	SC	SU	64755	78270
456 022	N	P	SC	SU	64756	78271
456 023	N	P	SC	SU	64757	78272
456 024	CX	P	SC	SU	64758	78273

Name (carried on PTSO): 456 024 Sir Cosmo Bonsor

CLASS 465   'Networker'   4-car Unit

DMSO(A)–TSO–TSOL–DMSO(B). Gangwayed within unit. Disc, rheostatic and regenerative brakes.
Traction Motors: Four Brush or four GEC Alsthom G352BY of 280 kW each per motor car.
Dimensions: 20.89 x 2.81 x . m (DMSO), 20.06 x 2.81 x . m (other cars).
Maximum Speed: 75 mph.   **Doors:** Power operated sliding plug.
Couplers: Tightlock.   **Bogies:** P3 (DMSO) and T3 (other cars).
Multiple Working: Classes 365, 465 & 466.

64759–64808. DMSO(A). Dia. EA268. Lot No. 31100 BREL York 1992–93. –/86. 39.2 t.
64809–64858. DMSO(B). Dia. EA268. Lot No. 31100 BREL York 1992–93. –/86. 39.2 t.
65700–65749. DMSO(A). Dia. EA269. Lot No. 31103 GEC-A B'ham 1992–93. –/86. 38.8 t.
65750–65799. DMSO(B). Dia. EA269. Lot No. 31103 GEC-A B'ham 1992–93. –/86. 38.9 t.
65800–65846. DMSO(A). Dia. EA268. Lot No. 31130 ABB York 1993–94. –/86. 38.9 t.
65847–65893. DMSO(B). Dia. EA268. Lot No. 31130 ABB York 1993–94. –/86. 39.0 t.
72028–72126 (even numbers). TSO. Dia. EH293. Lot No. 31102 BREL York 1992–93. –/86. 30.4 t.
72029–72127 (odd numbers). TSOL. Dia. EH292. Lot No. 31101 BREL York 1992–93. –/86. 30.5 t.
72719–72817 (odd numbers). TSOL. Dia. EH294. Lot No. 31104 GEC-A Birmingham 1992–93. –/86. 30.2 t.
72720–72818 (even numbers). TSO. Dia. EH295. Lot No. 31105 GEC-A Birmingham 1992–93. –/86. 29.1 t.
72900–72992 (evens). TSO. Dia. EH293. Lot No. 31102 ABB York 1993–94. –/90. 29.5 t.
72901–72993 (odds). TSOL. Dia. EH294. Lot No. 31101 ABB York 1993–94. –/86. 30.2 t.

Class 465/0. First batch built by ABB. Brush traction motors.

465 001	CS	F	SE	SG	64759	72028	72029	64809
465 002	CS	F	SE	SG	64760	72030	72031	64810
465 003	CS	F	SE	SG	64761	72032	72033	64811
465 004	CS	F	SE	SG	64762	72034	72035	64812
465 005	CS	F	SE	SG	64763	72036	72037	64813
465 006	CS	F	SE	SG	64764	72038	72039	64814
465 007	CS	F	SE	SG	64765	72040	72041	64815
465 008	CS	F	SE	SG	64766	72042	72043	64816
465 009	CS	F	SE	SG	64767	72044	72045	64817
465 010	CS	F	SE	SG	64768	72046	72047	64818
465 011	CS	F	SE	SG	64769	72048	72049	64819
465 012	CS	F	SE	SG	64770	72050	72051	64820
465 013	CS	F	SE	SG	64771	72052	72053	64821
465 014	CS	F	SE	SG	64772	72054	72055	64822
465 015	CS	F	SE	SG	64773	72056	72057	64823
465 016	CS	F	SE	SG	64774	72058	72059	64824

465 017	**CS**	F	*SE*	SG	64775	72060	72061	64825
465 018	**CS**	F	*SE*	SG	64776	72062	72063	64826
465 019	**CS**	F	*SE*	SG	64777	72064	72065	64827
465 020	**CS**	F	*SE*	SG	64778	72066	72067	64828
465 021	**NT**	F	*SE*	SG	64779	72068	72069	64829
465 022	**NT**	F	*SE*	SG	64780	72070	72071	64830
465 023	**CS**	F	*SE*	SG	64781	72072	72073	64831
465 024	**NT**	F	*SE*	SG	64782	72074	72075	64832
465 025	**NT**	F	*SE*	SG	64783	72076	72077	64833
465 026	**NT**	F	*SE*	SG	64784	72078	72079	64834
465 027	**NT**	F	*SE*	SG	64785	72080	72081	64835
465 028	**NT**	F	*SE*	SG	64786	72082	72083	64836
465 029	**NT**	F	*SE*	SG	64787	72084	72085	64837
465 030	**NT**	F	*SE*	SG	64788	72086	72087	64838
465 031	**NT**	F	*SE*	SG	64789	72088	72089	64839
465 032	**NT**	F	*SE*	SG	64790	72090	72091	64840
465 033	**NT**	F	*SE*	SG	64791	72092	72093	64841
465 034	**NT**	F	*SE*	SG	64792	72094	72095	64842
465 035	**NT**	F	*SE*	SG	64793	72096	72097	64843
465 036	**NT**	F	*SE*	SG	64794	72098	72099	64844
465 037	**NT**	F	*SE*	SG	64795	72100	72101	64845
465 038	**NT**	F	*SE*	SG	64796	72102	72103	64846
465 039	**NT**	F	*SE*	SG	64797	72104	72105	64847
465 040	**NT**	F	*SE*	SG	64798	72106	72107	64848
465 041	**NT**	F	*SE*	SG	64799	72108	72109	64849
465 042	**NT**	F	*SE*	SG	64800	72110	72111	64850
465 043	**NT**	F	*SE*	SG	64801	72112	72113	64851
465 044	**NT**	F	*SE*	SG	64802	72114	72115	64852
465 045	**NT**	F	*SE*	SG	64803	72116	72117	64853
465 046	**NT**	F	*SE*	SG	64804	72118	72119	64854
465 047	**NT**	F	*SE*	SG	64805	72120	72121	64855
465 048	**NT**	F	*SE*	SG	64806	72122	72123	64856
465 049	**NT**	F	*SE*	SG	64807	72124	72125	64857
465 050	**NT**	F	*SE*	SG	64808	72126	72127	64858

Class 465/1. Second batch built by ABB. Brush traction motors.

465 151	**NT**	F	*SE*	SG	65800	72900	72901	65847
465 152	**NT**	F	*SE*	SG	65801	72902	72903	65848
465 153	**NT**	F	*SE*	SG	65802	72904	72905	65849
465 154	**NT**	F	*SE*	SG	65803	72906	72907	65850
465 155	**NT**	F	*SE*	SG	65804	72908	72909	65851
465 156	**NT**	F	*SE*	SG	65805	72910	72911	65852
465 157	**NT**	F	*SE*	SG	65806	72912	72913	65853
465 158	**NT**	F	*SE*	SG	65807	72914	72915	65854
465 159	**NT**	F	*SE*	SG	65808	72916	72917	65855
465 160	**NT**	F	*SE*	SG	65809	72918	72919	65856
465 161	**NT**	F	*SE*	SG	65810	72920	72921	65857
465 162	**NT**	F	*SE*	SG	65811	72922	72923	65858
465 163	**NT**	F	*SE*	SG	65812	72924	72925	65859
465 164	**NT**	F	*SE*	SG	65813	72926	72927	65860
465 165	**NT**	F	*SE*	SG	65814	72928	72929	65861

465 166	**NT**	F	*SE*	SG	65815	72930	72931	65862
465 167	**NT**	F	*SE*	SG	65816	72932	72933	65863
465 168	**NT**	F	*SE*	SG	65817	72934	72935	65864
465 169	**NT**	F	*SE*	SG	65818	72936	72937	65865
465 170	**NT**	F	*SE*	SG	65819	72938	72939	65866
465 171	**NT**	F	*SE*	SG	65820	72940	72941	65867
465 172	**NT**	F	*SE*	SG	65821	72942	72943	65868
465 173	**NT**	F	*SE*	SG	65822	72944	72945	65869
465 174	**NT**	F	*SE*	SG	65823	72946	72947	65870
465 175	**NT**	F	*SE*	SG	65824	72948	72949	65871
465 176	**NT**	F	*SE*	SG	65825	72950	72951	65872
465 177	**NT**	F	*SE*	SG	65826	72952	72953	65873
465 178	**NT**	F	*SE*	SG	65827	72954	72955	65874
465 179	**NT**	F	*SE*	SG	65828	72956	72957	65875
465 180	**NT**	F	*SE*	SG	65829	72958	72959	65876
465 181	**NT**	F	*SE*	SG	65830	72960	72961	65877
465 182	**NT**	F	*SE*	SG	65831	72962	72963	65878
465 183	**NT**	F	*SE*	SG	65832	72964	72965	65879
465 184	**NT**	F	*SE*	SG	65833	72966	72967	65880
465 185	**NT**	F	*SE*	SG	65834	72968	72969	65881
465 186	**NT**	F	*SE*	SG	65835	72970	72971	65882
465 187	**NT**	F	*SE*	SG	65836	72972	72973	65883
465 188	**NT**	F	*SE*	SG	65837	72974	72975	65884
465 189	**NT**	F	*SE*	SG	65838	72976	72977	65885
465 190	**NT**	F	*SE*	SG	65839	72978	72979	65886
465 191	**NT**	F	*SE*	SG	65840	72980	72981	65887
465 192	**NT**	F	*SE*	SG	65841	72982	72983	65888
465 193	**NT**	F	*SE*	SG	65842	72984	72985	65889
465 194	**NT**	F	*SE*	SG	65843	72986	72987	65890
465 195	**NT**	F	*SE*	SG	65844	72988	72989	65891
465 196	**NT**	F	*SE*	SG	65845	72990	72991	65892
465 197	**NT**	F	*SE*	SG	65846	72992	72993	65893

Class 465/2. Built by GEC Alsthom. GEC traction motors.

465 201	**NT**	A	*SE*	SG	65700	72719	72720	65750
465 202	**NT**	A	*SE*	SG	65701	72721	72722	65751
465 203	**NT**	A	*SE*	SG	65702	72723	72724	65752
465 204	**NT**	A	*SE*	SG	65703	72725	72726	65753
465 205	**NT**	A	*SE*	SG	65704	72727	72728	65754
465 206	**NT**	A	*SE*	SG	65705	72729	72730	65755
465 207	**NT**	A	*SE*	SG	65706	72731	72732	65756
465 208	**NT**	A	*SE*	SG	65707	72733	72734	65757
465 209	**NT**	A	*SE*	SG	65708	72735	72736	65758
465 210	**NT**	A	*SE*	SG	65709	72737	72738	65759
465 211	**NT**	A	*SE*	SG	65710	72739	72740	65760
465 212	**NT**	A	*SE*	SG	65711	72741	72742	65761
465 213	**NT**	A	*SE*	SG	65712	72743	72744	65762
465 214	**NT**	A	*SE*	SG	65713	72745	72746	65763
465 215	**NT**	A	*SE*	SG	65714	72747	72748	65764
465 216	**NT**	A	*SE*	SG	65715	72749	72750	65765
465 217	**NT**	A	*SE*	SG	65716	72751	72752	65766

465 218	NT	A	SE	SG	65717	72753	72754	65767
465 219	NT	A	SE	SG	65718	72755	72756	65768
465 220	NT	A	SE	SG	65719	72757	72758	65769
465 221	NT	A	SE	SG	65720	72759	72760	65770
465 222	NT	A	SE	SG	65721	72761	72762	65771
465 223	NT	A	SE	SG	65722	72763	72764	65772
465 224	NT	A	SE	SG	65723	72765	72766	65773
465 225	NT	A	SE	SG	65724	72767	72768	65774
465 226	NT	A	SE	SG	65725	72769	72770	65775
465 227	NT	A	SE	SG	65726	72771	72772	65776
465 228	NT	A	SE	SG	65727	72773	72774	65777
465 229	NT	A	SE	SG	65728	72775	72776	65778
465 230	NT	A	SE	SG	65729	72777	72778	65779
465 231	NT	A	SE	SG	65730	72779	72780	65780
465 232	NT	A	SE	SG	65731	72781	72782	65781
465 233	NT	A	SE	SG	65732	72783	72784	65782
465 234	NT	A	SE	SG	65733	72785	72786	65783
465 235	NT	A	SE	SG	65734	72787	72788	65784
465 236	NT	A	SE	SG	65735	72789	72790	65785
465 237	NT	A	SE	SG	65736	72791	72792	65786
465 238	NT	A	SE	SG	65737	72793	72794	65787
465 239	NT	A	SE	SG	65738	72795	72796	65788
465 240	NT	A	SE	SG	65739	72797	72798	65789
465 241	NT	A	SE	SG	65740	72799	72800	65790
465 242	NT	A	SE	SG	65741	72801	72802	65791
465 243	NT	A	SE	SG	65742	72803	72804	65792
465 244	NT	A	SE	SG	65743	72805	72806	65793
465 245	NT	A	SE	SG	65744	72807	72808	65794
465 246	NT	A	SE	SG	65745	72809	72810	65795
465 247	NT	A	SE	SG	65746	72811	72812	65796
465 248	NT	A	SE	SG	65747	72813	72814	65797
465 249	NT	A	SE	SG	65748	72815	72816	65798
465 250	NT	A	SE	SG	65749	72817	72818	65799

CLASS 466   Networker 2-Car Unit

DMSO–DTSO. Gangwayed within unit. Disc, rheostatic and regenerative brakes.

Traction Motors: Four GEC Alsthom G352BYof 280 kW each.
Dimensions: 20.89 x 2.81 x . m (DMSO), 20.06 x 2.81 x . m (other cars).
Maximum Speed: 75 mph.   **Doors:** Power operated sliding plug.
Couplers: Tightlock.   **Bogies:** P3 (DMSO) and T3 (other cars).
Multiple Working: Classes 365, 465 & 466.

DMSO. Dia. EA271. Lot No. 31128 GEC Alsthom Birmingham 1993–94. –/86. 38.8 t.
DTSO. Dia. EE279. Lot No. 31129 GEC Alsthom Birmingham 1993–94. –/82. 33.2 t.

466 001	NT	A	SE	SG	64860	78312
466 002	NT	A	SE	SG	64861	78313
466 003	NT	A	SE	SG	64862	78314
466 004	NT	A	SE	SG	64863	78315
466 005	NT	A	SE	SG	64864	78316

466 006	**NT**	A	*SE*	SG	64865	78317
466 007	**NT**	A	*SE*	SG	64866	78318
466 008	**NT**	A	*SE*	SG	64867	78319
466 009	**NT**	A	*SE*	SG	64868	78320
466 010	**NT**	A	*SE*	SG	64869	78321
466 011	**NT**	A	*SE*	SG	64870	78322
466 012	**NT**	A	*SE*	SG	64871	78323
466 013	**NT**	A	*SE*	SG	64872	78324
466 014	**NT**	A	*SE*	SG	64873	78325
466 015	**NT**	A	*SE*	SG	64874	78326
466 016	**NT**	A	*SE*	SG	64875	78327
466 017	**NT**	A	*SE*	SG	64876	78328
466 018	**NT**	A	*SE*	SG	64877	78329
466 019	**NT**	A	*SE*	SG	64878	78330
466 020	**NT**	A	*SE*	SG	64879	78331
466 021	**NT**	A	*SE*	SG	64880	78332
466 022	**NT**	A	*SE*	SG	64881	78333
466 023	**NT**	A	*SE*	SG	64882	78334
466 024	**NT**	A	*SE*	SG	64883	78335
466 025	**NT**	A	*SE*	SG	64884	78336
466 026	**NT**	A	*SE*	SG	64885	78337
466 027	**NT**	A	*SE*	SG	64886	78338
466 028	**NT**	A	*SE*	SG	64887	78339
466 029	**NT**	A	*SE*	SG	64888	78340
466 030	**NT**	A	*SE*	SG	64889	78341
466 031	**NT**	A	*SE*	SG	64890	78342
466 032	**NT**	A	*SE*	SG	64891	78343
466 033	**NT**	A	*SE*	SG	64892	78344
466 034	**NT**	A	*SE*	SG	64893	78345
466 035	**NT**	A	*SE*	SG	64894	78346
466 036	**NT**	A	*SE*	SG	64895	78347
466 037	**NT**	A	*SE*	SG	64896	78348
466 038	**NT**	A	*SE*	SG	64897	78349
466 039	**NT**	A	*SE*	SG	64898	78350
466 040	**NT**	A	*SE*	SG	64899	78351
466 041	**NT**	A	*SE*	SG	64900	78352
466 042	**NT**	A	*SE*	SG	64901	78353
466 043	**NT**	A	*SE*	SG	64902	78354

CLASS 507   Merseyrail 3-Car Unit

BDMSO–TSO–DMSO. Gangwayed within unit. End doors. Disc & rheostatic brakes.
Traction Motors: Four GEC G310AZ of 82.125 kW per power car.
Dimensions: 20.02 x 2.82 x 3.58 m (outer cars), 19.92 x 2.82 x 3.58 m (inner car).
Maximum Speed: 75 mph.   **Doors:** Power operated sliding.
Couplers: Tightlock.   **Bogies:** BX1.
Multiple Working: Classes 455–457, 507 & 508.

BDMSO. Dia. EI202. Lot No. 30906 York 1978–80. –/74. 37.1 t.
TSO. Dia. EH205. Lot No. 30907 York 1978–80. –/82. 25.6 t.
DMSO. Dia. EA201. Lot No. 30908 York 1978–80. –/74. 35.6 t.

507 001	MT	A	MT	BD	64367	71342	64405
507 002	MT	A	MT	BD	64368	71343	64406
507 003	MT	A	MT	BD	64369	71344	64407
507 004	MT	A	MT	BD	64388	71345	64408
507 005	MT	A	MT	BD	64371	71346	64409
507 006	MT	A	MT	BD	64372	71347	64410
507 007	MT	A	MT	BD	64373	71348	64411
507 008	MT	A	MT	BD	64374	71349	64412
507 009	MT	A	MT	BD	64375	71350	64413
507 010	MT	A	MT	BD	64376	71351	64414
507 011	MT	A	MT	BD	64377	71352	64415
507 012	MT	A	MT	BD	64378	71353	64416
507 013	MT	A	MT	BD	64379	71354	64417
507 014	MT	A	MT	BD	64380	71355	64418
507 015	MT	A	MT	BD	64381	71356	64419
507 016	MT	A	MT	BD	64382	71357	64420
507 017	MT	A	MT	BD	64383	71358	64421
507 018	MT	A	MT	BD	64384	71359	64422
507 019	MT	A	MT	BD	64385	71360	64423
507 020	MT	A	MT	BD	64386	71361	64424
507 021	MT	A	MT	BD	64387	71362	64425
507 023	MT	A	MT	BD	64389	71364	64427
507 024	MT	A	MT	BD	64390	71365	64428
507 025	MT	A	MT	BD	64391	71366	64429
507 026	MT	A	MT	BD	64392	71367	64430
507 027	MT	A	MT	BD	64393	71368	64431
507 028	MT	A	MT	BD	64394	71369	64432
507 029	MT	A	MT	BD	64395	71370	64433
507 030	MT	A	MT	BD	64396	71371	64434
507 031	MT	A	MT	BD	64397	71372	64435
507 032	MT	A	MT	BD	64398	71373	64436
507 033	MT	A	MT	BD	64399	71374	64437

CLASS 508   3-Car Unit

DMSO–TSO–BDMSO. Gangwayed within unit. End doors. Disc & rheostatic brakes.
Traction Motors: Four GEC G310AZ of 82.125 kW per power car.
Dimensions: 20.02 x 2.82 x 3.58 m (outer cars), 19.92 x 2.82 x 3.58 m (inner car).
Maximum Speed: 75 mph.   **Doors:** Power operated sliding.
Couplers: Tightlock.   **Bogies:** BX1.
Multiple Working: Classes 455–457, 507 & 508.

Class 508/1. Standard design.

DMSO. Dia. EA208. Lot No. 30979 BREL York 1979–80. –/68. 36.2 t.
TSO. Dia. EH218. Lot No. 30980 BREL York 1979–80. –/86. 26.7 t.
BDMSO. Dia. EI203. Lot No. 30981 BREL York 1979–80. –/68. 36.6 t.

508 102	MT	A		WK(S)	64650	71484	64693
508 103	MT	A	MT	BD	64651	71485	64694
508 104	MT	A	MT	BD	64652	71486	64695
508 108	MT	A		BC(S)	64656	71490	64699

508 110	**MT**	A		SO(S)	64658	71492	64701
508 111	**MT**	A	*MT*	BD	64659	71493	64702
508 112	**MT**	A	*MT*	BD	64660	71494	64703
508 114	**MT**	A	*MT*	BD	64662	71496	64705
508 115	**MT**	A	*MT*	BD	64663	71497	64706
508 117	**MT**	A	*MT*	BD	64665	71499	64708
508 118	**MT**	A		KK(S)	64666	71500	64709
508 120	**MT**	A		KK(S)	64668	71502	64711
508 122	**MT**	A		KK(S)	64670	71504	64713
508 123	**MT**	A		BC(S)	64671	71505	64714
508 124	**MT**	A	*MT*	BD	64672	71506	64715
508 125	**MT**	A	*MT*	BD	64673	71507	64716
508 126	**MT**	A	*MT*	BD	64674	71508	64717
508 127	**MT**	A	*MT*	BD	64675	71509	64718
508 128	**MT**	A	*MT*	BD	64676	71510	64719
508 130	**MT**	A	*MT*	BD	64678	71512	64721
508 131	**MT**	A		KK(S)	64679	71513	64722
508 134	**MT**	A	*MT*	BD	64682	71516	64725
508 135	**MT**	A		NB(S)	64683	71517	64726
508 136	**MT**	A	*MT*	BD	64684	71518	64727
508 137	**MT**	A	*MT*	BD	64685	71519	64728
508 138	**MT**	A	*MT*	BD	64686	71520	64729
508 139	**MT**	A	*MT*	BD	64687	71521	64730
508 140	**MT**	A	*MT*	BD	64688	71522	64731
508 141	**MT**	A	*MT*	BD	64689	71523	64732
508 142	**MT**	A		WK(S)	64690	71524	64733
508 143	**MT**	A	*MT*	BD	64691	71525	64734

Class 508/2. Facelifted units for Connex South Eastern.

DMSO. Dia. EA211. Lot No. 30979 BREL York 1979–80. –/66. 36.2 t.
TSO. Dia. EH246. Lot No. 30980 BREL York 1979–80. –/79. 26.7 t.
BDMSO. Dia. EI204. Lot No. 30981 BREL York 1979–80. –/74. 36.6 t.

508 201	(508 101)	**CX**	A	*SE*	GI	64649	71483 64692
508 202	(508 105)	**CX**	A	*SE*	GI	64653	71487 64696
508 203	(508 106)	**CX**	A	*SE*	GI	64654	71488 64697
508 204	(508 107)	**CX**	A	*SE*	GI	64655	71489 64698
508 205	(508 109)	**CX**	A	*SE*	GI	64657	71491 64700
508 206	(508 113)	**CX**	A	*SE*	GI	64661	71495 64714
508 207	(508 116)	**CX**	A	*SE*	GI	64664	71498 64707
508 208	(508 119)	**CX**	A	*SE*	GI	64667	71501 64710
508 209	(508 121)	**CX**	A	*SE*	GI	64669	71503 64712
508 210	(508 129)	**CX**	A	*SE*	GI	64677	71511 64720
508 211	(508 132)	**CX**	A	*SE*	GI	64680	71514 64723
508 212	(508 133)	**CX**	A	*SE*	GI	64681	71515 64724

4.3. EUROSTAR EMUS (CLASS 373)

Eurostar EMUs are used on services between Britain and Continental Europe via the Channel Tunnel.

Each train consists of two Eurostar sets coupled, with a power car at each driving end. Services starting from/terminating at London Waterloo are formed of two 9-car sets coupled, whilst those to/from other British destinations (yet to commence) will be formed of two 7-car sets coupled. All sets are articulated with an extra motor bogie on the coach adjacent to the power car.

DM–MSOL–4TSOL–RB–2TFOL–TBFOL or DM–MSOL–3TSOL–RB–TFOL–TBFOL. Gangwayed within pair of units. Air conditioned.

Supply Systems: 25 kV a.c. 50 Hz overhead or 3000 V d.c. overhead or 750 V d.c. third rail (* also equipped for 1500 V d.c. overhead operation).
Wheel Arrangement: Bo–Bo + Bo–2–2–2–2–2–2–2–2.
Length: 22.15 m (DM), 21.85 m (MSOL & TBFOL), 18.70 m (other cars).
Maximum Speed: 300 km/h.
Built: 1992-93 by GEC Alsthom/Brush/ANF/De Dietrich/BN Construction/ACEC.
Note: DM vehicles carry the set numbers indicated below. No other external vehicle numbers are carried, hence allocated individual car numbers are not shown in this publication.

10-Car Sets. Built for services starting from/terminating at London Waterloo. Individual vehicles in each set are allocated numbers 7xxxx0 + 7xxxx1 + 7xxxx2 + 7xxxx3 + 7xxxx4 + 7xxxx5 + 7xxxx6 + 7xxxx8 + 7xxxx9, where xxxx denotes the set number.

DM. Dia. LA501. Lot No. 31118 1992–95. 68.5 t.
MSOL. Dia. LB202. Lot No. 31119 1992–95. –/52 1T. 44.6 t.
73xxx2 series TSOL. Dia. LC202. Lot No. 31120 1992–95. –/60 1T. 28.1 t.
73xxx3 series TSOL. Dia. LD202. Lot No. 31121 1992–95. –/60 2T. 29.7 t.
73xxx4 series TSOL. Dia. LE202. Lot No. 31122 1992–95. –/60 1T. 28.3 t.
73xxx5 series TSOL. Dia. LF202. Lot No. 31123 1992–95. –/60S 2T. 29.2 t.
RB. Dia. LG502. Lot No.31124 1992–95. 31.1 t.
73xxx7 series TFOL. Dia. LH102. Lot No. 31125 1992–95. 39/– 1T. 29.6 t.
73xxx8 series TFOL. Dia. LJ102. Lot No. 31126 1992–95. 39/– 1T. 32.2 t.
TBFOL. Dia. LK102. Lot No. 31127 1992–95. 27/– 1TD. 39.4 t.

3001	**EU**	EU	*EU*	NP		3014	**EU**	EU	*EU*	NP
3002	**EU**	EU	*EU*	NP		3015	**EU**	EU	*EU*	NP
3003	**EU**	EU	*EU*	NP		3016	**EU**	EU	*EU*	NP
3004	**EU**	EU	*EU*	NP		3017	**EU**	EU	*EU*	NP
3005	**EU**	EU	*EU*	NP		3018	**EU**	EU	*EU*	NP
3006	**EU**	EU	*EU*	NP		3019	**EU**	EU	*EU*	NP
3007	**EU**	EU	*EU*	NP		3020	**EU**	EU	*EU*	NP
3008	**EU**	EU	*EU*	NP		3021	**EU**	EU	*EU*	NP
3009	**EU**	EU	*EU*	NP		3022	**EU**	EU	*EU*	NP
3010	**EU**	EU	*EU*	NP		3101	**EU**	SB	*EU*	FF
3011	**EU**	EU	*EU*	NP		3102	**EU**	SB	*EU*	FF
3012	**EU**	EU	*EU*	NP		3103	**EU**	SB	*EU*	FF
3013	**EU**	EU	*EU*	NP		3104	**EU**	SB	*EU*	FF

3105	**EU**	SB	*EU*	FF	3215*	**EU**	SF	*EU*	LY
3106	**EU**	SB	*EU*	FF	3216*	**EU**	SF	*EU*	LY
3107	**EU**	SB	*EU*	FF	3217	**EU**	SF	*EU*	LY
3108	**EU**	SB	*EU*	FF	3218	**EU**	SF	*EU*	LY
3201	* **EU**	SF	*EU*	LY	3219	**EU**	SF	*EU*	LY
3202	* **EU**	SF	*EU*	LY	3220	**EU**	SF	*EU*	LY
3203	* **EU**	SF	*EU*	LY	3221	**EU**	SF	*EU*	LY
3204	* **EU**	SF	*EU*	LY	3222	**EU**	SF	*EU*	LY
3205	**EU**	SF	*EU*	LY	3223	**EU**	SF	*EU*	LY
3206	**EU**	SF	*EU*	LY	3224	**EU**	SF	*EU*	LY
3207	* **EU**	SF	*EU*	LY	3225*	**EU**	SF	*EU*	LY
3208	* **EU**	SF	*EU*	LY	3226*	**EU**	SF	*EU*	LY
3209	**EU**	SF	*EU*	LY	3227*	**EU**	SF	*EU*	LY
3210	**EU**	SF	*EU*	LY	3228*	**EU**	SF	*EU*	LY
3211	**EU**	SF	*EU*	LY	3229	**EU**	SF	*EU*	LY
3212	**EU**	SF	*EU*	LY	3230	**EU**	SF	*EU*	LY
3213	**EU**	SF	*EU*	LY	3231	**EU**	SF	*EU*	LY
3214	**EU**	SF	*EU*	LY	3232	**EU**	SF	*EU*	LY

8-Car Sets. Built for Regional Eurostar services. Individual vehicles in each set are allocated numbers 7xxxx0 + 7xxxx1 + 7xxxx3 + 7xxxx2 + 7xxxx5 + 7xxxx6 + 7xxxx7 + 7xxxx9, where xxxx denotes the set number.

DM. Dia. LA502. 68.5 t.
MSOL. Dia. LB203. –/48 1T. 44.6 t.
733xx3 series TSOL. Dia. LD203. –/58 2T. 29.7 t.
733xx2 series TSOL. Dia. LC203. –/58 1T. 28.1 t.
733xx5 series TSOL. Dia. LF203. –/58 1T. 29.2 t.
RB. Dia. LG503. 31.1 t.
733xxx7 series TFOL. Dia. LH103. 39/– 1T. 29.6 t.
TBFOL. Dia. LK103. 18/– 1TD. 39.4 t.

3301	**EU**	EU	*EU*	NP	3308	**EU**	EU	*EU*	NP
3302	**EU**	EU	*EU*	NP	3309	**EU**	EU	*EU*	NP
3303	**EU**	EU	*EU*	NP	3310	**EU**	EU	*EU*	NP
3304	**EU**	EU	*EU*	NP	3311	**EU**	EU	*EU*	NP
3305	**EU**	EU	*EU*	NP	3312	**EU**	EU	*EU*	NP
3306	**EU**	EU	*EU*	NP	3313	**EU**	EU	*EU*	NP
3307	**EU**	EU	*EU*	NP	3314	**EU**	EU	*EU*	NP

Spare DM:

3999	**EU**	EU	*EU*	NP

4.4. SERVICE EMUS

CLASS 305/9   3-Car Sandite & Route Learning Unit

BDT–MB–DT. Gangwayed within unit. Converted from Class 305/1.
Supply System: 25 kV a.c. 50 Hz overhead.
Traction Motors: Four GEC WT380 of 153 kW each.
Dimensions: 20.35 x 2.82 x 3.84 m (DT), 20.18 x 2.82 x 3.84 m (MB).
Maximum Speed: 75 mph.   **Doors:** Manually operated slam.
Couplings: Buckeye.   **Bogies:** Gresley.
Multiple Working: Classes 303–312 only.

BDT. Dia. EZ535. Lot No. 30570 York 1960. Converted by BR, Ilford. 34.5 t.
MB. Dia. EZ534. Lot No. 30571 York 1960. Converted by BR, Ilford. 56.4 t.
DT. Dia. EZ535. Lot No. 30572 York 1960. Converted by BR, Ilford. 31.5 t.

305 908	**N**	RT	*RT*	IL	977741 977742 977743

CLASS 316   3-Car Test Unit

PBDTB–MSO–DTCOL. Gangwayed within unit. Converted from Class 307. Test
bed for Class 323 electrical equipment.
Supply System: 25 kV a.c. 50 Hz overhead or 750 V d.c. third rail.
Traction Motors: Four Holec DMKT52/24 of 146 kW each.
Dimensions: 20.31 x 2.82 x 3.86 (outer cars); 20.18 x 2.82 x 3.86 m (MSO).
Maximum Speed: 75 mph.   **Doors:** Manually operated slam.
Couplings: Buckeye.   **Bogies:** B5–Gresley–B4.
Multiple Working:
PBDTB. Dia. EZ . Lot No. 30205 Eastleigh 1954–56. Converted BR, Derby 1992. . t.
M. Dia. EZ . Lot No. 30203 Eastleigh 1954–56. Converted BR, Derby 1992. . t.
DT. Dia. EZ . Lot No. 30206 Eastleigh 1954–56. Converted BR, Derby 1992. . t.

316 997	**BG**	SO	*SO*	ZA	75118 61018 75018

CLASS 930/0   2-Car Sandite & De-icing Units

DMB–DMB. Gangwayed within unit. Converted from Class 405.
Supply System: 750 V d.c. third rail.
Traction Motors: Two English Electric EE507 of 185 kW each per car.
Dimensions: 19.05 x 2.74 x 3.99 m.   **Multiple Working:** SR type.
Maximum Speed: 75 mph.   **Doors:** Manually operated slam.
Couplings: Buckeye.   **Bogies:** SR design.

DMB. Dia. EZ512. Various Lot Nos. Eastleigh 1946–51. 39.0 t.

930 001	**RK**	RT		AF(S)	975596 975605
930 002	**RK**	RT	*RT*	RE	975896 975897
930 003	**RK**	RT	*RT*	SU	975594 975595
930 004	**RK**	RT	*RT*	WD	975586 975587
930 005	**RT**	RT	*RT*	WD	975588 975589

930 006	**RK**	RT	*RT*	WD	975590	975591
930 007	**RK**	RT	*RT*	GI	975592	975593
930 008	**RT**	RT	*RT*	GI	975604	975597
930 009	**N**	RT	*RT*	BI	975598	975599
930 010	**RT**	RT	*RT*	BI	975600	975601
930 011	**RK**	RT	*RT*	SU	975602	975603

CLASS 930/0   Sandite & De-icing Trailers

DT. Non gangwayed. Converted from Class 416/2.
Dimensions: 20.44 x 2.82 x 3.86 m.   **Bogies:** Mk. 3D.
Maximum Speed: 75 mph.   **Doors:** Manually operated slam.
Couplings: Buckeye with additional Tightlock at non driving ends only.
Multiple Working: With Classes 317 and 319.

DT. Dia. EZ526. Lot No. 30117 Eastleigh 1954. 32.5 t.

| 930 078 | **RK** | RT | *RT* | HE | 977578 |
| 930 079 | **N** | RT | *RT* | SU | 977579 |

CLASS 930/0   3-Car Route Learning Unit

DM–TB–DM. Gangwayed within unit. Converted from Class 411/4.
Supply System: 750 V d.c. third rail.   **Dimensions:** 20.34 x 2.82 x 3.83 m.
Traction Motors: Two English Electric EE507 of 185 kW each per power car.
Maximum Speed: 90 mph.   **Doors:** Manually operated slam.
Couplings: Buckeye.   **Multiple Working:** SR type.
Bogies: Mk. 4 (motor), Commonwealth (unpowered).

977861. DM. Dia. EZ536. Lot No. 30111 Eastleigh 1956. 44.2 t.
TB. Dia. EZ542. Lot No. 30110 Eastleigh 1956. 36.2 t.
977862. DM. Dia. EZ536. Lot No. 30108 Eastleigh 1956. 43.5 t.

| 930 082 | **CX** | SC | *OT* | SU | 977861 | 977862 | 977863 |

CLASS 930/1   2-Car Tractor Unit

DMB–DMB. Gangwayed within unit.
Supply System: 750 V d.c. third rail.
Traction Motors: Two English Electric EE507 of 185 kW each per power car.
Dimensions: 20.42 x 2.82 x 3.86 m.
Maximum Speed: 90 mph.   **Doors:** Manually operated slam.
Couplings: Buckeye.   **Multiple Working:** SR type.
Bogies: Mk. 4 or Mk. 3B (motor), Commonwealth (unpowered).

977609. DMB. Dia. EZ522. Lot No. 30617 Eastleigh 1961. 40.5 t.
977207. DMB. Dia. EZ522. Lot No. 30388 Eastleigh 1958. 40.5 t.

| 930 101 | **N** | RT | | AF(S) | 977207 | 977609 |

CLASS 930/1   2-Car Sandite Unit

DMB–DMB. Gangwayed within unit. Converted from Class 416.
Supply System: 750 V d.c. third rail.
Traction Motors: Two English Electric EE507 of 185 kW each per power car.
Dimensions: 19.23 x 2.74 x 3.99 m.   **Multiple Working:** SR type.
Maximum Speed: 75 mph.   **Doors:** Manually operated slam.
Couplings: Buckeye.   **Bogies:** Central 40 inch.

977533. DMB. Dia. EZ512. Lot No. 4016 Eastleigh 1954–55. 40.5 t.
977534. DMB. Dia. EZ512. Lot No. 4099 Eastleigh 1955–56. 40.5 t.

| 930 102 | **RK** | RT | *RT* | FR | 977533 977534 |

CLASS 930/2   2-Car Sandite & De-icing Unit

DMB–DMB. Gangwayed within unit. Converted from Class 416/2.
Supply System: 750 V d.c. third rail.
Traction Motors: Two English Electric EE507 of 185 kW each per power car.
Dimensions: 20.44 x 2.82 x 3.86 m.   **Doors:** Manually operated slam.
Maximum Speed: 75 mph.   **Bogies:** Mark 3B.
Couplings: Buckeye.   **Multiple Working:** SR type.

977566/567. DMB. Dia. EZ525. Lot No. 30116 Eastleigh 1954–55. 40.5 t.
977804/864. DMB. Dia. EZ522. Lot No. 30119 Eastleigh 1954. 40.5 t.
977805/865/871. DMB. Dia. EZ522. Lot No. 30167 Eastleigh 1955. 40.5 t.
977872/924/925. DMB. Dia. EZ522. Lot. No. 30314. Eastleigh 1956–58. 40.5 t.
977874/875. DMB. Dia. EZ522. Lot No. 30114 Eastleigh 1954. 40.5 t.

930 201	**RK**	RT	*RT*	FR	977566 977567
930 202	**RK**	RT	*RT*	FR	977804 977805
930 203	**RK**	RT	*RT*	RE	977864 977865
930 204	**N**	RT	*RT*	RE	977874 977875
930 205	**RK**	RT	*RT*	RE	977871 977872
930 206	**RK**	RT	*RT*	WD	977924 977925

CLASS 931   2-Car Route Learning Unit

DT–DMB or DMB–DT. Gangwayed within unit. Converted from Class 416/2.
Supply System: 750 V d.c. third rail.
Traction Motors: Two English Electric EE507 of 185 kW each.
Dimensions: 20.44 x 2.82 x 3.86 m.   **Doors:** Manually operated slam.
Maximum Speed: 75 mph.   **Bogies:** Mark 3B.
Couplings: Buckeye.   **Multiple Working:** SR type.

977856. DT. Dia. EZ541. Lot No. 30168 Eastleigh 1955. 30.5 t.
977857. DMB. Dia. EZ522. Lot No. 30167 Eastleigh 1955. 40.5 t.
977917. DMB. Dia. EZ541. Lot No. 30119 Eastleigh 1954. 40.5 t.
977918. DT. Dia. EZ541. Lot No. 30120 Eastleigh 1954. 30.5 t.

| 931 001 | **N** | SE | *OT* | RE | 977856 977857 |
| 931 002 | **N** | SE | *OT* | RE | 977917 977918 |

CLASS 931 2-Car Tractor Unit

DMB–DMB. Gangwayed within unit. Converted from Class 416/2.
Supply System: 750 V d.c. third rail.
Traction Motors: Two English Electric EE507 of 185 kW each per power car.
Dimensions: 20.44 x 2.82 x 3.86 m.
Maximum Speed: 75 mph. **Doors:** Manually operated slam.
Couplings: Buckeye. **Bogies:** Mark 3B.
Multiple Working: SR type.

DMB. Dia. EZ525. Lot No. 30116 Eastleigh 1954-55. 40.5 t.

931 062	**N**	SE	*OT*	RE	977559 977560	The Sprinkler

CLASS 931 Tractor Unit

DM. Non gangwayed. Previously Class 419.
Supply System: 750 V d.c. third rail or battery power.
Traction Motors: Four English Electric EE507 of 185 kW each per power car.
Dimensions: 19.64 x 2.82 x 3.86 m.
Maximum Speed: 90 mph. **Doors:** Manually operated slam.
Couplings: Buckeye. **Bogies:** Mark 3B.
Multiple Working: SR type.

68002. DM. Dia. EX560. Lot No. 30458 Eastleigh 1959. 45.5 t.
68003–68010. DM. Dia. EX560. Lot No. 30623 Eastleigh 1960–61. 45.5 t.

9003	**B**	P		BM(S)	68003
9007	**J**	P		BM(S)	68007
9009	**J**	P		BM(S)	68009
931 090	**N**	P		BM(S)	68010
931 092	**N**	P	*OT*	BM	68002
931 094	**N**	P		BM(S)	68004
931 095	**J**	P		BM(S)	68005
931 098	**N**	P		BM(S)	68008

CLASS 932 3-Car Test Units

DM–TB–DM. Gangwayed throughout. Converted from Class 411. Test units for manufacturers traction packages. One driving motor car of 932 545 is now equipped with a pantograph.
Supply System: 750 V d.c. third rail (* or 15 kV a.c. 16.67 Hz overhead).
Traction Motors: Adtranz. († Two English Electric EE507 of 185 kW each (61948); Alstom (61949). **Dimensions:** 20.34 x 2.82 x 3.83 m.
Maximum Speed: **Doors:** Manually operated slam.
Couplings: Buckeye. **Multiple Working:** SR type.
Bogies: Mk. 4 (motor), Commonwealth (unpowered).
Non Standard Liveries:
• 932 545 is Adtranz blue with a white stripe.
• 932 620 has one side of each car painted in GEC Alsthom white and orange livery and the other side of each car painted in livery **P.**)

Note: 932 545 is currently based at the Adtranz works at Västerås, Sweden.

61358–61359. DM. Dia. EZ   . Lot No. 30454 Eastleigh 1958–59.
61948-61949. DM. Dia. EZ   . Lot No. 30708 Eastleigh 1963.
70330. TB. Dia. EZ   . Lot No. 30456 Eastleigh 1958–59.
70653. TB. Dia. EZ   . Lot No. 30709 Eastleigh 1963.

932 545 *	**0**	P	*AD*	Sweden	61359	70330	61358
932 620 †	**0**	P	*AM*	ZE	61948	70653	61949

CLASS 936/0   2-Car Sandite Unit

DM–DTB. Gangwayed throughout. Converted from Class 501.
Supply System: 750 V d.c. third rail.
Traction Motors: Four GEC of 137 kW each.
Dimensions: 18.47 x 2.90 x 3.86 m.   **Multiple Working:** SR type.
Maximum Speed: 70 mph.   **Doors:** Manually operated slam.
Couplings: Buckeye.   **Bogies:**

DM. Dia. EZ504. Lot No. 30326 Eastleigh 1957–58. 48.0 t.
DTB. Dia. EZ506. Lot No. 30328 Eastleigh 1957–58. 30.5 t.

936 003	**MD**	RT	*RT*	BD	977349	977350

CLASS 936/1   3-Car Sandite Unit

DT–MB–DT. Non gangwayed. Converted from Class 311.
Supply System: 25 kV a.c. 50 Hz overhead.
Traction Motors: Four AEI of 165 kW each.
Dimensions: 20.18 x 2.82 x 3.86 m.   **Multiple Working:** Classes 303–312.
Maximum Speed: 75 mph.   **Doors:** Power operated sliding.
Couplings: Buckeye.   **Bogies:** Gresley.

977844/847. DT. Dia. EZ543. Lot No. 30767 Cravens 1967. 34.4 t.
MB. Dia. EZ544. Lot No. 30768 Cravens 1967. 56.4 t.
977846/849. DT. Dia. EZ543. Lot No. 30769 Cravens 1967. 38.4 t.

936 103	**RK**	RT	*RT*	GW	977844	977845	977846
936 104	**RK**	RT	*RT*	GW	977847	977848	977849

CLASS 937   3-Car Sandite Unit

BDT–MB–DT. Gangwayed within unit. Converted from Class 308.
Supply System: 25 kV a.c. 50 Hz overhead.

For details see Class 308.

BDT. Dia. EZ545. Lot No. 30656 York 1961. 36.3 t.
MB. Dia. EZ546. Lot No. 30657 York 1961. 55.0 t.
DT. Dia. EZ547. Lot No. 30659 York 1961. 33.0 t.

937 990	**N**	RT	*RT*	EM	977876	977877	977878
937 991	**N**	RT	*RT*	IL	977926	977927	977928

CLASS 937 — 3-Car Sandite Unit

DT–MB–DT. Gangwayed within unit. Converted from Class 302.
Supply System: 25 kV a.c. 50 Hz overhead.
Traction Motors: Four English Electric EE536A of 143.5 kW each.
Dimensions: 20.36 x 2.82 x 3.86 m (driving cars), 20.18 x 2.82 x 3.86 m (MB).
Maximum Speed: 75 mph.   **Doors:** Manually operated slam.
Couplings: Buckeye.   **Bogies:** Gresley (MB), B4 or B5 (DT).
Multiple Working: Classes 303–312.

DT. Dia. EZ528. Lot No. 30435 York 1958–59. 32.5 t.
MB. Dia. EZ529. Lot No. 30434 York 1958–59. 55.3 t.

937 998	**RK**	RT	*RT*	IL	977604 977605 977606

UNCLASSIFIED — Generator Coach

QXA. Gangwayed throughout. Converted from Class 438. Works with 999550.
Dimensions: 20.18 x 2.82 x 3.81 m.
Maximum Speed: 90 mph.   **Doors:** Manually operated slam.
Couplings: Buckeye.   **Bogies:** B5 (SR).

QXA. Dia. QX174. Lot No. 30764 York 1966–67. 32.0 t.

–	**0**	SO	*SO*	ZA	977335

UNCLASSIFIED — LUL Track Recording Car

T. London Underground Track Recording Car. Converted from 1973 tube stock.
Dimensions:
Maximum Speed: 70 mph.   **Doors:** Power operated sliding.
Couplings: Buckeye.   **Bogies:** LT design.
Non Standard Livery: White with blue lower body stripe and red doors.
Note: Also carries LUL number TRC666.

T. Dia. EZ548. Met-Camm. 1974. Converted BREL Derby 1987. 23.8 t.

–	**0**	LU	*OT*	WR	999666

4.5. VEHICLES AWAITING DISPOSAL

25 kV a.c. 50 Hz OVERHEAD EMUS

Complete Units:

302 201	N	F	PY(S)	75085	61060	70060	75033
302 204	N	F	PY(S)	75088	61063	70063	75036
302 213	N	F	PY(S)	75097	61072	70072	75060
302 216	N	F	EM(S)	75100	61075	70075	75063
302 218	N	F	PY(S)	75191	61077	70077	75065
302 221	N	F	PY(S)	75194	61080	70080	75068
302 224	N	F	PY(S)	75197	61083	70083	75071
302 225	N	F	PY(S)	75198	61084	70084	75072
302 226	N	F	EM(S)	75199	61085	70085	75073
302 227	N	F	EM(S)	75325	61193	70193	75250
302 228	N	F	EM(S)	75201	61087	70087	75075
302 230	N	F	PY(S)	75205	61091	70091	75079

Spare Cars:

Cl. 307	BG	E	KN(S)	75023			
Cl. 308	N	A	CB(S)	70612	70621	70622	70631
				70640			

750 V d.c. THIRD RAIL EMUS

Complete Units:

4308	N	F	LM(S)	61275	75395		
4311	N	F	LM(S)	61287	75407		
5001	G	F	LM(S)	14001	15207	15101	14002
5176	B	F	LM(S)	14352	15396	15354	14351
6213	BG	F	LM(S)	65327	77512		
6308	N	F	LM(S)	14564	16108		
6309	N	F	LM(S)	14562	16106		
6402	N	F	LM(S)	65362	77547		
7001	N	P	ZG(S)	67300	67301		

Spare Cars:

Class 438	B	P	ZG(S)	70859	70812	

5. LOCO-HAULED NON-PASSENGER-CARRYING COACHING STOCK

USING THIS SECTION

The notes shown for locomotive-hauled passenger stock in Section 2 generally also apply to non-passenger-carrying coaching stock.

TOPS TYPE CODES

TOPS type codes for NPCCS are made up as follows:

(1) Two letters denoting the type of the vehicle:

AX	Nightstar Generator Van
AY	Eurostar Barrier Vehicle
NA	Propelling Control Vehicle.
NB	High Security Brake Van (100 m.p.h.).
NC	Gangwayed Brake Van modified for newspaper conveyance (100 m.p.h.).
ND	Gangwayed Brake Van (90 m.p.h.).
NE	Gangwayed Brake Van (100 m.p.h.).
NF	Gangwayed Brake Van with guard's safety equipment removed.
NG	Motorail Loading Wagon.
NH	Gangwayed Brake Van (110 m.p.h.).
NI	High Security Brake Van (110 m.p.h.).
NJ	General Utility Van (90 m.p.h.).
NK	High Security General Utility Van (100 m.p.h.).
NL	Newspaper Van.
NN	Courier Vehicle.
NO	General Utility Van (100 m.p.h. e.t.h. wired).
NP	General Utility Van for Post Office use or Motorail van (110 m.p.h.).
NR	BAA Container Van (100 m.p.h.).
NS	Post Office Sorting Van.
NT	Post Office Stowage Van.
NU	Brake Post Office Stowage Van.
NX	Motorail Van (100 m.p.h.).
NY	Exhibition Van.
NZ	Driving Brake Van (also known as driving van trailer).
QS	EMU Translator Vehicles.
YR	Ferry Van (special Southern Region version of NJ with two pairs of side doors instead of three).

(2) A third letter denoting the brake type:

A	Air braked
V	Vacuum braked
X	Dual braked

OPERATING CODES

Normal operating codes are given in parentheses following TOPS type codes:

BG	Gangwayed Brake Van.
BPOT	Brake Post Office Stowage Van.
DLV	Driving Brake Van (also known as driving van trailer – DVT).
GUV	General Utility Van.
PCV	Propelling Control Van.
POS	Post Office Sorting Van.
POT	Post Office Stowage Van.

HIGH SPEED IN JAPAN

by Peter Semmens

When Japan's legendary 'Bullet Trains' entered service in 1964, a new era in high speed rail travel had begun. Brand new trains operating over brand new railway lines cut journey times in half and opened the world's eyes to the possibilities of high speed rail travel. Never before had a new railway provoked such interest, with many new ideas now copied by engineers the world over.

HIGH SPEED IN JAPAN

SHINKANSEN – THE WORLD'S
BUSIEST HIGH-SPEED RAILWAY

Peter Semmens

With photographs by Mikio Niwa

HIGH SPEED IN JAPAN tells the story of Japan's high speed rail network from the earliest beginnings to the present day. Using unique first hand knowledge, author Peter Semmens guides the reader through the development of the network using a clear and explanatory narrative. Civil engineering challenges, day to day operating procedures, political aspects and the high speed trains themselves are all examined. A useful glossary and a chronology of events are also included.

The combination of highest quality photographic material and the exclusive knowledge of Peter Semmens make this the definitive work on the subject. It contains 122 colour illustrations, 13 black & white illustrations, 23 diagrams, 53 tables and 3 maps. A4 size. 112 pages. Hardback. **£16.95.**

Available from the Platform 5 Mail Order Department.
To place an order, please follow the instructions on the last page of this book.

5.1 LOCO-HAULED NON-PASSENGER CARRYING COACHING STOCK

5.1 AK51 (RK)   KITCHEN CAR

Dia. AK503. Mark 1. Converted from RBR. Fluorescent lighting. Commonwealth bogies. ETH 2X.

Lot No. 30628 Pressed Steel 1960–61. Converted by BR, Bounds Green 1989. 39 t.

Note: Kitchen cars have traditionally been numbered in the NPCCS series, but have passenger coach diagram numbers.

80041	(1690)	x	CC	RS	*ON*	BN

NN   COURIER VEHICLE

Dia. NN504. Mark 1. Converted 1986–7 from BSK. One compartment retained for courier use. Roller shutter doors. ETH 2.

80207. Lot No. 30721 Wolverton 1963. Commonwealth bogies. 37 t.
80211–7/23–5. Lot No. 30699 Wolverton 1962. Commonwealth bogies. 37 t.
80220. Lot No. 30573 Gloucester 1960. B4 bogies. 33 t.

Non-Standard Livery:
• 80211 is purple.

80207	(35466)	x	PC	VS	*ON*	SL
80211	(35296)		O	CN		FK
80212	(35307)	x	RM	E		OM
80213	(35316)	x	CH	O		CP
80216	(35295)	x	RM	E		OM
80217	(35299)	x	M	O	*OS*	GT
80220	(35276)	x	G	WT	*OS*	BQ
80223	(35331)	x	RY	CN		DY
80225	(35327)	x	BG	O		SZ

Name: 80207 is branded 'BAGGAGE CAR No.11'.

NP   POST OFFICE GUV

Dia. NP502. Mark 1. Converted 1991–93 from newspaper vans. Short frames (57 ft.). Originally converted from GUV. Fluorescent lighting, toilet and gangways fitted. Load 14 t. B5 bogies. ETH 3X.

Lot No. 30922 Wolverton or Doncaster 1977–8. 31 t.

80250	(86838, 94008)		RM	E	BK
80251	(86467, 94017)	x	RM	E	OM
80252	(86718, 94022)		RM	E	OM
80253	(86170, 94018)		RM	E	OM
80254	(86082, 94012)	x	RM	E	OM

80255	(86098, 94019)	x	**RM**	E		OM
80256	(86408, 94013)	x	**RM**	E		OM
80257	(86221, 94023)	x	**RM**	E		OM
80258	(86651, 94002)		**RM**	E		OM
80259	(86845, 94005)	x	**RM**	E		OM

NS (POS)   POST OFFICE SORTING VAN

Used in Travelling Post Office (TPO) trains. Mark 1. Various diagrams.

The following lots have BR Mark 1 bogies except * B5 bogies. (subtract 2 t from weight).

80303–80305. Lot No. 30486 Wolverton 1959. Dia. NS501. Originally built with nets for collecting mail bags in motion. Equipment now removed. ETH 3X. 36 t.
80306–80308. Lot No. 30487 Wolverton 1959. Dia. NS502. ETH 3. 36 t.
80309–80314. Lot No. 30661 Wolverton 1961. Dia. NS501. ETH 3. 37 t.
80315–80316. Lot No. 30662 Wolverton 1961. Dia. NS501. ETH 3X. 36 t.

80303	x*	**RM**	E	OM		80312	v	**RM**	E	OM
80305	v	**RM**	E	OM		80313	v	**RM**	E	ZH
80306	v	**RM**	E	OM		80314	x*	**RM**	E	OM
80308	x*	**RM**	E	OM		80315	v	**RM**	E	OM
80309	x*	**RM**	E	OM		80316	x*	**RM**	E	OM
80310		**RM**	E	OM						

The following lots are pressure ventilated and have B5 bogies.

80319–80327. Dia. NS504. Lot No. 30778 York 1968–9. ETH 4. 35 t.
80328–80338. Dia. NS505. Lot No. 30779 York 1968–9. ETH 4. 35 t.
80339–80355. Dia. NS506. Lot No. 30780 York 1968–9. ETH 4. 35 t.

80319		**RM**	E	E	EN		80338		**RM**	E		BK
80320		**RM**	E	E	EN		80339		**RM**	E	E	BK
80321		**RM**	E	E	BK		80340		**RM**	E	E	BK
80322		**RM**	E	E	EN		80341		**RM**	E	E	EN
80323		**RM**	E	E	EN		80342		**RM**	E	E	BK
80324		**RM**	E	E	EN		80343		**RM**	E	E	BK
80325		**RM**	E	E	EN		80344		**RM**	E	E	BK
80326		**RM**	E	E	EN		80345		**RM**	E	E	EN
80327		**RM**	E	E	BK		80346		**RM**	E	E	EN
80328		**RM**	E		OM		80347		**RM**	E	E	EN
80329		**RM**	E		OM		80348		**RM**	E	E	BZ
80330		**RM**	E		BK		80349		**RM**	E	E	EN
80331		**RM**	E	E	EN		80350		**RM**	E	E	BK
80332		**RM**	E	E	EN		80351		**RM**	E	E	EN
80333		**RM**	E	E	EN		80352		**RM**	E	E	BK
80334		**RM**	E	E	BK		80353		**RM**	E	E	EN
80335	x	**RM**	E		OM		80354		**RM**	E	E	BK
80336		**RM**	E		BK		80355		**RM**	E	E	EN
80337		**RM**	E	E	NC							

Names:

| 80320 | The Borders Mail | | 80327 | George James |

80356–80380. Lot No. 30839 York 1972–3. Dia. NS501. Pressure ventilated. Fluorescent lighting. B5 bogies. ETH 4X. 37 t.

80356	**RM**	E	*E*	BK		80369	**RM**	E	*E*	EN
80357	**RM**	E	*E*	BK		80370	**RM**	E	*E*	BK
80358	**RM**	E	*E*	EN		80371	**RM**	E	*E*	BZ
80359	**RM**	E	*E*	BK		80372	**RM**	E	*E*	EN
80360	**RM**	E	*E*	EN		80373	**RM**	E	*E*	EN
80361	**RM**	E	*E*	EN		80374	**RM**	E	*E*	EN
80362	**RM**	E	*E*	EN		80375	**RM**	E	*E*	BK
80363	**RM**	E	*E*	BK		80376	**RM**	E	*E*	BK
80364	**RM**	E	*E*	BK		80377	**RM**	E	*E*	EN
80365	**RM**	E	*E*	EN		80378	**RM**	E	*E*	EN
80366	**RM**	E	*E*	EN		80379	**RM**	E	*E*	EN
80367	**RM**	E	*E*	EN		80380	**RM**	E	*E*	BZ
80368	**RM**	E	*E*	BK					

Names:

80360	Derek Carter		80380	Ernie Gosling
80367	M G Berry			

80381–80395. Lot No. 30900 BREL Wolverton 1977. Dia NS531. Converted from SK. Pressure ventilated. Fluorescent lighting. B5 bogies. ETH 4X. 38 t.

80381	(25112)	**RM** E	*E*	EN		80389	(25103)	**RM** E		ZG
80382	(25109)	**RM** E	*E*	EN		80390	(25047)	**RM** E	*E*	EN
80383	(25033)	**RM** E	*E*	EN		80392	(25082)	**RM** E	*E*	EN
80384	(25078)	**RM** E	*E*	EN		80393	(25118)	**RM** E	*E*	EN
80385	(25083)	**RM** E	*E*	EN		80394	(25156)	**RM** E	*E*	EN
80386	(25099)	**RM** E	*E*	EN		80395	(25056)	**RM** E	*E*	EN
80387	(25045)	**RM** E	*E*	EN						

NT (POT)   POST OFFICE STOWAGE VAN

Mark 1. Open vans used for stowage of mail bags in conjunction with POS.

Lot No. 30488 Wolverton 1959. Dia. NT502. Originally built with nets for collecting mail bags in motion. Equipment now removed. B5 bogies. ETH 3. 35 t.

80400	**RM**	E	*E*	BK		80402	**RM**	E	*E*	BK
80401	**RM**	E	*E*	EN					

The following eight vehicles were converted at York from BSK to lot 30143 (80403) and 30229 (80404–80414). No new lot number was issued. Dia. NT503. B5 bogies. 35 t. (* Dia. NT501 BR2 bogies 38 t. ETH 3 (3X*).

80403	(34361)	**RM** E	*E*	BZ		80411	(35003)	*	**RM** E	*E*	BZ
80404	(35014)	**RM** E	*E*	BZ		80412	(35002)	*	**RM** E	*E*	EN
80405	(35009)	**RM** E	*E*	BZ		80413	(35004)	*	**RM** E	*E*	EN
80406	(35022)	**RM** E	*E*	EN		80414	(35005)	*	**RM** E	*E*	EN

Lot No. 30781 York 1968. Dia. NT505. Pressure ventilated. B5 bogies. ETH 4. 34 t.

80415	**RM**	E	*E*	EN		80416	**RM**	E	*E*	EN

80417	**RM**	E	*E*	EN		80422	**RM**	E	*E*	EN
80419	**RM**	E	*E*	EN		80423	**RM**	E	*E*	EN
80420	**RM**	E	*E*	BK		80424	**RM**	E	*E*	EN
80421	**RM**	E	*E*	EN						

Lot No. 30840 York 1973. Dia. NT504. Pressure ventilated. fluorescent lighting. B5 bogies. ETH 4X. 35 t.

80425	**RM**	E	*E*	BK		80428	**RM**	E	*E*	EN
80426	**RM**	E	*E*	EN		80429	**RM**	E	*E*	BK
80427	**RM**	E	*E*	EN		80430	**RM**	E	*E*	EN

Lot No. 30901 BREL Wolverton 1977. Converted from SK. Dia. NT521. Pressure ventilated. Fluorescent lighting. B5 bogies. ETH 4X. 35 t.

80431	(25104)	**RM**	E	*E*	EN		80436	(25077)	**RM**	E	*E*	EN
80432	(25071)	**RM**	E	*E*	EN		80437	(25068)	**RM**	E	*E*	EN
80433	(25150)	**RM**	E	*E*	BK		80438	(25139)	**RM**	E	*E*	BK
80434	(25119)	**RM**	E	*E*	EN		80439	(25127)	**RM**	E	*E*	BK
80435	(25117)	**RM**	E	*E*	EN							

NU (BPOT)   BRAKE POST OFFICE STOWAGE VAN

Dia. NU502. Mark 1. As NT but with brake compartment. Pressure ventilated. B5 bogies. ETH4.

Lot No. 30782 York 1968. 36 t.

80456	**RM**	E	*E*	EN		80458	**RM**	E	*E*	EN
80457	**RM**	E	*E*	EN						

PLATFORM 5 MAIL ORDER

NZ (DLV)   DRIVING BRAKE VAN (110 m.p.h.)

Dia. NZ501. Mark 3B. Air conditioned. T4 bogies. dg. Cab to shore communication. ETH 5X.

Lot No. 31042 BREL Derby 1988. 45.18 t.

82101	V	P	VW	OY	82127	V	P	VW	OY
82102		P	VW	OY	82128		P	VW	OY
82103		P	VW	OY	82129		P	VW	OY
82104		P	VW	PC	82130	V	P	VW	MA
82105	V	P	VW	PC	82131	V	P	VW	OY
82106	V	P	VW	OY	82132		P	VW	OY
82107		P	VW	PC	82133	V	P	VW	OY
82108		P	VW	PC	82134	V	P	VW	OY
82109		P	VW	PC	82135	V	P	VW	MA
82110	V	P	VW	PC	82136		P	VW	MA
82111		P	VW	PC	82137	V	P	VW	MA
82112		P	VW	PC	82138		P	VW	PC
82113		P	VW	OY	82139		P	VW	PC
82114		P	VW	PC	82140	V	P	VW	MA
82115		P	VW	PC	82141	V	P	VW	MA
82116		P	VW	PC	82142	V	P	VW	MA
82117	V	P	VW	PC	82143		P	VW	OY
82118		P	VW	OY	82144		P	VW	OY
82119	V	P	VW	MA	82145	V	P	VW	MA
82120	V	P	VW	MA	82146	V	P	VW	MA
82121	V	P	VW	PC	82147	V	P	VW	MA
82122	V	P	VW	MA	82148	V	P	VW	PC
82123	V	P	VW	PC	82149	V	P	VW	PC
82124		P	VW	PC	82150		P	VW	PC
82125		P	VW	PC	82151		P	VW	OY
82126	V	P	VW	OY	82152	V	P	VW	MA

Names:

82115	Liverpool John Moores University
82120	Liverpool Chamber of Commerce
82121	Carlisle Cathedral
82126	G8 Summit Birmingham 1998
82127	Abraham Darby
82132	INDUSTRY 96 West Midlands
82134	Sir Henry Doulton 1820–1897
82135	Spirit of Cumbria
82147	The Red Devils
82148	International Spring Fair
82149	101 Squadron

NZ (DLV)   DRIVING BRAKE VAN (140 m.p.h.)

Dia. NZ502. Mark 4. Air conditioned. BT41 bogies. dg. Cab to shore communication. ETH 6X.

Lot No. 31043 Metro-Camm. 1988. 45.18 t.

82200	**GN**	F	*GN*	BN	82216	**GN**	F	*GN*	BN
82201	**GN**	F	*GN*	BN	82217	**GN**	F	*GN*	BN
82202	**GN**	F	*GN*	BN	82218	**GN**	F	*GN*	BN
82203	**GN**	F	*GN*	BN	82219	**GN**	F	*GN*	BN
82204	**GN**	F	*GN*	BN	82220	**GN**	F	*GN*	BN
82205	**GN**	F	*GN*	BN	82221	**GN**	F	*GN*	BN
82206	**GN**	F	*GN*	BN	82222	**GN**	F	*GN*	BN
82207	**GN**	F	*GN*	BN	82223	**GN**	F	*GN*	BN
82208	**GN**	F	*GN*	BN	82224	**GN**	F	*GN*	BN
82209	**GN**	F	*GN*	BN	82225	**GN**	F	*GN*	BN
82210	**GN**	F	*GN*	BN	82226	**GN**	F	*GN*	BN
82211	**GN**	F	*GN*	BN	82227	**GN**	F	*GN*	BN
82212	**GN**	F	*GN*	BN	82228	**GN**	F	*GN*	BN
82213	**GN**	F	*GN*	BN	82229	**GN**	F	*GN*	BN
82214	**GN**	F	*GN*	BN	82230	**GN**	F	*GN*	BN
82215	**GN**	F	*GN*	BN	82231	**GN**	F	*GN*	BN

ND (BG)   GANGWAYED BRAKE VAN (90 m.p.h.)

Dia. ND501. Mark 1. Short frames (57 ft.). Load 10t. All vehicles were built with BR Mark 1 bogies. ETH 1. Vehicles numbered 81xxx had 3000 added to the original numbers to avoid confusion with Class 81 locomotives. The full lot number list is listed here for reference purposes with renumbered vehicles. No unmodified vehicles remain in service.

80525. Lot No. 30009 Derby 1952–3. 31 t.
80621. Lot No. 30046 York 1954. 31.5 t.
80700–80703. Lot No. 30136 Metro-Camm. 1955. 31.5 t.
80731–80791. Lot No. 30140 BRCW 1955–6. 31.5 t.
80805–80848. Lot No. 30144 Cravens 1955. 31.5 t.
80855–80962. Lot No. 30162 Pressed Steel 1956–7. 32 t.
80971–81014. Lot No. 30173 York 1956. 31.5 t.
81019–81051. Lot No. 30224 Cravens 1956. 31.5 t.
81055–81175. Lot No. 30228 Metro-Camm.1957–8. 31.5 t.
81182–81188. Lot No. 30234 Cravens 1956–7. 31.5 t.
81205–81265. Lot No. 30163 Pressed Steel 1957. 31.5 t.
81266–81309. Lot No. 30323 Pressed Steel 1957. 32 t.
81313–81497. Lot No. 30400 Pressed Steel 1957–8. 32 t.
81498–81568. Lot No. 30484 Pressed Steel 1958. 32 t.
81590. Lot No. 30715 Gloucester 1962. 31 t.
81604–81606. Lot No. 30716 Gloucester 1962. 31 t.

The following converted NDs are in service:

84025. ND rebogied with Commonwealth bogies (add 1.5 t to weight) and adapted 1998 for use as exhibition van at Lancastrian Carriage & Wagon Co. Ltd. , Heysham.
84382/7/477. Dia. NB501. High Security Brake Van. Converted 1985 at Wembley Heavy Repair Depot from ND. Gangways removed. B4 bogies.

84025	(81025)	v	**M**	RA	CP
84382	(81382, 80460)	x	**RX**	E	CC
84387	(81387, 80461)	x	**B**	E	CW
84477	(81477, 80463)	x	**B**	E	CW

NJ (GUV)   GENERAL UTILITY VAN

Mark 1. Dia. NJ501. Short frames (57 ft.). Load 14 t. Screw couplings. All vehicles were built with BR Mark 2 bogies. ETH 0 or 0X*. These vehicles had 7000 added to the original numbers to avoid confusion with Class 86 locomotives. The full lot number list is listed here for reference purposes with renumbered vehicles. No unmodified vehicles remain in service.

86081–86499. Lot No. 30417 Pressed Steel 1958–9. 30 t.
86508–86518. Lot No. 30343 York 1957. 30 t.
86521–86651. Lot No. 30403 York/Glasgow 1958–60. 30 t.
86656–86834. Lot No. 30565 Pressed Steel 1959. 30 t.
86836–86980. Lot No. 30616 Pressed Steel 1959–60. 30 t.

NE/NH (BG)   GANGWAYED BRAKE VAN (100/110 m.p.h.)

NE, as ND but rebogied with B4 bogies for 100 m.p.h running. NH are permitted to run at 110 m.p.h. with special maintenance. ETH 1 (* 1X). For lot numbers refer to original number series. Deduct 1.5t from weights. All NHA are *pg.

Non-standard Livery:
* 92116 is purple.

92100	(81391)	to		RV		CP
92111	(81432)	NHA		F		CP
92112	(81440)	x	**RY**	E		BK
92114	(81443)	NHA		F		LT
92116	(81450)	to	**0**	CN		FK
92146	(81498)	NHA		F		LT
92159	(81534)	NHA		F	*SR*	IS
92174	(81567)	NHA		F	*SR*	IS
92175	(81568)	pg		F	*GW*	LA
92193	(81604)	pg		E		PN
92194	(81606)	to		F	*GW*	LA
92211	(81267)	*	**R**	E		KM
92229	(80902)	*	**R**	E		KM
92234	(81336, 84336)	*	**RX**	E		DY
92238	(81563, 84563)		**RY**	E		DY
92243	(81489, 84489)	*	**R**	E		OM
92252	(80959)	x*	**RY**	E		CW
92258	(81346, 84346)		**RY**	E		OM

92259	(81313, 84313)	x		RY	E	BK
92261	(80988)	x*		RY	E	KM
92265	(80945)	x		RY	E	AN
92267	(81404, 84404)	x			E	CW
92271	(80962)	x*		R	E	OM

NE (BG)   GANGWAYED BRAKE VAN (100 m.p.h.)

As ND but rebogied with Commonwealth bogies. ETH 1 (1X*). For lot numbers refer to original number series. Add 1.5 t to weights to allow for the increased weight of the Commonwealth bogies.

92302	(81501, 84501)		RX	E	KM
92303	(81427, 84427)		RX	E	DY
92306	(81217, 84217)	*	RY	E	KM
92307	(80805)	*		E	KM
92309	(81043, 84043)	x*	RX	E	KM
92311	(81453, 84453)	x	RY	E	CW
92312	(81548, 84548)		RX	E	KM
92314	(80777)	x*	RY	E	CW
92316	(80980)	x*	RY	E	KM
92319	(81055, 84055)	*	RY	E	KM
92321	(81566, 84566)		RY	E	FK
92323	(80832)	*	R	E	KM
92324	(81087, 84087)		RY	E	KM
92325	(80791)		RY	E	KM
92328	(80999)	x*	RY	E	KM
92329	(81001, 84001)	*	RY	E	KM
92330	(80995)	x*	RY	E	KM
92332	(80845)	*	RX	E	KM
92333	(80982)	*	RY	E	KM
92334	(80983)	x*	R	E	BK
92337	(81140, 84140)	*	RX	E	KM
92340	(81059, 84059)	*	RY	E	KM
92341	(81316, 84316)	x	RY	E	KM
92343	(81505, 84505)	x	R	E	KM
92344	(81154, 84154)	*	RY	E	KM
92345	(81083, 84083)	x*	RY	E	KM
92346	(81091, 84091)		RY	E	KM
92347	(81326, 84326)		RX	E	DY
92348	(81075, 84075)	x*	R	E	KM
92350	(81049, 84049)	*	RY	E	DY
92353	(81323, 84323)		R	E	KM
92355	(81517, 84517)	x	RX	E	DY
92356	(81535, 84535)	x		E	KM
92357	(81136, 84136)		RX	E	KM
92362	(81188, 84188)	x	RY	E	KM
92363	(81294, 84294)	x	RY	E	CW
92364	(81030, 84030)	x*	R	E	KM
92365	(81122, 84122)		RX	E	KM
92366	(81551, 84551)		RX	E	KM

92369	(80960)	x*		E		DS
92370	(81324, 84324)		**RX**	E		KM
92377	(80928)	*	**RX**	E		DY
92379	(80914)	*	**RX**	E		KM
92380	(81247, 84247)	*	**R**	E		KM
92381	(81476, 84476)		**RX**	E		KM
92382	(81561, 84561)		**RX**	E		DY
92384	(80893)		**RY**	E		CW
92385	(81261, 84261)	x*	**RY**	E		KM
92387	(81380, 84380)	x		E		BK
92389	(81026, 84026)	*	**RY**	E		KM
92390	(80834)	*		E		KM
92392	(80861)	*	**RY**	E		KM
92395	(81274, 84274)			E		KM
92398	(80859)	x*	**RY**	E		KM
92399	(80781)	x*	**RY**	E		BK
92400	(81211, 84211)	*		E		CW
92401	(81280, 84280)	x	**RX**	E		KM
92402	(81099, 84099)	*	**RY**	E		KM
92403	(81273, 84273)	x	**RY**	E		OM
92404	(81051, 84051)	x		E		KM
92409	(81370, 84370)	x		E		OM
92410	(81469, 84469)	x		E		CW
92411	(81252, 84252)	x	**RY**	E		BK
92412	(81354, 84354)	*	**RY**	E		CW
92413	(81472, 84472)	x	**RY**	E		CW
92414	(81458, 84458)	x		E		OM
92415	(81388, 84388)		**RX**	E		KM
92416	(81250, 84250)	*	**RY**	E		KM
92417	(80885)	*	**RX**	E		KM
92418	(81512, 84512)	*	**RX**	E		OM

NF (BG)   GANGWAYED BRAKE VAN (100 m.p.h.)

As NE but with emergency equipment removed. For details and lot numbers
refer to original numbers. 92503–92740 have B4 bogies, 92804–92897 have
Commonwealth bogies.

b (Dia. NB501). High Security Brake Van. Converted at Wembley Heavy Repair Depot from ND in 1985. Gangways removed. Now used for movement of
materials between EWS maintenance depots.

92503	(80864, 92903)	x	**RY**	E		CU
92510	(80900, 92910)	x	**RX**	E		OM
92518	(80941, 92918)		**RX**	E		WI
92530	(81461, 84461)	xb	**RX**	E	*E*	EN
92542	(81207, 92942)		**RX**	E		KM
92547	(81216, 92947)		**RX**	E		BK
92550	(81220, 92950)		**RX**	E		BK
92558	(81228, 92958)		**RX**	E		BK
92562	(81232, 92962)		**RX**	E		WI
92566	(81238, 92966)			E		BK

92568	(81244, 92968)		**RX**	E	OM
92607	(81410, 92107)		**RX**	E	OM
92714	(81504, 92214)		**RX**	E	AN
92716	(81376, 92216)	x	**RY**	E	BK
92718	(81314, 92218)		**RX**	E	BK
92728	(80921, 92228)		**RX**	E	WI
92740	(80703, 92240)	x	**RY**	E	BK
92804	(81339, 92304)	x	**RX**	E	KM
92805	(81590, 92305)	x	**RX**	E	KM
92808	(80784, 92308)	x	**RX**	E	BK
92810	(81105, 92310)		**RX**	E	KM
92815	(80848, 92315)	*	**RX**	E	KM
92817	(80836, 92317)	x	**RX**	E	KM
92822	(80771, 92322)	x	**RX**	E	KM
92827	(80842, 92327)	x	**RX**	E	KM
92831	(81365, 92331)	x	**RX**	E	KM
92842	(81397, 92342)	x	**RY**	E	KM
92852	(81182, 92352)	*	**RX**	E	DY
92854	(81353, 92354)	x	**RX**	E	BK
92858	(81393, 92358)	x	**RX**	E	BK
92859	(81275, 92359)	*	**RX**	E	DY
92860	(81431, 92360)		**RX**	E	WI
92861	(81463, 92361)		**R**	E	KM
92867	(81293, 92367)	x	**RX**	E	KM
92872	(81362, 92372)	x	**RY**	E	CW
92873	(81528, 92373)		**RX**	E	KM
92876	(81374, 92376)	*	**RX**	E	KM
92883	(81429, 92383)	*	**RX**	E	OM
92886	(80843, 92386)	x	**RX**	E	KM
92888	(80868, 92388)	*	**RX**	E	BK
92893	(80701, 92393)	x	**RX**	E	BK
92894	(81322, 92394)		**RX**	E	BK
92897	(80700, 92397)	x*	**RY**	E	KM

NE/NH (BG)   GANGWAYED BRAKE VAN (100/110 m.p.h.)

Renumbered from 920xx series by adding 900 to number to avoid conflict
with Class 92 locos. Class continued from 92271.

92901	(80855, 92001)	NHA		F	*SR*	IS
92904	(80867, 92004)	*pg	**G**	VS	*ON*	SL
92907	(80880, 92007)	*pg	**RX**	E		KM
92908	(80895, 92008)	NHA		F	*SR*	IS
92912	(80910, 92012)	*pg		F		LM
92916	(80930, 92016)	x*pg	**RY**	E		KM
92917	(80940, 92017)	*to	**RX**	E		OM
92923	(80971, 92023)	*pg		F		LT
92926	(81060, 92026)	NHA		F		ZB
92927	(81061, 92027)	NHA		F		LT
92928	(81064, 92028)	NHA		F		LT

92929	(81077, 92029)	NHA	F		CP
92931	(81102, 92031)	NHA	F	SR	IS
92932	(81117, 92032)	NHA	F		ZD
92933	(81123, 92033)	NHA	F		LM
92934	(81142, 92034)	NHA	F		LT
92935	(81150, 92035)	*pg	F	SR	IS
92936	(81158, 92036)	NHA	F	SR	IS
92937	(81165, 92037)	NHA	F		ZH
92938	(81173, 92038)	NHA	F	SR	IS
92939	(81175, 92039)	NHA	F		LM
92940	(81186, 92040)	pg	F	GW	LA
92946	(81214, 92046)	NHA	F	SR	IS
92948	(81218, 92048)	NHA	F	SR	IS
92961	(81231, 92061)		F		LT
92986	(81282, 92086)	to	F		CP
92988	(81284, 92088)	to	F		LT
92991	(81308, 92091)	to	F		LT
92998	(81381, 92098)	NHA	F		LT

NL   NEWSPAPER VAN

Dia. NL501. Mark 1. Short frames (57 ft.). Converted from NJ (GUV). Fluorescent lighting, toilets and gangways fitted. Load 14 t. Not now used for news traffic. B5 Bogies. ETH 3X.

Lot No. 30922 BREL Wolverton or Doncaster 1977–8. 31 t.

94003	(86281, 93999)	x	**RX**	E	OM
94004	(86156, 85504)		**RY**	E	OM
94006	(86202, 85506)		**RX**	E	OM
94007	(86572, 85507)		**B**	E	OM
94009	(86144, 85509)		**RY**	E	OM
94010	(86151, 85510)	x	**RX**	E	OM
94011	(86437, 85511)		**RX**	E	OM
94015	(86484, 85515)	x	**B**	E	BK
94016	(86317, 85516)	x	**B**	E	OM
94020	(86220, 85520)	x	**RY**	E	OM
94021	(86204, 85521)	x	**B**	E	OM
94024	(86106, 85524)		**B**	E	OM
94025	(86377, 85525)		**RY**	E	OM
94026	(86703, 85526)	x	**RY**	E	OM
94027	(86732, 85527)		**R**	E	FK
94028	(86733, 85528)	x	**RX**	E	OM
94029	(86740, 85529)	x	**RY**	E	OM
94030	(86746, 85530)	x	**B**	E	OM
94031	(86747, 85531)	x	**B**	E	BK
94032	(86730, 85532)		**RX**	E	OM
94033	(86731, 85533)	x	**RY**	E	BK

NKA   HIGH SECURITY GENERAL UTILITY VAN

Dia. NK501. Mark 1. These vehicles are GUVs further modified with new floors, three roller shutter doors per side and the end doors removed. For Lot Nos. see original number series. Add 2 t to weight. Commonwealth bogies. ETH0X.

94100	(86668, 95100)	**RX**	E	*E*	BK
94101	(86142, 95101)	**RX**	E	*E*	BK
94102	(86762, 95102)	**RX**	E	*E*	BK
94103	(86956, 95103)	**RX**	E	*E*	BK
94104	(86942, 95104)	**RX**	E	*E*	EN
94106	(86353, 95106)	**RX**	E	*E*	BK
94107	(86576, 95107)	**RX**	E	*E*	EN
94108	(86600, 95108)	**RX**	E	*E*	BK
94110	(86393, 95110)	**RX**	E	*E*	BK
94111	(86578, 95111)	**RX**	E	*E*	EN
94112	(86673, 95112)	**RX**	E	*E*	EN
94113	(86235, 95113)	**RX**	E	*E*	BK
94114	(86081, 95114)	**RX**	E	*E*	BK
94116	(86426, 95116)	**RX**	E	*E*	BK
94117	(86534, 95117)	**RX**	E	*E*	BK
94118	(86675, 95118)	**RX**	E	*E*	EN
94119	(86167, 95119)	**RX**	E	*E*	EN
94121	(86518, 95121)	**RX**	E	*E*	BK
94123	(86376, 95123)	**RX**	E	*E*	BK
94126	(86692, 95126)	**RX**	E	*E*	BK
94132	(86607, 95132)	**RX**	E	*E*	EN
94133	(86604, 95133)	**RX**	E	*E*	BK
94137	(86610, 95137)	**RX**	E	*E*	EN
94138	(86212, 95138)	**RX**	E	*E*	EN
94140	(86571, 95140)	**RX**	E	*E*	BK
94146	(86648, 95146)	**RX**	E	*E*	BK
94147	(86091, 95147)	**RX**	E	*E*	BK
94148	(86416, 95148)	**RX**	E	*E*	EN
94150	(86560, 95150)	**RX**	E	*E*	BK
94153	(86798, 95153)	**RX**	E	*E*	EN
94155	(86820, 95155)	**RX**	E	*E*	EN
94157	(86523, 95157)	**RX**	E	*E*	EN
94160	(86581, 95160)	**RX**	E	*E*	BK
94164	(86104, 95164)	**RX**	E	*E*	EN
94166	(86112, 95166)	**RX**	E	*E*	BK
94168	(86914, 95168)	**RX**	E	*E*	BK
94170	(86395, 95170)	**RX**	E	*E*	BK
94172	(86429, 95172)	**RX**	E	*E*	EN
94174	(86852, 95174)	**RX**	E	*E*	EN
94175	(86521, 95175)	**RX**	E	*E*	BK
94176	(86210, 95176)	**RX**	E	*E*	EN
94177	(86411, 95177)	**RX**	E	*E*	BK
94180	(86362, 95141)	**RX**	E	*E*	EN

94182	(86710, 95182)	**RX**	E	*E*	BK
94190	(86624, 95350)	**RX**	E	*E*	EN
94191	(86596, 95351)	**RX**	E	*E*	BK
94192	(86727, 95352)	**RX**	E	*E*	EN
94193	(86514, 95353)	**RX**	E	*E*	EN
94195	(86375, 95355)	**RX**	E	*E*	BK
94196	(86478, 95356)	**RX**	E	*E*	BK
94197	(86508, 95357)	**RX**	E	*E*	BK
94198	(86195, 95358)	**RX**	E	*E*	BK
94199	(86854, 95359)	**RX**	E	*E*	BK
94200	(86207, 95360)	**RX**	E	*E*	EN
94202	(86563, 95362)	**RX**	E	*E*	BK
94203	(86345, 95363)	**RX**	E	*E*	BK
94204	(86715, 95364)	**RX**	E	*E*	BK
94205	(86857, 95365)	**RX**	E	*E*	BK
94207	(86529, 95367)	**RX**	E	*E*	BK
94208	(86656, 95368)	**RX**	E	*E*	EN
94209	(86390, 95369)	**RX**	E	*E*	BK
94211	(86713, 95371)	**RX**	E	*E*	EN
94212	(86728, 95372)	**RX**	E	*E*	EN
94213	(86258, 95373)	**RX**	E	*E*	EN
94214	(86367, 95374)	**RX**	E	*E*	BK
94215	(86862, 94077)	**RX**	E	*E*	BK
94216	(86711, 93711)	**RX**	E	*E*	EN
94217	(86131, 93131)	**RX**	E	*E*	BK
94218	(86541, 93541)	**RX**	E	*E*	BK
94221	(86905, 93905)	**RX**	E	*E*	BK
94222	(86474, 93474)	**RX**	E	*E*	EN
94223	(86660, 93660)	**RX**	E	*E*	BK
94224	(86273, 93273)	**RX**	E	*E*	BK
94225	(86849, 93849)	**RX**	E	*E*	BK
94226	(86525, 93525)	**RX**	E	*E*	BK
94227	(86585, 93585)	**RX**	E	*E*	BK
94228	(86511, 93511)	**RX**	E	*E*	BK
94229	(86720, 93720)	**RX**	E	*E*	BK

NAA   PROPELLING CONTROL VEHICLE

Dia. NA508. Mark 1. Class 307 driving trailers converted for use in propelling parcels trains out of termini. Fitted with roller shutter doors. Equipment fitted for communication between cab of PCV and locomotive. B5 bogies. ETH 2X.

Lot No. 30206 Eastleigh 1954–6. Converted at Hunslet-Barclay, Kilmarnock 1994–96.

94302	(75124)	**RX**	E	*E*	BK	94309	(75130)	**RX**	E	*E*	EN
94303	(75131)	**RX**	E	*E*	EN	94310	(75119)	**RX**	E	*E*	EN
94304	(75107)	**RX**	E	*E*	EN	94311	(75105)	**RX**	E	*E*	EN
94305	(75104)	**RX**	E	*E*	EN	94312	(75126)	**RX**	E	*E*	BK
94306	(75112)	**RX**	E	*E*	BK	94313	(75129)	**RX**	E	*E*	BK
94307	(75127)	**RX**	E	*E*	EN	94314	(75109)	**RX**	E	*E*	BK
94308	(75125)	**RX**	E	*E*	EN	94315	(75132)	**RX**	E	*E*	EN

94316	(75108)	**RX**	E	*E*	EN	94333	(75016)	**RX** E	*E*	EN
94317	(75117)	**RX**	E	*E*	EN	94334	(75017)	**RX** E	*E*	EN
94318	(75115)	**RX**	E	*E*	EN	94335	(75032)	**RX** E	*E*	BK
94319	(75128)	**RX**	E	*E*	EN	94336	(75031)	**RX** E	*E*	EN
94320	(75120)	**RX**	E	*E*	EN	94337	(75029)	**RX** E	*E*	EN
94321	(75122)	**RX**	E	*E*	EN	94338	(75008)	**RX** E	*E*	EN
94322	(75111)	**RX**	E	*E*	BK	94339	(75024)	**RX** E	*E*	BK
94323	(75110)	**RX**	E	*E*	EN	94340	(75012)	**RX** E	*E*	BK
94324	(75103)	**RX**	E	*E*	EN	94341	(75007)	**RX** E	*E*	BK
94325	(75113)	**RX**	E	*E*	EN	94342	(75005)	**RX** E	*E*	BK
94326	(75123)	**RX**	E	*E*	BK	94343	(75027)	**RX** E	*E*	EN
94327	(75116)	**RX**	E	*E*	EN	94344	(75014)	**RX** E	*E*	BK
94331	(75022)	**RX**	E	*E*	BK	94345	(75004)	**RX** E	*E*	EN
94332	(75011)	**RX**	E	*E*	EN					

NBA HIGH SECURITY BRAKE VAN   (100 m.p.h.)

Dia. NB501. Mark 1. These vehicles are NE further modified with sealed gang-ways, new floors, built-in tail lights and roller shutter doors. For Lot Nos. see original number series. 31.4 t. B4 bogies. ETH 1X.

94400	(81224, 92954)	**RX**	E	*E*	BK
94401	(81277, 92224)	**RX**	E	*E*	EN
94403	(81479, 92629)	**RX**	E	*E*	BK
94404	(81486, 92135)	**RX**	E	*E*	BK
94405	(80890, 92233)	**RX**	E	*E*	EN
94406	(81226, 92956)	**RX**	E	*E*	BK
94407	(81223, 92553)	**RX**	E	*E*	BK
94408	(81264, 92981)	**RX**	E	*E*	BK
94409	(81511, 92249)	**RX**	E	*E*	BK
94410	(81205, 92941)	**RX**	E	*E*	EN
94411	(81378, 92997)	**RX**	E	*E*	EN
94412	(81210, 92945)	**RX**	E	*E*	EN
94413	(80909, 92236)	**RX**	E	*E*	BK
94414	(81377, 92996)	**RX**	E	*E*	EN
94415	(81309, 92992)	**RX**	E	*E*	EN
94416	(80929, 92746)	**RX**	E	*E*	BK
94418	(81248, 92244)	**RX**	E	*E*	BK
94419	(80858, 92902)	**RX**	E	*E*	BK
94420	(81325, 92263)	**RX**	E	*E*	BK
94421	(81230, 92960)	**RX**	E	*E*	EN
94422	(81516, 92651)	**RX**	E	*E*	BK
94423	(80923, 92914)	**RX**	E	*E*	BK
94424	(81400, 92103)	**RX**	E	*E*	EN
94425	(80937, 92212)	**RX**	E	*E*	EN
94426	(81283, 92987)	**RX**	E	*E*	BK
94427	(80894, 92754)	**RX**	E	*E*	BK
94428	(81550, 92166)	**RX**	E	*E*	BK
94429	(80870, 92232)	**RX**	E	*E*	EN
94430	(80908, 92235)	**RX**	E	*E*	BZ
94431	(81401, 92604)	**RX**	E	*E*	BK
94432	(81383, 92999)	**RX**	E	*E*	EN

94433	(81495, 92643)	**RX**	E	*E*	EN
94434	(81268, 92584)	**RX**	E	*E*	BK
94435	(81485, 92134)	**RX**	E	*E*	EN
94436	(81237, 92565)	**RX**	E	*E*	BK
94437	(81403, 92208)	**RX**	E	*E*	EN
94438	(81425, 92251)	**RX**	E	*E*	BK
94439	(81480, 92130)	**RX**	E	*E*	BK
94440	(81497, 92645)	**RX**	E	*E*	BK
94441	(81492, 92140)	**RX**	E	*E*	BK
94442	(80932, 92723)	**RX**	E	*E*	BZ
94443	(81473, 92127)	**RX**	E	*E*	BK
94444	(81484, 92133)	**RX**	E	*E*	BK
94445	(81444, 92615)	**RX**	E	*E*	EN
94446	(80857, 92242)	**RX**	E	*E*	EN
94447	(81515, 92266)	**RX**	E	*E*	EN
94448	(81541, 92664)	**RX**	E	*E*	BK
94449	(81536, 92747)	**RX**	E	*E*	BK
94450	(80927, 92915)	**RX**	E	*E*	BK
94451	(80955, 92257)	**RX**	E	*E*	EN
94452	(81394, 92602)	**RX**	E	*E*	BK
94453	(81170, 92239)	**RX**	E	*E*	EN
94454	(81465, 92124)	**RX**	E	*E*	EN
94455	(81239, 92264)	**RX**	E	*E*	BK
94456	(80879, 92226)	**RX**	E	*E*	BK
94457	(81454, 92119)	**RX**	E	*E*	EN
94458	(81255, 92974)	**RX**	E	*E*	BK
94459	(81490, 92138)	**RX**	E	*E*	BK
94460	(81266, 92983)	**RX**	E	*E*	EN
94461	(81487, 92136)	**RX**	E	*E*	EN
94462	(81289, 92270)	**RX**	E	*E*	EN
94463	(81375, 92995)	**RX**	E	*E*	EN
94464	(81240, 92262)	**RX**	E	*E*	EN
94465	(81481, 92131)	**RX**	E	*E*	BK
94466	(81236, 92964)	**RX**	E	*E*	EN
94467	(81245, 92969)	**RX**	E	*E*	BK
94468	(81259, 92978)	**RX**	E	*E*	BK
94469	(81260, 92979)	**RX**	E	*E*	BK
94470	(81442, 92113)	**RX**	E	*E*	BK
94471	(81518, 92152)	**RX**	E	*E*	BK
94472	(81526, 92975)	**RX**	E	*E*	BK
94473	(81262, 92272)	**RX**	E	*E*	EN
94474	(81452, 92618)	**RX**	E	*E*	EN
94475	(81208, 92943)	**RX**	E	*E*	EN
94476	(81209, 92944)	**RX**	E	*E*	BK
94477	(81494, 92642)	**RX**	E	*E*	BK
94478	(81488, 92637)	**RX**	E	*E*	EN
94479	(81482, 92132)	**RX**	E	*E*	BK
94480	(81411, 92608)	**RX**	E	*E*	EN
94481	(81493, 92641)	**RX**	E	*E*	BK
94482	(81491, 92639)	**RX**	E	*E*	BK
94483	(81500, 92647)	**RX**	E	*E*	EN

94484	(81426, 92110)	**RX**	E	*E*	BK
94485	(81496, 92644)	**RX**	E	*E*	EN
94486	(81254, 92973)	**RX**	E	*E*	BK
94487	(81413, 92609)	**RX**	E	*E*	BK
94488	(81405, 92105)	**RX**	E	*E*	BK
94489	(81423, 92230)	**RX**	E	*E*	BK
94490	(81409, 92606)	**RX**	E	*E*	EN
94491	(80936, 92753)	**RX**	E	*E*	BK
94492	(80888, 92721)	**RX**	E	*E*	BK
94493	(80944, 92919)	**RX**	E	*E*	BK
94494	(81451, 92617)	**RX**	E	*E*	BK
94495	(80871, 92755)	**RX**	E	*E*	BK
94496	(81514, 92650)	**RX**	E	*E*	BK
94497	(80877, 92717)	**RX**	E	*E*	BK
94498	(81225, 92555)	**RX**	E	*E*	BK
94499	(81258, 92577)	**RX**	E	*E*	BK
94500	(81457, 92121)	**RX**	E	*E*	BK

NIA   HIGH SECURITY BRAKE VAN (110 m.p.h.)

Dia. NI501. Mark 1. These vehicles are NE further modified with sealed gangways, new floors, built-in tail lights and roller shutter doors. For Lot Nos. see original number series. 31.4 t. B4 bogies (special maintenance). ETH 1X. Note: At present these vehicles are operating at 100 m.p.h. as NBAs.

94501	(80891, 92725)	**RX**	E	*E*	BK
94502	(80924, 92720)	**RX**	E	*E*	BK
94503	(80873, 92709)	**RX**	E	*E*	BK
94504	(80935, 92748)	**RX**	E	*E*	BK
94505	(81235, 92750)	**RX**	E	*E*	BK
94506	(80958, 92922)	**RX**	E	*E*	BK
94507	(80876, 92505)	**RX**	E	*E*	BK
94508	(80887, 92722)	**RX**	E	*E*	BK
94509	(80897, 92509)	**RX**	E	*E*	BK
94510	(,)	**RX**	E		
94511	(,)	**RX**	E		
94512	(81265, 92582)	**RX**	E	*E*	BK
94513	(81257, 92576)	**RX**	E	*E*	BK
94514	(81459, 92122)	**RX**	E	*E*	BK
94515	(80916, 92513)	**RX**	E	*E*	BK
94516	(,)	**RX**	E		
94517	(81509, 92645)	**RX**	E	*E*	BK
94518	(,)	**RX**	E		
94519	(,)	**RX**	E		
94520	(,)	**RX**	E		
94521	(,)	**RX**	E		
94522	(,)	**RX**	E		
94523	(,)	**RX**	E		
94524	(,)	**RX**	E		
94525	(,)	**RX**	E		
94526	(,)	**RX**	E		

94527	(	,	)		**RX**	E	
94528	(	,	)		**RX**	E	
94529	(	,	)		**RX**	E	
94530	(	,	)		**RX**	E	
94531	(	,	)		**RX**	E	
94532	(	,	)		**RX**	E	
94533	(	,	)		**RX**	E	
94534	(	,	)		**RX**	E	
94535	(	,	)		**RX**	E	
94536	(	,	)		**RX**	E	
94537	(	,	)		**RX**	E	

NO (GUV)   GENERAL UTILITY VAN (100 m.p.h.)

Dia. NO513. Mark 1. Commonwealth bogies except where shown otherwise.
For Lot Nos. see original number series. Add 2 t to weight (Subtract 1 t for
B4). ETH 0X.

95105	(86126, 93126)			**RX**	E	KM
95109	(86269, 93269)	x		**B**	E	KM
95120	(86468, 93468)	x		**RY**	E	KM
95124	(86836, 93836)	x		**R**	E	KM
95125	(86143, 93143)	x		**B**	E	KM
95128	(86764, 93764)	x		**RY**	E	CW
95129	(86347, 93347)	x		**RY**	E	CW
95131	(86860, 93860)			**RX**	E	OM
95135	(86249, 93249)	x		**RY**	E	KM
95136	(86396, 93396)	x		**RX**	E	OM
95142	(86844, 93844)	x		**RX**	E	BK
95144	(86165, 93165)	x		**RY**	E	OM
95145	(86293, 93293)	x		**RX**	E	KM
95151	(86606, 93606)	x		**RX**	E	OM
95152	(86969, 93969)	x		**RY**	E	KM
95156	(86160, 93160)	x		**RX**	E	OM
95165	(86262, 93262)	x		**RX**	E	KM
95167	(86255, 93255)			**RX**	E	OM
95169	(86277, 93277)			**RX**	E	BK
95171	(86110, 93110)	x		**RX**	E	OM
95173	(86842, 94076)	x		**RX**	E	BK
95181	(86971, 95361)	x		**B**	E	BK
95190	(86643, 95393)	B4		**RY**	E	OM
95191	(86278, 95391)	x B4		**B**	E	OM
95192	(86495, 95392)	x B4		**R**	E	BK
95194	(86192, 93192)	x B4		**RX**	E	OM
95195	(86539, 93539)	x B4		**RX**	E	OM
95196	(86775, 93775)	x B4		**RX**	E	OM
95197	(86590, 93590)	x B4		**RX**	E	OM
95198	(86134, 93134)	x B4		**RX**	E	OM
95199	(86141, 93141)	x B4		**RX**	E	OM

NCX   NEWSPAPER VAN (100 m.p.h.)

Dia. NC501. Mark 1. Commonwealth bogies. BG modified to carry newspapers, but not now used for news traffic. For Lot Nos. refer to original number series. Add 2 t to weight. ETH3 (3X*).

95200	(81019, 84019)	x*	**RY**	E	BK
95201	(80875)	x	**RX**	E	KM
95204	(80947)	x*	**RX**	E	OM
95209	(81047, 84047)	x	**RX**	E	BK
95210	(80731)	x	**RX**	E	OM
95211	(80949)	x	**RY**	E	KM
95217	(81385, 84385)	x	**B**	E	OM
95223	(80933)	x*	**RY**	E	OM
95227	(81292, 95310)	x	**RX**	E	KM
95228	(81014, 95332)	x	**RX**	E	NC
95229	(81341, 95329)	x	**RX**	E	OM
95230	(80525, 95321)	x	**RX**	E	DY

NAA   PROPELLING CONTROL VEHICLE

Dia. NA508. Mark 1. Class 307 driving trailers converted for use in propelling parcels trains out of termini. Fitted with roller shutter doors. Equipment fitted for communication between cab of PCV and locomotive, but this is now isolated and these vehicles are in use as normal vans. B5 bogies. ETH 2X.

Lot No. 30206 Eastleigh 1954–6. Converted at RTC Derby 1993.

95300	(75114, 94300)	**RX**	E	*E*	EN
95301	(75102, 94301)	**RX**	E	*E*	EN

NOV   GENERAL UTILITY VAN (100 m.p.h.)

Dia. NO513. Mark 1. Commonwealth bogies. For Lot No. refer to original number series. Add 2 t to weight. ETH 0X.

95366	(86251, 93251)	v	**B**	E	GS

NRX   BAA CONTAINER VAN (100 m.p.h.)

Dia. NR503. Mark 1. Commonwealth bogies. Modified for carriage of British Airports Authority containers with roller shutter doors, roller floors and gangways removed. For Lot Nos. see original number series. Add 2 t to weight. Now used for movement of materials between EWS maintenance depots. ETH3.

95400	(80621, 95203)	x	**RX**	E	*E*	EN
95410	(80826, 95213)	x	**RX**	E	*E*	EN

NKA   HIGH SECURITY GENERAL UTILITY VAN

Dia. NK502. Mark 1. Commonwealth bogies. For Lot Nos. see original number series. Add 2 t to weight. These vehicles are GUVs further modified with new floors, two roller shutter doors per side, centre doors sealed and end doors removed. ETH 0X

95715	(86174, 95115)	R	E	*E*	EN
95727	(86323, 95127)	R	E	*E*	EN
95734	(86462, 95134)	RX	E	*E*	EN
95739	(86172, 95139)	R	E	*E*	EN
95743	(86485, 95143)	RX	E	*E*	EN
95749	(86265, 95149)	R	E	*E*	EN
95754	(86897, 95154)	R	E	*E*	EN
95758	(86499, 95158)	RX	E	*E*	EN
95759	(86084, 95159)	R	E	*E*	EN
95761	(86205, 95161)	RX	E	*E*	EN
95762	(86122, 95162)	RX	E	*E*	EN
95763	(86407, 95163)	R	E	*E*	EN

NX (GUV)   MOTORAIL VAN (100 m.p.h.)

Dia. NX501. Mark 1. For details and Lot Nos. see original number series. ETH 0 (0X*).

96100	(86734, 93734)	*B5		F	KN
96101	(86741, 93741)	*B5		F	ZW
96110	(86738, 93738)	*C		F	KN
96111	(86742, 93742)	*C		F	CP
96112	(86750, 93750)	*C		F	LT
96130	(86736, 93736)	*C		F	KN
96131	(86737, 93737)	*C		F	KN
96132	(86754, 93754)	*C		F	LT
96133	(86685, 93685)	C		F	LT
96134	(86691, 93691)	C		F	LT
96135	(86755, 93755)	C		F	LM
96136	(86735, 93735)	C		F	LT
96137	(86748, 93748)	C	B	F	ZN
96138	(86749, 93749)	C		F	LT
96139	(86751, 93751)	C		F	*VW*	MA
96141	(86753, 93753)	C	B	F	LT
96150	(86097, 93097)	*B5		F	KN
96155	(86334, 93334)	*B5		F	KN
96156	(86337, 93337)	*B5		F	KN
96157	(86344, 93344)	*B5		F	KN
96162	(86647, 93647)	*C		F	LT
96163	(86646, 93646)	*C		F	KN
96164	(86880, 93880)	*C		F	LT
96165	(86784, 93784)	*C		F	KN
96166	(86834, 93834)	*C		F	KN
96167	(86756, 93756)	*C		F	KN
96168	(86978, 93978)	*C		F	‡LT

96170	(86159, 93159)	x*C	F	KN
96171	(86326, 93326)	x*C	F	LT
96172	(86363, 93363)	x*C	F	KN
96173	(86440, 93440)	x*C	F	KN
96174	(86453, 93453)	x*C	F	LT
96175	(86628, 93628)	x*C	F	KN
96176	(86641, 93641)	x*C	F	KN
96177	(86980, 93980)	*C	F	CP
96178	(86782, 93782)	*C	F	KN
96179	(86910, 93910)	*C	F	LT
96181	(86875, 93875)	*C	F	LT
96182	(86944, 93944)	*C	F	CP
96185	(86083, 93083)	x*C	F	LT
96186	(86087, 93087)	x*C	F	LT
96187	(86168, 93168)	x*C	F	LT
96188	(86320, 93320)	x*C	F	KN
96189	(86447, 93447)	x*C	F	LT
96190	(86448, 93448)	x*C	F	LT
96191	(86665, 93665)	x*C	F	KN
96192	(86669, 93669)	x*C	F	KN
96193	(86874, 93874)	x*C	F	LT
96194	(86949, 93949)	x*C	F	LT
96195	(86958, 93958)	x*C	F	LT

NP (GUV)   MOTORAIL VAN (110 m.p.h.)

Dia. NP503. Mark 1. Vehicles modified with concertina end doors. For details
and Lot Nos. see original number series. B5 Bogies. ETH 0X.

96210	(86355, 96159)	F	LT
96212	(86443, 96161)	F	LT
96213	(86324, 96152)	F	KN
96215	(86351, 96158)	F	KN
96216	(86385, 96160)	F	KN
96217	(86327, 96153)	F	KN
96218	(86286, 96151)	F	LT

AX5G   NIGHTSTAR GENERATOR VAN

Dia. AX502. Mark 3A. Generator vans converted from sleeping cars for use on
'Nightstar' services. Designed to operate coupled between two Class 37/6 locomotives, with two Cummins diesel generator groups providing a 1500 V train
supply. Hydraulic parking brake. 61-way ENS interface jumpers. BT10 bogies.

Lot No. 30960. BREL Derby 1981–3. Converted ABB Doncaster. 46.1 t.

96371	(10545, 6371)	**EP**	EU	*EU*	NP
96372	(10564, 6372)	**EP**	EU	*EU*	NP
96373	(10568, 6373)	**EP**	EU	*EU*	NP
96374	(10585, 6374)	**EP**	EU	*EU*	NP
96375	(10587, 6375)	**EP**	EU	*EU*	NP

AY5 (BV)   EUROSTAR BARRIER VEHICLE

Dia. AY501. Mark 1. Converted from GUV. Bodies removed. B4 bogies.

96380–96382/9. Lot No. 30417 Pressed Steel 1958–9. 40 t.
96383. Lot No. 30565 Pressed Steel 1959. 40 t.
96384/6/7. Lot No. 30616 Pressed Steel 1959–60. 40 t.
96385. Lot No. 30343 York 1957. 40 t.
96388. Lot No. 30403 Cowlairs 1958–60. 40 t.

96380	(86386, 6380)	B	EU	*EU*	NP
96381	(86187, 6381)	B	EU	*EU*	NP
96382	(86295, 6382)	B	EU	*EU*	NP
96383	(86664, 6383)	B	EU	*EU*	NP
96384	(86955, 6384)	B	EU	*EU*	NP
96385	(86515, 6385)	B	EU	*EU*	NP
96386	(86859, 6386)	B	EU	*EU*	NP
96387	(86973, 6387)	B	EU	*EU*	NP
96388	(86562, 6388)	B	EU	*EU*	NP
96389	(86135, 6389)	B	EU	*EU*	NP

NG   MOTORAIL LOADING WAGON

Dia. NG 503. These vehicles have been converted and renumbered from weltrol wagons.

Built Swindon 1960. Wagon Lot No. 3102 (3192*).

96450	(B900920)		F	KN
96451	(B900912)		F	KN
96452	(B900917)		F	LT
96453	(B900926)	*	F	LT

NY   EXHIBITION VAN

Various interiors. Converted from various vehicle types. Electric heating from shore supply. New Lot Nos. were issued for some conversions, but not others.

Lot 30842 Swindon 1972–3. Dia. NY503. Converted from BSK to Lot No. 30156 Wolverton 1955.

Non-Standard Liveries:
•   Vary according to job being undertaken.

Mk4 denotes a Southern Region Mark 4 EMU trailer bogie.

99621	(34697)	x	BR1	0	E	OM	Exhibition Coach.
99625	(34693)	x	Mk4	0	E	OM	Generator Van.

Converted BR at Salisbury 1981 from RB to Lot No. 30636 Pressed Steel 1962. Dia NY523/4 respectively.

99645	(1765)	v	C	0	E	FK.	Club Car.
99646	(1766)	v	C	0	E	FK.	Club Car.

Converted Railway Age, Crewe 1996 from TSO to Lot No. 30822 Derby 1971.

| 99662 | (5689) | B4 | **0** | CN | FK |

Converted Railway Age, Crewe 1996 from SO to Lot No. 30821 Derby 1971. Originally FO.

| 99663 | (3194, 6223) | B4 | **0** | CN | FK |
| 99664 | (3189, 6231) | B4 | **0** | CN | FK |

Converted Railway Age, Crewe 1996 from TSO to Lot No. 30837 Derby 1972.

| 99665 | (5755) | B4 | **0** | CN | FK |

Converted Railway Age, Crewe 1996 from FO to Lot No. 30843 Derby 1972–3.

| 99666 | (3250) | B4 | **0** | CN | FK |

YR   FERRY VAN

Dia. YR025. This vehicle was built to a wagon lot although the design closely resembles that of NJ except it only has two sets of doors per side. Short frames (57ft.). Load 14 t. Commonwealth bogies.

Built Eastleigh 1958. Wagon Lot. No. 2849. 30 t.

| 889202 | | | **PC** | VS | *ON* | SL | BAGGAGE CAR No.8 |

QSA   EMU TRANSLATOR VEHICLES

These vehicles are numbered in the BR departmental number series but are included here as they are owned by leasing companies and used by them for moving their vehicles around the national system in the same way as other vehicles included in this book. Various diagrams. Converted from Mark 1 TSOs, RUOs and BSKs.

975864. Lot No. 30054 Eastleigh 1951–4. BR Mark 1 bogies.
975867. Lot No. 30014 York 1950–1. BR Mark 1 bogies.
975875. Lot No. 30143 Charles Roberts 1954–5. BR Mark 1 bogies.
975871–975978. Lot No. 30647 Wolverton 1959–61. Commonwealth bogies.
977087. Lot No. 30229 Metro-Cammell 1955–57. Commonwealth bogies.

975864	(3849)		F	*FT*	IL
975867	(1006)		F	*FT*	IL
975875	(34643)		F	*FT*	IL
975971	(1054)	**P**	P	*P*	CJ
975972	(1039)	**P**	P	*P*	CJ
975973	(1021)	**P**	P	*P*	CJ
975974	(1030)	**N**	A	*A*	IL
975975	(1042)	**P**	P	*P*	CJ
975976	(1033)		A		KN
975977	(1023)		A		KN
975978	(1025)	**N**	A	*A*	IL
977087	(34971)		F	*FT*	IL

5.2. NPCCS AWAITING DISPOSAL

This list contains the last known locations of coaching stock awaiting disposal. The definition of which vehicles are "awaiting disposal" is somewhat vague, but generally these are vehicles of types not now in normal service or vehicles which have been damaged by fire, vandalism or collision.

80735	PH
80865	Hornsey Sand Terminal
84197	Sheffield Midland Station
84361	CC
84364	DW
84519	Crewe Coal Sidings
92067	DW
92198	DW
92199	DW
93180	Derby South Dock Siding
93234	Hayes & Harlington
93259	LL
93358	MY
93446	CW
93457	Cricklewood Rubbish Terminal
93482	Bedford Civil Engineers Sidings
93542	Hayes & Harlington
93579	DY
93723	BY
93930	CW
93952	WI
93979	WI
96250	HY
96256	HY
96260	HY
96265	HY
99648	Eastleigh Locomotive Holding Sidings

6. CODES

6.1 LIVERY CODES

* denotes an obsolete livery style no longer used for repaints.

Code	Description
Code	*Description*
AC	ARC *(Yellow/silver. Cast numberplates).*
AL	Advertising livery *(See class heading).*
AO*	ARC *(Mustard with grey cabsides. Cast numberplates).*
AR*	Anglia Railways *(Turquoise blue with white stripe).*
B*	BR *(Blue).*
BG	BR *(Blue and grey lined out in white).*
BL*	BR *(Blue with yellow cabs, grey roof, large numbers).*
BR*	BR *(Blue with red solebar stripe).*
CC	BR/Strathclyde PTE *(Carmine & cream lined out in black and straw).*
CE*	BR Civil Engineers *(Yellow & grey with black cab doors and window surrounds).*
CH	BR or GWR style *(Chocolate and cream).*
CO	Centro *(Grey/green with light blue, white & yellow stripes).*
CR	Chiltern Railways *(Blue and white with a thin red stripe).*
CS	Connex *(Blue with white lower body and blue solebar).*
CT	Central Trains *(Details awaited).*
CX	Connex *(White with yellow lower body and blue solebar).*
DG*	BR Departmental *(Plain dark grey with black cab doors and window surrounds).*
DR	Direct Rail Services *(Dark blue with light blue roof).*
DS	Danske Statsbaner *(Blue and red with moon and star motifs).*
E	English Welsh & Scottish Railway *(Maroon bodyside & roof with gold stripe, gold reflective stripe at solebar level).*
EP	European Passenger Services *(Two-tone grey with dark blue roof).*
ET	Eurotunnel *(Two-tone grey and white with green and blue bands).*
EU	Eurostar. *(White with dark blue & yellow stripes).*
F*	BR Trainload Freight *(Two-tone grey with black cab doors and window surrounds. No logos).*
FA*	BR Trainload Construction *(Two-tone grey with black cab doors and window surrounds. Yellow & blue chequered logo).*
FC*	BR Trainload Coal *(Two-tone grey with black cab doors and window surrounds. Black & yellow logo).*
FD*	BR Railfreight Distribution *(Two-tone grey with black cab doors and window surrounds. Yellow & red logo).*
FE*	Railfreight Distribution International *(Two tone-grey with black cab doors and dark blue roof. Red & yellow logo).*
FF	Freightliner *(Two-tone grey with black cab doors and window surrounds. Freightliner logo).*
FG	Fragonset Railways *(Black with silver roof and a red bodyside band lined out in white).*
FL	Freightliner *(Dark green with yellow cabs).*
FM*	BR Trainload Metals *(Two-tone grey with black cab doors and window surrounds. Yellow & blue chevrons logo).*

FN* Foster Yeoman *(Blue/silver/blue. Cast numberplates)*.
FO* BR Railfreight *(Grey bodyside, yellow cabs, red buffer beam, large double-arrow logo)*.
FP* BR Trainload Petroleum *(Two-tone grey with black cab doors and window surrounds. Yellow & blue waves logo)*.
FR* BR Railfreight *(Grey bodyside, yellow cabs, red buffer beam/stripe at solebar level, large double-arrow logo)*.
FT Forward Trust Rail *(Blue and white lined out in straw)*.
FY Foster Yeoman *(Blue/silver. Cast numberplates)*.
G* BR *(Plain or two-tone green)*.
GE First Great Eastern *(Grey, green, blue and white)*.
GM Greater Manchester PTE *(Light grey/dark grey with red and white stripes)*.
GN Great North Eastern Railway *(Dark blue with a red stripe)*.
GS Great Scottish & Western Railway *(Maroon)*.
GW Great Western Trains *(Locos – Green; Other vehicles – Green & Ivory)*.
GX Gatwick Express *(Dark grey/white/burgundy/white)*.
GY Eurotunnel *(Grey and yellow)*.
HB* Hunslet-Barclay *(Two-tone grey with red solebar)*.
HX Heathrow Express *(Silver with black window surrounds)*.
I* BR InterCity *(Dark grey/white/red/light grey and yellow lower cabsides)*.
IM* BR Mainline *(Dark grey/white/red/light grey)*.
IS* BR InterCity Swallow *(Dark grey/white/red/white)*.
J* London & South East sector *(Two tone brown with orange stripe)*.
LH* BR Loadhaul *(Black with orange cabsides)*.
LS LTS Rail *(Grey/white/green/white/blue/white)*.
LN LNER *(Green and cream)*.
M BR *(Maroon, lined out in straw and black)*.
MD Mersey Travel departmental *(Yellow/black)*.
MG* BR Mainline Freight *(Two-tone grey with black cab doors and window surrounds)*.
ML* BR Mainline Freight *(Aircraft blue with silver stripe)*.
MM Midland Main Line *(Teal green with cream lower body sides and three orange stripes)*.
MT Mersey Travel *(Yellow/white with grey and black stripes)*.
N BR Network South East *(Grey/white/red/white/blue/white)*.
NB* North West Regional Railways *(Grey/white/blue/white/blue/white)*.
NS Northern Spirit *(Turquoise blue with lime green N)*.
NT Network South East *(Grey/red/white/blue/white)*.
NW North West Trains *(Blue with gold cant rail stripe and star)*.
O Non standard liveries *(see notes in class headings for details)*.
P Porterbrook Leasing Company *(Purple & grey)*.
PC* Pullman Car Company *(Umber & cream with gold lettering)*.
PS Provincial Services *(Dark blue/grey with light blue & white stripes)*.
R* Plain red.
RB Regency Rail Cruises *(Oxford blue and cream)*.
RE* Provincial Express *(Light grey/buff/dark grey with white, dark blue & light blue stripes)*.
RF* RFS (E) *(Light grey with yellow and blue stripes)*.
RG* BR Parcels *(Dark grey and red)*.
RK* Railtrack *(Orange with white and grey stripes)*.
RM Royal Mail *(Red with yellow stripes)*.

RN*	North West Regional Railways *(Dark blue/grey with green & white stripes)*.
RP	Royal Train *(Claret, lined out in red and black)*.
RR*	Regional Railways *(Dark Blue/Grey with light blue & white stripes, three narrow dark blue stripes at cab ends)*.
RT	Railtrack *(Yellow and blue)*.
RX*	Rail Express Systems *(Dark grey and red with blue markings)*.
RY*	Parcels Sector *(Red with yellow stripes)*.
S	Strathclyde PTE *(Orange/black lined out in white)*.
SL	Silverlink *(Indigo blue with white stripe, green lower body & yellow doors)*.
SN	Strathclyde PTE *(New livery, details to be advised)*.
SO	Serco Railtest *(Red/grey)*.
SR	ScotRail *(White, terracotta, purple and aquamarine)*.
ST	Stagecoach South West Trains *(White/orange/white/red/white/blue/white)*.
T*	Transrail *(Two-tone grey with Transrail logos)*.
TC*	BR Civil Engineers/Transrail. *(Yellow & grey with black cab doors and window surrounds. Transrail logo)*.
TR	Thameslink Rail *(Dark blue with a broad orange stripe and two narrower white bodyside stripes plus white cantrail stripe)*.
TW	Tyne & Wear PTE *(White/yellow with blue stripe)*.
TX	Northern Spirit Trans-Pennine Express *(Plum with yellow N)*.
U	Undercoat *(White or grey undercoat)*.
V	Virgin Trains *(Red & grey with three white stripes)*.
W*	Waterman Railways *(Locos – Black with cream and red lining; Other vehicles – Maroon with cream stripes)*.
WN	West Anglia Great Northern Railway *(White with blue, grey and orange stripes)*.
WV	Waterman Railways *(West Coast Joint Stock style lined purple lake)*.
WY*	West Yorkshire PTE *(Red/cream with thin yellow stripe)*.
Y	Plain yellow.
YN	West Yorkshire PTE *(Red with light grey N)*.

6.2 OWNER CODES

Code	Owner
14	75014 Locomotive Operators Group.
24	6024 Preservation Society.
50	The Fifty Fund
71	71A Locomotive Group.
90	Deltic 9000 Locomotives.
A	Angel Trains Contracts.
A4	A4 Locomotive Society.
AD	Adtranz (ABB Daimler-Benz Transportation).
AM	Alstom.
AR	Anglia Railways Train Services.
AY	Amey Fleet Services.
CA	Cardiff Railway Company.
CM	Cambrian Trains.
CN	The Carriage & Traction Company
CT	Central Trains.
DR	Direct Rail Services.
E	English Welsh & Scottish Railway.
ET	Eurotunnel.
EU	Eurostar (UK).
F	Forward Trust Rail.
FB	First Group.
FG	Fragonset Railways.
FL	Freightliner.
FS	Flying Scotsman Railways.
FY	Foster Yeoman.
GS	Great Scottish & Western Railway Co.
GW	First Great Western.
GX	Gatwick Express.
HA	Hanson Quarry Products (formerly ARC).
HD	Hastings Diesels.
HN	Harry Needle Industrial & Historical Locomotives.
HS	Harry Schneider.
HX	British Airports Authority.
IC	Imperial Chemical Industries.
IS	Ian Storey Engineering.
LF	Alan & Tracy Lear.
LU	London Underground.
LW	London & North Western Railway Co.
ME	Merseyrail Electrics.
MH	Mid Hants Railway.
MN	Merchant Navy Locomotive Preservation Society.
MM	Midland Mainline.
MO	Michael Owen.
NE	North Eastern Locomotive Preservation Group
NR	National Railway Museum.
NS	Northern Spirit.

NY	North Yorkshire Moors Railway.
O	Other owners (see class heading).
P	Porterbrook Leasing Company.
PE	Princess Elizabeth Locomotive Society.
RA	Railfilms.
RC	Railcare.
RF	RFS (E).
RM	Royal Mail.
RS	Rail Charter Services.
RT	Railtrack.
RV	Riviera Trains.
SB	Belgian National Railways.
SC	Connex South Central.
SE	Serco Railtest.
SF	French National Railways.
SH	Scottish Highland Railway Co.
SN	Société National de Chemins de fer Français.
SO	Serco Railtest.
SP	Scottish Railway Preservation Society
SR	ScotRail Railways.
SS	Sea Containers Rail Services.
SV	Severn Valley Railway.
SW	South West Trains.
VS	Venice Simplon Orient Express.
VW	Virgin West Coast.
WC	West Coast Railway Co.
WN	West Anglia Great Northern Railway.
WT	Wessex Trains.

6.3 LOCOMOTIVE POOL CODES

Code   Pool

SERCO RAILTEST
CDJD   Class 08.

CAMBRIAN TRAINS
CTLO   Operational Fleet
CTLS   Stored Fleet

FREIGHTLINER
DFFT   Class 47 (with tractive effort control and sanding equipment).
DFHZ   Class 57.
DFLC   Class 90.
DFLM   Class 47 (Multiple Working equipment).
DFLS   Class 08.
DFLT   Classes 37 & 47.
DFNC   Class 86.
DFYX   Class 47 (Stored).
DHLT   Class 47 (Awaiting maintenance).

ENGLISH WELSH & SCOTTISH RAILWAY
ENSN   Classes 08 & 09 (East Midlands).
EWEH   Classes 08 & 09 (Solent & Avon).
EWOC   Classes 08 & 09 (London, South East England & East Anglia).
FDSD   Classes 08 & 09 (South Yorkshire).
FDSI   Classes 08 & 09 (North Lincolnshire).
FDSK   Classes 08 & 09 (West Yorkshire & North Humberside)
FMSY   Classes 08 & 09 (Teesside & Tyneside).
(Continued with LBBS)

EUROSTAR (UK)
GPSN   Class 73.
GPSS   Class 08.
GPSV   Class 37.

TRAIN OPERATING COMPANIES
HASS   ScotRail Railways Class 08.
HBSH   Great North Eastern Railway Class 08.
HEBD   Merseyrail Electrics Class 73.
HFSL   Virgin Cross Country Class 08.
HFSN   Virgin West Coast Class 08.
HGSS   Central Trains Class 08.
HISE   Midland Mainline Class 08 (Derby).
HISL   Midland Mainline Class 08 (Neville Hill).
HJSE   First Great Western Class 08 (Landore).
HJSL   First Great Western Class 08 (Laira).
HJXX   First Great Western Class 08 (Old Oak HST & St. Phillips Marsh).
HLSV   Cardiff Railway Co. Class 08 (On loan to East Somerset Railway).
HQXX   West Anglia Great Northern Railway Class 03.
HSSN   Anglia Railways Class 08.
HWSU   Connex South Central Class 09.

HYSB	South West Trains Class 73.
IANA	Anglia Railways Class 86.
ICCA	Virgin Cross Country Class 86.
ICCP	Virgin Cross Country Class 43.
IECA	Great North Eastern Railway Class 91.
IECB	Great North Eastern Railway Class 89.
IECP	Great North Eastern Railway Class 43.
ILRA	Virgin Cross Country Class 47.
ILRB	Virgin Cross Country Class 47 (Reserve fleet).
IMLP	Midland Main Line Class 43.
IVGA	Gatwick Express Class 73.
IWCA	Virgin West Coast Classes 87 & 90.
IWCP	Virgin West Coast Class 43.
IWLA	First Great Western Class 47.
IWLX	First Great Western Class 47 (Reserve fleet).
IWPA	Virgin West Coast Class 86.
IWRP	First Great Western Class 43.

ROLLING STOCK MAINTENANCE COMPANIES

KCSI	Adtranz Class 08 (Ilford).
KDSD	Adtranz Class 08 (Doncaster).
KESE	Alstom Class 08 (Eastleigh).
KGSS	Railcare Class 08 (Glasgow).
KWSW	Railcare Class 08 (Wolverton).

ENGLISH WELSH & SCOTTISH RAILWAY
(Continued from FMSY)

LBBS	Classes 08 & 09 (South & West Midlands).
LGML	Classes 08 & 09 (Scotland and Carlisle).
LNCF	Classes 08 & 09 (South Wales & West of England).
LWSP	Classes 08 & 09 (North West England).
LNWK	Class 08 (On hire to Allied Steel & Wire, Cardiff).

(Continued with WAAN)

NON TRAIN OPERATING COMPANIES

MBDL	Non TOC owned diesel locomotives (see class headings).
MBEL	Non TOC owned electric locomotives (see class headings).

LEASING COMPANIES

SAXL	Forward Trust Rail (off lease).
SBXL	Porterbrook Leasing (off lease).
SCXL	Angel Train Contracts (off lease).
SDFR	Fragonset Railways, operational locomotives.
SDXL	Fragonset Railways, non-operational locomotives.

ENGLISH WELSH & SCOTTISH RAILWAY
(Continued from LNWK)

WAAN	Class 67.
WBAN	Class 66.
WCAN	Class 60.
WDAN	Class 59/2.
WEMF	A.C. electric locomotives (Network Freight).
WEMP	A.C. electric locomotives (Railnet & ScotRail).

WFAN	Class 58.
WGAN	Class 56.
WHBF	Class 47 (Network Freight).
WHCN	Class 47 (Rail Express Services – non Railnet).
WHDA	Class 47 (VIP).
WHDC	Class 47 (On hire to ScotRail).
WHDM	Class 47 (Rail Express Services – Railnet, Reliability Modifications).
WHDP	Class 47 (Rail Express Services – Railnet).
WHDT	Class 47 (Railtest).
WKBN	Class 37.
WKCD	Class 37 (On hire to First North Western).
WKCN	Class 37/4.
WKFN	Class 37/5.
WKGN	Class 37/7.
WKHN	Class 37/9.
WKMB	Class 37 (RETB equipped).
WKMS	Class 37 (Sandite equipment – used in sandite season only).
WMAN	Class 31.
WNWX	Main line locomotives – strategic reserve.
WNXX	Main line locomotives – stored.
WNYX	Main line locomotives – component recovery only.
WNZX	Main line locomotives – awaiting disposal.
WPAN	Class 73.
WSTT	Classes 08 & 09 – Remote control tests.
WSWX	Shunting locomotives – strategic reserve.
WSXX	Shunting locomotives – stored.
WSYX	Shunting locomotives – component recovery only.
WSZX	Shunting locomotives – awaiting disposal.
WTAN	Class 92 (Wembley–Frethun).
WTEN	Class 92 (Non-operational).
WTWN	Class 92 (WCML).

OTHER OPERATORS

XHSD	Direct Rail Services.
XHSS	Direct Rail Services – stored locos
XYPA	Mendip Rail Class 59/0.
XYPO	Mendip Rail Class 59/1.

6.4 OPERATION CODES

Code	Operator
A	Angel Trains Contracts.
AD	Adtranz.
AM	Alstom.
AR	Anglia Railways.
AY	Amey Railways.
CA	Cardiff Railways.
CR	Chiltern Railways.
CT	Central Trains.
DR	Direct Rail Services
E	English Welsh & Scottish Railway.
EU	Eurostar (UK).
FT	Forward Trust Rail.
GE	First Great Eastern.
GN	Great North Eastern Railway.
GW	First Great Western.
GX	Gatwick Express.
HX	Heathrow Express.
IL	Island Line.
LS	LTS Rail.
ME	Merseyrail Electrics.
MM	Midland Main Line.
NS	Northern Spirit.
NW	First North Western.
ON	Used normally on special or charter passenger services.
OR	Royal Train.
OS	Support Coach.
OT	Non revenue earning (e.g. Test Trains, Research, Route Learning).
P	Porterbrook Leasing.
RT	Railtrack.
SC	Connex South Central.
SE	Connex South Eastern.
SL	Silverlink.
SO	Serco Railtest.
SR	ScotRail.
SW	South West Trains.
TR	Thameslink Rail.
TT	Thames Trains.
VW	Virgin West Coast.
VX	Virgin Cross Country.
WC	West Coast Railway
WN	West Anglia Great Northern.
WW	Wales & West Passenger Trains

6.5 DEPOT & LOCATION CODES

* denotes unofficial code.

Code	Location	Operator
AF	Chart Leacon (Ashford, Kent) T&RSMD	Adtranz
AL	Aylesbury TMD	Adtranz (on behalf of Chiltern Railways)
AN	Allerton (Liverpool) T&RSMD	EWS
AY	Ayr SD	EWS
BA	Crewe Basford Hall Yard	Storage location only
BC	Birkenhead North CS	Storage location only
BD	Birkenhead North T&RSMD	Merseyrail Electrics
BH*	Billingham TMD	ICI
BI	Brighton T&RSMD	Connex South Central
BK	Barton Hill (Bristol) T&RSMD	EWS
BM	Bournemouth T&RSMD	South West Trains
BN	Bounds Green (London) T&RSMD	Great North Eastern Railway
BQ	Bury	East Lancashire Railway
BS	Bescot (Walsall) TMD	EWS
BT	Bo'Ness Station	Bo'Ness & Kinneil Railway
BY	Bletchley T&RSMD	Silverlink
BZ	St. Blazey (Par) T&RSMD	EWS
CB*	Crewe Brook Sidings	Storage location only
CC*	Cambridge Coalfields Sidings	Storage location only
CD	Crewe Diesel TMD	EWS
CE	Crewe International Electric T&RSMD	EWS
CF	Cardiff Canton (Loco) TMD	EWS
CF	Cardiff Canton (DMU/LHCS) T&RSMD	Wales & West/Cardiff Railways
CH	Chester SD	First North Western
CJ	Clapham Yard SD	South West Trains
CK	Corkerhill (Glasgow) TMD	ScotRail
CL	Carlisle Upperby (closed)	Storage location only
CP	Crewe CARMD	London & North Western Railway
CQ	Crewe (The Railway Age) T&RSMD	Carriage & Traction
CS	Carnforth T&RSMD	West Coast Railway
CU*	Carlisle Currock	EWS
CW*	Crewe South Yard	Storage location only
DI*	Didcot Railway Centre	Great Western Society
DR	Doncaster TMD	EWS
DS*	Doncaster Station	Storage location only
DW	Doncaster West Yard	Storage location only
DY	Derby Etches Park T&RSMD	Midland Mainline
EC	Edinburgh Craigentinny T&RSMD	Great North Eastern Railway
EH	Eastleigh TMD	EWS
EM	East Ham T&RSMD	LTS Rail
EN	Euston Downside CARMD	EWS
FB	Ferrybridge T&RSMD	EWS
FF	Forest (Brussels) T&RSMD	SNCB/NMBS
FH	Frodingham (Scunthorpe) (closed)	Storage location only
FK	Ferme Park CSD	Great North Eastern Railway

FR	Fratton T&RSMD	South West Trains
GD	Gateshead (closed)	Storage location only
GI	Gillingham T&RSMD	Connex South Eastern
GS	Gloucester Station	Storage location only
GW	Shields Road (Glasgow) T&RSMD	ScotRail
HA	Haymarket (Edinburgh) TMD	ScotRail
HE	Hornsey T&RSMD	West Anglia Great Northern Railway
HG	Hither Green TMD	EWS
HM	Healey Mills (Wakefield) SD	EWS
HT	Heaton (Newcastle upon Tyne) T&RSMD	Northern Spirit
HY*	Hinksey Yard (Oxford)	Storage location only
IL	Ilford T&RSMD	First Great Eastern
IM	Immingham TMD	EWS
IS	Inverness T&RSMD	ScotRail
IS	Inverness CARMD	ScotRail
KD	Carlisle Kingmoor TMD	Direct Rail Services
KK	Kirkdale SD	Merseyrail Electrics
KM	Carlisle Kingmoor Yard	Storage location only
KN*	MOD Kineton	Storage location only
KR	Kidderminster	Severn Valley Railway
KY	Knottingley T&RSMD	EWS
LA	Laira (Plymouth) T&RSMD	First Great Western
LB	Loughborough	Brush Traction
LC	Longsight Eurostar (Manchester) T&RSMD	Eurostar (UK)
LE	Landore (Swansea) T&RSMD	First Great Western
LG	Longsight Electric (Manchester) T&RSMD	Virgin Cross Country
LL	Liverpool Downhill CSD	Virgin West Coast
LM*	MOD Long Marston	Storage location only
LO	Longsight Diesel (Manchester) TMD	First North Western
LR	Leicester SD	EWS
LT*	MOD Longtown	Storage location only
LY	Le Landy (Paris) T&RSMD	SNCF
MA	Manchester Longsight CARMD	Virgin West Coast
MD	Merehead TMD	Mendip Rail
MG	Margam (Port Talbot) SD	EWS
MH	Millerhill (Edinburgh) SD	EWS
ML	Motherwell TMD	EWS
MY*	Mossend Yard	Storage location only
NB*	New Brighton EMU Sidings	Storage location only
NC	Norwich Crown Point T&RSMD	Anglia Railways/D9000 Locomotives
NL	Neville Hill InterCity (Leeds) T&RSMD	Midland Main Line
NL	Neville Hill DMU/EMU (Leeds) T&RSMD	Northern Spirit
NP	North Pole International (London) T&RSMD	Eurostar (UK)
NY	Grosmont T&RSMD	North Yorkshire Moors Railway
OC	Old Oak Common (London) TMD	EWS
OH	Old Oak Common Electric (London) T&RSMD	Siemens (on behalf of BAA)
OM	Old Oak Common (London) CARMD	First Great Western
OO	Old Oak Common HST T&RSMD (London)	First Great Western
OY	Oxley (Wolverhampton) T&RSMD	Virgin West Coast
PB	Peterborough SD	EWS
PC	Polmadie T&RSMD	Virgin West Coast

PH	Perth SD	EWS
PM	St. Phillips Marsh (Bristol) T&RSMD	First Great Western
PN*	Preston Station	Storage location only
PY*	MOD Pig's Bay (Shoeburyness)	Storage location only
RE	Ramsgate T&RSMD	Connex South Eastern
RG	Reading TMD	Thames Trains
RL	Ropley	Mid Hants Railway
RY	Ryde (Isle of Wight) T&RSMD	Island Line
SA	Salisbury TMD	South West Trains
SD	Sellafield TMD	Direct Rail Services/RFS(E)
SE	St. Leonards T&RSMD	St. Leonards Railway Engineering
SF	Stratford (London) SD	EWS
SG	Slade Green T&RSMD	Connex South Eastern
SK	Swanwick Junction (Derbyshire) T&RSMD	Midland Railway
SL	Stewarts Lane (London) T&RSMD	Gatwick Express
SM	Sheffield SD	Northern Spirit
SO	Southport EMU Sidings	Storage location only
SP	Springs Branch (Wigan) CRC	EWS
SU	Selhurst (Croydon) T&RSMD	Connex South Central
SZ	Southall T&RSMD	Flying Scotsman Railways
TE	Thornaby TMD	EWS
TM	Birmingham Railway Museum	Birmingham Railway Museum
TO	Toton (Nottinghamshire) TMD	EWS
TS	Tyseley (Birmingham) T&RSMD	Central Trains
TT*	Toton Training School (Nottinghamshire)	Storage location only
TU*	Toton Up Yard (Nottinghamshire)	Storage location only
WA	Warrington Arpley SD	EWS
WB	Wembley CSD	Virgin West Coast
WD	Wimbledon T&RSMD	South West Trains
WI*	Willesden Brent Sidings	Storage location only
WN	Willesden (London) TMD	Virgin West Coast
WR*	West Ruislip	London Underground
YM	National Railway Museum (York)	Science Museum
YO*	Yoker SD	ScotRail
YS*	York South Sidings	Storage location only
ZA	Railway Technical Centre, Derby	Serco Railtest/AEA Technologies
ZB	Doncaster	RFS (E)
ZC	Crewe	Adtranz
ZD	Derby Litchurch Lane	Adtranz
ZE*	Birmingham	Alstom
ZF	Doncaster	Adtranz
ZG	Eastleigh	Alstom
ZH	Glasgow	Railcare
ZI	Ilford	Adtranz
ZN	Wolverton	Railcare
ZP	Horbury (Wakefield)	Bombardier-Prorail
ZW	Stoke-on-Trent	Marcroft Engineering

6.6 DEPOT TYPE CODES

CARMD	Carriage Maintenance Depot
CRC	Component Recovery Centre
CSD	Carriage Servicing Depot
SD	Servicing Depot
TMD	Traction Maintenance depot
T&RSMD	Traction & Rolling Stock depot

6.7 GENERAL ABBREVIATIONS

a.c.	alternating current
BR	British Railways
BSI	Bergische Stahl Industrie
CARMD	Carriage Maintenance Depot
CS	Carriage Sidings
CSD	Carriage Servicing Depot
d.c.	direct current
DEMU	Diesel-electric multiple unit
Dia.	Diagram
DMU	Diesel multiple unit (general term)
EMU	Electric multiple unit.
FLT	Freightliner Terminal
ft.	feet
GNER	Great North Eastern Railway
GNR	Great Northern Railway
GWR	Great Western Railway.
h.p.	horsepower
HST	High Speed Train
Hz	Hertz
in.	inches
kN	kilonewtons
km/h	kilometres per hour
kW	kilowatts
lbf	pounds force
LMR	British Railways, London Midland Region
LMS	London Midland & Scottish Railway
LNER	London & North Eastern Railway
LNWR	London & North Western Railway
LT	London Transport
LUL	London Underground Limited
m.	metres
mm.	millimetres
m.p.h.	miles per hour
NPCCS	Non-Passenger-Carrying Coaching Stock
No.	number
RCH	Railway Clearing House
r.p.m.	revolutions per minute
RSL	Rolling Stock Library
SD	Servicing Depot
SR	British Railways, Southern Region
T	Toilets
t.	tonnes
TD	Toilets suitable for disabled passengers
T&RSMD	Traction & Rolling Stock Maintenance depot
TMD	Traction Maintenance Depot
TOPS	Total Operations Processing System
V	Volts
W	Wheelchair spaces
WRD	Wagon Repair Depot

6.8 BUILDER DETAILS

These are shown in class headings, the following abbreviations being used:

ABB Derby	ABB, Derby Carriage Works (now Adtranz Derby).
ABB Doncaster	ABB, Doncaster Works (now Adtranz Doncaster).
ABB York	ABB, York.
Adtranz Derby	Adtranz, Derby Carriage Works.
Alexander	Walter Alexander, Falkirk.
Alstom Birmingham	Alstom, Saltley, Birmingham.
Alstom Eastleigh	Alstom, Eastleigh Works.
Ashford	BR, Ashford Works.
Barclay	Andrew Barclay Ltd, Caledonia Works, Kilmarnock (now Hunslet-Barclay).
BRCW	Birmingham Railway Carriage & Wagon, Smethwick.
BREL Derby	BREL, Derby Carriage Works.
BREL Eastleigh	BREL, Eastleigh Works (later Wessex Traincare, now Alstom Eastleigh).
BREL Swindon	BREL, Swindon Works.
BREL Wolverton	BREL, Wolverton Works (now Railcare, Wolverton).
BREL York	BREL, York Works (later ABB York).
CAF	Construcciones y Auxiliar de Ferrocarriles, Zaragosa, Spain.
Cowlairs	BR, Cowlairs Works.
Cravens	Cravens, Sheffield.
Derby	BR, Derby Carriage Works (later BREL Derby, then ABB Derby, now Adtranz Derby).
Doncaster	BR, Doncaster Works (later BREL Doncaster, then BRML Doncaster, then ABB Doncaster, now Adtranz Doncaster).
Eastleigh	BR, Eastleigh Works (later BREL Eastleigh, then Wessex Traincare, now Alstom Eastleigh).
GEC-A Birmingham	GEC-Alsthom, Saltley, Birmingham.
Gloucester	Gloucester Railway Carriage & Wagon, Gloucester.
Hunslet-Barclay	Hunslet-Barclay, Caledonia Works, Kilmarnock.
Hunslet TPL	Hunslet Transportation Projects, Leeds.
Lancing	SR, Lancing Works (later BR, Lancing Works).
Leyland Bus	Leyland Bus, Workington.
Met-Camm.	Metropolitan-Cammell, Saltley, Birmingham (later GEC-A Birmingham, now Alstom Birmingham).
Pressed Steel	Pressed Steel, Linwood.
Railcare Glasgow	Railcare, Springburn Works, Glasgow.
Railcare Wolverton	Railcare, Wolverton.
Charles Roberts	Charles Roberts, Horbury Junction, Wakefield.
RTC	BR, Railway Technical Centre, Derby.
Swindon	BR, Swindon Works.
Wessex Traincare	Wessex Traincare, Eastleigh (now Alstom Eastleigh).
York	BR, York Carriage Works (later BREL York, then ABB York).

Note: The previous practice of showing dual builder details (e.g. Ashford/Eastleigh) where vehicle underframe and body were built at two separate locations has been discontinued as this is now the industry norm rather than an exceptional circumstance.

7. LIGHT RAIL & METRO SYSTEMS

USING THIS SECTION – LAYOUT OF INFORMATION

Vehicles are listed under each system heading in numerical order of painted number.

SYSTEM HEADINGS

For each system, the System Heading lists details of the system operator, guage, electical supply system, depots, workshops and other information as appropriate.

CLASS HEADINGS

Principal details and dimensions are quoted in metric and/or imperial units as considered appropriate bearing in mind common usage in the UK.

All dimensions and weights are quoted for vehicles in an 'as new' condition with all necessary supplies on board. Dimensions are quoted in the order Length – Width – Height. All lengths quoted are over either buffers, car ends or couplings as appropriate. All width and height dimensions quoted are maxima.

DETAIL DIFFERENCES

Only detail differences which currently affect the lines and types of service which vehicles may work are shown. All other detail differences are specifically excluded. Where such differences occur within a class or part class, these are shown alongside the individual vehicle number. Meaning of abbreviations is detailed in individual class headings. In all cases use of the an abbreviation indicates the equipment indicated is normally operable.

LIVERIES

Operator liveries are detailed under each system heading and any known variations are denoted by notes in class headings.

OWNERSHIP & OPERATION

All vehicles are assumed to be owned by their operator unless noted to the contrary.

DEPOT & WORKSHOP DETAILS

Details of maintenance depot and workshop locations for each system are quoted under each system heading.

SEATING

All seating accommodation is one class unless stated to the contrary.

NAMES

Only names carried with official sanction are listed in this publication. As far as possible names are shown in UPPER/lower case characters as actually shown on the name carried on the vehicle(s)

7.1 BLACKPOOL & FLEETWOOD TRAMWAY

Operator: Blackpool Transport Services Ltd.
Supply System: 660 V dc overhead.
Depot & Workshops: Rigby Road, Blackpool.
Livery: Cream and green, although many vehicles carry advertising liveries.

OPEN SINGLE DECK ('BOAT')CARS   A1–1A

Built: 1934 by English Electric.
Seats: 56.
Traction Motors: Two English Electric EE327 of 30 kW each.

600	602	604	605	606	607

PROTOTYPE 'ROADLINER'   Bo–2–Bo

Built: 1998
Seats: **Traction Motors:**
611

VANGUARD CAR   A1–1A

Built: 1987 by Blackpool & Fleetwood Tramway, Blackpool. Rebuilt from 'OMO Car' 7, originally built 1934–35 by English Electric. This is a replica 'toastrack' style vehicle.
Seats:
Traction Motors: Two English Electric EE327 of 30 kW each.

619

BRUSH RAILCOACHES   A1–1A

Built: 1937 by Brush, Loughborough.
Seats: 48.
Traction Motors: Two English Electric EE305 (*EE327) of 40 kW (*30 kW) each.
Note: 635 carries its original number, 298.

621	625	630	632	634	636
622*	626	631	633	635	637
623	627				

CENTENARY CLASS   A1–1A

Built: 1984-86 by East Lancashire Coachbuilders, Blackburn.
Seats: 52.
Traction Motors: Two English Electric EE305 of 40 kW each.

641	643	645	646	647	648
642	644				

CORONATION CLASS   Bo–Bo

Built: 1953 by Charles Roberts, Wakefield.   **Seats:** 56.
Traction Motors: Four Crompton Parkinson CP92 of 34 kW each.

660

PROGRESS TWIN CARS   A1–1A + 2–2

Motor + Driving Trailer.   **Seats:** 53 + 53.
Built: 1958-60 by Blackpool & Fleetwood Tramway, Blackpool (motor coaches)
or 1960 by Metropolitan Cammell, Birmingham (trailers). Motor coaches rebuilt from English Electric 'Railcoaches' built 1936.
Traction Motors: Two English Electric EE305 of 40 kW each per motor coach.

671 + 681	673 + 683	675 + 685	676 + 686	677 + 687
672 + 682	674 + 684			

ENGLISH ELECTRIC RAILCOACHES   A1–1A

Built: 1936 by English Electric. Rebuilt 1958-60 by Blackpool & Fleetwood
Tramway, Blackpool as towing cars, but non-driving trailers later withdrawn.
Seats: 48.
Traction Motors: Two English Electric EE305 of 40 kW each.

678	679	680

'BALLOON' DOUBLE DECK CARS   A1–1A

Built: 1934-35 by English Electric. 700–12 were originally open top cars. 706
has now reverted to open top. (* Rebuilt with new front end design and air-
conditioned cabs; † New interior including ice cream servery. 64 seats).
Seats: 94.
Traction Motors: Two English Electric EE305 of 40 kW each.
Notes: 700 carries its original number, 237.

700	704	709	713	718	722
701	706	710	715	719†	723
702	707*	711	716	720	724
703	708	712	717	721	726

Name: 706 Princess Alice

ILLUMINATED CARS A1–1A

Builders: Various. All conversions from earlier vehicles.
Traction Motors: English Electric.
Seats: See below.

732	Rocket	**Built:** 1961. **Seats:** 46.
733	Western Train loco & tender	**Built:** 1962. **Seats:** 35.
734	Western Train coach	**Built:** 1962. **Seats:** 60.
735	Hovertram	**Built:** 1963. **Seats:** 99.
736	Frigate	**Built:** 1965. **Seats:** 75.

JUBILEE CLASS A1–1A

Built: 1979-82 by Blackpool & Fleetwood Tramway, Blackpool. Rebuilt from 'Balloon Cars' 725 and 714 respectively.
Seats: 100.
Traction Motors: Two English Electric EE305 of 40 kW each.

761　　　|762

WORKS CARS

Miscellaneous vehicles not used for public service.

No.	Type of vehicle	Year Built
259	Permanent Way Car	1971
260	Crane Car	1973
752	Rail Grinding Car	1928
753	Overhead Line Car (Stored)	1958
754	Overhead Line Car	1993

VINTAGE CARS

The following vintage cars saw regular use on the Blackpool & Fleetwood system in 1998:

Car	Year Built
Blackpool & Fleetwood 2	1898
Blackpool & Fleetwood 31	1901
Blackpool & Fleetwood 40	1914
Blackpool & Fleetwood 167	1928
Bolton 66	1901
Stockport 5	1901

7.2 CROYDON TRAMLINK

Operator: Tramlink Croydon Ltd.
Supply System: 750 V dc overhead.
Depot & Workshops: Therapia Lane, Croydon.
Livery: Red and white.

SIX AXLE ARTICULATED CARS   Bo–2–Bo

Built: 1998-99 by Bombardier-Wien Schienenfahrzeuge, Austria.
Traction Motors: Four of 120 kW each.
Seats: 70.
Dimensions: 30.10 x 2.65 x 3.60 m.
Couplers: Scharfenberg.
Doors: Power operated sliding plug.
Maximum Speed: 80 km/h.
Weight: 36.3 t.
Brakes: Disc, regenerative and magnetic track.
Note: Car numbers subject to confirmation.

2530	2534	2538	2542	2546	2550
2531	2535	2539	2543	2547	2551
2532	2536	2540	2544	2548	2552
2533	2537	2541	2545	2549	2553

7.3 DOCKLANDS LIGHT RAILWAY (LONDON)

Operator: Docklands Railway Management Ltd.
Supply System: 750 V dc third rail (bottom contact).
Depots: Beckton, Poplar.
Livery: Blue with two narrow white stripes, a broad red stripe and red doors.

B90 CLASS   B–2–B

Built: 1991 by BN Constructions Ferroviaires et Métalliques, Brugge, Belgium.
Traction Motors: Two Brush of 140 kW each.
Seats: 66.   **Doors:** Power operated sliding.
Dimensions: 28.80 x 2.65 x 2.50 m.   **Maximum Speed:** 80 km/h.
Couplers: Scharfenberg.   **Weight:** 36.0 t.
Electric Brake: Rheostatic.

22	26	30	34	38	42
23	27	31	35	39	43
24	28	32	36	40	44
25	29	33	37	41	

B92 CLASS   B–2–B

Built: 1992-93 by Bombardier-BN, Brugge, Belgium.
Traction Motors: Two Brush of 140 kW each.
Seats: 66.   **Doors:** Power operated sliding.
Dimensions: 28.80 x 2.65 x 2.50 m.   **Maximum Speed:** 80 km/h.
Couplers: Scharfenberg.   **Weight:** 36.0 t.
Electric Brake: Rheostatic.
Note: * Livery turquoise blue & white.

45*	53	61	69	77	85
46	54	62	70	78	86
47	55	63	71	79	87
48	56	64	72	80	88
49	57	65	73	81	89
50	58	66	74	82	90
51	59	67	75	83	91
52	60	68	76	84	

0–4–0 DIESEL SHUNTER

Built: 1979 by GEC Traction, Newton-le-Willows.
Engine:
Transmission: Hydraulic.

Unnumbered

BATTERY/THIRD RAIL ELECTRIC LOCO   B

Built: 1991 by RFS Engineering, Kilnhurst.

BATTERY/THIRD RAIL ELECTRIC LOCO   B

Built: 1991 by RFS Engineering, Kilnhurst.
Electrical Equipment:

Unnumbered

DIESEL SHUNTER   B

Built: 1962 by Ruston & Hornsby, Lincoln.
Engine:
Transmission: Mechanical.

Unnumbered

7.4 GREATER MANCHESTER METROLINK

Operator: Serco Metrolink Ltd.
Supply System: 750 V dc overhead.
Depot & Workshops: Queens Road, Manchester.
Livery: White, dark grey and blue.

SIX AXLE ARTICULATED CARS   Bo–2–Bo

Built: 1991-92 by Firema Consortium, Caserta, Italy.
Traction Motors: Four GEC of 130 kW.
Dimensions: 29.00 x 2.65 x ?? m. **Seats:** 84.
Couplers: Scharfenberg. **Doors:** Power operated sliding.
Maximum Speed: 80 km/h. **Weight:** 45.0 t.
Brakes: Rheostatic, regenerative, disc and emergency track brakes.

1001	
1002	
1003	
1004	THE ROBERT OWEN
1005	
1006	
1007	
1008	MANCHESTER AIRPORT
1009	
1010	MANCHESTER CHAMPION
1011	
1012	
1013	THE FUSILIER
1014	THE CITY OF DRAMA
1015	SPARKY
1016	
1017	
1018	SIR MATT BUSBY
1019	
1020	THE DAVID GRAHAN CBE
1021	THE GREATER MANCHESTER RADIO
1022	THE GRAHAM ASHWORTH
1023	
1024	THE JOHN GREENWOOD
1025	
1026	THE POWER

MULTI-PURPOSE VEHICLE   B

Built: 1991 by RFS Industries, Kilnhurst.
Engine: Caterpillar 3306 PCT of 170 kW.
Transmission: Mechanical. Rockwell T280.
Maximum Speed: 40 km/h.

Unnumbered

Operator: Travel West Midlands Ltd.
Supply System: 750 V dc overhead.
Depot & Workshops: Wednesbury.
Livery: Dark blue and light grey with green stripe, yellow doors and red front end and roof.

SIX AXLE ARTICULATED CARS　　　　Bo–2–Bo

Built: 1998 by Ansaldo Transporti, Italy.
Traction Motors: Four
Seats: 58.
Dimensions: 24.00 x 2.65 x ?? m.
Couplers: Not equipped.
Doors: Power operated sliding plug.
Maximum Speed: 75 km/h.
Weight: 35.6 t.
Brakes: Rheostatic, regenerative, disc and magnetic track brakes.

01	04	07	10	13	15
02	05	08	11	14	16
03	06	09	12		

7.6 SOUTH YORKSHIRE SUPERTRAM

Operator: Stagecoach Supertram Ltd.
Supply System: 750 V dc overhead.
Depot & Workshops: Nunnery, Sheffield.
Livery: Stagecoach livery of white with orange, red and blue stripes.

EIGHT AXLE ARTICULATED CARS   B–B–B–B

Built: 1993-94 by Duewag, Düsseldorf, Germany.
Traction Motors: Four Siemens monomotors of 277 kW each.
Seats: 88.
Dimensions: 34.75 x 2.65 x 3.65 m.
Couplers: Not equipped.
Doors: Power operated sliding plug.
Maximum Speed: 50 mph.
Weight: 52.0 t.
Brakes: Rheostatic, regenerative, disc and magnetic track brakes.
Note: These cars have recently been renumbered by the addition of 100 to the previous number.

101	106	110	114	118	122
102	107	111	115	119	123
103	108	112	116	120	124
104	109	113	117	121	125
105	106				

WORKS CAR   Bo

Built: 1968 by Deutsche Reichsbahn, Berlin Schöneweide, East Germany. Converted to works car 1980. Acquired from Berlin Tramways (721 039-4) in 1996 for conversion to a Rail Grinder.
Traction Motors: Two LEW.
Dimensions: **Couplers:**
Maximum Speed:
Weight:

721 039-4

7.7 STRATHCLYDE PTE UNDERGROUND

Operator: Strathclyde PTE.
Supply System: 600 V dc third rail.
Gauge: 1220 mm (4 ft.).
Depot & Workshops: Broomloan, Glasgow.
Livery – Passenger vehicles: Orange (officially known as 'Strathclyde Transport Red') and black.
Livery – Locomotives: Yellow.

SINGLE POWER CARS   Bo–Bo

Built: 1977-79 by Metropolitan Cammell, Birmingham.
Refurbished: 1993–95 by ABB Derby.
Traction Motors: Four GEC G312AZ of 35.6 kW each.
Seats: 36.   **Doors:** Power operated sliding.
Dimensions: 12.81 x 2.34 x 2.65 m.   **Maximum Speed:** 54 km/h.
Couplers: Wedgelock.   **Weight:** 19.62 t.

101	107	113	119	124	129
102	108	114	120	125	130
103	109	115	121	126	131
104	110	116	122	127	132
105	111	117	123	128	133
106	112	118			

INTERMEDIATE TRAILERS   2–2

Built: 1992 by Hunslet-Barclay, Kilmarnock.
Seats: 40.
Dimensions: 12.70 x 2.34 x 2.65 m.
Couplers: Wedgelock.
Doors: Power operated sliding.
Maximum Speed: 54 km/h.
Weight: 17.25 t.

201	203	205	206	207	208
202	204				

BATTERY ELECTRIC LOCOS   Bo

Built: 1977 by Clayton Equipment, Hatton.
Battery: 94 cell Chloride lead acid, giving a nominal 188 volts.
Traction Motors: Two Clayton M5 of of 35.6 kW each.
Dimensions: 5.31 x ?.?? x 2.60 m.
Couplers: Wedgelock.
Weight: 14.8 tonnes.

L2	LOBEY DOSSER
L3	RANK BAJIN

BATTERY ELECTRIC LOCO   Bo

Built: 1974 by Clayton Equipment, Hatton. One of a pair of 914 mm. gauge locomotives built for use on the Channel Tunnel construction project. Both were converted to 1220 mm. gauge in 1976 or 1977 and used by contractors Taylor Woodrow on the Strathclyde Underground modernisation between 1977 and 1980 before being stored at Taylor Woodrow, Southall.

Both were purchased in a derelict condition by Strathclyde PTE in 1987, and one loco, L4, was rebuilt by Clayton in 1988 from the parts recovered from the two locomotives. L4 was further rebuilt by Hunslet-Barclay, Kilmarnock, in 1990 to make it compatible with L2 and L3.

Battery: 94 cell Chloride lead acid, giving a nominal 188 volts.
Traction Motors: Two Clayton M5 of 35.6 kW each.
Dimensions: 5.00 x 2.11 x 2.36 m.
Couplers: Wedgelock.
Weight:

L4   EL FIDELDO

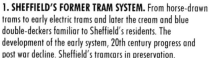

TRAM TO SUPERTRAM

by Peter Fox, Paul Jackson & Roger Benton

The official publication concerning the Sheffield Supertram system traces the history of Sheffield's old street tramway and tells the story behind the development of the new modern tramway network. It is lavishly illustrated in colour throughout, and includes maps of both old & new systems. The book is divided into three main sections:

1. SHEFFIELD'S FORMER TRAM SYSTEM. From horse-drawn trams to early electric trams and later the cream and blue double-deckers familiar to Sheffield's residents. The development of the early system, 20th century progress and post war decline. Sheffield's tramcars in preservation.

2. SUPERTRAM. The largest section of the book covers why the light rail option was chosen; Funding and implementation of the pioneering scheme; Construction - track, power supply, overhead line equipment, tramstops, Nunnery depot; The new trams; Operations and ticketing. Each of the three lines to Meadowhall, Halfway and Middlewood is described in detail.

3. SHEFFIELD TRAMWAY PICTORIAL. A combination of high quality photographs from both tramway eras.

48 pages. A4 size. 75 colour illustrations. **£4.95.**

Available from the Platform 5 Mail Order Department.
To place an order, please follow the instructions on the last page of this book.

7.8 TYNE & WEAR METRO

Operator: Nexus (Tyne & Wear PTE). **Supply System:** 1500 V dc overhead.
Depot & Workshops: South Gosforth.
Livery: Yellow and white unless otherwise indicated. **A** – Advertising livery;
B – Blue and yellow; **G** – Green and yellow; **R** – Red and yellow; **Locos** –
Green, with red solebar and black & yellow striped ends.

SIX AXLE ARTICULATED CARS　　　　　　　B–2–B

Built: 1978–81 by Metropolitan Cammell, Birmingham (4001/2 were built by
Metropolitan Cammell in 1976 and rebuilt 1984–87 by Hunslet TPL, Leeds.
Traction Motors: Two Siemens of 187 kW each.
Seats: 68 (*§ 84;† 70).   **Dimensions:** 27.80 x 2.65 x 3.15 m.
Couplers: BSI.   **Doors:** Power operated sliding plug.
Maximum Speed: 80 km/h.   **Weight:** 39.0 t.
Note: §‡ Denote Red Triangle coupling`code. Can only couple to other Red
Triangle coupling code cars.

4001	* Y	4019	R	4037 *	Y	4055	R	4073 *	Y
4002	* Y	4020	R	4038	R	4056 *	A	4074	R
4003	R	4021	R	4039	A	4057	R	4075	B
4004	‡ G	4022 *	Y	4040	R	4058 *	Y	4076 *	Y
4005	R	4023 *	Y	4041 *	Y	4059	R	4077	R
4006	R	4024 §	Y	4042 *	Y	4060	R	4078	R
4007	R	4025 *	Y	4043	R	4061 ‡	G	4079	R
4008	B	4026	R	4044	R	4062 *	Y	4080	R
4009	R	4027	R	4045	A	4063 *	A	4081 *	Y
4010	R	4028	R	4046	R	4064	R	4082	G
4011	* Y	4029 §	Y	4047 §	Y	4065	R	4083 *	A
4012	* A	4030	R	4048	B	4066	B	4084 *	Y
4013	* Y	4031 *	Y	4049	A	4067	R	4085	B
4014	R	4032	R	4050	R	4068	R	4086	B
4015	R	4033	R	4051	R	4069 *	Y	4087 †	A
4016	B	4034	R	4052 *	Y	4070	R	4088	R
4017	R	4035	R	4053 *	Y	4071 *	Y	4089	R
4018	* Y	4036	G	4054 *	Y	4072 §	Y	4090	R

Names:

4026	George Stephenson		4065	DAME Catherine Cookson
4041	HARRY COWANS		4077	Robert Stephenson
4060	Thomas Bewick		4078	ELLEN WILKINSON

BATTERY ELECTRIC LOCOS　　　　　　　　　　　　　　B

Built: 1989–90 by Hunslet TPL, Leeds.
Traction Motors: Two Hunslet-Greenbat T9-4P of 67 kW each.
Dimensions: 9.00 x ?.?? x ?.?? m.   **Couplers:** BSI.
Maximum Speed: 50 km/h.   **Weight:** 26.25 t.

BL1	BL2	BL3

PLATFORM 5 PUBLISHING LTD
MAIL ORDER

New Titles   Price

British Railways Locomotives & Coaching Stock 1999 .... 10.75
BR Pocket Book No. 1: Locomotives 1999 .... 2.70
BR Pocket Book No. 2: Coaching Stock 1999 .... 2.70
BR Pocket Book No. 3: DMUs & Light Rail Systems 1999 .... 2.70
BR Pocket Book No. 4: Electric Multiple Units 1999 .... 2.70
European Railway Atlas: Germany, Denmark, Austria, Switzerland (Ian Allan) ... 13.99
China Railway Atlas (Quail) 10.00
Narrow Gauge Railways of Portugal (Plateway) 24.95
The Hunslet Engine Works (Plateway) 25.00
Belfast & County Down Railway (Midland) 12.99
The Dublin & South Eastern Railway (Midland) 19.99
A Guide to Diesel & Electric Locomotives of Indian Railways (BORHT) 8.95
Beyer-Peacock: Locomotive Builders to the World (Venture) 32.50
Locomotive Rosters & News 1999 (DTA-LPA) 15.95
Steam & Rail in Germany (Loco International) 9.95
Broader Than Broad (Loco International) 5.95
Sussex Steam (Capital) 7.95
London Buses in the 1960s (Capital) 25.00
London Bus File 1946–49 (Capital) 10.95
The Piccadilly Line (Capital) 5.95
Luxury Travel (Capital) 16.95
The Postbus Handbook (British Bus) 12.50
Midland Railway System Maps Vol. 1: Settle–Carlisle (Kay) 4.95
Midland Railway System Maps Vol.5: Scotland + Index (Kay) 7.95
Mechanical Railway Signalling Part 2 (Kay) 12.50
Scenes From The Past 29: Woodhead Part 2 (Foxline) 14.95
Bus Review 13 (Bus Enthusiast) 7.50

Modern British Railways Titles

Preserved Locomotives of British Railways 9th ed. 7.95
Preserved Coaching Stock Part 1: BR Design Stock 7.95
Preserved Coaching Stock Part 2: Pre-Nationalisation Stock 8.95
Diesel & Electric Loco Register 3rd edition 7.95
Valley Lines - The People's Railway 9.95
Signalling Atlas and Signal Box Directory Great Britain & Ireland (Kay) 9.95
Departmental Coaching Stock 5th edition (SCTP) 6.95
On-Track Plant on British Railways 5th edition (SCTP) 7.95
Engineers Series Wagon Fleet 970000-999999 (SCTP) 6.95

British Rail Wagon Fleet - B-Prefix Series (SCTP) 6.95
British Rail Depot Directory (Metro) 6.95
Private Owner Wagons Vol. I (Metro) 7.95

Metro Systems

The Twopenny Tube (Capital) .... [History of the Central Line] ... 5.95
Circles Under the Clyde (Capital) .... [Glasgow Subway] . 15.95
London Underground Rolling Stock (Capital) 9.95
Underground Official Handbook (Capital) 7.95
Docklands Light Rail Official Handbook (Capital) 7.95
Underground Architecture (Capital) 25.00
Mr Beck's Railway Map (Capital) 12.95
World Metro Systems 2nd ed. (Capital) 10.95
The Berlin S-Bahn (Capital) 7.50
The Berlin U-Bahn (Capital) 7.50

Light Rail Transit and Trams

Tram to Supertram .... [Sheffield Trams] ... 4.95
Light Rail Review 3 .... 7.50
Light Rail Review 4 .... 7.50
Light Rail Review 5 .... 7.50
Light Rail Review 6 .... 7.50
Light Rail Review 7 .... 8.95
Light Rail Review 8 .... 9.50
Blackpool & Fleetwood 100 Years By Tram 19.95
Manx Electric 8.95
Light Rail in Europe (Capital) 9.95
London Tramways (Capital) 19.95
Freiburg: From Classic Tramway to Light Rail (LRTA) 17.70
The Tramways of Portugal (LRTA) 9.05

Overseas Railways

High Speed in Europe 9.95
High Speed in Japan 16.95
European Handbook No. 1: Benelux Railways 3rd ed. 10.50
European Handbook No. 3: Austrian Railways 3rd ed. 10.50
European Handbook No. 5: Swiss Railways 2nd ed. 13.50
European Handbook No. 6: Italian Railways 1st ed. 13.50
European Handbook No. 7: Irish Railways 1st ed. 9.95
TGV Handbook 2nd edition (Capital) 10.95
Railways Around Lake Luzern (Bairstow) 9.95
Railways in the Austrian Tirol (Bairstow) 8.95
Steam & Rail in Slovakia (Loco International) 9.95

Steam Locomotives of Czechoslovakia (Loco International) 16.95
Soviet Locomotive Types (Stenvall) 12.95
The Railways & Tramways of Hong Kong (Simms) 8.95
The Railways of Greece (Simms) 8.10
The Railways of Corsica (Simms) 5.10
The Railways of Tunisia (Simms) 8.50
Locomotives & Railcars of Bord Na Mona (Midland) 4.99
Johnson's Atlas & Gazetteer of the Railways of Ireland (Midland) 19.99
The Londonderry & Lough Swilly Railway (Midland) 8.99
The Cavan & Leitrim Railway (Midland) 8.99

Atlases, Maps and Track Diagrams

Railway Track Diagrams 1: Scotland & Isle of Man (Quail) 6.50
Railway Track Diagrams 2: England East (Quail) 7.95
Railway Track Diagrams 6: Ireland (Quail) 5.50
Railway Track Diagrams 7: NSW Metropolitan Areas (Quail) 6.50
London Transport Railway Track Map (Quail) 1.75
World Railway Gauge Map (Lascelles) 5.95
European Railway Atlas: France, Benelux (Ian Allan) 10.99

Historical Railway Titles

6203 'Princess Margaret Rose' 19.95
Steam Days on BR 1 - The Midland Line in Sheffield 4.95
Rails along the Sea Wall .... [Dawlish-Teignmouth Pictorial] ... 4.95
The Rolling Rivers 6.95
British Baltic Tanks 6.95
British Railways Locomotives - The First 12 Years (SCTP) 18.95
LNWR Branch Lines of West Leics & East Warwicks (Milepost) 7.95
Register of Closed Railways 1948-1991 (Milepost) 5.95
London Tilbury & Southend Railway Part 1 (Kay) 9.95
London Tilbury & Southend Railway Part 2 (Kay) 9.95
Bradshaw's Guide 1863 (Kay) 9.95
Midland Railway System Maps Vol. 2: Leicester–Leeds (Kay) 9.95
Midland Railway System Maps Vol. 3: Leicester–London (Kay) 8.95
Midland Railway System Maps Vol. 4: Birmingham–Bristol (Kay) 7.95

Loco & Coaching Stock Book Back Numbers

1986	3.30	1993	7.25
1987	3.30	1994	7.50
1988	3.95	1995	8.50
1989	4.95	1996	8.95
1990	5.95	1997	9.95
1991	6.60	1998	10.50
1992	7.00		

HOW TO ORDER

Telephone your order and credit card details to our 24-hour sales hotline:

0114-255-8000 (UK), +44-114-255-8000 (from overseas),
an answerphone is attached for calls made out of office hours. Or,
fax to: **0114-255-2471 (UK), +44-114-255-2471 (from overseas).**

We accept Credit/Debit Card payments by Visa, MasterCard/Access &
Eurocard / Delta & Switch. Please state type of card, card number, issue
no./date (for Switch Cards only), expiry date, and full name & address of
card holder.

!!! Please note - the minimum credit card order accepted is - £3.00   !!!

Or: Send your credit card details, cheque (sterling [drawn on a UK bank]
or euro), Eurocheque, money order or British Postal Order payable to
'PLATFORM 5 PUBLISHING LTD' at:

> **Mail Order Department (LCS99)**
> **Platform 5 Publishing Ltd**
> **3 Wyvern House, Sark Road**
> **SHEFFIELD, S2 4HG, ENGLAND**

Please add postage & packing: 10% UK; 20% Europe; 30% Rest of
World, 40p minimum. If p&p works out at less than 40p, then please add
on 40p, this is the minimum p&p accepted. ·

NOTE: Overseas postal prices are for despatch by Air Freight. Transit
time: Europe 2 weeks; Rest of World 4 weeks.

For a full list of titles available from Platform 5 Mail Order, please send a
SAE to the above address above.

Vouchers: When ordering publications in conjunction with a **Today's
Railways** subscription offer please add on post and packing **before** deducting
the voucher. Vouchers may **not** be combined.

Details correct as at 26th February 1999. Prices are not guaranteed and we reserve the right to
alter details without further notification. Please allow 28 days for delivery in the UK.